AF668267

Food Safety and Quality Control

Food Safety and Quality Control

Pulkit Mathur

Orient BlackSwan

All rights reserved. No part of this book may be (i) modified, reproduced or utilised in any form, or by any means, electronic or mechanical, including photocopying, recording or by any information storage and retrieval system, in any form of binding or cover other than in which it is published, without permission in writing from the publisher; or (ii) used or reproduced in any manner for the purpose of training, development or operation of artificial intelligence (AI) technologies and systems, including generative AI technologies, without permission in writing from the copyright holder.

FOOD SAFETY AND QUALITY CONTROL

ORIENT BLACKSWAN PRIVATE LIMITED

Registered Office
3-6-752 Himayatnagar, Hyderabad 500 029, Telangana, India
e-mail: centraloffice@orientblackswan.com

Other Offices
Bengaluru, Chennai, Guwahati, Hyderabad,
Kolkata, Mumbai, New Delhi, Noida, Patna

© Orient Blackswan Private Limited 2018
First published 2018
Reprinted 2022, 2026

ISBN 978-93-5287-379-1

Typeset in
Adobe Garamond Pro 11.5/13.6
by Shine Graphics, Delhi 110 094

Printed in India at
Kensington Printing & Packaging, Noida 201 301

Published by
Orient Blackswan Private Limited
3-6-752, Himayatnagar, Hyderabad 500 029, Telangana, India
e-mail: info@orientblackswan.com

Contents

Boxes

Figures

Tables

FOREWORD

There has been a paradigm shift in the way we look at food safety, with the enactment of the Food Safety and Standards Act, 2006. From a narrow focus on preventing adulteration, food safety today has become a more comprehensive concept to ensure food safety and hygiene across the value chain. It covers laying down science-based standards for articles of food and regulating their manufacture, storage, distribution, sale and import to ensure availability of safe and wholesome food to the citizens of the country.

India faces huge challenges in food safety and these challenges are complex due to the extremely diverse food system. Most food-borne illnesses occur due to risks caused by pathogens, chemicals, naturally occurring toxicants, allergens, etc., which may enter the food chain during cultivation, production, transportation, storage and improper handling. Addressing these challenges require collaborative efforts by food regulators, food businesses and the consumers.

I am happy to note that this textbook covers all aspects of food safety, viz. spoilage, food-borne diseases, contaminants, additives, adulteration, national laws and International standards. It will serve as a single reference point for the readers with invaluable resources of information, helping them understand the framework of the entire food chain, its challenges and risks. The panoramic approach of this book manages to address numerous food safety hurdles. It will definitely help students in moulding their future in the direction of developing strategies to overcome global food safety challenges, and provide the scope for research and development.

I congratulate Dr Pulkit Mathur for this remarkable textbook. Her sincere effort and pragmatic approach in collating the science of various food safety issues is commendable. I am sure that both students and the teaching faculty, and other stakeholders in the food sector would find this book very valuable.

New Delhi, April 2018

Pawan Agarwal
IAS, Secretary and CEO, FSSAI

PREFACE

Food can become contaminated at various stages from the point of production to consumption. Plant foods may be exposed to pesticides at the farm and seafood to heavy metals in polluted water. Animals treated with veterinary drugs that promote growth and control diseases may pass on residues to products like milk, eggs, meat and honey. Foods can get contaminated with harmful chemicals which leach out of equipment in processing plants or the material used for packaging. Or they may simply undergo spoilage due to microbial contamination. Hazards in food—whether physical, chemical or biological—can lead to foodborne illness and even death. Therefore, it has become vital to be mindful of food safety issues and try to ensure supply of safe food to all.

This book provides a comprehensive overview of food safety and methods of quality control. The initial chapters discuss the different types of hazards present in food viz. biological, chemical and physical. The sources of contamination of food have been traced and safety measures to prevent and control contamination are discussed. The risk of consuming contaminated food has also been discussed along with regulatory provisions for managing risks.

Factors affecting growth and survival of microbes have been discussed in relation to implications for food safety. Factors responsible for spoilage of food have been described with methods for preservation of food. Food-borne infections and intoxications, their routes of transmission and measures for prevention have been outlined. Pesticide residues, veterinary drug residues, heavy metals, mycotoxins, hazards introduced into foods from processing equipment, utensils and packaging materials have separate chapters dedicated to them for better understanding of these contaminants. Food additives used in the food industry have also been covered in a separate chapter, highlighting their use, abuse and health concerns. The menace of food adulteration has been discussed with methods to detect and avoid adulterated foods. Quality control and management have been discussed not only from the point of view of big food industries, but also for small-scale industries and street foods. The concept of risk analysis has been explained, highlighting the importance of using science-based standards for regulation. Later chapters discuss food laws and regulations in detail, both national and international regulations affecting smooth trade between nations; quality management systems; and how quality is assured in food service establishments and in the food industry. Principles and procedures of the Hazard Analysis Critical Control Point System have been described with the help of research studies which I have undertaken over the last decade. Importance of maintaining hygiene and sanitation in the food sector, methods of waste disposal and operations control have also been discussed. The last chapter is devoted to recent emerging concerns in food safety and how regulatory provisions need to cover any new hazard that might enter the food system.

The book has been prepared keeping in mind the syllabi of programmes like Home Science, Food Technology and Hotel Management. It has been written in a simple style with explanations of new terms and concepts for the benefit of the student. Exercises and activities at the end of each chapter will prepare the student for examinations. Useful weblinks have also been provided for those who wish to go deeper into the subject. Weblinks of videos on relevant topics have been provided to make learning more interesting. The book will also be useful for professionals working in the health and food sectors, as well as the consumer who wants to understand food safety issues.

I wish to thank my mentors, Dr Sushma Sharma, Reader (retd), Department of Food and Nutrition, Lady Irwin College; Dr Ramesh V. Bhat, International Food Safety Specialist, Retd. Deputy Director (Sr Gr.); and Dr V. Sudershan Rao, Scientist 'E' (retd), Food and Drug Toxicology Research Centre, National Institute of Nutrition, Hyderabad, who introduced me to the science of food toxicology. I also wish to thank my family for being my strength. I acknowledge the assistance rendered by my husband, Nikhil Mathur, in preparing the figures for this book and for being a constant source of motivation.

New Delhi, April 2018 **Pulkit Mathur**

1

INTRODUCTION TO FOOD SAFETY

HIGHLIGHTS

- History
- Relevance
- Types of hazards: biological, chemical, physical hazards
- Factors affecting food safety
- Ensuring safe food
- Emerging concerns of food safety

Why is it that we are not able to eat all kinds of plants as food? How did we learn which foods are edible and which are not? It would seem that man figured out what to eat and, more importantly, what not to eat by trial-and-error. Food which caused discomfort after ingestion or resulted in death was avoided and the information was passed down generations. You will notice that animals too have this sense of seeking and eating only those foods which agree with them. Man also realised that freshly plucked fruit and meat from a freshly hunted animal were safe to eat. Food which has been lying around for a while starts to smell and taste bad and if consumed, results in sickness, the usual symptoms being nausea, vomiting, diarrhoea, abdominal cramps and fever. These were probably the first instances of man being sensitive to the notion of safe food and realising that what he eats for his nourishment could well become his last meal if he was not careful.

HISTORY

Food is essential for our survival and well-being. However, it has to be safe and wholesome. References to consuming fresh and safe food are found in ancient Indian texts like the Vedas. The Vedas recommended certain dietary restrictions and spoke of fermented foods and food spoilage. Even though Confucius, the Chinese teacher and philosopher, warned people against consuming 'sour rice, spoilt fish and flesh or food kept for a long time' in 500 BCE, it was not until the CE 1600s that germs were actually isolated. But even then, the cause of illnesses was not very well understood. Table 1.1 traces some of the major events, discoveries and inventions in the history of food safety.

Table 1.1: Some Historical Moments in the Field of Food Safety

Time Period	*Scientist(s)*	*Contribution*
1673	Antonie van Leeuwenhoek	Invented the microscope which enabled scientists to see microbes and small organisms
1835	James Paget and Richard Owen	Described the parasite *Trichenella spiralis* found in pigs (illness known as Trichinosis today)
1847	Ignaz Semmelweiss	Hungarian physician who insisted that doctors wash hands before attending to childbirths. This simple precaution reduced maternal mortality from 10 per cent to 1.5 per cent
1857	William Taylor	Found that milk could transmit typhoid fever
1860s	Louis Pasteur	Research on process of pasteurisation and fermentation (see Figure 1.1)
1880s	Robert Koch and Julius Richard Petri	Standardised the process of growing pure strains of bacteria in the lab. The glass dishes designed to grow cultures of bacteria came to be known as petridishes. Koch also laid down criteria for showing that specific microbes caused specific diseases. These are known as the Koch Postulates.
1888	August Gartner	Identified that *Bacillus enteritidis* causes food-borne illness. He isolated it from a patient of food poisoning who had consumed meat of a cow suffering from diarrhoea.
1895	Emilie Pierre-Mare van Ermengem	*Clostridium botulinum* identified as the cause of botulism when people fell ill and few died after consuming uncooked salted ham in Belgium.
1913	–	The home refrigerator was invented
1914	M. A. Barber	Experimented on self to show that consumption of spoilt milk can result in food poisoning due to *Staphylococcus aureus*
1917		Frozen foods become available at the retail level in the USA
1920s	–	Home refrigerators with freezer compartments became commercially available (see Figure 1.2)
1937	–	Passage of the Agricultural Produce (Grading and Marking) Act, India
1954	–	Passage of the Prevention of Food Adulteration Act, India
1955	–	Fruit Products Order, India
1975–85	Various scientists	*C. jejuni*, *Y. enterocolitica*, *E. coli* O157:H7, and *Vibrio cholera* identified as causes for food-borne illness
1986	–	Passage of the Bureau of Indian Standards Act
2006	–	Passage of the Food Safety and Standards Act, India

Source: Adapted by Author from Pelczar et al. 1986 and Roberts 2001.

Artificial refrigeration was invented in the mid-1750s and commercial refrigeration came to be used only in the 1800s. Before that, people used different methods like burying food in snow, suspending it in a cool stream, waterfall or well water, or storing it in earthen pots which cooled food by evaporation of water, or in underground cellars which were cooler than the houses above them. Insulated iceboxes made of metal were packed with ice and used to keep food cold. Alexander Twining made it possible to have refrigerated trains in the 1860s to transport food to long distances by working on chemicals which could be used as refrigerants. Ancient Egyptians stored grain in silos which kept the grain cool and dry and hence safe to eat for a long period of time.

Canning was perhaps one of the first commercial methods of preservation. It was discovered by Nicolas Appert, who helped preserve food for Napolean's army by suggesting that they put the food in jars sealed with lids and then boil the jars till the food in them was fully cooked, in 1809.

Figure 1.1: Louis Pasteur in his Laboratory

Source: 'Portrait of Louis Pasteur in his Laboratory' by Wellcome Images (CC by 4.0; Wikimedia Commons).

Figure 1.2: General Electric's 'Monitor-Top' Refrigerator Introduced in 1927

Source: 'Monitor Top Style Refrigerator' by Magi Media (CC BY-SA 3.0; Wikimedia Commons).

Pickling, dehydration, smoking, freezing and salting have been used for centuries as ways to preserve food at home. Salting as a means of preservation was used by several ancient civilisations, including in India.

It was only in the early 1900s that American President Theodore Roosevelt introduced some sort of regulations on the food industry in the US, especially on the meat packing industry. The link between bacteria and human and animal diseases promoted a drive for sanitary conditions, both for human settlements and barnyards for animals. In 1962, the term 'potentially hazardous food' (PHF) was coined and was defined as perishable food that supports rapid and progressive growth of infectious or toxigenic microorganisms. Such food has to be kept under controlled temperature conditions and is also referred to as 'temperature controlled for safety' (TCS) food.

The Constitution of our country also has some provisions which protect the consumer. While Article 21 deals with the right to life in a healthy and safe environment, Articles 47 and 48 deal with the right to health and the right to a pollution-free environment, respectively.

RELEVANCE OF FOOD SAFETY AS A DISCIPLINE

Food is nourishment for our bodies and hence, wholesome safe food is a necessity and not a luxury. Food-borne diseases not only lead to a lot of physical suffering, but may also debilitate a person for life or result in death (see Figure 1.3). The economic consequences of a food-borne illness are massive, involving money spent on medical treatment, decrease in work capacity due to weakness after a food poisoning episode and loss of man hours spent away from work. In poor households, this becomes even more critical as they may not have sufficient resources for proper medical care and the vicious cycle of poverty may be perpetuated by the bread earner falling prey to illness. Vulncrable groups like children, pregnant and nursing mothers, and the elderly are especially at risk of health complications. The knowledge about keeping food safe is important to protect consumers from the ill effects of eating contaminated food. It is also important from the point of view of framing policies and laws which ensure food safety.

Producers of food also need to be aware of methods to keep food safe so that they do not incur financial losses when food products which are found to be sub-standard and unfit for human consumption are recalled. Companies are stuck in litigation for years if their product is found to be contaminated. Any outbreak of food-borne illness or presence of a contaminant can shatter brand image and result in loss of business. This can also severely affect trade as importing countries have very stringent quality checks before food is allowed to enter a nation's food supply.

Figure 1.3: Impact of Unsafe Food

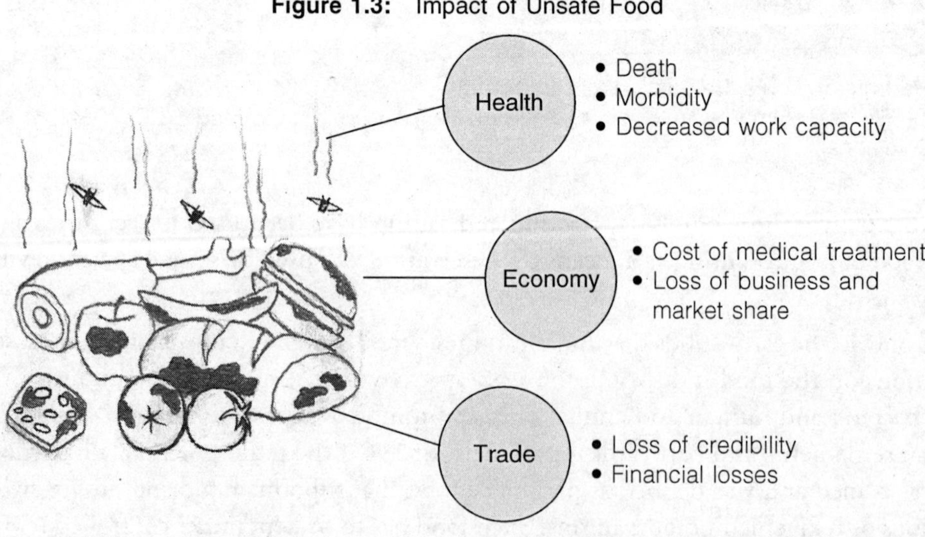

Source: Drawn by Author.

Shipments are often rejected and result in huge losses to the exporter. The image of the country also suffers as a result. Most importantly, the consumer needs to feel confident that the food he purchases and consumes is safe and wholesome.

Food safety is a multidisciplinary subject. There are many stakeholders in ensuring a safe food supply. Agriculturists, agriculture scientists and veterinarians are primarily responsible for preventing the contamination of food at the farm level. Developing pest-resistant varieties of crops and disease-resistant varieties of small livestock ensures minimum use of pesticides and medication. Clinicians are involved in diagnosing and treating people suffering from food-borne illnesses. Nutritionists are involved in promoting safe food-handling practices, both at the household and industry levels. Food technologists in food-processing industries oversee quality control procedures which reduce the risk of food-borne hazards. Engineers and physicists work on industrial and home equipment, like water purification machines, which can reduce contamination levels in foods. Lawyers and policy makers are important for drafting policies, legislations and putting the regulatory mechanism in place. Economists and businessmen look at trade-related issues pertaining to safe food.

HAZARDS IN FOODS

There are different kinds of hazards that may be present in our foods. Concern for these among the public is heightened only when one suffers from a food-borne illness. A **hazard** is defined as a probable source of danger or risk to health. Hazards can be categorised into biological, chemical and physical hazards (see Figure 1.4). **Biological hazards** in foods include protozoa, bacteria, yeasts, fungi, viruses and parasites like worms, which can cause disease in man. Some of these microbes may also produce toxins which can be life threatening for us.

Chemical substances which can pose a hazard to human health include those present in food as a result of contamination, such as heavy metals, pesticide residues, veterinary drug residues, chemicals leaching into the food as a result of contact with cooking/storage utensils or packaging material. Some chemicals may also have been intentionally added as adulterants or food additives.

Physical hazards are substances which pose a threat to health by their physical presence. In this category, we have substances which are present as chance contaminants or intentional adulterants in foods like husk, straw, chips and stones in cereal grains and pulses, or iron filings in semolina (*suji*) or tea leaves.

The presence of these hazards in foods not only makes these unsafe for consumption, but also decreases the quality of the food. The cost of treating food-borne illnesses and the number of man hours lost during each illness episode is bad for the economy. Repeated illness further aggravates malnutrition in the population, debilitating the workforce of the country. Hence it is vital to monitor hazards lurking in our food supply and find ways of reducing them.

Figure 1.4: Hazards Lurking in our Food

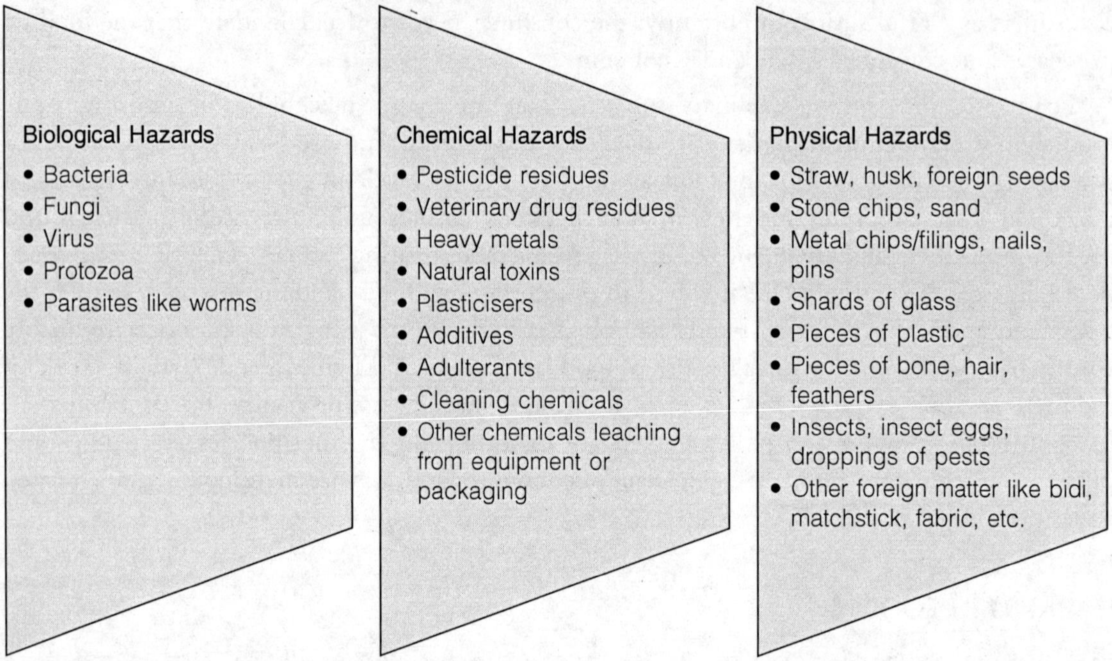

Source: Drawn by Author.

Biological Hazards

Hazards of biological origin usually include microorganisms and parasites which may be present in food or water. A microorganism is a single-cell organism and can usually be seen only with the help of a microscope. Protozoa, bacteria, virus and fungi are examples of microbes capable of producing disease in man. Parasites like worms can also be transmitted via food. It is important to know how these biological hazards enter our food supply so that preventive measures can be taken to reduce the hazards posed by them.

Protozoa (singular—protozoan) are single-celled organisms belonging to the animal kingdom. They are microscopic in size, varying between 5 and 250 µm in diameter. The protozoan cell consists of **cytoplasm**, which is surrounded by a special **cell envelope**. The cell has at least one **nucleus**. Other organelles normally found in a eukaryotic cell are found embedded in the cytoplasm, like the **endoplasmic reticulum**, **golgi bodies**, **ribosomes**, **mitochondria** and **vacuoles**. In addition, there are groups of **fibrils** which by contraction aid in the movement of the protozoan. The cell may also have **cilia** (hair-like structures) or **flagella** (whip-like structures) with the help of which the protozoan can move. Protozoans like the amoeba move with the help of foot-like structures (**pseudopodia**). They form **cysts** which can survive adverse environmental conditions. The active feeding stage of the Protozoan lifecycle which causes illness in humans is called the **trophozoite**.

The most important disease-causing protozoan is an amoeba called *Entamoeba histolytica*, which causes amoebiasis. Faecal contamination of food (especially raw vegetables) and water spreads this disease. Depending on the severity of infection, symptoms can range from mild diarrhoea to serious dysentery and even death. Prevention lies in the safe disposal of human excreta and simple hygienic practices of washing hands before eating and after a visit to the toilet. Food handlers, whether at home or in commercial settings like hotels and restaurants, should be periodically examined for infection and should also be educated about basic practices of personal hygiene.

Cryptosporidiosis is an illness in which the parasite ***Cryptosporidium parvum*** is present in the intestinal tract. The parasite produces cysts which are passed from the body through stool. People with strong, healthy immune systems usually recover on their own after a mild episode. People with weak immune systems may have symptoms such as nausea, vomiting, stomach ache and watery diarrhoea for longer periods, and repeated illness episodes. Cryptosporidium can be found naturally in lakes and streams. People who drink water from streams or lakes may swallow the cysts. Cryptosporidium can also spread from one person to another directly or via objects or food contaminated by human or animal faeces.

The ***Giardia*** parasite (see Figure 1.5) lives in the intestine of infected humans or animals and causes the disease **giardiasis**. Millions of germs can be released from an infected human or animal. *Giardia* is found in soil, food, water or surfaces that have been contaminated with the faeces from infected humans or animals. Because the parasite is protected by an outer shell, it can survive outside the body and in the environment for long periods of time. Swallowing water in swimming pools, hot tubs, fountains, lakes, rivers, springs, ponds or streams contaminated with sewage or faeces from humans or animals can cause the infection.

Figure 1.5: Parasites

1.5A: Amoeba

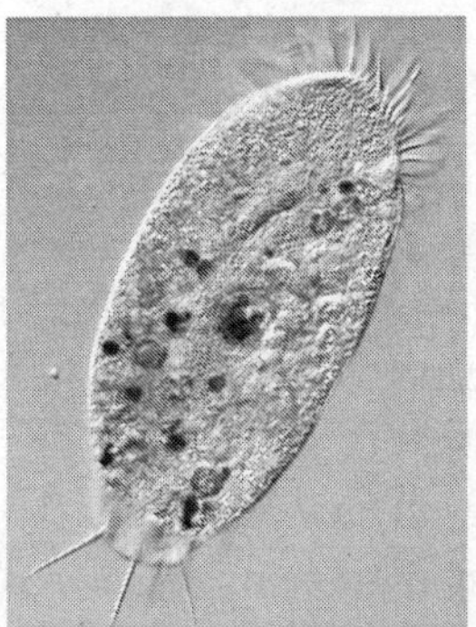

Source: 'Zdjęcie ameby, widok spod mikroskopu' by Picturepest (CC by 2.0; Wikimedia Commons).

1.5B: *Cryptosporidium parvum*

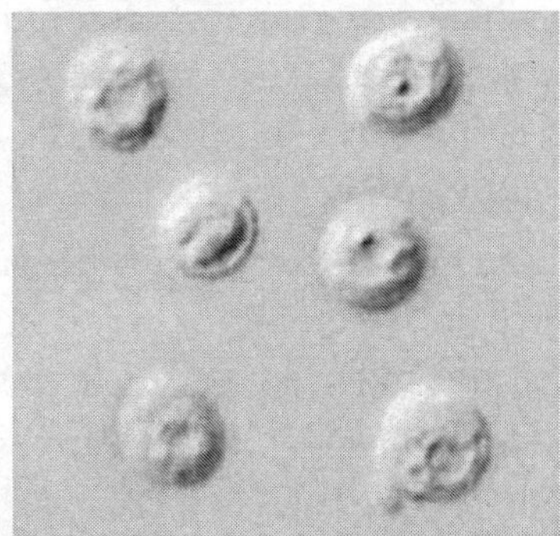

Source: US 'Oocysten von C. parvum' (CC0 1.0; Wikimedia Commons).

1.5C: Scanning Electron Micrograph of *Giardia lamblia*

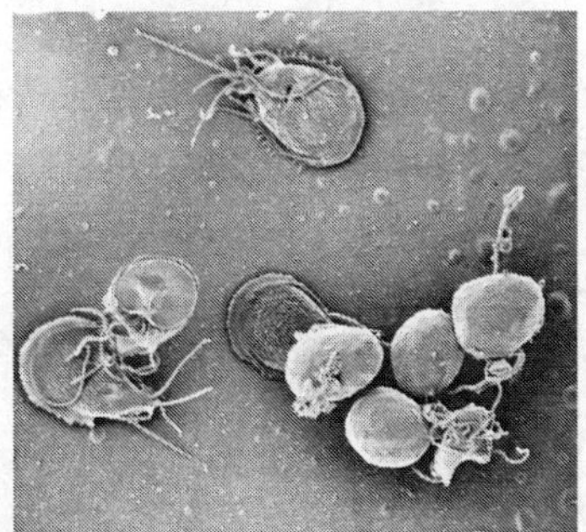

Source: 'Giardia lamblia culture' by US Department of Health and Human Services (CC0 1.0; Wikimedia Commons).

A single-celled parasite called ***Toxoplasma gondii*** causes a disease known as **toxoplasmosis.** The parasite usually causes serious illness in people with compromised immune systems and in pregnant women. ***Toxoplasma gondii*** causes the disease **toxoplasmosis**. This parasite gets transmitted through the faecal–oral route. Eating or handling raw or undercooked meat or drinking contaminated water can result in this illness.

Bacteria are single-celled organisms present all around us in the soil, water, dust and air. They are also present on our skin and in our gut as a part of the natural flora. They vary in size—mostly between 0.5 and 1.0 μm in diameter. Their shape is governed by the rigid **cell wall**, which is composed of lipids, proteins and polysaccharides. Some bacterial cells are surrounded by a viscous substance forming a covering layer or **envelope/capsule** around the cell wall. Some bacteria also have hair-like structures called **flagella** which protrude through the cell wall and help the bacteria to move. These may cover the surface of the bacteria or may be restricted to one or both ends. Bacteria may also have short, hollow filamentous appendages called **pili** that are numerous in number and are used by the bacteria to attach themselves to surfaces and also in the transfer of genetic material during sexual reproduction.

Depending on the species, the bacteria may be spherical (coccus), rod-like (bacillus) or helical (spirillum) in shape. In some species of bacteria, the cells are arranged in groups. The commonly found groupings are in pairs (for example, diplococcus), in chains (for example, streptococcus), in clusters (for example, staphylococcus) and filaments (for example, Streptomyces), as shown in Figure 1.6. The internal structure is fairly simple, with cell organelles like **ribosomes**, **vacuoles** and concentrated deposits of certain substances in the cytoplasm. The **nuclear substance** is not enclosed by a nuclear membrane. Unlike animal and plant cells, bacterial cells do not have an endoplasmic reticulum.

Some of these bacteria are actually useful to man, helping us digest food, synthesise vitamins, preventing the growth of unfavourable microbes and also helping in the production of fermented food products like batter for *idli*, *dosa*, *dhokla*, etc., and beverages (wine, apple cider, etc.). Other bacteria, however, cause problems when they gain entry into our body through food and water. Some of these bacteria are also capable of producing toxins (poisonous substances). Consumption of food contaminated with bacteria and their toxins makes us ill. Some diseases caused by bacteria are typhoid, cholera, diphtheria and dysentery.

Contamination of food with bacteria is indicative of low standards of personal and public hygiene. Food can get contaminated in a number of ways. For instance, if food handlers do not wash their hands after visits to the toilet or do not keep the cooking and chopping area thoroughly clean, millions of bacteria can enter the food. Washing all raw ingredients with clean water also helps to get rid of surface bacteria. Cooking food at high temperatures often kills most of the disease-causing bacteria. Refrigerating food when not in use prevents the bacteria from multiplying as low temperatures do not favour bacterial growth. After doing everything right, if people do not wash their hands before they start eating food, they may land up ingesting the harmful bacteria they have collected on their hands from other contaminated surfaces.

Figure 1.6: Basic Morphological Differences between Bacteria

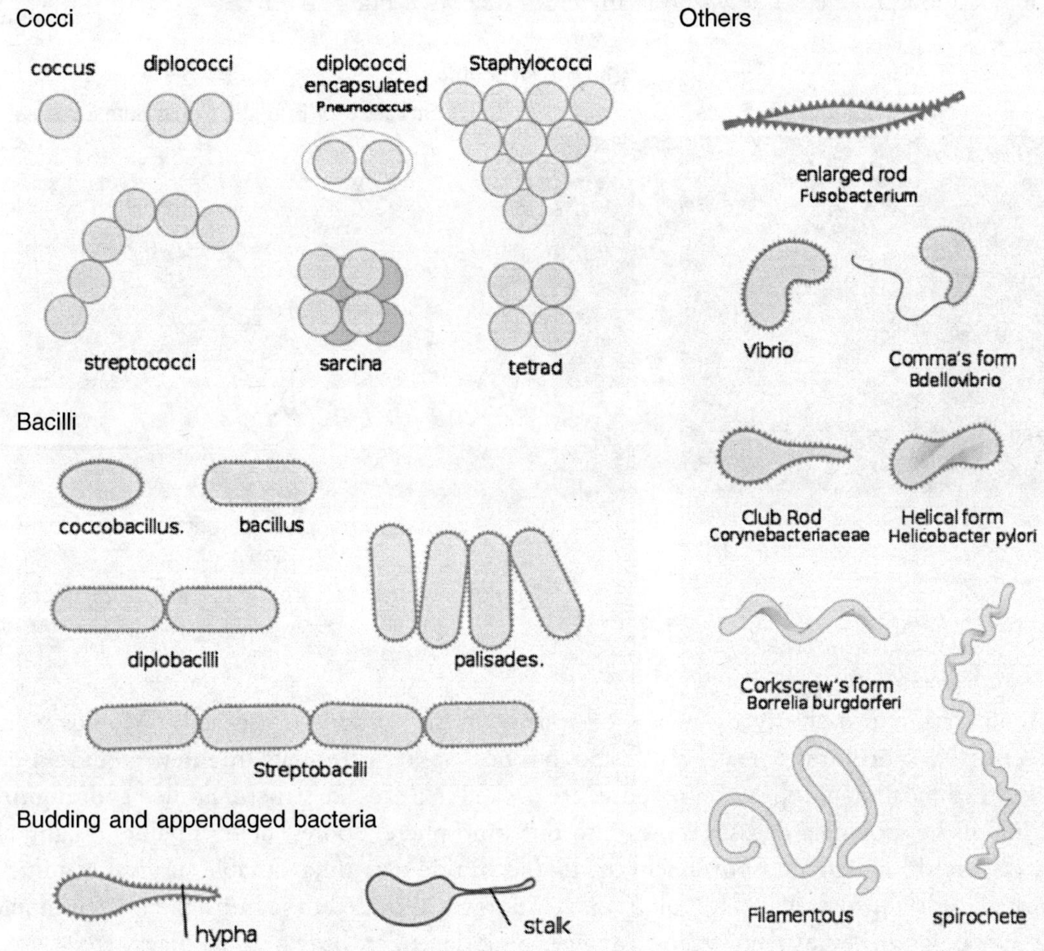

Source: 'Basic morphological differences between bacteria' by Mariana Ruiz LadyofHats (CC0 1.0; Wikimedia Commons).

Fungi were earlier considered to be plants, but are now a separate kingdom. Some fungi grow on dead organic matter while others are like parasites, living on plants, animals and humans. Like bacteria, some fungi are harmful to man, while others are beneficial. You must have seen a cottony mass of delicate threads growing on rotten fruits, vegetables or stale moist bread. Fungal growth can be in a variety of colours ranging from white, black, grey to green, blue, yellow, orange and pink. The growth may be a fluffy or a compact mass, dry powdery or sticky, and these characteristics actually help in identification of the type of fungus.

The term 'mould' or 'mold' is commonly applied to multicellular, filamentous fungi. The mould consists of a mass of branching, intertwined filaments called **hyphae** (singular hypha), and the entire mass of these hyphae is known as the **mycelium.** The hyphae may grow within the food or into the air above the food. The hyphae may be divided into cells by cross walls or they may be long filament-like without any cross walls (see Figure 1.7).

Figure 1.7: Fungi

1.7A: Fungus on Fruits

Source: Author.

1.7B: Structure of Fungus: Penicillium Species

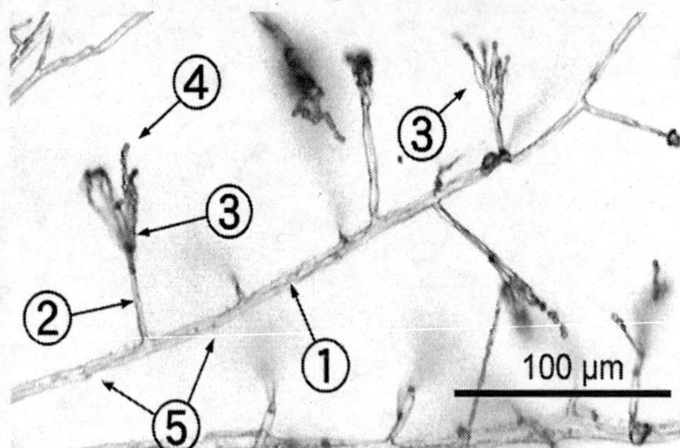

1. hypha 2. conidiophore 3. phialide 4. conidia 5. septa

Source: 'Microscopic Image of *Penicillium* sp.' by Adrian J. Hunter (CC BY-SA 3.0; Wikimedia Commons).

Moulds reproduce chiefly by means of **spores**, mostly produced asexually. Moulds which produce sexual spores are generally not found in foods. Spores germinate into new moulds, much like seeds. In most mould species, the spores are packed in a sac-like structure called **sporangium**. Bursting of the sporangia releases spores into the atmosphere. Spores, being small and light, are easily dispersed through air. Spores help the mould to tide over unfavourable survival conditions as they are resistant to drying. The colour of the spores is also used to identify the type of mould. They may be green, blue-green, yellow, orange, pink, lavender, brown, gray, black, etc.

Moulds can be quite toxic for man and animals as some of them produce toxic substances known as **mycotoxins**. Aflatoxin, a mycotoxin, has been implicated as a cause of liver damage and cancer. Ergot alkaloids cause ergotism, a disease with symptoms of nausea, vomiting, giddiness and sleepiness. Fumonisins have resulted in a fatal disease in horses and in humans, it has been linked to cancer of the oesophagus. Trichothecenes have been implicated in acute human diseases with symptoms of gastrointestinal upset, nausea, vomiting and diarrhoea. Zearalenone may adversely affect the reproductive system of animals. Patulin is an irritant to the stomach causing nausea, vomiting, haemorrhage and ulceration. Ochratoxin A mainly affects the kidneys. These mycotoxins have been discussed in detail in Chapter 5 of this volume.

Moulds also cause a lot of food spoilage. However, some moulds have been used traditionally in the food industry for the production of foods like cheese, fermented foods like soy sauce, *miso* (Japanese seasoning produced by the fermentation of soybean), among many others. Moulds are also grown for the enzymes they are capable of producing, such as amylases. Mushrooms are also a type of fungi, and although many of them are toxic, a number of varieties are eaten by us (see Figure 1.8).

Figure 1.8: Varieties of Edible Mushrooms

Source: 'Natural Edible mushroom at Vinjamur, Nellore' by YVSREDDY (CC BY-SA 3.0; Wikimedia Commons).

Yeast is also a fungus but it is unicellular (single-celled), as seen in Figure 1.9. Yeast is generally a useful fungus and is widely used in the food processing industry for making alcoholic beverages like beer and wine and for imparting flavour and sponginess to bread. Yeast is a good source of vitamin B and can be taken in dried form in tablets. Yeasts are also grown for the enzymes they can produce.

Figure 1.9: *Saccharomyces cerevisiae* Cells as Seen under a Microscope

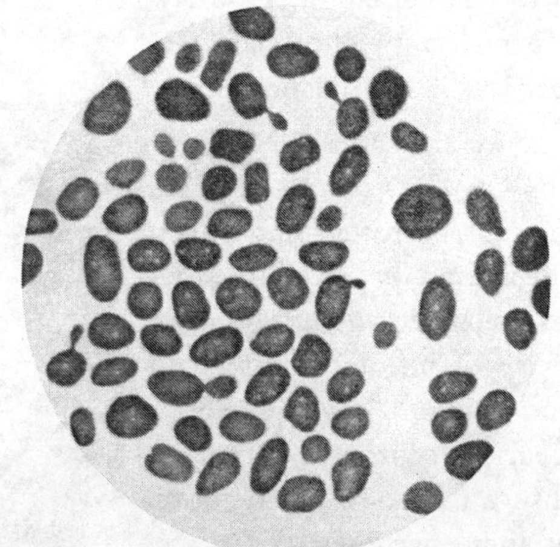

Source: '14353' by the US Centers for Disease Control and Prevention (CC0 1.0; Public Health Image Library).

Yeasts are microscopic and differ greatly in their size and shape. They can be oval or spherical, lemon-shaped, pear-shaped, cylindrical, triangular or even elongated like the hypha in a mould. Like a plant cell, they have a **cell wall**, a **nucleus**, **cytoplasm**, **water vacuoles, fat globules** and **granules**. Their growth on food can be seen as either a film on the surface of liquids or coloured spots on solids. Yeasts reproduce either asexually by budding, or sexually, resulting in the production of spores.

A variety of yeasts cause spoilage of food products; for instance, various species of the genus *Candida* lead to spoilage of butter, margarine and foods high in acid and salt. *Torulopsissphaerica* ferments lactose and may spoil milk products. Other species can spoil sweetened condensed milk, fruit-juice concentrates and acidic foods. Yeasts belonging to the genus *Rhodotorula* cause discolouration of a number of foods, such as coloured spots on meats or pink areas in sauerkraut. *Saccharomyces* species of yeast cause spoilage of dry fruits, concentrated fruit juices, honey, maple syrup and other high-sugar solutions. Some species of this genus can also cause spoilage of foods with a high salt concentration, such as meats, cucumbers preserved in brine, and soy sauce. Some species of yeast are also useful to man. *Saccharomyces cerevisiae* is the yeast commonly used for the leavening of bread (see Figure 1.9) and for the production of wines and alcohol. *Saccharomyces fragilis* and *Saccharomyces lactis* may be used for the fermentation of milk and milk products.

Viruses cannot be seen with the help of the normal optical microscopes because of their minute size (the average virus may be one-hundredth the size of a bacterial cell). More powerful microscopes like electron microscopes have been used to study the morphology of the virus. These cannot be grown on artificial laboratory media. They require living cells to grow and reproduce, and hence sometimes are referred to as *obligate intracellular parasites.* Viruses cause diseases not just in humans but also plants, animals and other microorganisms. When not inside a cell, viruses exist as independent particles known as virions.

Size and shape are characteristic properties of each type of virus. The virus is composed of a central core of **genetic material (DNA or RNA)** surrounded by a protein coat or **capsid**. In some viruses, an outer membrane-like structure made of lipoproteins is present. This is called the **envelope**. Most viruses have a very simple and symmetrical structure like a helical or icosahedral form (see Figure 1.10). Viruses generally lack metabolic machinery of their own to generate energy or to synthesise proteins. They depend on the host cells to carry out these functions.

Figure 1.10: Rotaviruses: the one on the right is coated with antibodies that stop its attaching to cells and infecting them

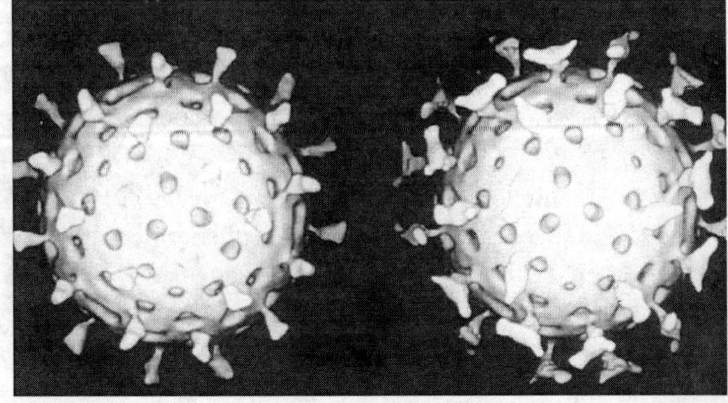

Source: 'Rotavirus with antibody' by Graham Colm (CC BY-SA 3.0; Wikimedia Commons).

Several viruses have been known to cause diseases in humans. Viruses that infect our intestinal tract are shed in extremely high numbers in the faeces of infected individuals and current sewage water treatment practices fail to ensure the complete removal of these pathogens. We are exposed to enteric viruses through various routes: shellfish grown in contaminated waters, food crops grown in land irrigated with wastewater and/or fertilised with sewage, sewage-polluted recreational waters (like swimming pools, water rides in parks) and contaminated drinking water. These viruses cause a wide variety of illnesses in man like hepatitis A, gastroenteritis and poliomyelitis.

Worms or **helminths** are also capable of causing diseases in man (see Figure 1.11). They live like parasites in their host, which can be an animal or man. Some examples of worms which can cause serious illness in man are round worms, tapeworms, hookworms and threadworms. The round worm (*Ascaris lumbricoides)* larvae find entry into humans through improperly washed food and hands contaminated with faecal matter. The general symptoms of round worm infection are loss of appetite, paleness and abdominal pain. A large number of round worms can get entangled and cause intestinal obstruction, which may need to be surgically removed. Proper cooking of food can destroy the eggs of the worm. Other preventive measures involve maintaining a high standard of hygiene, especially when handling food.

Figure 1.11: Helminths

1.11A: *Trichinella Spiralis* Larvae

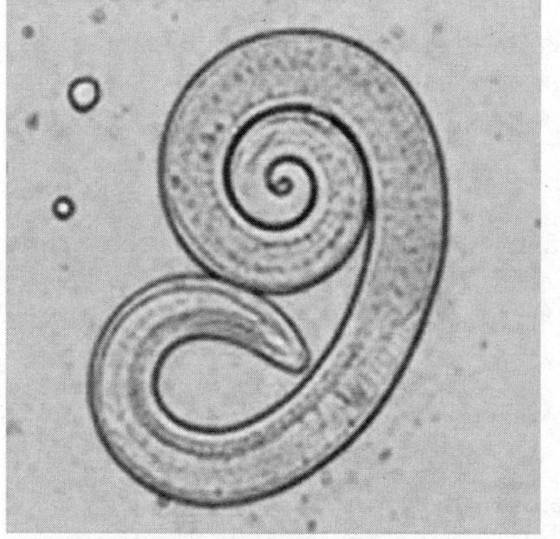

Source: 'Trichinella spiralis larvae' by US Centers for Disease Control and Prevention (CCO 1.0; Wikimedia Commons).

1.11B: *Taenia Solium* or Tapeworm (Head)

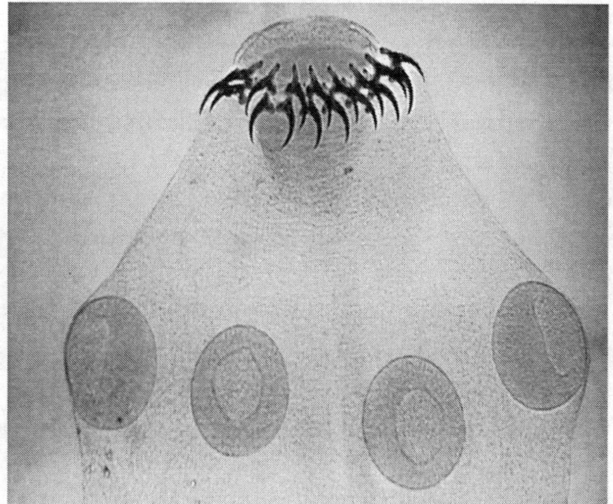

Source: 'Taenia Solium' by US Centers for Disease Control and Prevention (CCO 1.0; Wikimedia Commons).

There are many types of tapeworms, but the most common one is called *Taenia solium.* This worm has two hosts—pig and man. Infected individuals excrete eggs of the worm in the stool. Pigs feeding on stool-contaminated food get infected. The eggs develop into embryos in the pig's intestine. The embryos then pass through the intestinal wall and lodge themselves in the muscles of the pig. When undercooked pork is eaten by man, these embryos are released in his intestine and they attach themselves to the intestinal wall. Symptoms usually include loss of appetite, abdominal pain and stunted growth in children. Preventive measures include thorough inspection and cooking of pork. Hookworm and threadworms are usually not transmitted by infected food, but improper personal hygiene can increase the chances of spreading infection (especially from dirty hands to mouth). Sanitary disposal of faecal matter and personal hygiene are very important in controlling all worm infections. Washing hands is perhaps the simplest but the most important precaution one can take to avoid all microbial and worm infections.

Physical Hazards

In recent years, there has been a substantial improvement in the quality of food available in big cities of our country due to several factors like large-scale food production and distribution, which necessitated mechanisation. Greater market competition has encouraged manufacturers to sell cleaner food which is packaged, and hence better protected from not only pests but also environmental contamination. Physical hazards like husk, stones, straw, insect and pest excreta and dirt have substantially reduced. These physical hazards, besides increasing the work we needed to do in order to get the food to be fit for consumption, also pose a threat to our health. Hard materials like pieces of stone can chip our tooth enamel; straw, twigs and husk, if swallowed, may get lodged in or irritate the intestine.

Some foods like tea leaves and semolina (*suji*) are processed between iron rollers. As a result, small iron filings scrape off the rollers and may get mixed with these foods. Iron filings can irritate our intestine or get imbedded in the lining of the intestine and lead to serious problems. Sometimes, the silver foil used to decorate traditional Indian sweets may be replaced by aluminium foil to cheat the customer. Aluminium foil is tougher to crumble and does not get digested. Hence it can cause damage to the intestine. Several things which can cause us harm can unintentionally enter our food. For instance, while opening a soft drink bottle, you may have experienced chips of glass falling from the neck of the bottle into the soft drink. If these are accidently swallowed, they can seriously injure the intestine. Similarly, while using plastic plates, glasses and cutlery, bits of plastic may find their way into our food and drink.

Chemical Hazards

Chemical hazards are substances which are dangerous to us by virtue of the harm they cause by altering our body's metabolism or by causing toxic reactions in our body. Contamination of foodstuffs with chemical hazards can occur from various sources in the environment (see Figure 1.12). Waste from our homes, offices and industries (detergents, soaps, pesticides, discarded batteries, effluents of factories—which is a cocktail of chemicals—heavy metals, etc.) is disposed daily either into our rivers and seas or buried in dumping grounds. Smoke from industries as well as exhaust fumes from vehicles and machinery pollute the atmosphere. The waste thus contaminates the air we breathe, the water we drink or the soil in which we grow our food. These toxic chemicals present in the soil, water and air are taken in by the plants, and land and marine animals. Animals feeding on these plants accumulate these harmful chemicals and hence the meat, milk and eggs we get from these animals get contaminated. Since man is on top of the food chain, consuming both contaminated plants and animals, he is the worst affected.

Figure 1.12: Sources of Contamination in the Food Chain

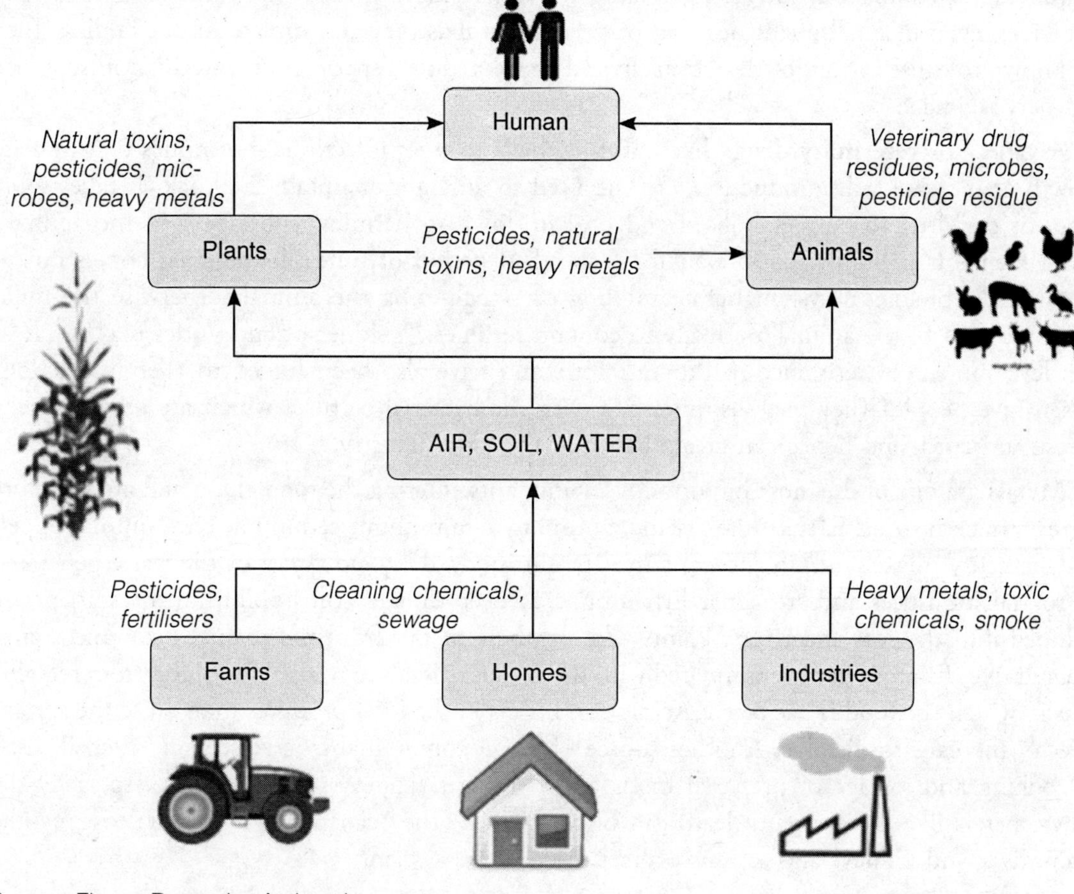

Source: Figure Drawn by Author; Images:
Human: 'Icon of man and woman holding hands' by AIGA (CC0 1.0; Wikimedia Commons).
Plant: 'corn plant' by Onsemeliot (CC0 1.0; Openclipart).
Animals: '9 Free Vector Animal Farm' by Mauricio Duque (CC0 1.0; Snap2objects).
Farm: 'Farm tractor' by tmjbeary (CC0 1.0; Openclipart).
Home: 'tango go home' by warszawianka (CC0 1.0; Openclipart).
Industry: 'factory' by AX11 (CC0 1.0; Openclipart).

The agricultural sector utilises a number of chemicals in the form of **fertilisers** and **pesticides** to improve the crop yield. Fertilisers provide extra nutrients for plant growth. Pesticides are used to protect the crops from pests, such as insects, rodents, mould and bacteria. A significant amount of these chemicals leach into the rivers (especially from farms bordering river banks) and other water bodies. These also enter and collect in the soil. These chemicals remain in the environment for quite some time after their application in the form of residues. So, for instance, if a crop has

> After washing utensils with a scouring powder/detergent/soap, do you sometimes notice a white glaze/deposit? This is a residue of the scouring powder which if you don't remove properly, will be consumed by you with the next meal you serve in that utensil!

recently been sprayed with a pesticide, a suitable time gap should be given before the crop is harvested, depending on how long it takes for the residues of the pesticides to disintegrate. Pesticides, even in small quantities, can be very harmful as they accumulate in our bodies. They are known to cause cancer, birth defects, liver damage, reduced sperm count, sterility, miscarriage and nerve damage.

A variety of **veterinary drugs** like antimicrobials to treat infections, hormones to stimulate growth or increase milk production, etc. are used to raise and maintain livestock. It takes some time for the drug to be metabolised and broken down to harmless substances in the animal's body. Hence it is important to wait for a specified period of time till the drug comes out of the animal's biological system before milking or slaughtering the animal; otherwise the milk, meat and eggs of the animal are likely to contain residues. Residues of antibiotics may result in the development of resistance to the antibiotic and have also been linked to allergic reactions in sensitive people. They may also interfere with the bacterial cultures which are used to make cheese and curd, and hence can create havoc in the food industry.

Metals are one of the most important contaminants entering the food chain and are therefore a great concern to us. Metals like arsenic, antimony, aluminium, cadmium, chromium, copper, lead, mercury, nickel and tin can contaminate our foods. They are a part of the waste generated by several industries and are generally dumped in deep ditches (thus polluting the soil) or are dumped into the seas and rivers. Plants take up these metals from the polluted soil and water. Sea and river fish may get contaminated with the metals. Metals may also enter food from metallic cans in which the food is packaged. Acidic conditions in the food products may cause the surface layer of the cans to dissolve. Another source of metal contaminants is vessels and utensils used in cooking and storage of prepared foods and beverages. Some of these metals, especially the heavy metals like mercury and lead, can be very toxic. They can damage our vital organs like brain, liver and kidneys and seriously affect the nervous system.

A wide range of other chemical hazards can find their way into our food. **Plastics** are widely used in contact with foodstuffs, namely in food processing equipment, utensils, and as packaging material. In their manufacture, numerous additives like plasticisers are used. In addition, the polymerisation process may leave trace quantities of residual monomer or low-molecular-mass polymer in the plastic. Bisphenol A (BPA) is used for making plastic utensils and bottles or in epoxy resins, which are used to coat water pipes and the insides of food and beverage cans. It leaches out into food and water and is considered very harmful for our body as it is an endocrine disruptor (affecting the action of natural hormones in the body).

After reading the newspaper, have you noticed how dirty your hands become? This is a result of printing ink coming off onto your hands. Hence it is advisable not to wrap food in or eat any food being served on sheets of newspaper, a practice followed by several street food vendors and even in homes for absorbing oil from fried foods.

Foods also contain a wide range of **natural chemical compounds** which may act as toxicants or anti-nutritional factors (interfering with the way our body utilises nutrients). The harmful effects of consuming these range from mild symptoms of gastric distress to even death. Some examples of **naturally occurring toxicants** are seafood toxins, biogenic amines, alkaloids and toxic amino acids. Shellfish poisoning, epidemic dropsy and lathyrism are some of the disease conditions arising out of consuming foods containing these natural toxins. Some of the chemicals which act as **anti-nutritional factors** are trypsin inhibitors, phytates, oxalates, tannins and cyanogenic glycosides.

Sometimes chemicals are intentionally added to foods for a technological purpose, for instance, to impart colour and flavour to the food, to increase the shelf life of the food or to impart desirable texture to the finished food product. These chemicals are known as **food additives**. The problem with these additives arises when we consume a large quantity. A number of additives like preservatives and colouring agents have been associated with allergic reactions in sensitive people. The malpractice of adding inferior quality ingredients and masking their use with the help of additives is also widely prevalent across the world. These inferior quality ingredients are called **adulterants**, which at times can be very toxic mostly because of the use of inedible substances. Sometimes these can even result in death.

FACTORS AFFECTING FOOD SAFETY

Whether our food supply is safe or not is determined by a host of factors. Knowledge about these is useful in learning how to keep food safe by preventing contamination. The first thing is to identify the source of contamination. Usually the most common source is man, who contaminates the food supply due to his poor personal hygiene. Food handlers suffering from diseases tend to transmit the germs to the food they are handling. If the raw food material is not thoroughly cleaned before cooking, you start with a high microbial or chemical contaminant load in the food. Buying food from safe sources, from vendors who keep the produce in a hygienic and sanitary environment, improves the likelihood of food being safe to consume. Cooking doesn't always destroy all the microbes, especially if the heat treatment has been mild or for a short period of time. Raw foods like vegetable and fruit salads tend to be highly contaminated if not handled properly. Both raw and cooked foods need to be held at appropriate temperatures to prevent the growth of microbes. Contaminated equipment and utensils for food preparation and storage can contaminate the food even if one started with relatively good quality, clean raw ingredients.

When you look at any food-borne illness, there are four important factors (see Figure 1.13) which determine how serious the outcome will be. The first factor is the **pathogen/contaminant**. How virulent the strain of microbe is and the extent to which the contaminant is present in the environment will determine the likelihood of a serious outbreak of food poisoning. Poor agricultural practices like indiscriminate use of fertilisers and pesticides, and poor handling and storage of produce can heavily contaminate the food. Unregulated use of antibiotics and hormones for milk, meat, egg and honey production can result in residues of these medications in these products. Pollutants in the environment and insanitary conditions increase the likelihood of pathogens and contaminants being present in the food environment.

The second factor is the presence of a **suitable food vehicle** which will pick up the pathogen and/or contaminant and transmit it to the human body. Most food items and of course water and beverages are good vehicles for pathogens as they have all the nourishment the microbes need to grow and thrive. These foods, if left exposed to the environmental contaminants, or in contact with packaging material and storage utensils which can leach chemicals, or if inappropriately handled by patients harbouring infectious agents (for instance, with unclean hands), will increase the possibility of a food poisoning outbreak.

A **conducive environment** for the propagation and growth of the harmful microbe is also an important factor. Usually every microbe has an optimum temperature, pH, level of moisture and oxygen which is most suitable for its survival and multiplication. These conditions determine the likelihood of the pathogen surviving in the food before it enters the host in substantial numbers so as to produce symptoms of illness. That is why sometimes you may just have a mild stomach upset because of a pathogen, while if the same microbe had a chance of growing and increasing its numbers or producing a toxin, the result could be a very severe food poisoning episode, needing hospitalisation. Usually holding food at room temperature for long periods results in the rapid multiplication of bacteria. That is why it is recommended to keep hot foods at a high temperature and cold foods at refrigeration or freezing temperatures if there is a time lag of more than two hours between preparation and consumption of cooked food.

Figure 1.13: Factors Necessary for Food-borne Illness to Occur

Pathogen/ Contaminant
- Presence of disease-causing strain of microbe
- Contaminant present as a result of poor agricultural, animal husbandry or food processing/storage practices

Food vehicle
- Appropriate food which premits survival of microbes
- Contamination of food with microbes or chemical/physical hazards through poor handling practices
- Food left exposed to contaminants in environment

Conducive environment
- Optimum temperature, moisture, pH, nourishment available for microbes to grow and multiply
- Inappropriate holding temperature for food or food kept at room temperature for a long time
- Inadequate screening for quality of raw materials going into a product and no process for decontamination or purification

Susceptible host
- Poor immunity
- Poor health
- Children, elderly, pregnant and nursing mothers (vulnerable groups)

Source: Drawn by Author.

Where contaminants are concerned, if there is no screening or testing of raw ingredients for level of contamination, then the spread of the contaminant is facilitated. Milk plants, for instance, have a quality assurance department which tests all consignments of milk being brought to the plant for processing. Besides quality parameters like fat content, the laboratory looks for possible presence of adulterants and other chemical contaminants like neutralisers, added urea as well as levels of acidity, which are indicative of microbial load. Acceptance of contaminated milk can spell trouble for the processing plant as contaminated milk has a greater chance of curdling and jamming all the pipes of the plant. Hence the milk processing plants are extremely cautious and reject contaminated batches of milk. Industries which do not check raw materials or do not take measures to reduce contamination in raw materials end up producing food which is unsafe. Just imagine if a factory processing wheat to produce flour for bakeries does not bother to remove/reduce pesticides from the wheat by thorough washing! The flour produced will be contaminated with residues and subsequently all products made from this flour in different industries like bread, buns, biscuits, etc., will be contaminated.

Finally, **the presence of a susceptible host** is necessary for any episode of food-borne illness. The most vulnerable age groups are the elderly, young children and infants whose immune systems are not so efficient, as also pregnant women and nursing mothers who are under a lot of physiological stress. People who do not have a good constitution or are just recovering from some other ailment are also more vulnerable to food poisoning than healthy young adults. People with ailments that have resulted in a compromised immune system are also especially susceptible. That is why you may have noticed that sometimes, even though all members of a family ate the same food, only a few actually suffered from the food poisoning, or the degree to which all were affected varied.

ENSURING SAFE FOOD

The different hazards described in this chapter enter our food supply through different routes. The approach now adopted is to look at food from the level of the primary producer of the food right up to the end consumer. This approach is referred to as the 'farm-to-fork approach'. Figure 1.14 looks at the different levels at which food safety needs to be monitored. Level 1 is at the **farm level** where the food crops are grown, and the farmer needs to ensure good agricultural practices so that food does not become contaminated at this level. The dairy farmer or the animal rearer similarly needs to maintain his livestock/fish/poultry and adopt good practices to avoid residues and other contaminants in his produce. **Primary level** of processing may sometimes be at the farm level or at mills or abattoirs nearby where operations of cleaning, chaffing, winnowing, milling, slaughter, aging are carried out. At the **secondary level** of processing, some of the value-added products are made and other complex processing and packaging operations are conducted. Both at primary and secondary levels, utmost care and sanitary conditions need to be maintained to ensure that the food does not get contaminated.

Good manufacturing practices (**GMP**) go a long way in ensuring the same. Storage at appropriate temperatures and appropriate handling practices are important. Ultimately the food is transported to the regional, national and international markets and care needs to be taken that appropriate temperature conditions are maintained, and the packaging is of a quality that protects the food from physical and chemical contamination. Product formulation is also important from the point of view of the shelf life of the product. Food cooked at the household level is as much at risk of being contaminated as food cooked and served by mass caterers at weddings, in restaurants, hostels, hospitals, etc.

As already discussed, poor **handling and storage practices** result in food and water getting contaminated with microbes. If microbes find suitable conditions to grow and multiply, they can lead to serious food-borne infections and intoxications. Cooking or heating food and water to sufficient temperatures usually destroys the microbes, but then care needs to be taken that the cooked food is not re-contaminated or stored at ambient temperature for long as that would encourage surviving microbes to grow and multiply.

Personal hygiene plays a major role in the transmission of germs and perhaps is responsible for most of the food poisoning outbreaks. Dirty hands especially have been recognised as one of the most important sources of contamination. Washing hands before eating or handling food, not sneezing or coughing on food and covering any wounds, boils, sores, etc., while handling food are simple precautions.

Good agricultural practices involve controlled use of fertilisers and pesticides. Good animal husbandry practices would ensure that chemicals and residues of veterinary drugs do not enter the food chain. **Proper waste disposal**, both at domestic and industrial levels, taking care not to pollute the environment is critical if we wish to prevent contamination of the food we eat and the water we drink.

Additives are chemicals which make it possible to produce value-added food products. We must be careful not to misuse the technology and endanger lives by using too much or additives of inferior quality. Unscrupulous traders would have to be kept in check by a strong, **well-implemented law** to ensure that they do not adulterate our food and drink with harmful substances.

Hence, **awareness and education** are vital among food producers, handlers, consumers and of course the policy makers to ensure that food is not contaminated. **Risk analysis** is a process which evaluates the risk posed by different hazards (risk assessment), looks at ways to mitigate or manage the risks (risk management) and also looks at how to effectively communicate the risk to food producers and consumers (risk communication).

EMERGING CONCERNS OF FOOD SAFETY

Food-borne illnesses have been influenced by several factors in the past and these factors continue to change the kind of hazards present in our food supply. Changing agricultural practices, food processing and distribution systems, the extent of environmental pollution, population demographics, consumer preferences, lifestyles and demand are trends which pose new challenges to food safety.

Figure 1.14: Levels at which Food Safety Needs to be Ensured

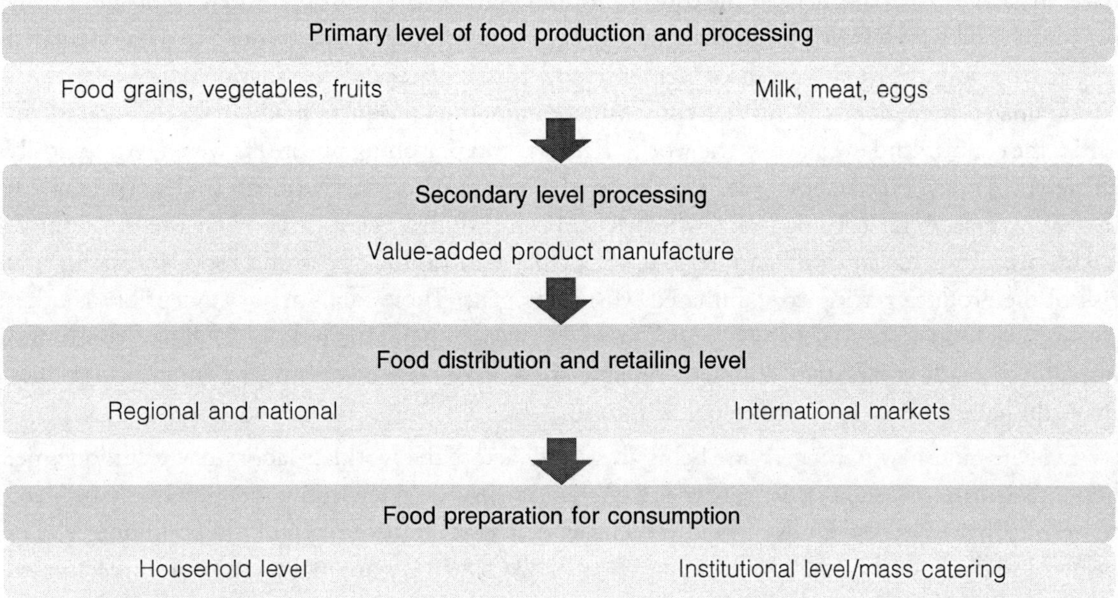

Source: Drawn by Author.

Introduction of new agricultural chemicals like pesticides and synthetic fertilisers can lead to newer chemicals entering the food chain. With greater realisation about the health effects of these chemicals, the global trend is towards minimum use of chemicals and use of environment-friendly substances which do not persist in plants and in the soil. Biotechnology is also being used to produce more pest-resistant crops which will not require large quantities of pesticides. Yet contamination and survival of pathogens in fresh produce is an increasing problem, referred to as *internalisation* (penetration of pathogens like bacteria into internal tissues of plants). Washing then becomes ineffective in removing these pathogens. New strains of pathogens are emerging; some of these can be found in foods that were earlier not identified as likely vehicles. Maintenance of livestock and poultry on a large commercial scale has necessitated the use of antibiotics and other hormones for growth purposes. International trade of animals for breeding purposes may also allow movement of pathogens across national boundaries. Feeds for livestock have also undergone transformations in an effort to increase meat production. This had led to the spread of a new kind of infection due to prions, proteinaceous substances present in the offal of sheep, which was fed to cattle as feed. The disease called Bovine Spongiform Encephalitis (BSE) led to the death of several cattle in Europe, leading to a ban on beef import in several countries.

Industrialisation and growth of cities also increases the problem of environmental pollution. Pollutants like heavy metals and other industrial chemicals enter the food chain at various levels. Changing population demographics, with an increase in the elderly population across several countries of the world, has resulted in a greater proportion of the vulnerable population.

Changing consumer preferences and an increase in the scale of food production and distribution have, to a large extent, influenced the concern for food safety. The consumer today wants minimally processed food with few or no additives, and a year-round supply of fresh foods. This has increased imports by countries and the movement of food across state and international boundaries. A contaminated ingredient can further contaminate numerous products made from this ingredient across the country and even across the world. Earlier, food poisoning outbreaks were geographically clustered. Today this is not true, thanks to the increase in international trade. There is an increasing market for organic foods which have been produced with little or no use of synthetic chemicals. However, animal manure is used for the cultivation of organic food, increasing the risk of the produce getting contaminated with pathogens. These foods are as susceptible as other commercial food crops to getting contaminated due to poor handling practices. Hence, consumers need to be made aware that although organic foods have less of chemical contaminants, they may still have a heavy load of biological hazards.

Evolving and new pathogens are being identified across the world as laboratory techniques get better. Scientists are also discovering that bacteria can survive in environments previously believed to be safe, that is, in new kinds of food vehicles as well as at temperature and pH conditions earlier believed to destroy all microbes. For example, *E. coli* O157:H7, originally found in undercooked ground beef, has shown up in foods as diverse as salami, apple cider, raw milk and lettuce, and in lower pH conditions than originally thought. It is now known that *Yersinia enterocolitica* and *L. monocytogenes* can survive and multiply at refrigeration temperatures.

With an increase in food security-related programmes in developing countries like India, there has been a strong concern for the safety of food dished out in large supplementary feeding programmes like the Mid-day Meal Programme and the Integrated Child Development Scheme (ICDS) supplementary feeding programme, in which hot cooked meals are fed to millions of children across the country every day. Any outbreak of food poisoning can prove to be a huge setback for the programmes. Hence, food safety management tools such as Hazard Analysis Critical Control Point (HACCP) are becoming essential. Regulations and policies need to be in place to ensure a safe food supply for a nation. However, these have to be carefully drafted so that while ensuring the safety of citizens, they do not stifle innovation and entrepreneurship in the food industry or put hurdles in the way of trade between nations. A potential threat to the food supply is also from terrorism. Deliberate contamination of food and water supply with virulent pathogens has been the theme of many a book or movie, and now it may even be a very serious threat. Governments need to keep the food supply of the country safe from possible threats of contamination by terrorists. Food defence technology research is happening alongside research in control of other food-borne hazards.

SUMMARY

- Different types of hazards may lurk in our foods which make the food unsafe for us to consume.
- Hazards can be classified as biological, chemical and physical hazards.

- Biological hazards in foods include microscopic animals and plants—protozoa, bacteria, fungi, viruses and parasites like worms—which can cause disease in man.
- Chemical hazards can come in our food from several sources—industrial effluents, untreated sewage, household chemical wastes, fertilisers, pesticides, veterinary drugs, packaging material (metals and plastics), naturally occurring contaminants in plants and animals, anti-nutritional substances, food additives and adulterants.
- Physical hazards like chips of stone, glass, husk, straw, twigs, iron filings and bits of other metals like aluminium can also be present in our food.
- Personal hygiene plays a major role in the transmission of germs and is responsible for most of the food poisoning outbreaks.
- A farm-to-fork approach is adopted in ensuring safe food for the population.
- It is important to reduce our exposure to these hazards. Safe disposal of industrial and household chemical waste and appropriate treatment of sewage before it is released into the seas and rivers or utilised for agriculture, good agricultural and animal husbandry practices, good personal hygiene and maintaining sanitation in areas where food is handled will go a long way in making food safe for us.

KEY WORDS

Additives: Substances added to foods to perform certain functions in foods

Adulterants: Inferior substances added intentionally to food and which decrease the food quality

Anti-nutritional substances: Substances interfering with the way our body utilises nutrients

Effluent: Sewage or industrial waste discharged into the river or sea

Endocrine disruptor: Chemical substances which can cause disturbances in our hormones leading to severe consequences like cancer, birth defects and developmental disorders

Hazard: A danger or risk

Livestock: Farm animals

Parasite: An organism living in or on another and benefiting at the expense of the other

Pathogen: Disease-causing microbe

Residue: What is left over or remains

Toxicant/Toxin: Poison

Veterinary: Of or for diseases and injuries of farm and domestic animals, or their treatment

Virion: The infectious form of a virus as it exists outside the host cell, consisting of a nucleic acid core, a protein coat and, in some species, an external envelope

EXERCISES

1. What do you understand by the term 'hazard'? How are hazards classified?
2. What are the toxins produced by fungi called? Give an example.
3. What is a protozoan? Give an example of a protozoan that is food-borne.
4. Describe how pesticides enter our food.
5. What are veterinary drug residues?
6. Name some anti-nutritional substances.
7. Why is it so important to ensure food safety?

REFERENCES

Frazier, W. C., and D. C. Westhoff, adapted by N. M. Vanitha, *Food Microbiology* (5th edition), New Delhi: McGraw Hill Education (India), 2014.

Pelczar, M. J. Jr, E. C. S. Chan, and N. R. Krieg, *Microbiology* (5th edition), New Delhi: Tata McGraw-Hill, 1986.

Roberts, Cynthia A., 'Food Safety', *Encyclopedia of Food and Culture*. http://www.encyclopedia.com/topic/Food_safety.aspx (accessed 8 February 2016).

———, *The Food Safety Information Handbook*, USA: Oryx Press, 2001.

ONLINE SOURCES

History of Food Safety. Available at http://www.food-safety-and-you.com/HistoryofFoodSafety.html#The Pre-Refrigeration Era (accessed 12 April 2018).

Food Safety for Pantries: Types of Food Hazards. Available at https://www.youtube.com/watch?v=oosN3jms0Y8 (accessed 12 April 2018).

Potentially Hazardous Food. Available at https://www.youtube.com/watch?v=wxC6CWHUs8k (accessed 12 April 2018).

Presentations and Monographs on Food and Water Safety, Website of International Life Sciences Institute, India. Available at http://www.ilsi-india.org/ilsi-india-conference-recommendation/food-water-safety.htm (accessed 12 April 2018).

2

GROWTH OF MICROBES IN FOOD

HIGHLIGHTS

- Physiological requirements of different microbes
- Growth and reproduction in microbes
- Factors affecting growth and survival of microbes
- Use of microbes in the food industry
- Implications for food safety

Our food serves as sustenance for many other organisms as well. Unseen by the naked eye, many of these microscopic organisms survive not only in our food, but also in our environment. They grow wherever they find suitable temperature, pH, moisture and oxygen, along with a steady supply of nutrients. Thousands reside on our skin, especially on our hands as we touch different things in our environment. No wonder then, that the most important step in ensuring that we do not contaminate our food is to wash our hands thoroughly before handling food.

Bacteria, viruses, fungi and protozoa are some of the major groups of microorganisms present in our food. All of them are not harmful; some of them are actually beneficial for our health. Some others are used in the preparation of certain food items as well as in other industries.

This chapter describes the factors important for the growth and survival of microbes, and also deals with the different types of microbes which may be useful for us and are used in the food industry. It also highlights the precautions one needs to keep in mind while introducing microbes into our food, especially at the industry level.

PHYSIOLOGICAL REQUIREMENTS OF DIFFERENT MICROBES

Bacteria show wide variations in their requirements for environmental conditions which favour their growth. Most bacteria which have been implicated in human diseases grow best within the temperature range of 25–40°C, though several species have been known to survive extreme temperatures because of the ability to form spores. The level of oxygen in the environment affects the growth of bacteria, with most bacteria requiring air for their growth and survival. Some others are capable of surviving without oxygen. The optimum pH for growth lies between 6.5 and 7.5 for most bacteria, the range for survival being 5–9.

Moulds need moisture, warmth, nutrients and oxygen to grow and multiply. Mould growth in a food is favoured only when the moisture content of the food is more than 15 per cent. The optimal temperature for growth for most moulds is 25–30°C. However, mould growth has been reported at temperatures as low as –5 to –10°C. Some moulds can thrive at high temperatures also. Most moulds grow well in a food with acidic pH. Among all microbes, moulds are known to grow on a variety of things besides food; for example, wood, leather, walls, etc. They are capable of producing a number of enzymes which can utilise a number of substances as foods.

Most **yeasts** grow well when there is plenty of moisture available. They require less moisture as compared to bacteria, but more moisture than most moulds. They are also able to grow in high concentrations of salt or sugar. The range of temperature for the growth of most yeasts is similar to that of moulds, with the optimum around 25–30°C and the maximum about 35–47°C. Yeasts grow best under aerobic conditions and in a slightly acidic medium (pH 4–4.5).

Protozoa are usually found where there is water or moisture—in fresh water bodies, seas and even moist soil. Protozoa, which are parasitic in nature, have been found in humans and animals. Most protozoa thrive best in a pH range of 6.0 to 8.0 and temperatures between 16 and 25°C. If conditions are not favourable in the environment, they become dormant or form cysts, which can survive the harsh environmental conditions.

GROWTH AND REPRODUCTION IN MICROBES

Usually when microbes enter a food product, they are in small numbers. Finding a suitable environment for survival triggers them to multiply in number. Different microbes reproduce in different ways, both sexually and asexually. Bacteria generally reproduce by binary fission (see Figure 2.1), which is an asexual form of reproduction in which, after replicating its genetic material, the cell divides into two nearly equal-sized daughter cells.

Bacterial cells which are multiplying by binary fission in favourable environments tend to follow the growth curve given in Figure 2.2. There are four distinct phases which can be recognised in the growth curve. These are:

1. *Lag phase*: This is the initial phase of growth when the bacterial cells are adjusting to the growth medium, and hence there may be little or no increase in the number of cells.
2. *Log phase or exponential phase*: Once the bacterial cells adjust to the environment they start multiplying rapidly, doubling their numbers at regular intervals, and that is why the growth is referred to as exponential. So, two cells give rise to four, four to eight and so on.
3. *Stationary/resting phase*: As the bacterial cells multiply, the nutrients in the medium start getting depleted and waste products of the bacteria start accumulating, thus making the

Figure 2.1: Binary Fission in a Prokaryotic Cell

: Plasmid
: Ribosome

1 2 3 4 5 6

Notes: 1. The bacterium before binary fission, when the DNA is tightly coiled. 2. The DNA of the bacterium has uncoiled and replicated. 3. The DNA is pulled to the separate poles of the bacterium as it increases in size to prepare for splitting. 4. The growth of a new cell wall begins to separate the bacterium. 5. The new cell wall fully develops, resulting in the complete split of the bacterium. 6. The new daughter cells have tightly coiled DNA rods, ribosomes and plasmids; these are brand new organisms.

Source: 'Binary fossion' by Ecoddington (CC BY-SA 3.0; Wikimedia Commons).

Figure 2.2: Growth Curve of Bacteria

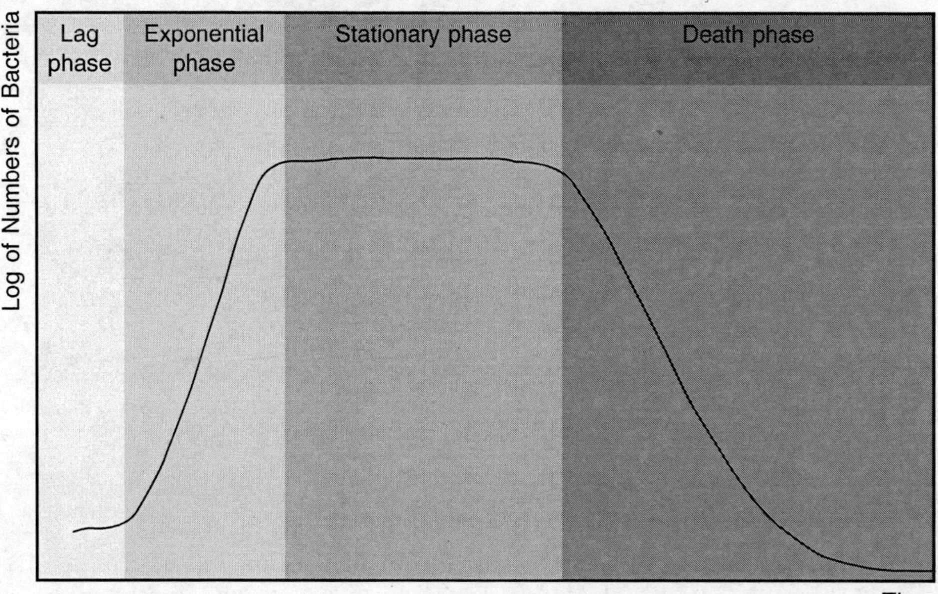

Source: Drawn by Author.

environment less hospitable. The death rate equals the growth rate and there is no net increase in the number of bacteria.

4. *Death phase*: With the nutrients now totally exhausted, the death rate is very fast and the number of bacteria decreases exponentially. The environment (medium) in which the bacteria were growing has a build-up of toxic waste products and is incapable of supporting growth.

Usually in some bacteria, when the environment becomes inhospitable, there is production of spores. Spores inside the bacterial cell are referred to as **endospores**. These spores are very hardy and some can even tolerate heat, ultraviolet light and chemicals. When conditions are favourable the spores germinate, producing fresh vegetative cells.

Moulds can reproduce sexually or asexually. They form spores which, when released, can form new mycelium in favourable environments. The *Aspergillus* and *Penicillium* species form **exospores** which are free conidia, while *Rhizopus* and *Mucor* form **sporangiospores**, which are housed in a sac and which burst to release the spores. Fragmentation of the hyphae also produces spores, which are called **arthrospores**. Sexual spores called **oospores** are formed by only a few fungi.

Yeasts, on the other hand, reproduce asexually by the process of **budding**. A small bud (daughter cell) is formed on the parent cell on its outer surface (see Figure 2.3). As the daughter cell grows, the nucleus of the parent cell divides and one nucleus migrates to the daughter cell. The daughter cell then breaks off from the parent cell and forms a separate cell. Some yeasts also reproduce by binary fission or by sexual reproduction. In sexual reproduction, haploid spores are formed by meiosis. These spores then mate to form the diploid cell.

Figure 2.3: Budding in Yeast

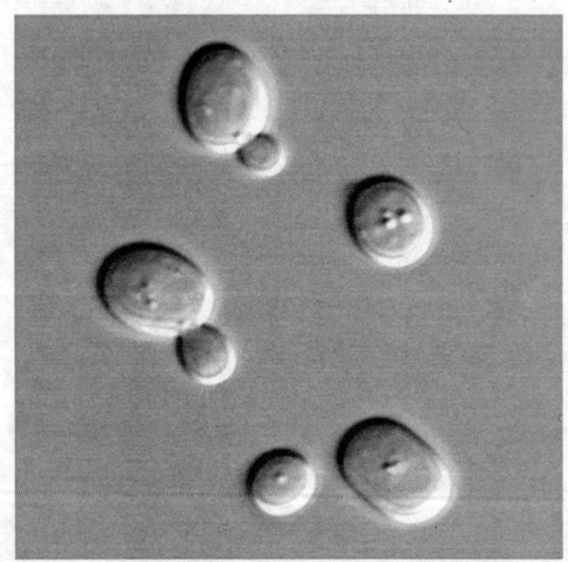

Source: 'Saccharomyces cerevisiae cells in DIC microscopy' by Masur (CC0 1.0; Wikimedia Commons).

Protozoans usually reproduce asexually. Under adverse conditions, they may reproduce sexually. This ensures the mixing of genetic material and hence better adaptation to the adverse environment.

Viruses have a very different method of reproduction. They latch on to the host cell and inject their nuclear material into the host cell. Then the genetic material uses the metabolic processes of the host cell to replicate its nuclear material and form new viral cells. The host cell ultimately bursts to release the new viruses.

FACTORS AFFECTING GROWTH AND SURVIVAL OF MICROBES

Knowledge of the factors that favour or inhibit the growth of microorganisms is essential for us to control their growth and multiplication, when used in the industry for the preparation of certain foods as well as when we wish to prevent them from spoiling our food or causing food poisoning. By adjusting, for instance, the conditions of storage and processing, we can speed up or slow down the growth of microbes according to our requirements. The chief factors that influence microbial activity in a food are hydrogen–ion concentration, moisture, oxidation–reduction (O–R) potential, temperature, nutrients and the presence of inhibitory substances or barriers. Each microorganism has a maximal, optimal and minimal requirement level for each of these factors. Optimal levels correspond with maximum growth of the microbe. When any of these conditions are unfavourable, most microbes tend to slow down their activity (become dormant) while some others die. Let us look at each of these factors.

Moisture

Microorganisms need water for growth, though the amount needed by each type of microbe varies. The water requirement is best expressed in terms of **available water or water activity (a_w).** This is defined as the vapour pressure of the water in the food divided by the vapour pressure of pure water. The value of a_w for pure water is taken as 1.00. If we multiply this ratio by 100, we obtain the **equilibrium relative humidity (ERH)** that the foodstuff would produce if enclosed with air in a sealed container at constant temperature. Thus, a food with an a_w of 0.6 would produce an ERH of 60 per cent.

Maintaining a relative humidity corresponding to a_w lower than that of the food being stored would tend to dry the surface of the food; conversely, if the relative humidity were higher than that corresponding to a_w, the food surface would pick up moisture. So water activity is actually a measure of ‘free’ water in a food, as opposed to ‘bound’ water. Water activity can also be expressed as per cent equilibrium relative humidity divided by 100. It is different from per cent moisture content, which refers to the total water in a food product which is available or bound. Although moist foods are likely to have greater water activity than dry foods, it may not be the norm. Foods having the same moisture content may have different water activities.

Each microorganism needs a maximal, optimal and minimal a_w in the food substance for growth. As the a_w is reduced below the optimal level, there is a decrease in the rate of growth and metabolism. Most bacteria grow well in a medium with an a_w approaching 1.00 (at 0.990 to 0.998), that is, they grow best in low concentrations of sugar or salt, although there are notable exceptions. The a_w would have to be below 0.60 to stop all chances of mould growth. The available water in a food can be reduced by several methods, which would then help in controlling the number of microbes in a food. These methods include adding salt or sugar, dehydration, forming hydrophilic colloids or crystallisation. In general, bacteria require more moisture than yeasts and yeasts more than mould. Fresh meat has an a_w of around 0.99, milk 0.97, dried fruit 0.6, biscuits 0.4–0.6, while milk powder and instant coffee have an a_w of 0.2 or below.

Osmotic pressure is related to the water activity of foods. A high solute concentration leads to a high osmotic pressure and a low water activity. Similarly, dilute solutions will have a low osmotic pressure and a high water activity. The cell membrane of bacteria allows water to pass in and out of the cell. This process is known as osmosis. When bacteria are placed in a solution with a high concentration of sugar or salt, water from the bacterial cells moves out, thus shrinking and killing the cells. Microorganisms that can grow in high concentrations of solutes, like sugar and salt, obviously have a low minimal a_w. **Halophilic** bacteria (those that thrive in high salt concentrations) require a certain minimal concentration of dissolved sodium chloride for growth. **Osmophilic** yeasts (adapted to environments with high osmotic pressures) grow best in high concentrations of sugar.

Oxidation–Reduction (O–R) Potential

The type of organisms which can grow in a food and the chemical changes that can happen in the food are determined by the reducing and oxidising power of the food (O–R potential), and by the amount of oxygen available where the food is kept/stored. The O–R potential of the food is determined by the oxygen tension of the atmosphere about the food. How much of air is in contact with the food will influence the oxygen tension. Atmospheric air has a high oxygen tension, but the head space in a can of food (space between the top layer of food and the lid of a can) would have a low oxygen tension.

> Modifying the atmosphere in which a food is packed also helps to increase its shelf life. Typically, the amount of oxygen is reduced in such packages and the concentration of gases like carbon dioxide or nitrogen is increased. This is known as **modified atmosphere packaging (MAP)**. It helps to slow down the growth of aerobic microbes as well as the spoilage caused by oxidative processes.

Bacteria display such a wide variety of responses to oxygen in the atmosphere that they can be classified into the following categories:

1. ***Aerobic*** bacteria are those that require free oxygen for growth and can grow well when incubated in the presence of air (which is 21 per cent oxygen by volume).
2. ***Anaerobic*** bacteria do not use oxygen to obtain energy and hence can grow without it. In fact, if oxygen is present in the environment, it hinders their growth and survival. Some, however, can tolerate low levels of oxygen (*non-stringent or tolerant anaerobes*), but others (*stringent, obligate or strict anaerobes*, for example *Clostridium spp.*) cannot tolerate even low levels and may die upon brief exposure to air.
3. ***Facultatively anaerobic*** bacteria, such as *Staphylococcus spp.* and *E. coli*, do not require oxygen for growth, although they may use it for energy production if it is available. They are not inhibited by oxygen and usually grow as well in the presence of oxygen as they do in its absence.
4. ***Microaerophilic*** bacteria require low levels of oxygen for growth, but cannot tolerate the level of oxygen present in the atmosphere.

The redox potential of a food is a measure of potential difference. The electrical units of millivolts (mV) designated as Eh are used to measure the redox potential in a system or food. In the oxidised range, the redox potential is positive while in the reduced range, it is negative. The redox potential of a food is affected by its chemical composition, the processing treatment given to the food, as well as the storage condition with respect to the gaseous environment. A high (oxidising) potential favours aerobes while a low (reducing) potential favours anaerobes.

Moulds require oxygen for their growth; most yeasts are also aerobic. During the growth of microbes like anaerobic bacteria, the O–R potential of a food may get lowered. This would restrict the growth of other aerobic microbes.

While packaging food, the shelf life can be extended by removing the air totally from the package, as is seen in shrink-wrapped and vacuum-packaged foods. Alternately, keeping a small head space in containers like cans and bottles can reduce oxygen tension, thus preventing microbial growth and also undesirable oxidative chemical changes.

Temperature

The rate of metabolic reactions of microbes is influenced by temperature. The temperature that allows for most rapid growth during a short period is known as the optimum growth temperature. Based on the temperature at which bacteria thrive, they are divided into three main groups:

1. ***Psychrophiles*** are bacteria which are able to grow at 0°C or lower, though they grow best at higher temperatures (10–20°C), the maximum temperature being 20°C.
2. ***Mesophiles*** grow best within a temperature range of approximately 25–40°C. For example, all bacteria which are pathogenic for humans and warm-blooded animals are mesophiles, most growing best at the human body temperature (37°C).
3. ***Thermophiles*** grow best at temperatures above 45°C. Some thermophilic bacteria have been detected in hot water or sulphur springs also. These bacteria can survive at very high temperatures.

Most moulds and yeasts do not grow well above 35–37°C. They grow very well at room temperature, some even grow at refrigeration temperatures. Knowledge of the maximum temperature the microbe can tolerate is important to decide the conditions under which processing needs to be done for food products containing useful microbes, and for the selection of cooking methods to destroy harmful microbes, their toxins and their spores.

Hydrogen–Ion Concentration (pH)

Just like temperature, every microbe has a minimal, a maximal and an optimal pH for growth. The inherent pH of foods varies, although most are neutral or acidic. Foods with low pH values (below 4.5) are usually not readily spoiled by bacteria and are more susceptible to spoilage by yeasts and moulds. Some foods have a low pH because of inherent acidity; others, like fermented products, have a low pH because of acidity that develops due to microbial activity.

Moulds can grow over a wider range of pH values than most yeasts and bacteria. Most yeasts do not grow well in alkaline substrates and prefer acidic pH (nearing 4.0–4.5). Most bacteria are favoured by a pH near neutrality (between 6.0 and 8.0). Hence, acidic foods tend to have a better shelf life (like pickles, fermented beverages, etc.). They are spoilt mostly by yeasts and moulds.

Buffers have a very important role to play in the food processing industry as they resist change in pH in a food. Each **fermentation process** requires a specific pH for best results. The pH during a fermentation process changes by itself. To control this pH change, buffers may be used. For instance, during fermentation of the dough for baking of bread, the pH decreases with the release of carbon dioxide and other organic acids. The flour and milk act as natural buffering agents, resisting change in pH. Chemical buffers like calcium carbonate may alternately be used to maintain pH during the fermentation process. Buffers maintain the physical, chemical and microbiological stability of foods.

Nutrient Content

Microbes, like other living organisms, need a source of nutrition. Nutrients present in food are used by microbes for their growth and maintenance. Microbes need the same nutrients that we do—a source of energy (carbohydrates or fats), protein, vitamins and minerals. The kind of microorganisms that are likely to grow on a food product can be determined by the kind and amount of different nutrients present in the food stuff, as each microbe has a specific requirement.

Carbohydrates in foods (especially sugars) are most commonly used as the source of **energy**. Complex carbohydrates like cellulose can be used only by a few microbes. Starch also can be utilised only by a limited number of organisms. When carbohydrates are unavailable, some microbes can utilise fats and proteins as an energy source. Microorganisms differ in their ability to use various **nitrogenous compounds** as a source of nitrogen for growth. Only some types of microbes are proteolytic in nature, that is, they break down proteins. When nutrients are in short supply, the growth of microbes is naturally restricted. Some microbes are unable to manufacture some or all the vitamins needed by them. These must then be present in the foodstuff on which they are growing. Organisms requiring special accessory growth substances might be prevented from growing if one or more of these **vitamins** or **minerals** are lacking. Cooking and processing reduces the quantity of vitamins, especially vitamins B and C, which are heat labile.

Moulds in general can utilise many more kinds of food as compared to bacteria. This is because most of the common moulds possess a variety of enzymes that help digest simple and complex substances. That is the reason why moulds can grow on such a variety of surfaces, ranging from different types of food to walls, books, clothes, leather, etc.

Based on nutritional requirements, bacteria can be divided into two categories—autotrophic and heterotrophic. **Autotrophic** bacteria can synthesise complex nutrients like carbohydrates, proteins and vitamins with the help of simpler substances available in their environment. The **heterotrophic** bacteria, on the other hand, require several preformed organic compounds. This category is the most common.

Autotrophic bacteria are further classified into **chemosynthetic** and **photosynthetic** bacteria, depending on whether they use inorganic chemical reactions as the source of energy (such as *Nitrobacter* and sulphur bacteria *Thiobacillus*) or sunlight (such as green and purple bacteria, Cyanobacteria) to produce food, respectively. Ultraviolet light is, however, harmful to the microbes as it can damage their nucleic acids and result in the death of cells.

Heterotrophic bacteria are further classified as parasites, saprophytes and symbionts. **Parasites** live on other organisms called hosts, from whom they derive their food, usually causing harm to the hosts; for instance, *Streptococcus*, *Mycobacterium tuberculosis,* etc. Disease-causing microbes are referred to as pathogens. **Saprophytes** feed on dead organic matter like soil bacteria and fungi like *Mucor,* while **Symbionts** live in a symbiotic relationship with other plants or animals for mutual benefit. For instance, a few species of *Rhizobium* live on the root nodules of leguminous plants, fixing nitrogen for the plant in exchange for protection. Similarly, several microbes reside in our intestine, including *Escherichia coli,* feeding on undigested matter and manufacturing vitamins B_{12} and K which can be used by the host.

Other Factors

As microbes exist in a variety of environments, some of them have other special requirements which help them to grow and thrive. Phototrophic bacteria, as the name suggests, need **light** to synthesise their food. Bacteria found in deep ocean trenches cannot grow in the laboratory unless the growth medium is subjected to similar **pressure** in which they survive in nature.

In addition, certain substances naturally present in foodstuffs may act as **inhibitors** of growth for some microbes. Examples of inhibitors present naturally are *lysozyme* in egg white, *lactenins* and *anticoliform* factors in freshly drawn milk, *allicin* in garlic and *eugenol* in cloves. Some of these chemicals are produced by plants and animals as a defence mechanism against microbial attack, and knowledge about these can be used by us to preserve foods. These chemicals can be extracted and added to other foods as well.

Synthetic chemicals are now manufactured and used to control the growth of microbes in foods. These are called **preservatives** and are used as food additives; for example, sodium benzoate, potassium metabisulphite, etc. are some commonly used food preservatives. These will be discussed in detail in chapter 10 of this volume.

A microorganism growing in a food may produce one or more **inhibitory substances** which prevent the growth of other microbes. For instance, propionic acid produced by the bacteria in Swiss cheese inhibits the growth of moulds. Nisin production by *Streptococcus* inhibits the growth of *Clostridium* during the curing of cheese. Heating or other forms of food processing may sometimes result in the formation of inhibitory compounds in foods. Heating fat hastens its oxidation, producing inhibitory compounds in the process. Browning concentrated sugar syrups may result in the production of furfural, which inhibits fermenting organisms.

Some foods are naturally protected from attack by microbes due to the presence of a **protective covering** or **layer**. For instance, eggs have an outer shell, fruits and vegetables have peels, etc. In fact, intact tissues are difficult for microbes to invade. Damage to or removal of these protective layers while peeling, cutting, chopping and mashing during cooking and processing exposes the cells of tissues to microbes. Hence, you will see that cut fruits spoil faster than whole fruits.

USE OF MICROBES IN THE FOOD INDUSTRY

Since time immemorial, microbes have been used for the preparation of fermented foods and beverages across cultures. They may comprise anywhere between 5 and 40 per cent of the diet of individuals across communities. Preparation of bread, wine, cheese and pickle is perhaps common to most cultures of the world. Each country and region has its own tradition of preparing these and other foods with the help of microbes. Plant and animal source foodstuffs are fermented either naturally because of the microflora naturally present in these foods, or by the addition of microbes (which is referred to as a starter culture). As understanding of the underlying process grows, many of these traditional foods are now being produced commercially. Discussed here are examples of fermented foods from across the globe.

Figure 2.4: Foods Prepared Using Microbes

2.4A. Breads

Source: 'Foccacia' by Jeremy Keith (CC BY 2.0; Wikimedia Commons).

2.4B. Variety of cheeses

Source: 'Cheese for sale in Freiburg im Breisgau' by Daderot (CC0 1.0; Wikimedia Commons).

Milk-based Preparations

Amasi is a popular fermented milk preparation of South Africa that tastes like cottage cheese or plain yoghurt. It is traditionally prepared by fermenting unpasteurised milk in special containers made of calabash (a gourd) or in a hide sack. Commercially, it is prepared using a culture of *Lactococcuslactis*.

Blue cheese is made using the *Penicillium* mould. It has a strong characteristic smell and flavour. In the European Union, many blue cheeses such as Roquefort, Danablu, Cabrales, Gorgonzola and Blue Stilton carry a protected designation of origin, that is, they can bear the name only if manufactured in a particular region of a certain country.

Source: 'Du Roquefort, fromage de l'Aveyron' by Thesupermat (CC BY-SA 4.0; Wikimedia Commons).

Chaas or ***Chaach***, also known as *Mattha*, is a curd-based drink which is consumed plain or with a variety of spices, which varies with the region of India it is made in.

Cheese is a product made by fermenting coagulated milk. Use of different types of moulds produces different kinds of cheeses, the flavour and texture of which varies across the world and even from farm to farm in the same region.

Curd or ***dahi*** is produced by using starter cultures of lactic acid bacteria (*Lactobacillus* spp.) from previously set curd. It is traditionally eaten in India along with meals, and is also used to make beverages like *lassi*.

Kefir is a milk-based, mildly alcoholic beverage popular in Eastern Europe and West Asian countries. The milk is inoculated with a starter culture of lactic acid bacteria and yeast. Traditionally, the fermentation was carried out in skin bags hung from the doorway. It is good for the immune system and has traditionally been used in the treatment of tuberculosis and cancer.

Koumiss is a naturally fermented dairy product used in the Caucasus region. It is traditionally made from mare's milk and is popular among the nomads and cattle breeders of Central Asia. It contains about 1–3 per cent alcohol. It is also recommended for the treatment of tuberculosis.

Yoghurt is produced using a culture of *Lactobacillus delbrueckii* subsp. *bulgaricus* and *Streptococcus thermophilus* bacteria.

Most fermented foods also have health promoting benefits. Curd and yoghurt have live bacteria which are referred to as probiotic bacteria. Probiotic bacteria are defined as live microbes which when given in adequate amounts, confer health benefits on the host. The health benefits attributed to these bacteria are listed in Box 2.1.

Cereal / Pulse-based Preparations

Several Asian countries consume fermented soybean foods as a part of their daily diet. Here are examples of some more traditional fermented products made from cereal grains or pulses. Traditional south Indian dishes like ***idli*** (steamed preparation) and ***dosa*** (thin pancake-like preparation) are prepared from fermented batters of rice and black gram *dal*. The batter is usually left to ferment overnight. The microorganisms involved in this preparation include *Leuconostoc mesenteroides*, *Streptococcus faecalis* and *Pediococcus cerevisiae*.

Box 2.1: Health Benefits of Probiotics

Probiotic bacteria like species of *Lactobacilli*, *Bifidobacteria* and *Streptococcus thermophiles* are considered beneficial for our health. They are good bacteria which are normally present in our gut. They promote digestion, protect the intestinal lining, prevent diarrhoea and balance the pH in the intestine. They also provide immunity to the body against pathogenic bacteria, protect against certain infections and reduce the risk of some cancers. Probiotic preparations are recommended after a course of antibiotics to re-establish the gut flora, which is partially destroyed by antibiotics.

A probiotic microbe should be non-pathogenic, genetically stable, and resistant to acid, bile and digestive enzymes of the gastrointestinal tract. Only then would it be able to survive during the gastrointestinal transit and reach the gut, where it must grow and proliferate.

There are several food products in the market which contain probiotics. These include milk, curd, milk-based beverages, ice cream, and even types of coffee and green tea!

Vada is made from the soaked, ground paste of black gram *dal* which has been fermented overnight, and then made into the shape of a doughnut before deep frying.

Appam is a pancake made from fermented rice batter and coconut milk. It is a popular preparation in the south Indian states, especially Tamil Nadu and Kerala, and also in Sri Lanka, where it is called 'hoppers'.

Breads such as sourdough bread and others which depend on yeast to raise the dough are examples of fermented breads. The yeast *Saccharomyces cerevisiae*, also known as baker's yeast, is most commonly used for raising the dough as the fermentation process leads to the production of carbon dioxide.

Bhatura is a deep-fried preparation made from refined wheat flour (*maida*) dough with curd as a starter. The major organisms involved in fermentation are *Streptococcus* and *Lactobacillus* species which are present in curd.

Dhokla is a Gujarati preparation made of rice and chickpea batter which has been fermented. It may also be made with semolina and chickpea flour. It is a steamed preparation. The major organisms involved in fermentation are *Leuconostoc mesenteroides* and *Streptococcus faecalis.* A similar preparation made with chickpeas alone is called *khaman.*

Miso is a popular Japanese seasoning prepared by fermenting soybean with the fungus *Aspergillus oryzae* and salt. Sometimes rice, barley and other ingredients are also added, producing different types of miso. Miso is mostly used for the preparation of miso soup.

Naan is an Indian flat bread made with refined wheat flour using yeast or curd.

Natto is a popular Japanese breakfast dish made by fermenting soybeans with *Bacillus subtilis var. natto.* It is typically eaten with rice.

Soy sauce is a widely used condiment in Asian countries, made from a fermented paste of soybeans and roasted grains. The chief mould used is of the *Aspergillus* species, mostly *Aspergillus oryzae* and yeast. The liquid soya sauce is separated from the fermented slurry, filtered and pasteurised.

Tempeh is an Indonesian preparation made by fermenting soybeans using natural cultures. Traditionally, it is wrapped in banana leaves. A mild acidulant, usually vinegar, may be added to lower the pH and create a selective environment that favours the growth of the tempeh mould over competitors. The chief organism in this preparation is *Rhizopus oligosporus* or *Rhizopus oryzae*. A portion of the previous batch of tempeh usually serves as the starter culture. It is a dense cake which can be sliced or crumbled and added to dishes, or roasted or fried and added to preparations. It has an earthy flavour and goes well with several dishes.

Tofu is made by coagulating soybean milk and then pressing the resultant soft white coagulum into blocks just like *paneer* is prepared in India. Tofu has a subtle flavour and is added to sweet and salty dishes. It can also be fermented to produce a kind of condiment in East Asian cuisine. *Mucor* and *Rhizopus* species of moulds are typically used as inoculum.

Worcestershire sauce is a condiment mix of British origin. The ingredients include barley malt vinegar, molasses, sugar, salt, anchovies, garlic and onions, among other ingredients. Fermentation is carried out by halophilic bacteria.

Vegetable/Fruit-based Preparations

Kanji is a fermented drink made in India, especially in winter and around the festival of Holi. It is made with black carrots, beetroots, mustard seeds and asafoetida (*heeng*). Some preparations have *vadas* of black gram.

Kimchi is a fermented vegetable preparation popular in Korea and other Southeast Asian countries.

Pickles of a variety of fruits and vegetables are made by letting them ferment. Cucumber pickle is made by fermentation with *Lactobacillus plantarum*.

Sauerkraut is fermented cabbage produced with the help of lactic acid bacteria, including *Leuconostoc*, *Lactobacilli* and *Pediococcus*. It is a sour preparation with a distinct flavour.

Meat Preparations

Traditionally, Eskimos have practised fermentation of animal products, such as whole fish, fish heads, walrus, sea lion and whale flippers, beaver tails, seal oil, birds, etc., for an extended period before being consumed. Minced meat filled in intestinal casings and left to ferment after adding a starter culture is common across several cultures across the world. A variety of fermented sausages and salami are consumed in several countries and are known by different names, like *som moo* in Vietnam, *chorizo* in the Iberian Peninsula, *sujuk* in Turkey, pepperoni in America and *saucisson* in France. These are prepared using a variety of lactic acid bacteria or mould as starter cultures. Some commonly used bacteria are *Lactobacillus plantarum*, *Pediococcus* and *Micrococcus* species. Fish sauce and shrimp paste/sauce are popular ingredients in several dishes of East and Southeast Asia and Chinese cuisine that are also fermented.

Alcoholic Preparations

Carbohydrates, on fermentation, produce alcohol. Traditionally, alcoholic beverages were prepared by natural fermentation of cereal grains or fruit. Yeasts have also been used in the production of alcoholic beverages. Pure cultures are now used commercially for fermentation, leading to the production of products that are consistent in quality and have a characteristic flavour.

Beer is perhaps one of the oldest and the most widely consumed alcoholic beverages in the world. It is prepared by brewing, a process of fermentation of cereal grains. Most beers are made from malted barley, although wheat, rice, millet or corn are also used to produce different varieties of beer. Brewer's yeast is used for fermentation. The dominant types of yeast used to make beer are the top-fermenting (yeasts rise to the surface during the process of fermentation creating a foam head) *Saccharomyces cerevisiae* and bottom-fermenting (tend to settle at the bottom of the fermenter as fermentation nears completion) *Saccharomyces pastorianus*. Flowers of the hop vine (called hops) are used for flavouring.

Rice beer is popular in north-eastern India. The rice is fermented with a mix of yeasts and mould (*Rhizopus, Aspergillus* and *Mucor* species). **Ale** is a type of beer produced using a warm fermentation process. Yeasts such as *Saccharomyces cerevisiae* are used for the fermentation, which is carried out at warm temperatures between 15 and 20°C, and occasionally as high as 24°C.

Wine is produced by the fermentation of grapes, followed by an ageing process before it is ready for consumption. Wines are also made from other fruits like pomegranate, cherry, berries, apple, etc., and from rice (called *sake*). Residues of wine have been discovered in ceramic jars dating back 8,000 years. Traditionally the grapes were crushed in huge containers with bare feet, the whole family often joining in the ceremonial process! The pulp of grapes (must) is fermented with yeast, which converts the sugar of the grapes to alcohol and carbon dioxide. This is followed by bacterial fermentation (using lactic acid bacteria). For ageing, the wine may be kept in oak barrels which impart the wine a flavour of their own. Wines from specific regions of the world have a specific flavour of their own.

Champagne is a product of secondary fermentation. Fresh must, yeast and sugar are added to wine to create carbonation. It is a sparkling wine.

Distilled alcoholic products like rum, brandy and whiskey are made by distillation of the fermented products. **Rum** is distilled from fermented sugarcane juice or molasses, while **brandy** is made from distilling fruit wines. **Whiskey**, on the other hand, is made by distilling fermented mash of wheat, barley, corn, rye or other malted grains. Fermentation is usually carried out by yeasts like *Saccharomyces cerevisiae*. Whiskey is typically aged in wooden casks.

Other Products

Amino acids are widely used for their nutritional and flavour-enhancing properties in the food industry. Amino acids like branched chain amino acids, taurine and lysine are added to energy drinks, food supplements and health foods. Monosodium glutamate (ajinomoto) is made from the amino acid glutamic acid. *Corynebacterium glutamicum* is used to produce glutamate and other amino acids. *Brevibacterium lactofermentum* is used for lysine and threonine production. Strains of *Escherichia coli* are also used in the production of several amino acids.

Antibiotics are naturally produced by moulds and bacteria to discourage the growth of other microbes in the same medium. Ever since the discovery of Penicillin in 1928 by Alexander Fleming, man has identified several antibiotics from a variety of moulds and bacteria for use in the treatment of human and animal infections. The genus of the bacteria *Streptomyces*, for example, can produce bioactive secondary metabolites such as antifungals, antivirals, antitumorals, anti-hypertensives, immunosuppressants, and especially antibiotics like streptomycin, neomycin and tetracycline.

Citric acid is another widely used chemical, mostly as an acidulant, flavouring agent and preservative in the food industry. It is produced by the mould *Aspergillus niger*, which converts sugar in molasses to citric acid.

Enzymes are widely used in the food industry in the manufacture of different foods and beverages. These enzymes are commercially prepared using microbes. Table 2.1 gives a listing of enzymes obtained from different microbes. Enzymes to break down pectin (pectolytic enzymes) during processing of fruits are obtained from a variety of fungi.

Table 2.1: Some Enzymes Used in the Food Industry

Enzyme	Microbe from which the enzyme is obtained	Used in manufacture of these Products
α-amylase	*Aspergillus oryzae*	Bread
Thermostable α-amylase	*Bacillus stearothermophilus* or *Bacillus licheniformis*	Glucose, crystalline dextrose, dextrose syrup, maltose and maltodextrins
Amyloglucosidase	*Aspergillus niger*	Beer and other spirits
Cellulase	*Trichoderma viride*	Clarified juices
Lipases	*Mucormiehei* *Aspergillus niger*	Cheese
Proteases	*Aspergillus niger* *Bacillus amyloliquefaciens*	Cheese

Source: Adapted by Author from Frazier and Westhoff 2014 and Gurung et al. 2013.

Vinegar (5–20 per cent solution of acetic acid in water with other trace chemicals and flavourings) is made by further oxidation of the alcohol, typically produced by fermentation of carbohydrates present in starchy vegetables, malted cereals or fruit juices using acetic acid bacteria.

Vitamins can be produced commercially by growing microbes on feedstocks. This type of production is more economical than chemical synthesis of the vitamin. Microbes are used for the production of B vitamins like riboflavin, vitamin B12, niacin, pyridoxine, etc.

IMPLICATIONS FOR FOOD SAFETY

Bacteria and moulds can form spores which can survive inhospitable conditions. Protozoa survive adverse environmental conditions by forming a resistant cyst or going into a dormant stage. When conditions become favourable again for their growth, these spores or cysts germinate into the vegetative cells. Most of these spores and cysts are very hardy and can survive normal pasteurisation and cooking temperatures. For example, the spores of *Clostridium botulinum* have been reported to resist boiling for several hours. Subsequently, if the food is left at room temperature for a long time, the spores may germinate and lead to food poisoning.

Knowledge of the factors affecting the growth and survival of microbes helps us in controlling them. These factors can be classified as intrinsic and extrinsic (see Figure 2.5). *Intrinsic factors* relate to the food and *extrinsic* to the environment in which the food is kept. It helps us to predict which microbes are likely to grow under the prevalent conditions of moisture, temperature, pH and gaseous environment in different kinds of food, thus helping us to work out the best storage conditions to improve shelf life. These factors can be used as critical control points in HACCP (Hazard Analysis Critical Control Point) plans to control the growth of spoilage/harmful organisms. For instance, we know that it would be difficult for bacteria to grow below a_w 0.6, pH 4.5 and temperatures higher than 70°C.

This also helps us in the food industry, where we use these microbes for the preparation of fermented products like curd, yoghurt, cheese, beverages, etc. It also helps us to prevent transmission of disease and infection by undesirable microbes and prevent the spoilage of materials by microorganisms.

Figure 2.5: Intrinsic and Extrinsic Factors Affecting Growth of Microbes in Food

Intrinsic Factors	**Extrinsic Factors**
• pH of the food	• relative humidity
• oxidation-reduction potential	• ambient temperature
• water activity	• concentration of gases in storage atmosphere
• temperature of food	
• nutrient content	
• inhibitory substances	
• protective layer/covering	

Source: Drawn by Author.

By modifying the environment in which the microbes are growing, we can either kill the microbes or at least restrict their growth. Lowering the pH, that is, making the food acidic, usually restricts the growth of most harmful bacteria. An unfavourable water activity will result in a reduction in the rate of growth. Hence, reducing the moisture content of foods by drying or by adding solutes like sugar or salt in high concentrations can help in food preservation. Heating the food to high temperatures can destroy microbes and spores. Storing food at low temperatures of the refrigerator or freezing slows down the growth of most organisms. Making the gaseous environment unfavourable by either removal or addition of oxygen also helps, depending on the type of microbe. The growth of an aerobic microbe is restricted by restricting the supply of oxygen, such as by packaging the food in vacuum or in a nitrogen environment. Exposing the organism to oxygen is detrimental to the growth of anaerobic microbes. Organisms might be prevented from growing if one or more of nutrients like carbohydrates, proteins and vitamins were lacking. The addition of inhibitory substances like preservatives will also achieve the desired results.

SUMMARY

- The chief factors that influence microbial activity in a food are hydrogen–ion concentration, moisture, oxidation–reduction (O–R) potential, temperature, nutrients and the presence of inhibitory substances.
- Finding a suitable environment for survival triggers microbes to multiply in number. Different microbes reproduce in different ways—both sexually and asexually.
- Microbes are used for the preparation of fermented foods and beverages across cultures. These foods may constitute 5–40 per cent of the diet of individuals, depending on the community to which they belong.
- Preparation of bread, wine, cheese and pickle is perhaps common to most cultures of the world.
- Bacteria and moulds can form spores which can survive inhospitable conditions, while protozoa survive adverse environmental conditions by forming a resistant cyst or going into a dormant stage.
- The principles of food preservation are based on the factors influencing the growth of microbes. Microbes can be destroyed, or their growth slowed down by suitably changing the pH of the food (generally lowering the pH), drying the food, adding solutes like salt or sugar in high concentrations, heating the food to high temperatures, storing it at low temperatures, making the gaseous environment unfavourable by either removal or addition of oxygen, depending on the type of microbe.
- Addition of inhibitory substances like preservatives or by limiting an important nutrient in the medium will also achieve the desired results.

KEY WORDS

Aerobic: Requiring oxygen or air for survival and growth.

Anaerobic: Refers to microbes which grow best in the absence of free oxygen.

Asexual reproduction: Not involving the fusion of male and female gametes.

Binary fission: Division in half; a kind of asexual reproduction.

Diploid: Nucleus containing two complete sets of chromosomes, one from each parent.

Facultative: Refers to microbes which grow well, either aerobically or anaerobically.

Halophilic: Refers to microbes which require a salt-rich environment for growth and survival.

Haploid: Nucleus having a single set of unpaired chromosomes.

Meiosis: Type of cell division that results in daughter cells with half the chromosome number of the parent cell.

Mesophiles: Refers to microbes which grow best within a temperature range of approximately 25 to 40°C.

Microaerophilic: Bacteria which require low levels of oxygen for growth, but cannot tolerate the level of oxygen present in air.

Mycotoxin: Toxic substances produced by moulds.

Osmophilic: Refers to microorganisms adapted to environments with high osmotic pressures, such as high sugar concentrations.

Parasite: An organism living at the expense of another organism (called the host).

Pathogenic: Disease-causing.

Psychrophiles: Refers to microbes able to grow at 0°C or lower.

Thermophiles: Refers to microbes which grow best at temperatures above 45°C.

EXERCISES

1. How are viruses different from other microbes?
2. What is the difference between yeasts and moulds?
3. What microbes grow better in an acidic pH?
4. What microbes require more moisture for their growth?
5. Classify the bacteria according to the temperature at which they grow.
6. What are microaerophilic bacteria?
7. List some foods made with the help of microbes, which you regularly consume.
8. What are probiotics? Why are they beneficial for our health?
9. What are the food safety implications of knowing the different factors which affect microbial survival?

REFERENCES

Enei, H., and Y. Hirose, 'Recent Research on Development of Microbial Strains for Amino Acid Production', Available at http://www.nottingham.ac.uk/ncmh/documents/bger/volume-2/bger2-4.pdf (accessed 2 March 2016).

Frazier, W. C., and D. C. Westhoff, adapted by N. M. Vanitha, *Food Microbiology* (5th edition), New Delhi: McGraw Hill Education (India), 2014.

Gurung, N., S. Ray, S. Bose, and V. Rai, 'A Broader View: Microbial Enzymes and their Relevance in Industries, Medicine, and Beyond', *BioMed Research International* 2013, 2013, 18 pages, Available at http://dx.doi.org/10.1155/2013/329121 (accessed 14 March 2016).

Tamang, J. P., 'Benefits of Traditional Fermented Foods', *Our* World, 2010, Available at http://ourworld.unu.edu/en/benefits-of-traditional-fermented-foods (accessed 14 March 2016).

ONLINE SOURCES

Types of Fermented Foods, Available at https://en.wikipedia.org/wiki/List_of_fermented_foods (accessed 12 April 2018).

Types of Cheeses, Available at https://en.wikipedia.org/wiki/List_of_cheeses (accessed 12 April 2018).

ICMR-DBT Guidelines for Evaluation of Probiotics in Food, Available at http://icmr.nic.in/guide/PROBIOTICS_GUIDELINES.pdf (accessed 12 April 2018).

3

FOOD SPOILAGE AND PRESERVATION

HIGHLIGHTS

- Factors responsible for food spoilage
- Chemical changes due to spoilage
- Spoilage of different types of food
- Principles of preservation
- Methods of food preservation

Food, like any organic matter, is perishable. The quality of food deteriorates over time, faster for some foods than others. Several physical and chemical changes in the food lead to spoilage. These changes may be a result of microbes growing in the food, pests feeding on it or reaction of food ingredients with the environment. Naturally present enzymes in food may also deteriorate food quality. Different foods spoil because of the interplay of a number of factors. These factors primarily depend on the composition of the food item and the conditions of the storage environment. Knowledge about how food spoils will help in finding ways to prevent spoilage or at least ways to slow down the process and hence increase the shelf life of foods. With advances in science and technology we now have a number of methods to preserve foods, thus improving their safety as well as utility. In this chapter, we discuss the various factors which are responsible for spoilage in different foods as well as describe the different methods of increasing shelf life of foods by preventing spoilage.

FACTORS RESPONSIBLE FOR FOOD SPOILAGE

Spoilage is the deterioration of the quality of food resulting in physical and chemical changes which ultimately make the food inedible. A number of factors determine why and how our food spoils (see Figure 3.1). Usually, a single factor does not act in isolation.

For most foods, it is a number of factors acting in tandem which ultimately lead to the physical and/or chemical changes referred to as spoilage. For instance, cooked food left uncovered or packaged food left open is exposed to the *oxygen* and *moisture* in the air. Dry foods like biscuits and wafers would readily pick up moisture from the air and lose their crisp texture.

Microbes grow better in foods with higher moisture content. They feed on the nutrients in the food and produce metabolic waste products which may spoil the taste of the food as well as make it unsafe for human consumption. At the same time, the fat in the food product is susceptible to oxidative change (rancidity) if exposed to air. The *physical state* and *biological structure* of the food also determines whether and how it gets spoilt. For instance, whole grains have a longer shelf life as compared to powdered or broken grain, which has a greater surface area exposed to the environment. Whole pulses with seed coat also keep longer than washed/polished pulses as the seed coat acts as a protective barrier. Similarly, nuts in shells and vegetables/fruits with tougher skins keep longer.

Figure 3.1: Factors Responsible for Food Spoilage

Microorganisms and pests like insects

Extrinsic and intrinsic factors—temperature, moisture, air, light, pH

Natural enzymes in plants and animals

Physical factors and chemical contaminants

Source: Drawn by Author.

Let us examine in detail how different factors affect the quality of food.

When is food considered to be spoilt?

Different communities have different criteria for food being considered to be spoilt and unfit for consumption. People in Greenland, for instance, consider *kiviak* (fermented whole birds) and *hakarl* (fermented shark) as delicacies. Others would label the dishes putrid and unfit for consumption. Changes which are objectionable for some may be desirable for some others. As long as the food does not lead to illness, it may be considered fit for consumption, provided that it also meets the desired stage of development/maturity and texture as well as flavour.

Microorganisms use our food as a source of nutrients for their own growth. The characteristics of food determine the kind of microbes that are likely to grow on it. We have already learnt in the previous chapter that microbial growth is influenced by factors like hydrogen-ion concentration or the pH of the food, moisture content, the amount of oxygen available, temperature, nutrients present in the food and the presence of inhibitory substances.

Besides making food unsafe to eat, microbes tend to spoil the appearance of the food product as well as alter other sensory properties like taste and aroma. Thus, spoilt milk will taste sour and will split on heating. Over-ripe fruits which get infested with fungus smell and taste bad.

However, sometimes the taste and texture of the food is not altered and in such cases, the consumer falls prey to food poisoning, as he does not realise that the food is spoilt.

Pests like insects, birds and rodents may also spoil food, especially cereal grains, fruits and vegetables by feeding on them and bruising them in the process. Bruised, broken or cut food items are further susceptible to microbial attack, resulting in further decay. Exposed to light and air, oxidation reactions may cause further spoilage. Insect-infested food is anyway unappetising to consume.

Temperature of storage further determines whether microbes are able to grow and survive. Most microbes grow best at room temperatures ranging between 25–40ºC. The greater the number of microbes, the faster the spoilage. Storage at high temperatures may also lead to loss of volatile flavouring substances, destruction of nutrients and breakdown of other food components, thus leading to deterioration in food quality. Freezing may alter the texture of fruits and vegetables, making them mushy on thawing.

Moisture is an important requirement for microbial growth. Hence foods with a higher **water activity** (**a_w**) are more prone to spoilage by microbes. Foods which pick up moisture from the environment also tend to spoil faster. High levels of moisture in foods or in the storage environment may spoil the texture of food due to formation of lumps, especially in powdered spices and flour, and loss of crispness of products like wafers and biscuits.

Exposure to air induces oxidation reactions which may result in undesirable changes in colour, flavour and nutrient content. Fats in foods may also become rancid. Most microbes also need air to grow and survive.

Light has been shown to destroy certain vitamins like riboflavin, vitamin A and E present in food. It may also be responsible for loss in colour and oxidation of fats.

pH of a food also determines whether a food is susceptible to microbial spoilage. Most microbes grow best near neutral pH.

Nutrient content of foods determines which microbes are likely to cause spoilage as microbes have different requirements for nutrients. Foods like milk and milk products, eggs and meat are rich in all nutrients and provide the ideal substrate for a variety of microbes to grow and thrive. These foods are hence likely to be the most contaminated with a wide range of microbial flora.

Enzymes are naturally present in foods of plant and animal origin. These enzymes continue to be active even when the food is harvested from the plant or the animal is slaughtered. They bring about several physical and chemical changes in the food. Fruit ripening is one such change which may continue in some fruits even after it is plucked from the parent plant. If the activity of the enzymes is not decreased or stopped, then the fruit may become over-ripe and ultimately rot. Enzymes may also result in browning reactions; for instance, when fruits like apples, bananas and pears, or vegetables like potatoes and aubergine are cut and left exposed to the air, they start turning brown and are unappetising to consume.

Physical changes in food can spoil the appearance of the food, like those induced by burning (charring), pressure (where a food loses its shape and size becoming unappealing; for instance, squashed tomatoes or cherries won't find many buyers) or drying (where for instance, the surface of breads, cakes, etc. may dry out and harden). The presence of foreign bodies also makes food inedible, as you will surely reject food in which you see a finger nail or animal/human hair. Presence of chemical contaminants also renders food unfit for human consumption.

Figure 3.2: Classification of Food Based on Shelf Life

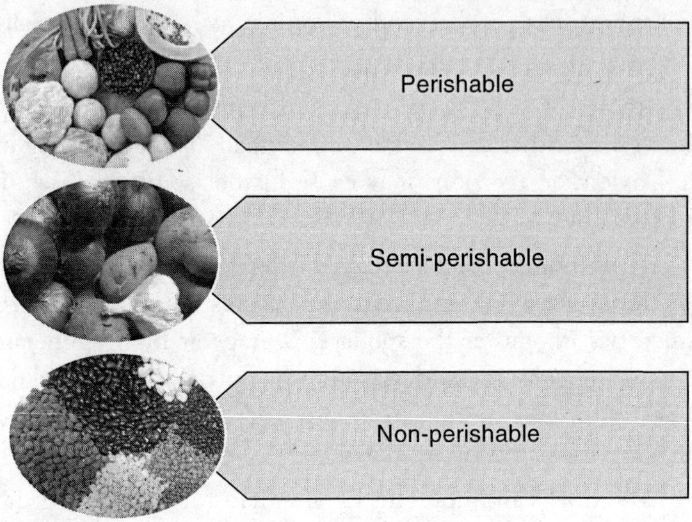

Perishable

Semi-perishable

Non-perishable

Source: Drawn by Author.

Figure 3.2 depicts the classification of food by the ease with which they spoil. *Perishable foods* which spoil readily include milk, meat, poultry, fish, eggs and most fruits and vegetables. Hence you cannot imagine storing these at room temperature without them getting spoilt. Some would not even last a hot summer day without getting spoilt. Keeping these in a refrigerator or freezer is important to prevent their spoilage.

Semi-perishable foods are those which can be kept at room temperature for a brief period of time (couple of weeks to a few months) without them spoiling; for instance, potatoes, onions, nuts, wheat flour, semolina, vermicelli, rice flakes, etc. They would naturally keep for a longer period of time if the temperature and moisture of the storage environment are kept favourable.

Non-perishable foods are those which do not spoil for a longer period of time (months or years) provided they are stored and handled carefully. Examples include rice, sugar, dry pulses, beans, etc.

CHEMICAL CHANGES DUE TO SPOILAGE

When microbes act on foods, a variety of chemical reactions ensue because of their metabolic activity. Various components of food undergo different reactions and result in the production of a number of products.

Changes in Proteins

Proteins in foods may be broken down by microbial enzymes to peptides. These may impart a slight bitter taste to the food. Proteinases and peptidases may hydrolyse proteins to form a variety of peptides or amino acids. These, in the case of some foods like cheeses, may actually impart a desirable flavour. However, this is very subjective. Blue cheese is considered to be a delicacy but some may easily be put off by fungus visible as streaks on its surface (see Figure 3.3) or by its pungent smell and sharp taste.

Figure 3.3: Blue Cheese with Bluish-green *Penicillium* Mould

Source: 'Bleu de Gex' by Myrabella (CC BY-SA 3.0; Wikimedia Commons).

Anaerobic decomposition of proteins and its breakdown products may result in obnoxious foul smells due to the production of sulfides, mercaptans, ammonia and putrescine. These changes are referred to as ***putrefaction***. Aerobic degradation is usually referred to as ***decay***. Amino acids may be deaminated (removal of amino group $-NH_2$) or decarboxylated (removal of a carboxyl group –COOH) to a variety of compounds like amines, keto acids, ammonia, acetic acid, carbon dioxide, etc. The degradation of amino acids is of primary significance in the spoilage of foods which are rich in protein.

Changes in Fats

Enzymes produced by microbes decompose the fat to glycerol and fatty acids, ketones and alcohols. Autoxidation of fats in foods due to exposure to air is a more common cause of spoilage (***rancidity***) than microbial spoilage. Rancidity can be of two types—hydrolytic (breakdown of fat-releasing free fatty acids in presence of moisture) and oxidative (oxidation of the unsaturated fatty acids upon exposure to air).

Changes in Carbohydrates

Carbohydrates are the preferred energy source for microbes. If available in a food, these are readily used. Complex carbohydrates are broken down to simple sugars. This results in softening of the texture of foods. Under aerobic conditions, glucose, the simplest sugar, is oxidised to carbon dioxide and water. Anaerobically it undergoes fermentation of any of the six types as shown in Table 3.1. A variety of other products like organic acids, fatty acids, aldehydes and ketones are also possible when different microorganisms act on sugars.

Changes in Other Substances

Alcohols are usually oxidised to their corresponding organic acids; for instance, ethanol is converted to acetic acid. *Acetaldehyde* may be oxidised to acetic acid or reduced to ethanol. Glycosides release

Table 3.1: Types of Fermentation Reactions which Decompose Simple Carbohydrates

Type of fermentation	*Microbe involved*	*Chief products formed*
Alcoholic	Yeasts	Ethanol + CO_2
Simple lactic	Homofermentative lactic acid bacteria	Lactic acid
Mixed lactic	Heterofermentative lactic acid bacteria	Lactic, acetic acids, ethanol, glycerol, CO_2
Coliform type	Coliforms	Lactic, acetic, formic acids, ethanol, CO_2, H_2
Propionic	Propioni bacteria	Propionic, succinic, acetic acids, CO_2
Butyric-butyl-isopropyl	Anaerobic bacteria	Butyric, acetic acids, CO_2, H_2

Source: Adapted by Author from Frazier and Westhoff 2014.

sugar upon hydrolysis. *Pectic substances* like protopectin present in foods derived from plants are converted to pectin. Pectinesterases may further breakdown pectin to give pectic acid and D-galacturonic acid. Some of these changes happen naturally in fruits during ripening. However, beyond a point, the fruit may become overripe and be rejected as unfit for consumption because of deterioration of flavour and texture. *Organic acids* present as salts in foods may be oxidised by microbes to carbonates, causing the medium to become more alkaline. Under aerobic conditions, there can be a complete oxidation of organic acids to carbon dioxide and water, or they may be broken down to other products similar to those from sugars.

SPOILAGE OF DIFFERENT TYPES OF FOOD

After understanding that foods spoil at different rates depending on their nature and favourability of conditions for their growth, let us study in detail how each food group spoils and the organisms which are primarily responsible for spoilage.

Spoilage in Milk and Milk Products

If you have ever visited a farm or dairy and witnessed the milking process, you will be able to list a number of ways in which the milk can become contaminated on the farm itself. Aseptically drawn milk also has bacteria like Streptococci and Micrococci. However, if the yard/shed where the cows and buffaloes are housed is not kept clean and the body of the animal is covered with mud, dung or is in contact with contaminated water from stagnant pools, there is a high risk of the milk being contaminated with pathogenic microorganisms. In fact, it is recommended to clean the udders and surrounding skin of the animal with a germicidal solution before milking.

The other significant sources of contamination include any surface with which the milk comes into contact—milk pail/can, milking machine pipelines, strainers, homogenisers, separators, filters, stirrers, valves, bulk milk coolers, tankers which transport the milk and different parts of the milk vending machines. The workers who handle the milking process or machinery can also be a source of contamination and they need to follow all precautions of personal hygiene as do food handlers of any food industry or food service establishment. The water used for all cleaning purposes itself needs to be free of contamination. All milk-contact surfaces need to be kept clean and sanitised. Residue milk should always be removed from containers before fresh milk is filled, as several bacteria would have grown in the residue milk. The design of the equipment should be such that it facilitates easy cleaning, sanitising and drying.

Milk is an excellent medium for growth as it is rich in nutrients, high in moisture and has a near neutral pH. *Acid-forming bacteria* spoil milk by souring which is due to the production of lactic acid. Heating acidic milk usually results in the milk splitting. *Lactics* and many other bacteria spoil milk by **lactic acid fermentation.** Some of the bacteria like species of *Clostridium*, *Bacillus* and *Coliform* lead to formation of gas, which can be seen in the form of froth on milk or bubbles in curd. The bacteria may also result in breakdown of milk proteins and production of a bitter flavour because of the production of peptides (breakdown products of proteins). **Ropiness** and **sliminess**, usually seen in milk and cream, are caused by bacteria. Ropiness mostly on surface of milk is caused by *Alcaligenes viscolactics*, while ropiness throughout the milk is caused by many bacteria, such as certain species of *Enterobacter*, *Streptococcus*, *Lactobacillus* and *Micrococci*. Psychrotrophic (those which survive at low temperatures), gram-negative, rod-shaped bacteria often tend to spoil milk which has been refrigerated. Thermodurics (those microbes which withstand the pasteurisation temperature and can survive at high temperatures) also adversely affect keeping quality.

Milk fat in milk and milk products may be decomposed by the action of bacteria, yeasts and moulds. Fat in milk products may also become **rancid** on storage due to oxidation of fatty acids and hydrolysis. Milk powder becomes brown due to **maillard reaction** (non-enzymatic browning reaction between reducing sugars and amino acids). Spoilage of milk and milk products usually results in the production of **off-flavours** like sour, bitter, musty, stale and sometimes even a burnt flavour like that of overheated milk. **Colour changes** in milk and milk products like butter and cheese are mostly due to surface growth of bacteria or moulds. Red, pink, yellow and brown-coloured growth has been seen in cream of milk, surface of butter and cheese.

Spoilage in Meat, Fish, Poultry and Eggs

Meat, poultry and eggs can get contaminated very easily as most animal and poultry rearers are not able to maintain hygiene and sanitation on their farms. The hide, hooves, hair, feathers of animals and birds, and eggshells are exposed to dirt and faecal matter and hence, intestinal bacteria. Handling of the meat after slaughter can further add to the contamination, especially from knives, cleavers, containers, air of the slaughter house, and clothing and hands of workers. Grinders, spices and other ingredients which go into the production of meat products like sausages can also add to the contamination.

These foods serve as an excellent medium of growth for microbes as they have high moisture content, nearly neutral pH and are a rich source of almost all nutrients. **Bacteria**, **yeasts** and **moulds** are all responsible for spoilage (see Table 3.2). This may result in the production of **slime** on the surface, patches of **discolouration** and an **off-taste** and **smell**. Bacteria can spoil

Table 3.2: Microbes which Cause Spoilage in Meat and Meat Products

Sign of spoilage	*Microbes involved*
Surface slime	*Pseudomonas, Alcaligenes, Streptococcus, Leuconostoc, Bacillus, Micrococcus, Lactobacillus* and yeasts
Change in colour (from red to green, brown or grey) because of oxidative changes. Patches and spots of red, yellow, purple, green or brown colours may also be seen on surface	*Lactobacillus, Leuconostoc* (production of peroxides or sulfides) *Serratia* (red spots), *Micrococcus, Flavobacterium* (yellow), *Chromobacterium* (greenish-blue, brownish-black), *Cladosporium* (black spot), *Penicillium* (green patches), *Sporotrichum, Geotrichum* (white spot)
Phosphorescence (glowing on surface of meat)	*Photobacterium* spp.
Lipolysis (breakdown of fat) and oxidative rancidity	*Pseudomonas, Achromobacter* and some yeasts. Exposure to air, light and metals like copper may hasten rancidity
Off-odour and flavour (taints, putrefaction or souring)	*Clostridium, Coliforms* (acid and gas formation leading to souring), *Pseudomonas, Alcaligenes* and *Proteus* (putrefactive bacteria), *Actinomycetes* (which give a musty flavour) and yeasts
Whiskers (white fuzzy growth)	*Thamnidium, Mucor, Rhizopus*

Source: Adapted by Author from Frazier and Westhoff 2014.

the meat or meat products even if they are vacuum packaged. Anaerobic and facultative bacteria can act in the absence of oxygen or at low levels of oxygen to cause **putrefaction** and **souring**. The sour odour may be due to the production of volatile acids and growth of yeasts. Faecal coliform bacteria, *Clostridium* and *Salmonella* are commonly found pathogens in meat and meat products. Green rot in eggs caused by *Pseudomonas fluorescens* makes the white of the egg bright green in colour. In black rots, the yolk becomes black and gives a brownish tinge to the whole egg when it breaks. This is mostly caused by the *Proteus* spp. In cases of storage in conditions of high humidity, surface spoilage of eggs may take place in the form of fuzzy growth, which progresses to spoil the egg inside once the mycelia of the mould gain entry through the shell. Pink and red rots have also been seen in eggs.

Eggs can spoil by **physical changes** too—cracked shells may lead to moisture loss from the egg and microbes on the shell may gain entry. As an egg stales, the air cell enlarges, the white becomes more alkaline and thinner, the yolk membrane also weakens and breaks easily when the egg is cracked and contents taken out in a utensil. **Chemical changes** may also lead to the spoilage of these foods. Fats of meat, poultry and fish are susceptible to **oxidative changes** making it rancid. High-fat meat like pork is especially

Why do fish and seafood spoil faster than the other meats?

- The natural enzymes in fish cause faster deteriorative changes
- The pH of the flesh (not being as acidic as meat) favours microbial growth
- The unsaturated oils in fish undergo oxidative rancidity faster than saturated fats in other meats

prone to this kind of spoilage. Unlike meats which are rich in saturated fat, fatty fish that have more of unsaturated fat are prone to faster spoilage. Spoilt fish has a putrid odour and is unfit for human consumption. Fish and other seafood are more perishable than the other meats. Spoilt or stale fish is also likely to have sunken eyes, grey gills, scales falling off and flesh easily separable from bone. Prompt cooling helps to slow down the spoilage. That is why you will find fish being kept on ice by retailers.

Cathepsins are **natural enzymes** present in meat which breakdown proteins and help in tenderising meat during ageing (a process carried out by hanging beef in a refrigerated atmosphere). However, if the meat is left for longer periods of time or the temperature of the cold storage is not maintained, then the meat may spoil, leaving a sour taste and odour. This is a result of hydrolysis of proteins by the meat enzymes and microbial action. More microbes are encouraged to grow with increase in simple nitrogenous compounds, made available for their use by the hydrolytic enzymes.

Spoilage in Vegetables and Fruits

Although **plant pathogens** (disease-causing microbes) can spoil fruits and vegetables while they are growing in the field, what is discussed here pertains only to harvested horticultural products which spoil because of changes during ripening or due to **microbial contamination**. Vegetables and fruits can easily get contaminated with soil and dirt during harvesting and packing. **Mechanical damage** like cuts and bruises (due to poor handling or by animals, birds or insects) may make them more vulnerable to decay and growth of microbes, which would otherwise have not been able to penetrate the peel. Although it is difficult to estimate how much of the produce is lost in India annually, various estimates have put it to the tune of 15–50 per cent. This has usually been attributed to inappropriate storage and transport. Sometimes, the processing plants serve as sources of contamination depending on the levels of sanitation of the factories and processing equipment (peelers, corers, choppers, conveyor belts, filters, etc.), hygiene of handlers and quality of water used for washing.

Changes during **ripening** include the action of enzymes which result in softening of the flesh, conversion of complex to simpler substances (especially sugars) and development of flavour with decrease in astringency. Although these changes are desirable from the point of view of their acceptability for humans, they also make the fruit or vegetable a more suitable medium for microbes to grow. Organisms get transferred from spoiling fruits and vegetables on to other produce in contact during storage or transport.

Vegetables and fruits have a lot of moisture and have carbohydrates, making them a suitable medium for growth. A lot of the spoilage in fruits and vegetables may be a result of **saprophytic organisms** (which feed on dead or decaying matter), invading after plant pathogens have caused the preliminary damage. **Sliminess** or **souring** may be seen in vegetables which have been piled up and kept in moist and hot conditions. **Fungal spoilage** may result in either wet (water-soaked) areas or as dry spots with hard discoloured areas. There may be areas where the mycelia of the fungus is clearly visible as a fuzzy growth (see Figure 3.4). The typical types of spoilage seen in vegetables and fruits as shown in Table 3.3. The term '**rot**' is usually given to the changes seen.

Juices of fruits and vegetables spoil by **fermentation** of sugars and organic acids and **slime** production by lactic acid bacteria (*Lactobacillus* and *Leuconostoc* spp.)

Table 3.3: Types of Spoilage Commonly Seen in Fruits and Vegetables

Type of spoilage	*Vegetables/fruits affected*	*Microbes involved*	*Appearance*
Bacterial soft rot	Broccoli, radish, cabbage, garlic, cauliflower, onion, green beans, carrots	*Erwinia*, *Pseudomonas*, *Clostridium*, *Bacillus* spp.	Water-soaked appearance, soft and mushy with foul odour
Rhizopus soft rot	Cucumber, pumpkin, watermelon, peach, cantaloupe	*Rhizopus* spp.	Soft and mushy, cottony growth with black dots
Blue mould rot	Apple, peach, lemon	*Penicillium* spp.	Bluish-green-coloured growth
Pink mould rot	Cantaloupe, melons, strawberries	*Trichothecium roseum*	Pink spores
Green mould rot	Tomato	*Cladosporium* spp.	Greenish growth
Grey mould rot	Tomato, watermelon, cabbage, apple, cauliflower, onion	*Botrytis* spp.	Grey-coloured growth
Black mould rot	cabbage, cauliflower, sweet potato, onion, peach	*Aspergillus niger*	Black spots or smut (like those seen on onions)
Alternaria rot	Pepper, sweet potatoes, lemon, figs	*Alternaria* spp.	Greenish brown to black spots
Anthracnose	Bananas, avocados	*Colletotrichum* spp.	Spots on leaves, fruit or pods
Downy mildew	Cucumber, grapes, cantaloupes	*Phytophthora* spp., *Bremia* spp.	White wooly mass

Source: Adapted by Author from Frazier and Westhoff 2014 and Jay et al. 2005.

Spoilage in Cereals and Cereal Products

Cereal grains get contaminated with dirt, filth and microbes during the process of harvesting, threshing, winnowing and packaging, as most of these operations take place in fields, on the open ground. The surface of the grains may contain millions of bacteria and mould spores. However, if the grains are dry, the low water activity discourages the growth of microbes. Insects may, however, infest the grains and lead to damage and spoilage. Flour of cereals is more prone to spoilage as compared to whole grains as it is easier for pests and microbes to feed on it. Also, the increased surface area exposes the lipids to air, causing rancidity. That is why wheat and rice grains taste fine and are good to eat even after several months or more than a year; however, the shelf life of flour is not more than three months. Refined wheat flour (*maida*) and all other types of flour which undergo bleaching as a part of processing have a lower microbial load as a result of treatment with bleaching agents like benzoyl peroxide or an oxide of chlorine or nitrogen. Washing and milling processes also reduce the microbial load of the grains. However, blending and conditioning of bleached flour can lead to an increase in microbial load if strict hygienic standards are not maintained.

Cereal products like bread, biscuits and cakes may not have viable microbes when fresh out of the oven. These may, however, subsequently get contaminated if exposed to air during cooling or slicing and packaging, and if handled using insanitary equipment or surroundings. Bacteria which cause **ropiness in bread** may survive the baking process as they form spores which are resistant to heat. The area where ropiness develops becomes soft and sticky and the slimy material can actually be drawn out into threads and hence the name 'ropy' bread. This can be prevented by use of chemical preservatives in bread.

Figure 3.4: Visible Mould Growth on Custard Apple and Bread

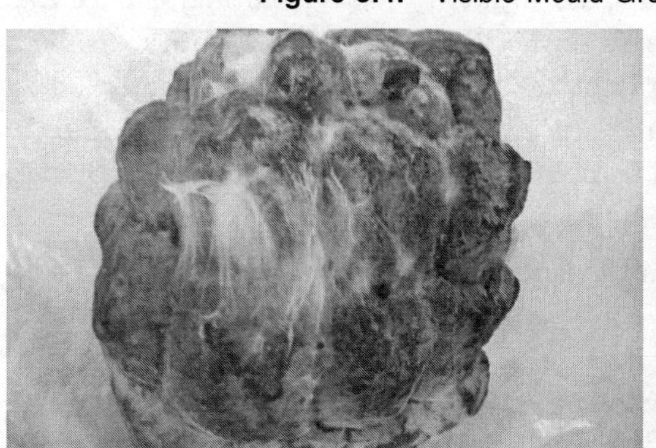

Source: Author.

Moisture levels above 12–13 per cent encourage microbial growth and hence spoilage of cereals. Undesirable bacteria which are found to decrease shelf life of cereal products include:

- Bacteria causing ropiness in bread (*Bacillus subtilis, Bacillus licheniformis*)
- Acid-forming bacteria which cause **sourness of dough and flour**. This may be followed by alcoholic fermentation by yeasts and then conversion of alcohol to acetic acid by *Acetobacter* species.

Besides bacteria, growth of moulds like *Aspergillus* and *Fusarium* may lead to production of **mycotoxins in cereals and cereal products**. Aflatoxin in corn and rice, and deoxynivalenol in wheat flour can potentially pose a threat to animal or human health as well as result in economic loss. *Mucor*, *Rhizopus* (white and black cottony growth), *Monilia* (pink or reddish growth) and *Penicillium* (green growth) mould can be seen on the surface of baked products like bread and cakes and result in their spoilage (see Figure 3.4).

Most cereal grains and their products like pastas and breakfast cereals are very low in moisture content and unless stored in warm and moist conditions or contaminated by unclean equipment, they seldom spoil. Moist pastas and dough, even when refrigerated, may show signs of **swelling due to gas formation** by bacteria.

Products which are rich in fat like biscuits and cookies usually spoil because of the fat becoming rancid on exposure to air.

Spoilage in Sugars and Sugary Products

Table sugar is sucrose made usually from sugarcane or beets. It is a dry crystalline product and has a low microbial load, and therefore does not spoil easily, unless it is handled or packaged in an unhygienic manner. Sugarcane juice, molasses (viscous by-product formed during refining of sugar from sugarcane or beets), syrups made with sugar and honey have higher moisture levels and may spoil.

Sugarcane itself may be highly contaminated depending on how it was harvested and transported to the factories. Cutting, extraction and clarification of the juice may reduce the vegetative cells of bacteria and yeasts and these may further be reduced during the remaining steps of sugar manufacture like sedimentation, filtration, evaporation and crystallisation. Spores of **thermophilic bacteria** may, however, survive the process. Other microbes may be added to the product during packaging from contaminated equipment and poor handling.

The extent of microbial load and spoilage of **candies** and **confectioneries** made from sugar is determined by how contaminated the ingredients are and how contaminated the surfaces and air are during handling and packaging. Confectionery for which the processing temperature does not reach pasteurisation temperature, like chocolates with creamy centres have often been incriminated in food poisoning episodes (salmonellosis). However, hard candies or those made by hot processing methods, like caramels, jellies and fudges, are less likely to harbour microbes.

Spoilage of sugars or sugary products is mostly caused by microbes which are **osmophillic** (adapted to conditions of high osmotic pressure due to high concentration of sugar) or **xerotolerant** (tolerant of dry conditions). These are generally yeasts (such as *Saccharomyces*) and certain moulds. Some species of *Bacillus* and *Leuconostoc* bacteria may also lead to spoilage of sugars especially raw juice of sugarcane or beet. Honey is chiefly spoiled by species of *Zygosaccharomyces* or *Torula*. An off-flavour slowly develops and there is darkening of the colour of the honey and crystallisation along with fermentation. Syrups with lower concentrations of sugar may allow growth of moulds on the surface. Poorly stored or preserved jam may sometimes show growth of moulds on the surface.

> Presence of organisms which have low heat resistance in a canned food is an indication that there has been a leakage in the can. The microbes have gained entry after the heat treatment. Bulging or swollen cans should be discarded as it is an indication of either chemical or biological spoilage. Rusted and leaky cans should also be rejected.

Spoilage in Canned Foods

Foods packaged in cans are usually heated to high temperatures. Hence, chances of **biological spoilage** arise only if there has been inadequate heating or contamination during cooling and sealing. This results in microbes or their spores surviving in the canned food. If the can is not of good quality material and cracks, or develops small perforations, or the seams are defective, then again, microbes can enter the can. Alcoholic yeasts and bacteria of the *Bacillus* species are gas producers, resulting in formation of carbon dioxide. Some of the bacteria, especially the anaerobes, may result in the production of **off-odours** (acid or putrid) depending on the type of organism present. This type of spoilage results in swelling of cans, or if the product is bottled, the gas can be seen in the form of foam or bubbles. However, spoilage need not always be evident by **gas production**. Some bacteria simply result in a decrease in pH levels and cause **souring**. Home-canned products are usually spoilt by yeasts and moulds. The different types of microbial/ biological spoilage seen in canned foods are summarised in Table 3.4.

Table 3.4: Types of Biological Spoilage of Canned Foods

Type of microbe	*Type of spoilage*	*Microbes involved*	*Foods affected*
Thermophilic spore-forming bacteria	*Flat sour spoilage*: development of lactic acid (which causes souring) but no gas, so the cans do not swell	*Bacillus* spp.	Low-acid foods like peas and corn, acid foods like tomato
	TA (thermophilic anaerobic) spoilage: spoilt food has a sour or 'cheesy' odour. There is both acid and gas (CO_2 + H_2) production but not hydrogen sulfide production. There is a 'hard swell' in cans which may eventually burst	*Clostridium thermosaccharolyticum*	Microbe feeds on carbohydrates and is found in a variety of ingredients used in canned foods such as vegetables, sugar and cereal
	'*Sulfur Stinker' or Sulfide spoilage*: production of hydrogen sulfide gas. In corn there may be grey-black discolouration of liquid and kernels.	*Desulfotomaculum nigrificans*	Low-acid foods like peas and corn
Mesophilic spore-forming bacteria	*Sugar fermenting (butyric acid type of fermentation)* with production of CO_2 + H_2 and swelling of can. Putrefactive or proteolytic species	*Clostridium* spp.	Acidic to medium-acid foods like tomatoes, pineapple, pear by sugar fermenting bacteria, low-acid foods like peas, meat, fish and poultry by putrefactive anaerobes
	Production of gas by some aerobic species causing swelling in cans of cured meat	*Bacillus* spp.	Seafood, meat, evaporated milk and low-acid, home-canned foods

(*Contd*)

(*Contd*)

Type of microbe	*Type of spoilage*	*Microbes involved*	*Foods affected*
Non-spore forming bacteria	Some of these cause formation of acid, while the heterofermentative species may result in formation of CO_2 and swelling of can	*Streptococcus thermophiles*, *Micrococcus*, *Lactobacillus*, *Microbacterium*, *Leuconostoc*	Fruits, tomatoes, meat and ham
Yeasts	Fermentation with production of CO_2 and swelling of cans, film yeasts may grow on surface of food	Fermentative yeasts and film yeasts, such as *Saccharomyces* spp.	Canned fruits, jams, jellies, fruit juices, syrups, sweetened condensed milk
Moulds	Growth of mycelia on the food along with fermentative changes by some species	Moulds like *Aspergillus*, *Penicillium*, *Citromyces*	Home-canned foods like jams, jellies, candied fruit, marmalades

Source: Adapted by Author from Frazier and Westhoff 2014 and Jay et al. 2005.

Spoilage in canned food can be also be due to chemical causes. **Chemical spoilage** mostly occurs due to **hydrogen swell.** The acid in the food reacts with the iron of the can producing hydrogen gas (see Box 3.1). Food may also interact with the metals in the can producing **discolouration**, **off-flavour** and perforation of the metal. There may also be loss of nutritive value of food due to destruction of vitamins.

Box 3.1: Causes of Spoilage in Canned Foods

Biological spoilage

- Sub-optimal heat treatment (which does not kill all the microbes and their spores)
- Inadequate or slow cooling after the heat sealing (permitting the thermophilic spore formers to grow)
- Poorly evacuated cans in which some air remains (so aerobic microbes can also grow)
- Excessive microbial load of raw ingredients (hence all are not destroyed during the processing)
- Improper sealing at seams (which permits entry of microbes later)
- Leakage due to punctures/holes as a result of manufacturing defects or rough handling of cans (results in release of vacuum, entry of microbes after processing, usually from contaminated cooling water in which cans are immersed)

Chemical spoilage

- Improper lining and lacquering of inner surfaces of cans (which allows the metal to react with food)
- Presence of sulphur or phosphorus in foods (which react with the metal)
- Highly acidic foods (which react with the metal)
- High storage temperatures (promote reaction of food components with metal)
- Poorly ventilated production and storage areas (heat and moisture promote reaction of food ingredients with metal of cans)

PRINCIPLES OF PRESERVATION

In order to prevent food spoilage, a number of things need to kept in mind by the food industry, food service establishments and people at home. These principles to be followed for preservation of food are illustrated in Figure 3.5.

Figure 3.5: Principles of Food Preservation

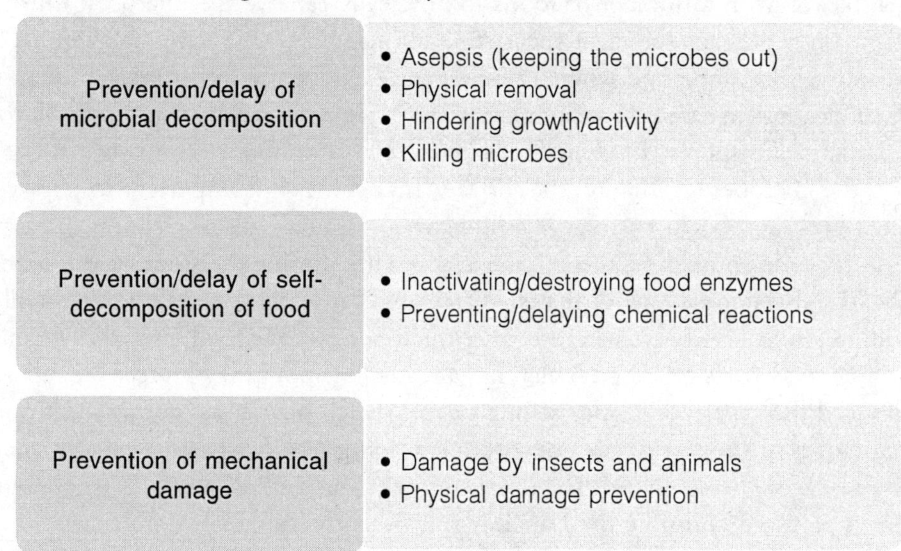

Source: Adapted by Author from Frazier and Westhoff 2014.

Prevention/Delay of Microbial Decomposition

The first logical step in protecting our food from microbes is to keep microbes away from food. In case that is not feasible (technologically or due to prohibitive costs), or if the food is already contaminated, then microbes need to be either removed from the food, killed or conditions made so unfavourable that they are not able to grow or survive. In the previous chapter, conditions favouring the growth and survival of microbes have already been discussed in detail.

Keeping microbes away from food is also referred to as ***asepsis***. This is done by keeping the environment in which food is processed or stored absolutely clean and sanitised (using chemicals, heat or irradiation). Aseptic handling, processing and packaging ensure that microbes do not gain entry into a food product. The natural protective covering on food also protects it from microbial attack like the peels of fruits and vegetables, the shell of an egg, skin/membranes/ fat layer on meat. If the protective covering is damaged, microbes gain access to the food and decompose it. A number of packaging materials and techniques are now available to prevent the entry of microbes during storage. The container—whether a pouch, bottle or can—needs to be sealed. The package should be strong and not easily damaged during handling and transport. Newer product formulation technology is striving for food microstructure (structure of food at the microscopic level), which does not allow microbes access to nutrient-rich portions of the food by use of films and emulsions.

Removal of microbes must be done if the 'bioburden' of microbes in a food is high, which means that if a food has a high microbial count because of the nature of the food or because of contamination during processing or storage, it would need to be treated to physically remove the microbes. Methods like filtration, centrifugation, sedimentation, clarification, washing or trimming have been employed with a number of foods to physically remove the microbes. Out of all the methods, *filtration* is perhaps the most successful, and has been used with clear liquids like fruit juices, beer, soft drinks, water and wine. The filter can be a membrane or made of diatomaceous earth, sintered glass or unglazed porcelain, etc. *Centrifugation* is mostly used for milk to remove suspended particles and spores. *Washing* foods before consumption is done to get rid of soil and dirt as well as the microbes residing on the surface. That is why it is important to wash vegetables and fruits first and then begin cutting. Washing when you have already chopped the vegetable defeats the purpose by providing the microbes access to the inner tissues of the food. It also enhances the loss of water-soluble nutrients. Water used for washing should undoubtedly be free from contamination; otherwise, it will introduce microbes into the food instead of washing them away. *Trimming* away parts of a food which has already got spoilt may protect the rest of it. You may have noticed the vegetable vendor selling carrots which have some portions cut out. This is to prevent microbes in the rotting portions from spreading to other parts. Similarly, many times at home, if a block of cheese or fruit has fungus growing on a small portion, people tend to cut off the affected part and consume the remaining 'apparently' fungus-free portion.

Hindering the growth or activity of the microbes is done by providing conditions which are unsuitable for their growth or survival. This can easily be done by:

- altering the temperature of storage: keeping the food hot (>60°C) or refrigerated (<5°C) or frozen
- restricting the amount of water available for the microbe to use: by drying the food, adding salt, sugar or other solutes
- modifying the atmosphere around the food: by restricting the oxygen (vacuum packing, nitrogen or carbon dioxide packing)
- altering the pH to make it unfavourable: by adding acids, fermentation
- use of chemical compounds or preservatives which inhibit the growth of microbes like inorganic compounds (sulphites, nitrites), organic substances (benzoates, sorbates, etc.), antibiotics and smoke

Microbes which have already entered the food and cannot be removed physically have to be ***inactivated*** or ***killed***. This is done by heat treatment of food to temperatures capable of destroying the harmful microbes. So milk is usually *pasteurised*, while canned foods may need to be *sterilised*. *Irradiation* of food is also used to destroy the microbes. *Mechanical destruction* of microbes by grinding or high pressure is also possible, though not frequently used.

Prevention/Delay of Self-decomposition of Food

Destruction of food enzymes is done by heat treatment of foods. *Blanching* is a pre-treatment given to fruits and vegetables before dehydration, freezing or canning. In this process, the food is scalded or plunged into boiling water for some time and then cooled in tap water or cold water. It is not a drastic heat treatment, but is effective in inactivating the enzymes. Normal cooking temperatures will also destroy the food enzymes, as most of them get inactivated around 79.4°C. These enzymes are also responsible for hydrolytic rancidity of fats. Microbial enzymes also lead to food spoilage and these enzymes can also be destroyed by heating.

Preventing/delaying chemical reactions like oxidation which lead to food spoilage, especially rancidity in fats and fat rich foods or dry foods, is possible by limiting exposure to air (by covering/wrapping the food, vacuum packaging, modified atmosphere packaging) or by using antioxidants (natural ones like vitamin E, vitamin C and beta carotene or synthetic chemicals like BHT, BHA, TBHQ, gallates, etc.). Storing food at refrigeration and freezing temperatures can prevent rancidity by reducing autoxidation. Storing food in coloured or opaque containers prevents oxidation catalysed by light.

Prevention of Mechanical Damage

Damage by insects and animals is prevented by adequately packaging the food with material which is not easy to tear or make holes in. Storage areas should be pest-free. This is ensured by appropriately designing storage areas, storing food material safely at a height to keep it beyond the reach of rodents, and use of pesticides and insecticides. Irradiation is also useful in killing insects living on some vegetables.

Physical damage to food is prevented by appropriate handling and storage. Packaging in special cartons and containers prevents physical damage; for instance, egg trays/cases are used to protect eggs, special foam wrapping is used for fruits like apples and pears, separators are used in cartons, etc. so that food or its packaging is not damaged. Damaged packaging or shell/skin/peel gives easy access to microbes and encourages oxidative damage as well.

METHODS OF FOOD PRESERVATION

The principles of food preservation are used for identifying methods which can be used to delay or prevent food spoilage (see Table 3.5). The methods have been broadly discussed in the previous section. In this section, some of these will be discussed in detail. Most methods are based on factors affecting growth and activity of microbes. Microbes can be destroyed or their growth slowed down by suitably changing the pH of the food (generally lowering the pH), drying the food, adding solutes like salt or sugar in high concentrations, heating the food to high temperatures, storing it at low temperatures, and making the gaseous environment unfavourable by either removal or addition of oxygen, depending on the type of microbe. Addition of inhibitory substances like preservatives or by limiting an important nutrient in the medium will also achieve the desired results.

Table 3.5: Methods of Preservation of Food

Principle	*Method used*
Asepsis	Microstructure design of foods, decontamination of all ingredients and surfaces which the food will touch, clean handling, processing and packaging
Removal of microbes	Filtration, centrifugation, sedimentation, clarification, washing or trimming
Hindering growth and activity	Addition of acidic ingredients, fermentation (increasing acidity); drying, adding salt, sugar, solutes (restricting available water); cooling, refrigerating or freezing (lowering temperature); vacuum packing, modified atmosphere packing (restricting oxygen availability); addition of chemical preservatives (antimicrobial compounds)
Killing microbes	Pasteurisation, boiling, sterilisation (heat treatment); irradiation
Inactivation of food enzymes	Blanching, other heat treatments
Delay of chemical reactions	Antioxidants used in foods, packaging techniques
Physical damage, damage by pests/insects	Pest/insect proofing, packaging and storage areas, use of insecticides and pesticides, appropriate packaging to prevent mechanical damage

Source: Drawn by Author.

Altering the pH

Increasing the acidity of foods, either by fermentation or the addition of weak acids like lemon juice or vinegar, has been used as a preservation method since ancient times. In their natural state, most foods such as meat, fish and vegetables are slightly acidic while most fruits are moderately acidic. A few foods such as egg white are alkaline. Less heat is needed to inactivate microbes if the food has an acidic pH.

Dehydration

Dried foods are preserved because the available moisture is too low for the microbes to grow. Since enzymes function in an aqueous medium, their activity is also controlled on removal of moisture. Dehydration also concentrates the food, increasing the proportion of solutes and thereby osmotic pressure. Drying of foods is a common practice; for instance, *papad*s and extruded products like *wadi*s made of pulse flour are often laid out in the sun to dry in traditional Indian households. In coastal areas, you may see fish being sun-dried. Fruits may be dried at home or in processing units using special dehydrating equipment. Foods prepared for astronauts are also dehydrated using ultra-modern dehydrators and are vacuum packed to increase shelf life. Air or sun drying is dependent on weather conditions. Food left out in the open to dry may also become contaminated with dust. The industry uses a variety of dehydrators for removing moisture from a variety of foods.

The process of dehydration typically involves surrounding the food with warm air. Circulating air tends to pick up more moisture. Heating in vacuum results in loss of water from foods at much lower temperatures. This has another advantage in that the natural characteristics of the food are retained better. Food dehydration at the industrial level may be done by freeze-drying. Food is flash frozen and put into a reduced-pressure system which causes the water to sublimate directly from the solid to the gaseous phase. Although freeze-drying is more expensive than traditional dehydration techniques, it reduces the change in flavour, texture and nutritional value. Instant coffee is sometimes freeze-dried. Fruits may also be freeze-dried to preserve them. Liquids are generally spray-dried or drum-dried. For instance, milk produced in excess can easily be converted into milk powder, which has a better shelf life.

Limitations of dehydration include high processing cost, especially if expensive equipment is used. Texture, colour and flavour can get adversely affected, with the food product turning brown. Rehydration of certain products may become difficult if not processed properly.

Refrigeration and Freezing

This is another method of preservation which has been practised for centuries. People stored food in cool cellars or lowered them in containers into wells or earthen pots containing water. Hunters and gatherers, especially those living in snowbound areas, would bury their food in snow or ice, thus preserving it for some time. Refrigeration slows down the microbial activity and prevents their replication. Freezing food slows down decomposition by turning residual moisture into ice, inhibiting the growth of most microbes. Some microbes may also die as a result of being frozen. Freezing also ties up most of the moisture available and in the process increases the concentration of dissolved substances in the unfrozen moisture. Enzymes in vegetables may still adversely affect the flavour and texture during freezing. These enzymes must therefore be destroyed by heating before the vegetables are frozen. A variety of freezing equipment and processes are now available. Food basically needs to be stored at –18°C. You are already familiar with the freezer compartment of home refrigerators. In retail outlets and supermarkets, you may also have seen the sliding-top freezers in which ice cream is stored or the big open freezers which line nearly a full wall of the store.

The way the food is frozen will determine the texture and quality of the food product. Quicker freezing generates smaller ice crystals and helps retain cellular structure. This is done by exposing foods to very low temperatures. **Cryogenic freezing** is the quickest freezing technology available due to the ultra-low liquid nitrogen temperature (-196°C). **Slow freezing**, which is followed at the household level, results in coarse or bigger crystals, which tend to rupture plant and animal cells thus affecting the texture of the food. Commercially, some fruits and vegetables may be first dehydrated to about half their weight and then frozen. This is known as **dehydro-freezing** and significantly reduces the cost of packing, storing and shipping as the weight and volume of the food decreases.

> **Hurdle technology** is an intelligent combination of hurdles for microbes which ensure that they are eliminated from the food or their activity controlled. The right combination of methods would ensure that all disease-causing microbes have been safely controlled or eliminated from the final food product. For instance, during preparation of a food product, the raw ingredients may be subjected to high temperature, a preservative or antioxidant added to the product and the product aseptically packaged using vacuum packaging.

Several foods are frozen at the home level and several others are available in markets in a frozen form. Typically, we freeze vegetables which are cheap in a particular season; for instance, during winter, peas are shelled, blanched in hot water and then packed into polythene bags and frozen. Raw meat, fish and poultry are also stored in the freezer compartment. Sometimes, cooked preparations which we want to eat after a few days are also frozen. Several 'fry and eat' frozen snacks are available in the market along with frozen vegetables like peas, mixed vegetables and sweet corn. Ice cream and other frozen desserts are also very popular.

Modified Atmosphere Packaging

Storage in controlled atmospheres with high levels of carbon dioxide was practiced in the early 1930s on ships which transported fruits. The composition of the internal atmosphere of packages of food is now controlled to increase shelf life. The process involves reducing the quantity of oxygen drastically as oxygen is vital for microbes to survive and multiply. The speed of oxidation reactions also slows down. This is done by replacing oxygen with an inert gas like nitrogen or with carbon dioxide. This kind of packaging is mostly used for fresh and minimally processed foods like fruits, vegetables, meat and fish. The mixture of gases in the package depends on the type of product, packaging material and storage temperature. *Vacuum packaging* is used for several foods like peanuts and processed meats, which are shrink-wrapped with absolutely no air in the package. This protects the food from oxidative and microbial damage.

Preservatives

Preservatives are *substances which when added to food retard, inhibit or arrest the activity of microorganisms.* The Food Safety and Standards Act (FSSA), 2006 in India specifies the different types of preservatives which can be added to foods in our country. These preservatives have been classified as Class I and Class II preservatives. Included under Class I preservatives are natural food ingredients which we use in food preparation, like common salt, sugar, dextrose, glucose syrup, spices, vinegar or acetic acid, honey and edible vegetable oils. You will find most of these preservatives in food items like pickles, relishes, *chutneys* and pastes which we make at home. There is no restriction on the addition of these preservatives in any food item unless otherwise specified under the FSSA.

Class II preservatives are chemicals like benzoic acid, sulphurous acid, nitrates or nitrites of sodium or potassium, sorbic acid, including its sodium, potassium and calcium salts, propionic acid, including its calcium or sodium salts and its esters, lactic acid, including its sodium, potassium or calcium salts, acid calcium phosphate, nisin, sodium diacetate and methyl or propyl parahydroxy-benzoate. The use of Class II preservatives is restricted to only certain foods and the amount of the preservative which can be added to these foods is also specified under the FSSA. Also, the presence of a Class II preservative in any food has to be declared on the packaging of the food.

Heat Treatment

Heat is known to kill microbes. The vegetative cells die first at lower temperatures (most getting killed at 70°C), while spores need higher temperatures and take longer to get destroyed.

Pasteurisation is mainly used for milk and fruit juices. It is a relatively mild heat treatment where temperatures are kept below 100°C. Usually, milk is pasteurised at 72°C for 15 seconds. This must be followed by chilling the milk because although most disease-causing microbes would have been killed, some other microbes may have survived and can spoil the milk.

Ultra-heat treatment (**UHT**) of milk may also be done. This involves heating milk to 93.4°C for 3 seconds or 149.5°C for one second. This milk is usually sold packaged in tetra packs which do not need refrigeration and usually have a shelf life of 3 months if unopened. Juices are also packaged in tetra packs after pasteurisation and usually have a shelf life of 6 months until opened.

Sterilisation is done at a very high temperature of 121°C, at which all the microbes are destroyed in the food product. Most canned and bottled foods are sterilised. Usually, the air inside cans is also drawn out. This further restricts the growth of aerobic bacteria. One drawback of the method is that the taste and appearance of the food gets altered when heated at such high temperature. Heat labile nutrients also get destroyed.

Irradiation

Food is usually irradiated using either of the three sources of ionising radiation—gamma rays from radioactive cobalt 60 or cesium137, X-rays, or a beam of high-energy electrons. The SI unit of the dose of ionising radiation is gray (Gy). One gray is defined as the *absorption of one joule of energy by one kilogram of food matter*.

Ionising radiation kills microbes by causing damage to the structure of the microbial cells, like the cell membranes. It may lead to the production of free radicals which cause irreversible alterations in DNA and RNA structures. If oxygen is present during irradiation, the damage done to microbial cells is greater; higher the dose of radiation, greater the damage. At low doses, the damaged DNA may be repaired by specialised enzymes present in the microbe.

> **Radicidation** is the treatment of food with ionising radiation in doses (<1 kilogray), which will reduce the number of microbes to an undetectable level. It is usually used for increasing shelf life or inhibiting sprouting.
>
> **Radurisation** is the treatment of food with ionising radiation in doses (1–10 kilograys), which will substantially reduce the number of microbes which cause spoilage, and hence increase shelf life of foods. This can be equated with the process of pasteurisation and is used to target specific organisms.
>
> **Radappertisation** is the treatment of food with ionising radiation in doses (20–30 kilograys), which will reduce the number of microbes to a level at which they are undetectable and the product is virtually sterile.

Generation of free radicals may, however, affect the quality of food as well. Foods containing high amounts of fat are highly vulnerable to oxidation and rancidity as a result of irradiation. This adversely affects the sensory quality of the food. The problem is usually overcome by first vacuum packaging and then holding the high-fat food to be irradiated at sub-freezing temperatures during irradiation. Proteins are not affected to a great extent. Irradiation does not inactivate enzymes naturally present in food at the usual doses. Large carbohydrate molecules are however broken down by irradiation, reducing gelling power of starches. Vitamins A, E and thiamine present in

Table 3.6: Different Methods of Preservation Used for Food Products

Food	*Product*	*Method*
Milk	Milk powder	Dehydration
	Liquid milk	Pasteurisation and refrigeration
	Cheese	Heat during preparation, preservative, pasteurisation, dehydration, smoking, irradiation of rooms
	Condensed milk	Heat, canning, high osmotic pressure (due to addition of sugar and concentration of solutes)
Fruit	Whole fruit	Asepsis during packaging, transport and storage, washing, chilling, freezing, canning, pickling, modified atmosphere storage, dehydration, chemical preservatives
	Fruit juice/beverages	Addition of acid, chemical preservative, pasteurisation, aseptic (tetra pack) packaging
Vegetables	Whole or cut vegetables	Asepsis during packaging, transport and storage, washing, blanching, chilling, freezing, canning, preservatives, pickling (high osmotic pressure), dehydration, irradiation (potatoes, onion, garlic)
Meat	Raw meat	Asepsis, canning, chilling, freezing, irradiation (UV rays), dehydration, brining (high osmotic pressure)
	Meat products	Asepsis, canning, chilling, freezing, dehydration, curing, smoking, preservatives, spices
Cereals and cereal products	Grains	Dried and stored in containers protected from insects/ vermin
	Bread, cakes, baked goods	Cleaning and sanitation of equipment, heat, refrigeration, chemical preservatives, irradiation of equipment and rooms with UV rays
Sugar and sugar products	Sugars	Refining process destroys many microbes, SO_2, sugar is kept dry and stored in containers to keep vermin out
	Cane or sugar beets	Stored in controlled environment
	Syrups and beverage concentrates	Heat, high sugar concentration (high osmotic pressure), chemical preservatives
	Honey	Pasteurisation

Source: Drawn by Author.

food are lost during the process of irradiation. Removing air during the process of irradiation helps in reducing loss of these vitamins.

Irradiation of food is followed in several countries for certain foods and specific purposes. It is used widely for preventing sprouting in stored onions, potatoes and garlic and also for increasing the shelf life of fruits like strawberries, mangoes, pears, grapes, cherries, red currants, and for insect dis-infestation of pulses, peanuts, dried fruits, papayas, wheat and ground-wheat products.

Studies have indicated that irradiation of food does not cause any harmful change in food and doses up to 10 kilograys is generally considered to be safe for food products.

No single method is considered foolproof and usually, a combination of methods is used in the food industry to preserve our foods (see Table 3.6). The combination is carefully chosen for each type of food to improve the effectiveness of the preservation methods.

SUMMARY

- Spoilage is the deterioration of the quality of food, resulting in physical and chemical changes which ultimately make the food inedible.
- A number of factors determine why and how our food spoils. This includes biological factors like microorganisms, pests, insects or even the natural enzymes present in foods of plant and animal origin. Extrinsic and intrinsic factors like temperature and moisture of the food and storage environment, pH of the food, its exposure to air (oxygen) and light influence shelf life or the period till which the food can be safely consumed.
- Foods can be classified as perishable, semi-perishable and non-perishable depending on how fast they spoil.
- Chemical changes occur in foods due to spoilage. Proteins, fats and carbohydrates are broken down by natural or microbial enzymes into a variety of other compounds which result in undesirable changes in appearance, texture and flavour of food.
- Spoilage of different types of food is determined by the kind of microbes which are naturally present in them or contaminate them during handling, processing and storage.
- Milk and milk products, meat, fish, poultry and eggs are excellent growth media for a variety of microbes and spoil easily.
- Fruits and vegetables are spoiled mostly by moulds and the spoilage is referred to as 'rot'.
- Cereals and cereal products mostly have low water activity and spoil when storage conditions are inappropriate. Ropiness and mould growth are two common kinds of spoilage seen in bread.
- Sugars and sugar products spoil because of osmophilic microbes (some bacteria, yeasts and moulds) which can tolerate high sugar levels.
- Canned foods spoil by both biological (bacteria and yeasts) and chemical causes (interaction of food ingredients like acid, sulphur, phosphorus with lining of cans).
- Principles of preservation include prevention/delay of microbial decomposition by keeping the microbes away from the food by following asepsis, physically removing the microbes from the food, hindering their growth or activity or simply killing the microbes in the food product.
- Food can also be preserved by preventing or delaying the self-decomposition of the food by inactivating food enzymes and preventing or delaying the chemical reactions which can lead to spoilage.
- Prevention of the mechanical damage to foods by insects, animals and other physical causes like poor handling is also important. Physically damaged foods are more susceptible to attack by microbes, insects and pests as well as more exposed to the environmental air and moisture which can hasten spoilage.
- Commonly used methods of food preservation followed at home and in the industry include aseptic handling, processing, packaging and storage; filtration, centrifugation, sedimentation, clarification, washing or trimming (for physical removal of microbes); dehydration, chilling, refrigeration, freezing, vacuum or modified atmosphere storage and packaging, fermentation, use of acidic ingredients or chemical preservatives (for making conditions unfavourable for growth and survival of microbes); killing microbes by heat treatment like pasteurisation, boiling, sterilisation or by irradiation.
- Using a combination of these methods which is ideally suited to prevent spoilage in a particular food product is referred to as *hurdle technology*.

KEY WORDS

Clarification: Treating water with flocculation reagents and then removal of the solid particles by physical methods. The bacteria get trapped in the solid clumps and is removed along with it.

Gram negative: Gram staining is a staining technique used to identify bacteria. A violet dye is applied, followed by a decolourising agent and a red dye. Gram negative bacteria are those which lose the violet dye and take on the red stain.

Hurdle technology: An intelligent combination of methods of food preservation which act as hurdles for microbes ensuring that they do not survive or/and they are not able to multiply—this results in a safe final product.

Modified atmosphere packaging: The composition of the internal atmosphere of packages of food is controlled to increase shelf life by reducing the quantity of oxygen and replacing it with an inert gas like nitrogen or with carbon dioxide.

Osmophilic: Microbes adapted to conditions of high osmotic pressure; for instance, due to high concentration of sugar.

Psychrotrophic bacteria: Bacteria that are capable of surviving or even thriving in a cold environment; they are responsible for spoiling refrigerated foods.

Radappertisation: The treatment of food with ionising radiation in doses (20–30 kilograys), which will reduce the number of microbes to a level at which they are undetectable and the product is virtually sterile.

Radicidation: The treatment of food with ionising radiation in doses (> 1 kilogray), which will reduce the number of microbes to an undetectable level. It is usually used for increasing shelf life or inhibiting sprouting.

Radurisation: The treatment of food with ionising radiation in doses (1–10 kilograys), which will substantially reduce the number of microbes which cause spoilage and hence increase shelf life of foods; this can be equated with the process of pasteurisation and is used to target specific organisms.

Saprophytic organisms: Those which feed on dead or decaying matter.

Thermoduric bacteria: Heat resistant bacteria which survive temperatures used in milk processing including pasteurisation; also cause spoilage in milk products like milk powders.

Xerotolerant: Also referred to as xerophiles, these are microbes tolerant of dry conditions or low water activity.

EXERCISES

1. Why do foods spoil? Discuss factors which decrease the shelf life of a food product.
2. How are foods classified based on their shelf life? Give examples.
3. How do the following foods spoil? Discuss giving details of the spoilage microorganisms:
   a. Meat
   b. Eggs
   c. Milk
   d. Fruits
4. What are the basic principles used to preserve foods?
5. Discuss how moisture levels in foods can be controlled to extend their shelf life.
6. Explain how controlling the temperature of foods can help in preservation.
7. Write a short note on chemical preservatives in food. (*Hint: You can also take some points for this answer from the chapter on food additives.*)

REFERENCES

Food Preservation, Encyclopaedia Britannica, Available at https://www.britannica.com/topic/food-preservation/Food-irradiation#ref502403 (accessed 12 April 2018).

Frazier, W. C., and D. C. Westhoff, adapted by N. M. Vanitha, *Food Microbiology* (5th edition), New Delhi: McGraw Hill Education (India), 2014.

Jay, J, M., M. J. Loessner, and D. A. Golden, *Modern Food Microbiology* (7th edition), USA: Springer, 2005.

Srilakshmi, B. *Food Science* (6th edition), New Delhi: New Age International, 2015.

ONLINE SOURCES

Food Spoilage and its Prevention—by IGNOU, Available at https://www.youtube.com/watch?v=CkoOm4Lxmjk (accessed 13 April 2018).

Food Spoilage Microbes, Available at https://www.youtube.com/watch?v=BlKP35bct2o (accessed 13 April 2018).

10 Food Preservation Methods, Available at https://www.youtube.com/watch?v=AulCuXNjl94 (accessed 13 April 2018).

4

FOOD-BORNE DISEASES

HIGHLIGHTS

- Food-borne infections and intoxications
- Foods implicated in food-borne disease outbreaks
- Routes of transmission of microbes
- Investigating food-borne disease outbreaks
- Prevention and control measures

It would be difficult to find an individual who has not had some form of gastrointestinal upset resulting from intake of food. The cause of symptoms like nausea, vomiting, diarrhoea and abdominal pain or discomfort may be different—overeating, allergies, reactions to toxins present in plants, animals, or exposure to microbial toxins. Food-borne diseases continue to wreak havoc in developing countries of the world, especially those in the tropical belt, but are fairly common in the developed countries as well. They pose a serious public health hazard resulting in huge economic losses due to loss of life and costs of treatment.

Most food-borne diseases have been attributed to microbial contamination of food. Warm temperatures and high moisture content serve as ideal conditions for the growth of microorganisms like bacteria and fungi in stored food products. Several microbes are known to produce toxic metabolites which have been the cause of many serious, and in some instances fatal, poisonings in man and animals. Separate chapters have been dedicated to poisonings caused by fungal metabolites or mycotoxins, chemicals, naturally occurring toxicants in plants and animals. Discussed here are the most commonly occurring bacterial, viral and protozoan hazards responsible for food-borne diseases, their mode of transmission, and control measures necessary to prevent and control the spread of these infections. A separate section explains how food-borne disease outbreaks are investigated to identify the causative organisms.

FOOD-BORNE INFECTIONS AND INTOXICATIONS

Food-borne diseases can be of two types—poisonings (intoxication) and infections. **Poisoning** is caused by the ingestion of toxins produced by a microbe, plant or animal or ingestion of a toxic chemical. An **infection** is caused by the entry of a microbe into the body through ingestion of contaminated foods and the reaction of the body to them or to their metabolites. In an infection, the microbes invade the gut lining and then multiply within the host, causing symptoms. On the other hand, toxins are preformed in the food; after ingestion of contaminated food, the toxin causes the adverse effects. Hence, the symptoms of an intoxication appear much earlier (minutes to a few hours), whereas for symptoms of infections to appear, it may take several hours to a few days. Infections are usually transmitted from person to person through the faecal–oral route. Poor personal hygiene, cross-contamination from raw foods to cooked foods, touching food with bare hands, all facilitate transmission of microbes. Symptoms are mostly gastrointestinal. Intoxications are more a result of inadequate cooking of foods and cooked foods being stored at room temperatures, allowing microbes to multiply and produce toxins. Intoxications cannot be transmitted from person to person. Also, the toxins need not just affect the gastrointestinal system; they may affect other systems as well, such as the nervous system. Microbes like bacteria, fungi, virus and protozoa have been implicated in different food-borne disease outbreaks.

Important bacterial agents implicated in food-borne intoxications are *Staphylococcus aureus* and *Clostridium botulinum.* Bacteria most commonly implicated in food infections are *Salmonella spp.*, *Shigella spp.*, *Camplylobacterjejuni*, *Vibrio cholerae* and *Bacillus cereus.* The viruses and protozoa implicated in food-borne disease outbreaks mostly cause infections. These have been listed in Table 4.1.

Table 4.1: Microbes Implicated in Food-borne Illness

Microbe	*Food implicated*	*Symptoms*
Bacteria		
Bacillus cereus	Cooked rice, cooked meats, vegetables, starch puddings, raw milk, dairy products	Diarrhoea, abdominal cramps, nausea, vomiting, fever and body aches
Campylobacter jejuni	Fish, meat, vegetables	Diarrhoea, inflammation of the intestinal wall
Clostridium botulinum	Cooked meat, fish and poultry, fruits, vegetables, canned or bottled foods	Difficulty in breathing, weakness of muscles, abdominal distension, paralysis which can result in death due to respiratory failure
Escherichia coli (several strains)	Raw milk, ground meat products, undercooked meat, cheese and raw vegetables	Diarrhoea, abdominal cramps, bloody stools and vomiting. Serious illness can result in renal failure in children.
Salmonella spp.	Meat, poultry, raw milk, eggs	Gastroenteritis (enteric fever), nausea, vomiting, abdominal pain and diarrhoea
Shigella spp.	Shellfish, raw vegetables, salads, cream-filled bakery products, ice cream and cheese	Diarrhoea, stools containing blood, mucus and pus

(*Contd*)

(*Contd*)

Microbe	*Food implicated*	*Symptoms*
Staphylococcus aureus	Raw milk, raw and cooked meats, custard- or cream-filled pastries, egg foods, cheese, prawns, salads	Nausea and vomiting with occasional abdominal cramping and diarrhoea.
Vibrio cholerae	Shellfish, salads	Cholera (rice water stools)
Virus		
Enteric adenoviruses	Contaminated food or beverages	Persistent diarrhoea, nausea and vomiting
Hepatitis A Virus	Milk and other beverages; shellfish (raw oysters and clams)	Jaundice; loss of appetite; gastrointestinal disturbance
Norwalk or Norwalk-like viruses	Shellfish, salad ingredients, water, ice, eggs and ready-to-eat foods	Nausea, vomiting, diarrhoea, stomach cramps
Poliovirus types I, II, III (Poliomyelitis)	Milk; possibly other beverages and prepared foods	Fever; vomiting; headache; pain in muscle groups; paralysis of leg
Rotaviruses, adenoviruses, caliciviruses, astroviruses	Contaminated food or beverages, raw shellfish	Fever; headache; abdominal pain; vomiting and watery diarrhoea
Protozoa		
Cryptosporidium parvum	Raw milk, raw sausage	Watery diarrhoea, abdominal cramping, and lack of appetite
Entamoeba histolytica	Vegetables, fruits	Dysentery with diarrhoea, weakness, nausea and vomiting
Giardia lamblia	Vegetables, fruits	Diarrhoea, flatulence, greasy stools that tend to float, stomach cramps, nausea
Toxoplasma gondii	Undercooked meat, raw vegetables	Swollen lymph glands or muscle aches and pains, fever, damage to the brain, eyes, or other organs in severe infection

Source: Adapted by Author from NCDC 2009, Narayan and Albrecht n.d., and WHO n.d.

Gastroenteritis means inflammation of the stomach and the small and large intestines. It may be caused by bacteria (such as *Salmonella* or *Escherichia coli*), or parasites (such as *Giardia*), by viruses or by medications or other medical conditions, although the symptoms for all may be very similar. As the contaminated food first enters the gastrointestinal tract, the first symptoms are intestinal discomfort, nausea, vomiting, pain and diarrhoea. In some infections, the symptoms are restricted to gastrointestinal, while in some others the infection is more invasive. The microbes invade the intestinal mucosa, move into the blood and travel to other tissues of the body like the muscles and the liver. **Systemic infections** (those which spread throughout the body) do not necessarily cause more severe symptoms.

Figure 4.1 elaborates the mechanism by which the different microbes act in the gastrointestinal tract of humans. **Non-inflammatory enterotoxins** typically act in the proximal part of the small

Figure 4.1: Types of Food Poisonings

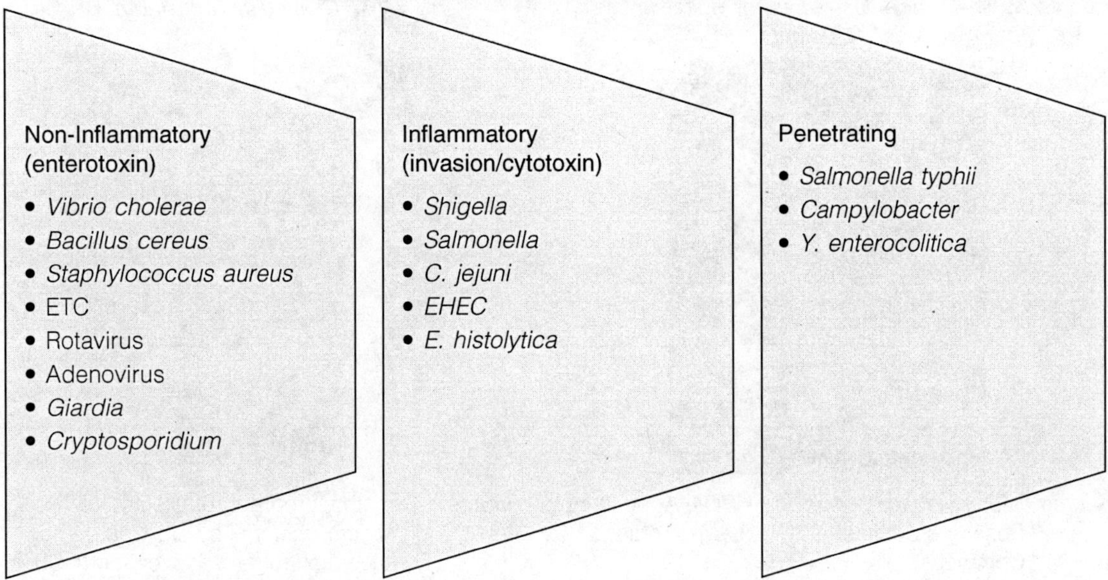

Source: Adapted by Author from NCDC 2009.

intestine and result in a watery diarrhoea. **Inflammatory reactions** are seen in infections by certain microbes which invade the intestinal lining mostly in the distal part of the small intestine or colon. They may produce cytotoxins (chemicals poisonous for cells) and result in dysentery or inflammatory diarrhoea in which leukocytes (white blood cells) are seen in stool samples. Other microbes may penetrate the intestinal mucosa in the distal part of the small intestine producing enteric fever and leukocytes in the faecal samples.

FOODS IMPLICATED AND THE ROUTES OF TRANSMISSION OF MICROBES

Bacterial Poisonings

Most food-borne illnesses have been attributed to bacteria.

Bacillus Cereus is a rod-shaped, facultatively aerobic, spore-forming bacterium. The optimum temperature for the growth of the organism is 30°C and a pH range of 4.9–9.3. It causes gastroenteritis of two types—diarrhoeal and emetic (vomiting). The diarrhoeal illness occurs usually within 6–15 hours of consuming contaminated foods. The stools are watery and accompanied by abdominal cramps and pain. Usually, in the case of diarrhoeal poisoning, a wide variety of foods are implicated, like meat, fish, milk and vegetables. The illness, characterised primarily by vomiting and nausea, is attributed to contaminated starchy foods like rice, potatoes and preparations like puddings, soups and pastas; this is called emetic poisoning. The person usually recovers within 24 hours.

Figure 4.2: Pathogenic Bacteria

4.2A: The Typical Corkscrew or Spiral Shape of *C. Jejuni.*

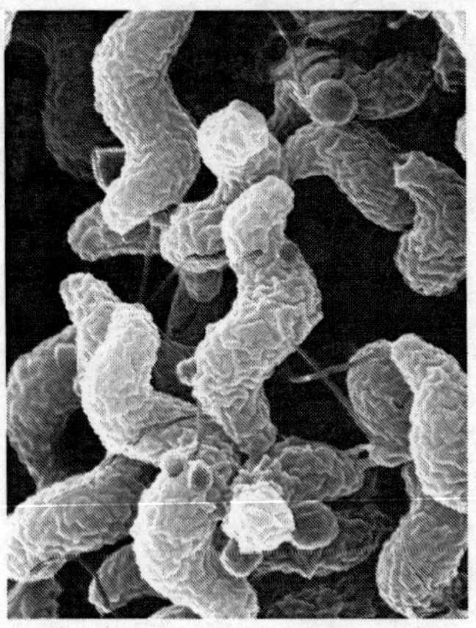

Source: '*Campylobacter jejuni*' by USDA Agricultural Research Service (CC0 1.0; Wikimedia Commons).

4.2B: *Clostridium botulinum*

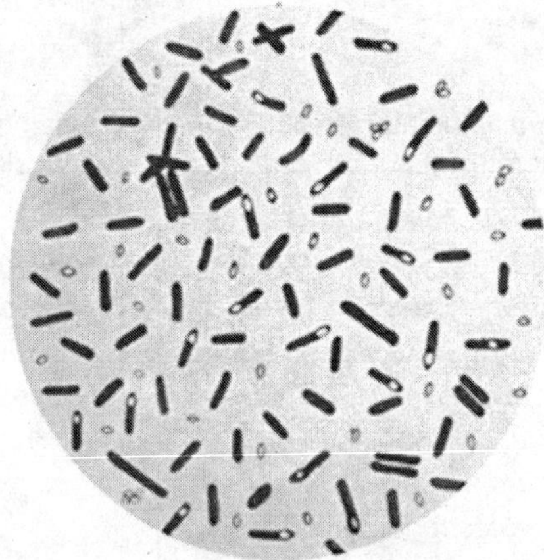

Source: 'A photomicrograph of Clostridium *botulinum bacteria*' by US Centers for Disease Control and Prevention (CC0 1.0; Wikimedia Commons).

Campylobacter jejuni is a slender, curved, rod-shaped bacterium (see Figure 4.2A), microaerophilic requiring low levels (3–5 per cent) of oxygen. **Campylobacteriosis** (illness caused by *C. jejuni*) is characterised by symptoms of watery or sticky diarrhoea, which may contain blood and white blood cells. Other symptoms often present are fever, abdominal pain, nausea, headache and muscle pain. The incubation time is usually two to five days after ingestion of the contaminated food or water and symptoms last for seven to 10 days. People rarely get the infection from other people. Faecal matter from infected animals contaminating our food and water is the main source of infection. Raw milk and raw chicken is frequently contaminated by *C. jejuni.* The bacteria may be carried by flies from the faecal matter to the food.

Clostridium botulinum is an anaerobic, spore-forming, rod-shaped bacterium which causes the disease botulism (see Figure 4.2B). This is a severe type of food poisoning caused by the ingestion of foods containing a potent neurotoxin which can result in death, an example of microbial **intoxication**. The symptoms appear 18–36 hours after ingestion of the contaminated food, although in some cases these may appear earlier than or as late as eight days, making it difficult to pin down the source of infection. Symptoms consist of lassitude (weariness), weakness and vertigo (dizziness), usually followed by double vision and progressive difficulty in speaking and swallowing. Difficulty in breathing, weakness of muscles, abdominal distension and constipation may also be common symptoms. Being a nerve toxin, it leads to paralysis which progresses from the eyes,

Standard abbreviations used for different types of *E. coli*:

Enteropathogenic *E. coli*: EEC

Enterohemorrhagic *E. coli*: EHEC

Enterotoxigenic *E. coli*: ETEC

Shiga toxin producing *E. coli*: STEC

face to the throat, chest and the extremities, ultimately resulting in respiratory failure and consequent death. There is an antitoxin that can be administered to affected individuals and save their lives.

The worst type of *E. coli*, known as *E. coli* O157:H7, causes bloody diarrhoea and can sometimes cause kidney failure and even death. It produces the Shiga toxin, which destroys red blood corpuscles and injures the kidney, and the patient may require dialysis and blood transfusion.

Being an anaerobic bacterium, it grows best in canned or bottled products from which air has been removed. Most outbreaks have been linked to inadequately processed or canned foods. Sausages, meat products, canned vegetables and seafood products have been the most frequent vehicles for transmission. Almost any type of food that is not very acidic (pH above 4.6) can support growth and toxin production by *C. botulinum*. The toxin has been detected in a considerable variety of foods, such as canned corn, peppers, green beans, soups, beets, asparagus, mushrooms, ripe olives, spinach, tuna fish, chicken, meats, ham, sausage, lobster, and smoked and salted fish.

Escherichia coli is present as a part of the normal microflora of intestines of humans and some animals (see Figure 4.3A). Some enteropathogenic serotypes have been implicated in food poisoning outbreaks. These are referred to as **enteropathogenic *E.coli*** (**EEC**). Some strains are known to produce enterotoxins, which result in cholera-like illness in humans with 'rice-water stools'. These **enterotoxigenic strains** produce two types of enterotoxins—one which is heat stable and one heat labile. These are believed to be responsible for diarrhoeal diseases in infants as well as for '**traveller's diarrhoea**'. The second type of illness is caused by strains of EEC which are **invasive** in nature, penetrating epithelial cells of the colon and resulting in dysentery-like symptoms and colitis (inflammation of colon). There is profuse watery diarrhoea accompanied by abdominal cramps, fever and chills. Another strain called the **hemorrhagic *E. coli*** can result in bloody diarrhoea and severe abdominal pain. Optimal temperature for growth of the organism is 37°C and optimal pH 7.0–7.5. Foods implicated include undercooked meats, raw milk, cheese made from unpasteurised milk, contaminated water, sprouts, raw fruits and vegetables. Cooked foods which have not been preserved or refrigerated properly tend to allow the organism to grow rapidly. Adequate heating to pasteurisation temperatures easily destroys the bacteria. Incubation time ranges from eight to 44 hours.

Salmonella is a rod-shaped bacterium which causes the disease **Salmonellosis**, which is one of the most frequently occurring bacterial food infections. The bacteria grow well over a wide range of temperature and pH. They grow well at room temperature but the optimum temperature is 37°C. *S. typhi* produces **typhoid fever** and *S. paratyphior S. enteritidis* causes **paratyphoid fever** in humans. Other members of Salmonella genus are responsible for the other milder forms of the disease. Humans and animals can both be a source of contamination as they may be suffering from the disease or may be carriers of the organisms. Poultry (chicken, ducks, turkey, etc.) are important food sources that may be contaminated by this bacteria. The organisms may be present in the flesh or in the eggs. That is why it is important to select eggs which are not contaminated with faeces. The organism may be found in the yolk of eggs, deposited there by an infected hen prior to shell formation. It is hence not advisable to consume raw or half-cooked eggs (where the yolk is still runny). Rodents (mice, rats), cockroaches and flies can also transmit the organisms from faecal matter to unprotected food. Meat and meat products, dishes and foods made with egg which have not been sufficiently heated, and milk and milk products are some of the foods implicated in disease outbreaks.

The disease has an incubation time of 12–36 hours and sometimes as long as 72 hours. Acute symptoms include nausea, vomiting, abdominal cramps, diarrhoea and fever. Diarrhoea may be preceded by a headache and chills. Stools are greenish and foul smelling, and the patient feels restless, faint and weak. Recovery is usually within a week, but may be prolonged if the patient is malnourished or has a low immunity level, or has ingested a heavy dose of the bacteria. It also depends on the strain of the bacteria consumed.

Figure 4.3: Bacteria Implicated in Food-borne Diseases

4.3A: Electron Microscope Picture of *E. coli*

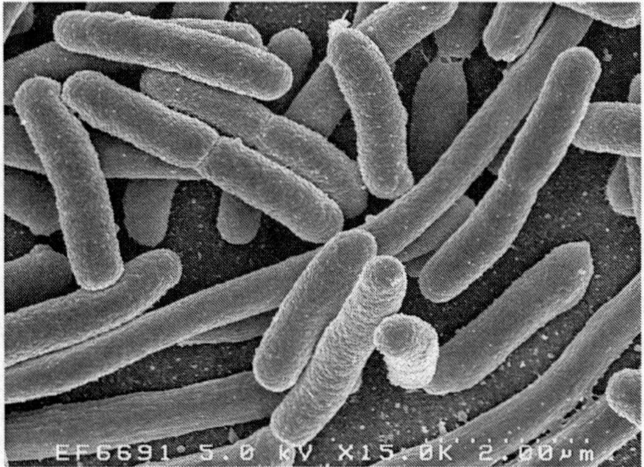

Source: 'E. coli' by Elapied (CC0 1.0; Wikimedia Commons).

4.3B: *Shigella* in a Stool Sample

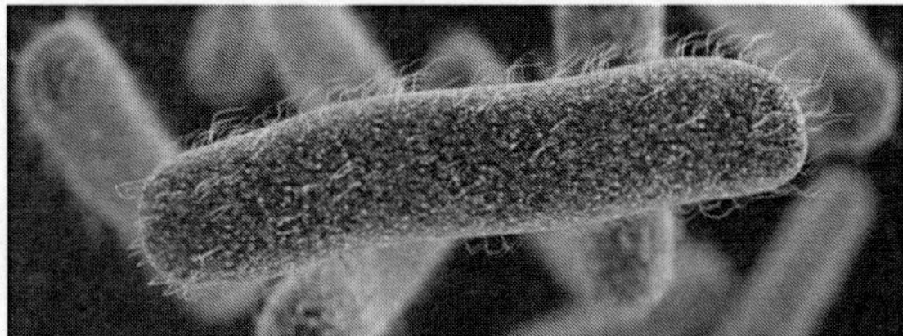

Source: '21920', US Centers for Disease Control and Prevention (CC0 1.0; Public Health Image Library).

Shigella are non-spore forming rod-shaped bacteria (see Figure 4.3B), which cause **shigellosis** (**bacillary dysentery**). *Shigella* rarely causes diseases in animals. It is principally a disease of humans (and other primates such as monkeys and chimpanzees). The incubation time is usually less than four days. Species commonly leading to illness are *Shigella sonnei*, *S. flexneri*, *S. dysenteriae* and *S. boydii*. Symptoms include abdominal pain, cramps, fever, vomiting, diarrhoea with watery stools which may contain blood, pus or mucus. The disease is caused when *Shigella* organisms attach to, and penetrate, the epithelial cells of the intestine. After invasion, they multiply intracellularly, and the spread results in tissue destruction. Infections are associated with ulceration, rectal bleeding and drastic dehydration which can result in death.

The *Shigella spp.* are highly infectious agents that are transmitted by the faecal–oral route. The organism is frequently found in water polluted with human faeces. Salads, raw vegetables, milk and dairy products, and poultry are foods generally implicated in poisoning outbreaks. Unsanitary handling of foods by food handlers is also a common cause of contamination.

Staphylococcus aureus is a spherical bacterium (coccus) which, on microscopic examination, appears in pairs, short chains, or grape-like bunches (see Figure 4.4A). Some strains of this organism are capable of producing a highly heat-stable toxin that causes illness in humans. The toxin is referred to as an **enterotoxin** because it causes inflammation of the lining of the intestinal tract. Staphylococcal poisoning also comes under the category of microbial intoxications. Most toxin-producing strains have the ability to coagulate blood plasma and are referred to as '**coagulase-positive**'.

Figure 4.4: Electron Microscopic Images

4.4A: *Staphylococcus aureus*

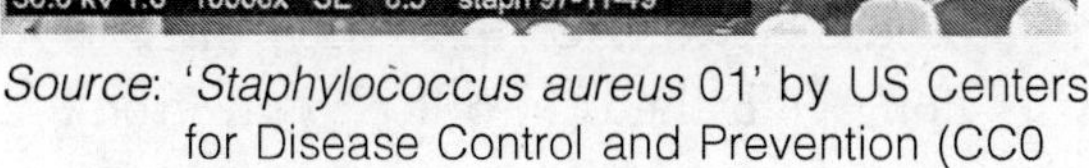

Source: '*Staphylococcus aureus* 01' by US Centers for Disease Control and Prevention (CC0 1.0; Wikimedia Commons).

4.4B: *Vibrio cholera*

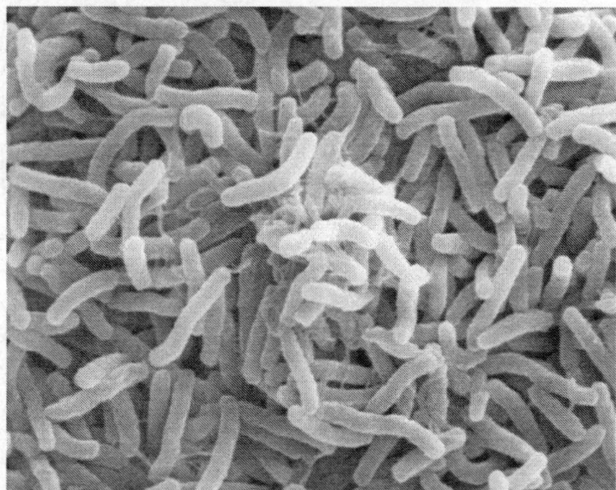

Source: 'Cholera bacteria SEM' by Zeimusu (CC0 1.0; Wikimedia Commons).

The onset of symptoms is usually rapid (generally within two to four hours), depending on individual susceptibility to the toxin, the amount of contaminated food eaten, the amount of toxin in the food ingested and the general health of the victim. The most common symptoms are nausea, vomiting, retching (making sounds or movements of vomiting), abdominal cramping and prostration (lying stretched out, inability to get up). Some individuals may not always demonstrate all the symptoms associated with the illness. In more severe cases, headache, muscle cramping and transient changes in blood pressure and pulse rate may occur. Recovery generally takes two to three days or longer depending on the severity of the case. Death from staphylococcal food poisoning is very rare, although such cases have occurred among the elderly, infants and severely debilitated persons.

Foods usually implicated in staphylococcal food poisoning include meat and meat products, poultry and egg products, salads, bakery products such as cream-filled pastries, pies and sandwich fillings, and milk and dairy products. Foods that require considerable handling during preparation and that are kept at room temperatures or slightly elevated temperatures meant to keep food warm after preparation are frequently involved in staphylococcal food poisoning. The bacterium multiplies rapidly at 20–45°C and pH range of 4.8–8.0. The organism is also fairly tolerant to salt (up to 10–20 per cent NaCl) and sugar (up to 50–60 per cent sucrose) and hence, easily grows in different preparations.

Staphylococci are perhaps the most ubiquitous microbes existing on a variety of surfaces, water and food. The strains which cause food poisoning enter foods from humans or animals, the primary reservoirs. Staphylococci are present in the nasal passages (they are a common cause of sinus infections), throats, boils, infected wounds, hair and skin of humans. In cows, the bacteria are known to cause mastitis. Milking infected cows introduce the bacteria into milk.

Vibrio cholera is the bacterium responsible for cholera, a disease which has plagued our country since ancient times. It finds mention in the *Susruta Samhita*, an ancient Sanskrit text on medicine and surgery. Although the reservoir of the disease-causing germ is believed to have originated in India, cholera is now an endemic in several countries of the world. Researchers have estimated that there are 1.4 to 4.3 million cases and 28,000 to 142,000 deaths worldwide due to cholera every year. The bacterium is rod-shaped (see Figure 4.4B) and facultatively anaerobic, transmitted man-to-man via faecal contamination of water and food.

Symptoms vary from mild to profuse, watery diarrhoea, with characteristic rice-water stools. Onset of the illness is generally sudden, with incubation periods varying from six hours to five days. Abdominal cramps, nausea, vomiting, dehydration and shock are some other symptoms; after severe fluid and electrolyte loss, death may occur. Illness is caused by the ingestion of viable bacteria, which attach to the wall of the small intestine and produce **enterotoxin**. The production of cholera toxin by the attached bacteria results in the watery diarrhoea associated with this illness. The illness is generally self-limiting. Antibiotics have been demonstrated to shorten the course of the illness. It is vital to give oral rehydration salts along with fluids in order to save the life of the infected person.

Viral Food-borne Illnesses

The study of water-borne viruses gained importance after a large hepatitis outbreak was declared in New Delhi between December 1955 and January 1956. The origin of the outbreak was the contamination by sewage of the river Yamuna, which is the source of water for the city. Alum and chlorine treatment of the water, which is used to prevent bacterial infections, could not control the viruses. As many as 30,000 cases of hepatitis were reported among the population. Efforts also began to detect the polio virus in water.

Viruses are shed in extremely high numbers in the faeces of infected individuals. These then contaminate our food and water. We are exposed to enteric viruses through various routes:

- shellfish grown in contaminated waters
- food crops grown in land irrigated with wastewater and/or fertilised with sewage
- sewage-polluted recreational waters (like swimming pools, water rides in parks), and
- contaminated drinking water

Usually, water-borne infections are acquired through the ingestion of contaminated water or shellfish. Shellfish, being filter feeders, tend to concentrate viruses and bacteria in their edible tissues. Concentrations of these microorganisms in shellfish may be expected to be much higher than in the surrounding water. Millions of people die each year from gastroenteritis, and rotaviruses alone are responsible for most of the children dying from diarrhoea. Hepatitis A, poliomyelitis, astrovirus, adenovirus, parvovirus, coronavirus, Norwalk, other small, round-structured viruses, and hepatitis E, are other significant viruses that may be acquired by ingestion of contaminated water or shellfish.

Viral gastroenteritis, often called the '**stomach flu**', is an infection caused by a variety of viruses resulting in vomiting or diarrhoea (see Figure 4.6). Food may be contaminated by food preparers or handlers who have viral gastroenteritis, especially if they do not wash their hands thoroughly after using the bathroom or changing diapers and nappies. Shellfish may be contaminated by sewage. Persons who eat raw or undercooked shellfish harvested from contaminated waters may get diarrhoea. Drinking water can also be contaminated by sewage and be a source of the spread of these viruses. Viral gastroenteritis occurs in people of all ages and backgrounds. Rotavirus infection is the most common cause of diarrhoea in infants and young children under five years. Adenoviruses and astroviruses cause diarrhoea mostly in young children, but older children and adults can also be affected. Norwalk and Norwalk-like viruses are more likely to cause diarrhoea in older children and adults.

Adenovirus (serotypes 40 and 41) are known as the enteric adenoviruses as they have been implicated in causing viral gastroenteritis. They have been found to be the second most common cause of diarrhoea in young children, after rotaviruses. The virus is transmitted mainly by the faecal–oral route. The incubation time can range from three to 10 days. Affected individuals, usually children, have persistent diarrhoea which may last for 10–14 days. There may also be mild vomiting and fever. This type of gastroenteritis does not seriously affect the health of the individual unless s/he is malnourished.

Astroviruses were first described during an outbreak in 1975. This virus is endemic worldwide and a common cause of diarrhoea among children under seven. Transmission is person-to-person via the faecal–oral route, and consumption of contaminated food and water. The incubation period is short, between one to four days, with symptoms of watery diarrhoea, nausea, headache, abdominal cramps, low-grade fever and sometimes vomiting.

Norwalk virus was first identified in 1972 after an outbreak of gastrointestinal illness in Norwalk, Ohio, USA. Later, other viruses with similar features were described and called Norwalk-like viruses. Humans are the only known hosts, the viruses being transmitted by the faecal–oral route. Symptoms include nausea, vomiting, diarrhoea, stomach cramps, with recovery within two to three days. Outbreaks in developed countries where such contamination is rare are often linked to eating raw or insufficiently steamed shellfish, especially oysters and clams. Shellfish become contaminated via stool from sick food handlers or from raw sewage dumped overboard by commercial ships and boats. Salad ingredients too are often implicated in Norwalk outbreaks. Contaminated water, ice, eggs and ready-to-eat foods are other sources of infection.

Rotavirus, identified in 1973, is capable of surviving in the environment for months. It is also resistant to hand washing, which makes it a difficult virus to avoid. It enters the cells lining the intestinal tract and multiplies in the cytoplasm. It leads to atrophy of the villi. Symptoms include watery diarrhoea, vomiting, abdominal pain and fever. Rotavirus infection is very common in India resulting in the death of thousands of children due to dehydration. Vaccination is now available to protect children from this deadly virus. Spread of infection is mainly person-to-person through the faecal–oral route, through fomites (objects capable of carrying the germ), and of course through consumption of contaminated food and water. The incubation time is less than four days.

Figure 4.5: Viruses which Cause Gastroenteritis

4.5A: Astrovirus

Source: 'Astrovirus' by Jer Cas (CC BY-SA 4.0; Wikimedia Commons).

4.5B: Rotavirus

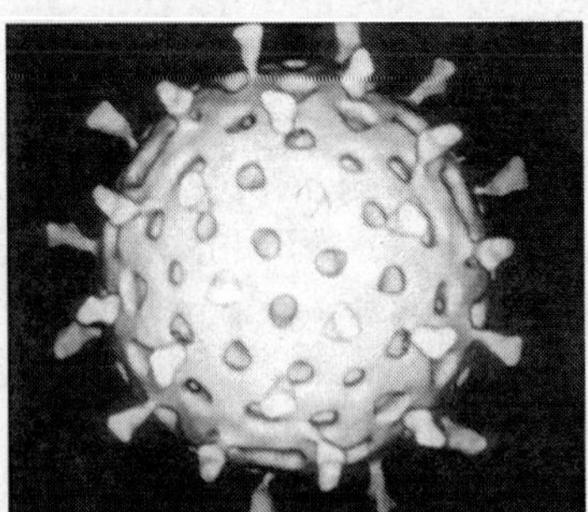

Source: 'Rotavirus' by Wikipedia (CC BY-SA 3.0; Wikimedia Commons).

4.5C: Norwalk Virus (3D Print)

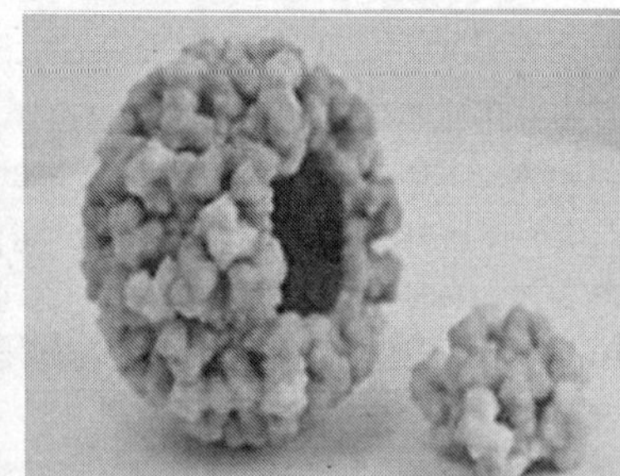

Source: 'Norwalk Virus' by NIAID (CC0 1.0; Wikimedia Commons).

Hepatitis A, also referred to as 'infectious' hepatitis, is the most common type of hepatitis. It is caused by the hepatitis A virus (HAV), an enterovirus which multiplies only in the liver cells. It is spread from person to person through faecal contamination of food and drinking water. Foods usually implicated include shellfish, cut fruits, salads, ice, milk and milk products, cold cuts of meat, sandwiches, etc. The incubation period for hepatitis A varies from 10 to 50 days, which means that infected persons can spread the disease before they realise they have it. Symptoms include sudden onset of fever, nausea, vomiting, abdominal pain and feeling of being very tired. This is followed by jaundice. Other symptoms include pain in the liver area, dark urine and light-coloured stools. The disease is usually mild and recovery is complete in one to two weeks, though occasionally, the symptoms can be severe and recovery can take several months.

Poliomyelitis is also an infectious disease caused by an enterovirus, which primarily infects the human alimentary tract. The virus enters through the mouth (via faeces-contaminated food and water) and then multiplies in the throat and intestines. It then enters the blood stream, travelling to the central nervous system, destroying nerves—especially those which activate muscles. The incubation period is four to 35 days. The initial symptoms include fever, headache, vomiting, fatigue, stiffness in neck and pain in the limbs. The muscles of the legs are affected more often than the arm muscles. The limb becomes floppy and lifeless, a condition known as **acute flaccid paralysis (AFP)**. Although it can strike at any age, it mainly afflicts children under five. India was declared a 'polio-free' nation by the WHO in 2014. Now, 80 per cent of the world's population lives in polio-free regions. The aim is to make the world polio-free by 2018.

Man is the only known reservoir of polio infection. The virus is transmitted by the faecal–oral route and can survive for months in the external environment like water or faeces. During the acute phase of the disease, when the virus occurs in the throat, close personal contact with an infected person facilitates the spread by droplets sprayed during coughing or sneezing.

Protozoan Infections

Cryptosporidium is a microscopic parasite which causes watery diarrhoea, the condition being referred to as **crytosporidiosis**. The parasite is covered by an outer shell which enables it to survive in the environment for long periods of time. The parasite is mostly spread through contaminated water—not just drinking water but also recreational water in swimming pools and water parks which may be ingested, especially by children. The parasite is also tolerant to chlorine in water and hence chlorination does not always protect people. It lives in the intestines of infected humans and animals and is shed in stools. If contaminated water is used to wash or prepare food items, these can spread the parasite. Symptoms appear two to 10 days after exposure and include abdominal cramps, nausea, vomiting, fever, dehydration and weight loss.

Entamoeba histolytica is the cause of what is also referred to as '**amoebic dysentery**'. It is spread through faecal contamination of food, water or simply hands which have come in contact with contaminated surfaces. The parasites form cysts which enable them to survive in the environment for a long period of time. In many cases, the parasites remain in the intestine, while in rare cases they may invade the intestinal mucosa or travel via the blood stream to the liver, brain and lungs. A mild form of the infection may result in just loose stools with cramps in the abdomen. However, severe dysentery cases result in bloody stools, pain and fever. People who become infected may develop symptoms after two to four weeks of exposure.

Giardia lamblia infection leads to a condition called **giardiasis**. *Giardia* is a microscopic parasite spread through contaminated food and water, as well as person-to-person contact. Swallowing contaminated water from recreational pools or shallow unprotected wells, as are common in several rural areas of India, can also result in infection. Symptoms, which appear one to three weeks after exposure, include watery, foul-smelling diarrhoea, alternating with greasy stools. Abdominal cramps with bloating and flatulence are common with general malaise, nausea and weight loss. Giardia parasites also live in the intestines of humans and animals, and form cysts which help them survive for months outside the body.

Toxoplasma gondii causes the infection known as **toxoplasmosis**. Contaminated drinking water, undercooked or raw meat, or food contaminated by knives, chopping boards used earlier for raw meats, as also hands contaminated by touching garden soil, manure, or litter boxes of pets like cats, can result in spreading the infection. It is also possible to transmit the parasite from mother to child *in utero*. Symptoms include fever, swollen lymph glands and pain in muscles. Sometimes there may be eye damage as well.

INVESTIGATING FOOD-BORNE DISEASE OUTBREAKS

Unless the food poisoning episode is serious enough to make us bedridden, we take it as a given consequence of eating food prepared outside the house. Sometimes the 'stomach upset' is blamed on the weather or on having 'hot foods'. Rarely would the affected individual or his family lodge a formal complaint with the seller of the implicated food or with the health authorities. Hence, all the human epidemiological data which is available with the health authorities of a country are based on large food poisoning outbreaks which debilitated or killed a large number of people. You may have seen news items about entire wedding parties landing up in the hospital after feasting or school children taking ill after consuming mid-day meals served to them.

Food-borne diseases are monitored by the National Centre for Disease Control which is under the Directorate General of Health Services, government of India. It is interesting to understand how food-borne disease outbreaks are investigated and documented so that similar outbreaks can be prevented in the future.

Objectives of Investigation

It is important in a food-borne illness outbreak to first identify the food which was the source of the pathogen or chemical which led to the illness. The organism or chemical which was responsible also needs to be identified. This is easier said than done as symptoms for most poisonings are similar (nausea, vomiting, diarrhoea and stomach cramps). Vomit and stool samples may not be available in all cases unless prompt investigation was launched. Incubation time may be a few days for several pathogens and hence linking the disease to the food may be difficult in such scenarios. Once the food source has been established, it is also vital to determine how the food became contaminated. This helps to take corrective measures so that there is no repetition of the outbreak. Educating the public about appropriate precautions to be taken is a necessary measure for preventing death and disability due to food-borne diseases.

Process of Investigation

The investigating team should reach the field as soon as it is informed of a potential food-borne disease outbreak. Reports usually come in from treating hospitals, news agencies and sometimes even police complaints. Promptness in responding to reports is vital to a good investigation. Just like a forensic team does its investigation, this team collects samples of suspected foods and ingredients and inspects the premises where it was stored, cooked and served. All samples need to be collected aseptically and refrigerated/kept cool if perishable. Samples are sealed and appropriately labelled before being sent for laboratory analysis. If the food is no longer available by the time the investigating team arrives at the scene of the outbreak, rinsings of utensils and even food thrown in garbage may sometimes have to be collected. The field team also interviews the people affected, those involved in food handling as well as physicians who are treating the affected individuals to get details about symptoms shown by the afflicted. It also makes sense to interview the people who ate at the function but did not develop any symptoms as this helps to narrow down the food to be implicated. The source of the implicated food may also need to be tracked to see at which stage the contamination took place (see Figure 4.6). Blood samples may also need to be taken along with stool and vomit samples to trace the cause of the outbreak. An epidemiologist may need to step in for interpreting the data collected.

Figure 4.6: Important Information to be Gathered during the Investigation

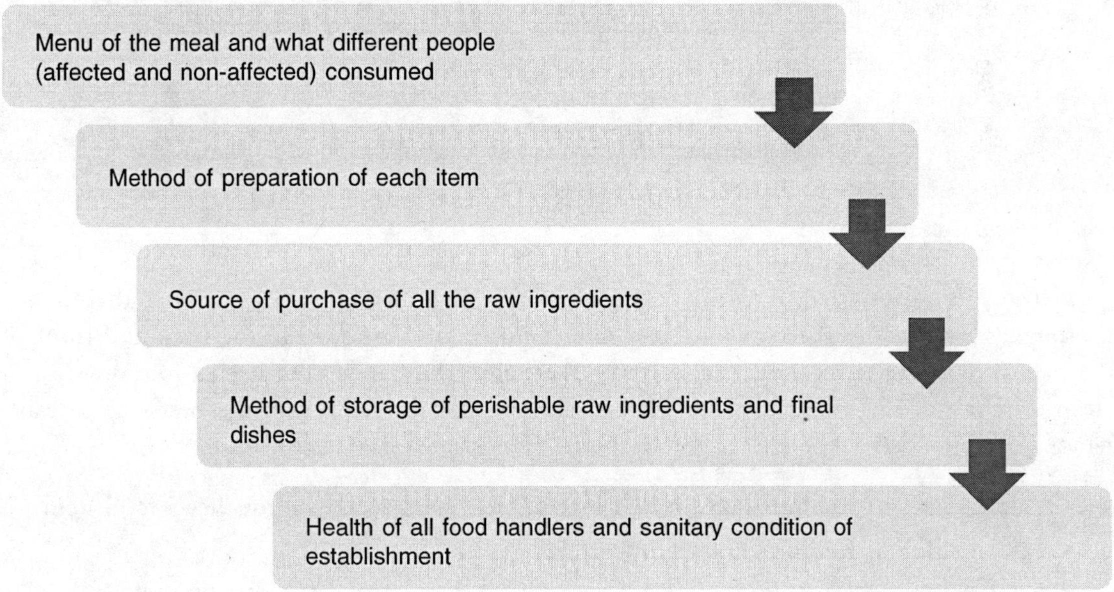

Menu of the meal and what different people (affected and non-affected) consumed

Method of preparation of each item

Source of purchase of all the raw ingredients

Method of storage of perishable raw ingredients and final dishes

Health of all food handlers and sanitary condition of establishment

Source: Drawn by Author.

PREVENTION AND CONTROL MEASURES

It is a common misconception that we can get food poisoning only when we eat food prepared outside our home, such as from street food vendors or restaurants. Many food-borne illnesses originate in our own kitchens due to poor handling or storage. One may even wonder how faecal–oral transmission of pathogens takes place (who does not wash their hands after touching faeces!). People do wash their hands in most cases, but maybe not thoroughly. Soap is many times not available in toilets of small establishments and even homes of the poor. They use public taps to wash their children after defecation and may not carry soap along to wash their hands. Harried mothers may just cursorily wash their hands after changing diapers of their children. When water used for growing vegetables or fish in ponds itself is contaminated with faeces, there is no way of knowing about the safety of the vegetables/fish (see Figure 4.7). Unless thoroughly cooked, these foods can then lead to food-borne illnesses.

Figure 4.7: How Microbes are Transmitted from Person-to-Person via the Faecal–Oral Route

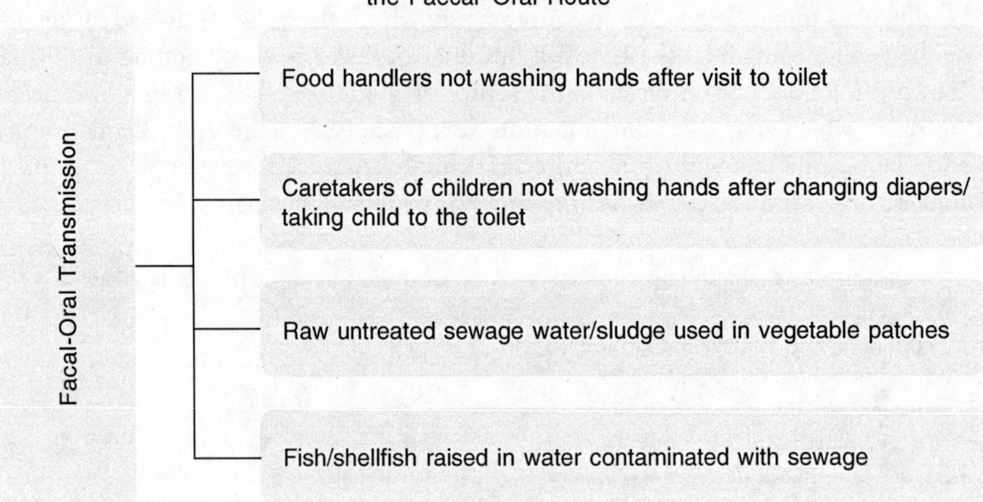

Source: Drawn by Author.

Hence, it is obvious that to reduce the chances of getting infection, one must wash their hands thoroughly at least for 20 seconds (ideally one minute), rubbing soap in the back and front of the palms, in between the fingers and under the nails. The hands then need to be dried on a clean towel/air dried. Watch the YouTube video provided by WHO on the best way to wash hands (link provided at the end of the chapter). Hands need to be washed:

- before, during and after food preparation; in fact, every time one touches a food item
- before eating or feeding another individual
- before and after tending to a cut or wound
- before and after tending to a sick person
- after visiting a toilet yourself or helping a child/elderly/patient clean up after visiting the toilet/changing diapers
- after touching any pet
- after touching garbage
- after sneezing, coughing or blowing one's nose

Other **precautions** which need to be taken include:

- Cooking, eating and food storage areas need to be kept absolutely clean.
- Raw fruits and vegetables should be washed properly before eating.
- Storing foods at appropriate temperatures is important. Refrigerating, freezing or keeping temperatures above 65°C for hot foods helps to keep conditions unfavourable for the growth and multiplication of microbes.

- Cross-contamination should be prevented by keeping raw foods away from cooked as well as raw non-vegetarian foods away from vegetables and fruits, as the former tend to have a high microbial load. Chopping boards and knives used should be separate or should be thoroughly washed before using for another food.
- Foods should be thoroughly cooked, all the way to the core of thick foods. Special thermometers are available to measure the core temperatures, so that one can make sure that microbes being harboured deep inside thick cuts of meat, for instance, have been completely destroyed.
- Food which needs to be refrigerated needs to be chilled rapidly rather than be left at room temperature to be cooled. Dishes in large containers may have improper cooling even in refrigerators. Ideally, the time lag between cooking and eating a food, or leaving cooked food at room temperature, should not be more than two hours.
- Leftovers which had been refrigerated, or cooked food to be eaten at a later time, need to be reheated thoroughly at least to a temperature of 71°C before consumption. This is done to make sure that all microbes which multiplied during storage get destroyed.
- Wear gloves while handling soil and manure during gardening/farming.

C. jejuni is a relatively fragile organism sensitive to environmental stresses. Hence, exposure to 21 per cent oxygen, drying, heating, use of disinfectants, acidic conditions can easily destroy the microbe. Properly cooking chicken, pasteurising milk and chlorinating drinking water generally kills the bacteria and prevents severe outbreaks.

Avoidance of contamination of the food with ***Salmonella*** from sources such as diseased human beings, animals and carriers, and ingredients carrying the organisms, such as contaminated eggs, is an important measure in preventing outbreaks. Cooking or pasteurisation of food or food ingredients can destroy the organism. Growth of the organism can be prevented in the foods by adequately refrigerating them. Of course, care and cleanliness in food handling and preparation are important.

> WHO is committed to building the capacity of nations to detect, control and prevent food-borne infections. The **Global Foodborne Infections Network** (**GFN**) is a network of institutions and individuals committed to enhancing the capacity of countries to detect, respond and prevent food-borne and other enteric infections.

Maintaining adequate levels of hygiene and sanitation is perhaps the most important step in preventing the spread of **cholera**. Washing hands thoroughly after each visit to the toilet and not letting patients or carriers of this infection handle food go a long way in checking the spread of infection. Chlorinating the water, boiling water before use, and using clean water for washing raw vegetables and fruits are important safety measures to take, especially in summer months and during monsoons.

The ***C. botulinum*** toxin is heat labile and can be destroyed if heated at 80°C for 10 minutes or longer. Maintenance of appropriate temperatures during food processing is therefore crucial in the control of this illness. Puffed or swollen cans of food should be rejected as they are indicative of bacterial spoilage which has resulted in gas production. Raw or precooked foods that have been frozen, thawed and held at room temperatures should be avoided. The most important precaution is to always maintain good sanitation throughout production and handling.

The means of prevention of outbreaks of **staphylococcal poisoning** include prevention of contamination of the food by following general methods of maintaining hygiene and sanitation. Ingredients like milk and cream should be pasteurised, and food handlers should not be carriers of this organism. Growth of the bacteria can also be prevented by adequate refrigeration of foods or by making the pH of the foods slightly acidic.

Most incidences of **shigellosis** involve contaminated water. Protection of water sources from contamination and boiling of drinking water are two important measures to prevent outbreaks. Clean water should be used for washing and cooking. Food handlers should follow strict hygienic practices to avoid contaminating water and foodstuffs. Heating foods to appropriate temperatures in order to destroy the microbes also helps. Foods should be refrigerated immediately if they are not being consumed.

Hepatitis A vaccines are now available, which provide long-term protection. Individuals who have been infected have a lifelong protection against re-infection. Other preventive measures include proper hand washing after using the toilet or changing soiled diapers and nappies, especially before handling food. Good personal hygiene habits need to be inculcated from childhood (see Figure 4.8). Drinking boiled water or water treated by ultraviolet rays, especially during the rainy season and during epidemics, also checks the spread of infection. **Polio** is also preventable by vaccination and maintaining hygiene and sanitation at the community level. Proper disposal and treatment of sewage is vital in preventing many food-borne ailments. Open defecation should be discouraged and public toilets constructed for the use of people on the move and those living in slums. According to a report by the United Nations Children's Fund (UNICEF), 626 million people in India practise open defecation. Poor sanitation, lack of access to clean water and inadequate personal hygiene are responsible for an estimated 88 per cent of childhood diarrhoea in India. Prime Minister Narendra Modi's ***Swachh Bharat Abhiyan*** (Clean India Mission) launched on 2 October 2014 aims to eradicate open defecation by 2019. Provision of clean drinking water for all is also vital for ensuring prevention of water-borne illnesses.

India's Fight against Polio

1978: Vaccination against polio started under the Expanded Program on Immunisation (EPI)

1985: The Universal Immunisation Program (UIP) was launched to cover all the districts of the country

1988: Global Polio Eradication Initiative of the World Health Organization

1992: UIP became a part of Child Survival and Safe Motherhood (CSSM) programme

1995: India launched Pulse Polio immunisation programme as a part of UIP, which aimed at 100 per cent coverage

1997: UIP became a part of Reproductive and Child Health (RCH) programme. This programme led to a significant increase in coverage, up to 95 per cent

2011: No reported cases of polio

2014: Country declared polio-free by WHO

Figure 4.8: Good Personal Hygiene Habits should be Inculcated from Childhood

Source: 'Kids washing hands' by Angelica Brasil (CC BY-SA 3.0; Wikimedia Commons).
'lavado de manos' by jaramillosergio (CC0 1.0; Openclipart).

SUMMARY

- Food-borne illnesses can be of two types—one caused by the ingestion of toxins (intoxication) and the other resulting from ingestion of microbes which multiply in the body of the host, producing symptoms (infection).
- Important bacterial agents implicated in food-borne intoxications are *Staphylococcus aureus* and *Clostridium botulinum. Salmonella* spp., *Shigella* spp., *Camplylobacterjejuni*, *Vibrio cholerae* and *Bacillus cereus* are bacteria implicated in food infections.
- Viruses that infect our intestinal tract may be food- or water-borne. Humans are exposed to enteric viruses through various routes: shellfish grown in contaminated waters, food crops grown in land irrigated with wastewater and/or fertilised with sewage, sewage-polluted recreational waters (like swimming pools, water rides in parks) and contaminated drinking water. These viruses cause a wide variety of illnesses in man like hepatitis A, gastroenteritis (adenovirus, astrovirus, norwalk virus, rotavirus) and poliomyelitis.
- Infections can also be caused by parasites (protozoa) like *Cryptosporidium*, *Entamoeba histolytica*, *Giardia lamblia* and *Toxoplasma gondii.*
- Symptoms are usually restricted to the gastrointestinal tract—nausea, vomiting, diarrhoea and abdominal cramps, but may also become systemic if the infection/toxin travels to other parts of the body, sometimes resulting in death. Dehydration is a special concern, especially in small children.
- Most of the food-borne diseases are transmitted person-to-person by the faecal–oral route.
- The principal means of prevention of outbreaks of poisoning include prevention of contamination of the food. This is achieved by general methods of maintaining hygiene and sanitation. Hand washing is vital to prevent any spread of infection.
- Boiling/treating drinking water, washing all foods thoroughly before eating, cooking foods thoroughly and storing them at low (refrigeration) temperatures or at high temperatures, reheating to appropriate temperatures, preventing cross-contamination from raw to cooked foods and from raw meats to raw vegetables and fruits, etc. are important safety measures.

KEY WORDS

Colitis: Inflammation of colon.

Debilitated: Weakened, feeble.

Endemic: (here refers to diseases) Confined to a particular place.

Enteric: Related to the intestine.

Enteropathogenic: Tending to produce disease in the intestinal tract.

Enterotoxin: A toxic substance produced by certain bacteria that on ingestion causes violent vomiting and diarrhoea.

Enterotoxigenic: Those microbes which produce enterotoxins.

Fomites: Objects or substances (such as skin cells, hair, clothing, bedding, etc.) capable of carrying infectious organisms and hence transferring them from one individual to another.

Food handlers: People involved in food preparation or service.

Gastroenteritis: Inflammation of the membrane lining the intestines and the stomach.

Lassitude: Weariness of body or mind.

Morbidity: Sickness.

Mortality: Death.

Pathogen: Any disease producing agent, especially a microbe.

Prostration: Lying down.

Retching: Vomiting, or making an effort to vomit.

Sewage: Waste matter (such as human excreta) which passes through sewers.

Systemic infection: Infection spread in a large part of the body as opposed to in a localised area.

Vertigo: Dizziness.

EXERCISES

1. Differentiate between food infection and intoxication giving appropriate examples.
2. Name the organism responsible for causing cholera. How would you prevent the spread of the disease in a community?
3. What are the symptoms of hepatitis A infection? How does the hepatitis A virus spread?
4. How is polio transmitted? What is being done to prevent the spread of polio?
5. What disease do the Norwalk viruses cause? What symptoms are associated with the Norwalk virus infection?
6. What is the single most important precaution which prevents adenovirus infection?
7. The Health Department has just been informed about a food poisoning episode in a school. Outline the process the investigation should follow.
8. What is the best way to wash hands thoroughly? List the activities before or after which individuals should definitely wash their hands.

REFERENCES

Frazier, W. C., and D. C. Westhoff, adapted by N. M. Vanitha, *Food Microbiology* (5th edition), New Delhi: McGraw Hill Education (India), 2014.

NCDC, 'Food Borne Diseases', *CD Alert*, 13 (4), December 2009, pp. 1–12, Available at http://www.ncdc.gov.in/writereaddata/linkimages/Dec_091047732317.pdf (accessed 16 July 2016).

Lakshminarayanan, S., and R. Jayalakshmy, 'Diarrheal Diseases among Children in India: Current Scenario and Future Perspectives', *J Nat Sci Biol Med* 6 (1), January–June 2015, pp. 24–28.

Narayan, N., and H. Albrecht, 'Virology', in *Viral Agents of Gastroenteritis*, Microbiology and Immunology Online, University of South Carolina School of Medicine, Available at http://www.microbiologybook.org/virol/rotaviruses.htm (accessed 10 June 2016).

Vemula, R. S., R. Naveen Kumar, and K. Polasa, 'Foodborne Diseases in India: A Review', *British Food Journal* 114 (5), 2012, pp. 661–80.

WHO, 'World Health Organisation Fact Sheets', WHO, Geneva, Available at http://www.who.int/mediacentre/factsheets/ (accessed 24 June 2016).

ONLINE SOURCES

Global Foodborne Infections Network (GFN), Available at http://www.who.int/gfn/en/ (accessed 13 April 2018).

Information about Different Parasites, Available at https://www.cdc.gov/parasites/ (accessed 13 April 2018).

Procedures for Investigation of a Food Borne Disease Outbreak – WHO Manual, and for clinical features of each type of food borne pathogen for diagnosis, Available at http://www.who.int/foodsafety/publications/foodborne_disease/outbreak_guidelines.pdf (accessed 13 April 2018).

WHO: How to Handwash? With Soap and Water, Available at https://www.youtube.com/watch?v=3PmVJQUCm4E (accessed 13 April 2018).

WHO Estimates of the Global Burden of Foodborne Diseases (2007–15), Available at http://apps.who.int/iris/bitstream/10665/199350/1/9789241565165_eng.pdf?ua=1 (accessed 13 April 2018).

5

MYCOTOXINS

HIGHLIGHTS

- Types of fungal toxins
- Impact on health
- Prevention and control measures

Fungus is, perhaps, the only microorganism which can be seen with the naked eye. Hot and humid weather conditions favour the growth of fungi not just on food but also on other surfaces like walls, leather goods and even clothes. Fruits, bread, vegetables, cheese and nuts (even those left in refrigerators) tend to support mould growth. Usually, people tend to just chop off the part of the vegetable or fruit which appears mouldy and consume the portion which does not 'look' mouldy. However, one needs to be very careful as the other portion may also have been contaminated by toxins produced by the fungus growing on the food. Such toxins are referred to as ***mycotoxins***. These are actually secondary metabolites (organic compounds produced by the organism but not directly involved in the normal growth, development and reproduction of the organism) of moulds and are a cause of illness and economic loss to us. Although thousands of moulds are capable of growing on food, only a few mould species produce mycotoxins. To produce mycotoxins, fungi require nutrients, moisture, a certain relative humidity, proper temperatures and neutral to slightly alkaline conditions. If all these conditions are suitable for the fungus to grow, the fungus may produce the toxin. Diseases caused by the growth of fungus on a host are termed as ***mycoses*** (like athlete's foot) while diseases caused due to exposure to toxic fungal metabolites or mycotoxins are called ***mycotoxicoses*** (such as aflatoxicosis caused by aflatoxins).

TYPES OF FUNGAL TOXINS

Not all toxins produced by fungi are termed as mycotoxins. Toxins produced by mushrooms (which are a kind of fungi) are not considered to be mycotoxins, even though they can be fatal to humans. Some toxins produced by fungi which are toxic to bacteria are referred to as antibiotics, while those which are toxic for plants are called phytotoxins. Mycotoxins are harmful to vertebrates, including many animals and man. These have been found in many types of foods for human consumption, particularly cereals and nuts. Meat, eggs and milk from animals that have fed on mycotoxin-contaminated feed can be an indirect route of exposure for humans. Some examples of mycotoxins are aflatoxins produced by the fungi *Aspergillus flavus* and *Aspergillus parasiticus*, ergot alkaloids produced by the *Claviceps* spp.; trichothecenes, fumonisin and zearalenone produced by the *Fusaria* species; and ochratoxin by *Aspergillus ochraceus* and *Penicillium* species. These may be produced on the food while it is still in the field or during the storage period, depending on when the food gets contaminated with the fungus. *Claviceps* affects cereals during the pre-harvest stages; *Fusarium* contamination generally occurs under the field conditions and persists during early storage; and *Aspergillus* and *Penicillium* are typical storage fungi, infecting agricultural commodities due to improper storage. Infection with *A. flavus* can also occur in the field. Currently, there are more than 300 known types of mycotoxins but the attention is usually focussed on the ones which are very toxic to us or those that are carcinogenic. These are discussed here in no particular order but by name of the mycotoxin. This is because they are difficult to classify and categorise into groups according to chemical structure, fungus producing them or target organ for toxicity, primarily due to overlapping of categories.

> Turkey X disease was a mysterious outbreak among turkey in England which resulted in the death of nearly 100,000 poults. The disease was ultimately linked to the peanut meal consumed by the turkey which was infested with the mould *Aspergillus flavus*. The term mycotoxin was subsequently coined in 1962 to describe the secondary metabolites (aflatoxins) and opened a new chapter in the field of food safety.

Aflatoxin is perhaps the most researched mycotoxin in India. It is produced by the fungi *Aspergillus flavus* and *Aspergillus parasiticus* found on foods like rice, corn, wheat, sorghum, maize, groundnut, dried coconut, soybean, cottonseed, tree nuts (like pistachios, walnuts, brazil nuts and pecans) and spices. The growth of the fungus and the production of aflatoxin is influenced by certain environmental factors like climate, agricultural practices, susceptibility of commodities to fungal invasion and conditions of storage (specifically the temperature and humidity). The major aflatoxins of concern are designated B_1, B_2, G_1 and G_2 based on blue or green fluorescence under ultraviolet light. These toxins are usually found together in various foods and animal feeds in various proportions; however, aflatoxin B_1 is usually predominant and is the most toxic. When animals consume aflatoxin-contaminated feed, the toxins appear in their milk and consequently in milk products, and are referred to as aflatoxin M_1 and M_2 (see Figure 5.1).

Ergot is actually a plant disease caused by the fungus *Claviceps purpurea*. Crops like pearl millet, wheat, sorghum and rye are often infected during the flowering stage by the fungus. The infected flower, instead of developing into a normal grain, develops into a dark black mass often referred to as 'ergot'. The ergot contains mycotoxins (alkaloids in nature). The alkaloids responsible for the toxic symptoms in ergoty rye and wheat belong to the ergotoxine and ergometrine group of alkaloids while those belonging to the ergot of pearl millet belong to the clavine group.

Besides aflatoxin and the ergot alkaloids, several other commonly occurring mycotoxins have been a source of concern for humans.

Figure 5.1: Cows Feeding on Aflatoxin B_1-contaminated Feed Produce Milk Containing Aflatoxin M_1 as they Metabolically Transform the Toxin

Source: 'cow on farm' by Johnny_automatic (CC0 1.0; Openclipart).
'Lady Milking a Cow' by j4p4n (CC0 1.0; Openclipart).

It is important to note that not all *Aspergillus* species produce aflatoxin. *Aspergillus oryzae* and *Aspergillus sojae* are widely used in Asian food fermentations such as soy sauce, miso and sake.

Ochratoxin A, a potent toxin mainly affecting the kidneys, is a commonly occurring mycotoxin produced by *Aspergillus ochraceus*, *Aspergillus melleus*, *Aspergillus carbonarius*, *Penicillium verrucossum* and *Aspergillus niger*, among some other species. It is found as a natural contaminant of cereals like barley, rye, oats, wheat, corn, cocoa beans, coffee beans, cassava flour, fish, peanuts, poultry eggs and milk, and found in a wide range of stored and processed foods like coffee, beer, dried fruit, wine, cocoa and nuts. This indicates that Ochratoxin A is a moderately stable molecule which can survive most food processing. Thus, different procedures are needed to reduce the levels of this mycotoxin in our food. *Aspergillus niger* is also used in the industrial production of enzymes and citric acid for human use. It is important to make sure that strains which are for this purpose are not toxin-producing strains.

The **trichothecene mycotoxins** (TCT) are a group of over 100 fungal metabolites having the same basic structure. They are further categorised into type A and B, according to their structure. Examples of type-A TCT include T-2 toxin (T-2), HT-2 toxin (HT-2) and diacetoxyscirpenol (DAS). Fusarenone-X (FUX), deoxynivalenol (DON) and nivalenol (NIV) are some of the common naturally occurring type-B TCT. Though a number of fungal genera can produce TCT, mycotoxins produced by *Fusarium* spp. are most commonly seen. Trichothecenes occur in cereal grains such as wheat, barley, maize, oats, rice, soybeans and in derived products, and have been a problem in a number of countries in Asia, Africa, South America, Europe and North America. They are also commonly found in poultry feeds.

Deoxynivalenol, also known as **DON** or **vomitoxin**, is formed by *F. graminearum* and *F. culmorum*. The main commodities affected are cereals and grains like wheat, barley, oats, rye, maize, sorghum and rice. High humidity and temperatures favour the production of this toxin.

Fumonisins (B1 and B2) are metabolites of several species of *Fusarium*, like *Fusarium proliferatum* and *Fusarium verticillioides*. The most toxic among the toxins is fumonisin B1. *Fusarium verticillioides* is present in virtually all corn samples; however, the presence of the fungus does not necessarily mean that fumonisin is also present, as most strains do not produce the toxin.

Zearalenone has been used as a drug to treat postmenopausal symptoms and as an oral contraceptive in some countries.

Patulin is produced by certain fungal species of *Penicillium*, *Aspergillus* and *Byssochlamys* growing on fruit, including apples, pears and grapes. *Penicillium expansum*, a blue mould, is responsible for the production of patulin in apple juice. Its use as an antibiotic was explored before the toxic effects became apparent in both plants and animals.

Zearalenone can be produced by a number of species of *Fusarium*, like *F. culmorum*, *F. culmorum*, etc. These species affect cereals, especially during cool, wet, growing and harvest seasons. The mycotoxin has been detected in wheat, barley, rice, maize, oats, sorghum and other cereals. The most important effect of this mycotoxin is on the reproductive system of animals. It is a non-steroidal compound that exhibits oestrogen-like activity in certain farm animals such as cattle, sheep and pigs.

Moniliformin is produced by several *Fusarium* species (mainly *F. proliferatum*) and is usually found on the corn kernel. It can survive for years in the soil and be passed on to crops in subsequent seasons. The structure of this mycotoxin is distinctly different from fumonisin B1, which is produced by the same fungal species.

IMPACT ON HEALTH

It is not simple to assess the risk posed by mycotoxins to human or animal health. Unless chemically analysed, it is difficult to predict whether a food visibly affected by fungi has mycotoxins in it or not. There are many physical, chemical and biological factors which determine whether and to what extent the fungi will produce toxins. These are:

- **physical factors** like temperature, relative humidity and insect infestation;
- **chemical factors** like use of fungicides and/or fertilisers; and
- **biological factors** such as competing microbes which do not allow toxigenic fungi to thrive

In general, monogastric animals (animals with a single-chambered stomach, like humans, dogs, rats, etc.) are more at risk of suffering from the harmful effects of mycotoxins as compared to ruminants. This is because ruminants (animals having a complex stomach with chambers, like sheep, goats, cows, buffaloes, oxen, camels, etc.) have microbes in their rumen (first stomach), which can degrade the toxin.

Diseases in animals and human beings resulting from the consumption of mycotoxins are called **mycotoxicoses**. Several mycotoxins have also been linked to increased incidence of cancer in human beings. These include aflatoxin, zearalenone, patulin, ochratoxin and fumonisin. Table 5.1 summarises how different mycotoxins affect the health of man and his domestic animals.

Table 5.1: Some Commonly Found Mycotoxins and their Effects on Health

Mycotoxin	*Fungus*	*Foods likely to be contaminated*	*Toxic effects*
Aflatoxin	*Aspergillus flavus*, *A. parasiticus*, some *Penicillium* spp.	Peanuts, unrefined peanut oil, peanut butter, rice, wheat, oats, corn, barley, millets, sorghum, soybeans, peas, sweet potato	Hepatotoxin, Hepatocarcinogen (Group 1, that is those which have been shown to be carcinogenic to humans), genotoxic, immune suppressant
Ergot alkaloids	*Claviceps* spp.	Bajra, sorghum, wheat and rye	Convulsive and gangrenous symptoms
Fumonisins	*Fusarium* spp.	Maize	Possible carcinogens (Group 2B, or those which are possibly carcinogenic to humans), different effects in different animals: promote tumour in rats and cause equine leukoencephalomalacia and porcine pulmonary oedema
Deoxynivalenol and other trichothecenes	*Fusarium* spp.	Wheat, rice, maize, oats, barley, sorghum, rye, vegetables and various other crops	primary inhibition of protein synthesis, necrosis of the oral mucosa and dermatitis if skin gets in contact with the toxin, haemorrhaging in the digestive tract, and decreased bone marrow and immune function
Zearalenone	*Fusarium* spp.	Wheat, rice, maize, barley	Toxic to the reproductive tract of animals, has been shown to have oestrogenic effects in farm animals
Ochratoxin A	Some *Aspergillus* and *Penicillium* spp.	Mainly in cereals—corn, wheat, barley, but also found in peanuts, white beans, eggs, wine, coffee, spices and dried fruits	Possible carcinogens (Group 2B), nephrotoxic and nephron carcinogenic, toxin, an immune suppressant and a potent teratogen
Patulin	*Penicillium*, *Aspergillus* and *Byssochylamys* moulds	Apples, apple juice and cider, fruits	Irritant to the stomach, causing nausea, vomiting and even ulceration in severe cases; genotoxic, neurotoxic, also known to cause reproductive toxicity

(*Contd*)

(*Contd*)

Mycotoxin	*Fungus*	*Foods likely to be contaminated*	*Toxic effects*
Moniliformin	*Fusarium* spp. (mainly *F. proliferatum*)	Corn, other cereals	Reproductive toxicity in fowl, myocardiac damage; toxicity to humans not clearly demonstrated
Citrinin	Species of *Penicillium*, *Aspergillus*	Wheat, oats, rye, corn, barley and rice	Yellow rice disease in Japan, nephrotoxin

Source: Adapted by Author from Zain 2011 and Bennett and Klich 2003.

Aflatoxicosis is the poisoning that results from ingestion of aflatoxins in contaminated food or feed. Aflatoxin is a potent liver toxin and carcinogen. Field outbreaks of diseases have been observed in turkeys, ducks, chickens, swine, cattle, dogs and trout. In each species, the liver is the primary target organ of acute injury.

Acute aflatoxicosis occurs when moderate to high levels of aflatoxins are consumed. Chronic aflatoxicosis is caused due to ingestion of low to moderate levels of aflatoxins over an extended period of time. The effects are usually subclinical and difficult to diagnose. It leads to immune suppression, cancer, impaired feed efficiency (conversion of food which is eaten into useful components of the body) and slower rates of growth, with or without obvious clinical symptoms of aflatoxin toxicity. Impairment of immunity could decrease resistance to infections.

Ergotism is a complex disease that results from the ingestion of grains and cereals infected with ergot by humans and domestic animals. Symptoms of ergotism have been recorded since ancient times in manuscripts as well as paintings, one of which by Matthias Grünewald dates back to 1512–16 CE. The disease was initially attributed to witchcraft due to the convulsive symptoms exhibited by patients. It was also referred to as '*St Anthony's Fire*', named after an

Figure 5.2A: Advanced Ergotism with Gangrene

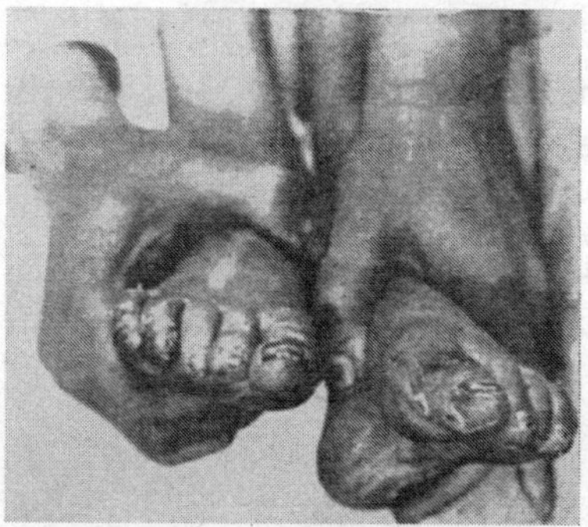

Source: 'Advanced ergotism with gangrene' by G Barger (CC0 1.0; Wikimedia Commons).

Figure 5.2B: Convulsive Ergotism

Source: 'Convulsive ergotism' by T.O. Heusinger (CC0 1.0; Wikimedia Commons).

> You may be surprised to learn that ergot is also used in the preparation of medicines and the recreational drug LSD (d-lysergic acid diethylamide). Two of the alkaloids of ergot—ergotoxine and ergotamine—have been found to have medical use in the treatment of migranes, Parkinsonism and cerebrovascular insufficiency.

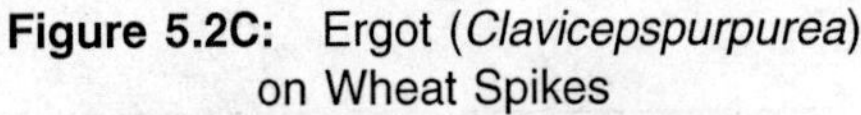
Figure 5.2C: Ergot (*Clavicepspurpurea*) on Wheat Spikes

Source: 'Ergot (Claviceps purpurea) on wheat spikes' by JoJan (CC BY-SA 2.5; Wikimedia Commons).

Tricothecenes have been proposed as possible biological warfare agents. They were implicated in the episode of 'yellow rain', a sticky yellow liquid dropped by planes in Laos and in Cambodia in the 1970s and early 1980s. Thousands of people died as a result of the attacks. The allegations were not substantiated.

institution dedicated to St Anthony in medieval Europe. Two sets of symptoms are seen in ergotism—convulsive and gangrenous. Usually gastrointestinal symptoms like nausea, vomiting and diarrhoea precede the central nervous system effects. The visuals in Figure 5.2 depict a patient suffering from advanced ergotism exhibiting gangrene and in the throes of convulsions.

Convulsive symptoms include muscle spasms, seizures, convulsions or, in some cases, confusion, delusions and hallucinations, itching and paresthesia. In **gangrenous ergotism**, the victim may lose parts of their extremities, such as toes or fingers, due to constriction in the blood vessels extending to the extremities. Decreased blood flow to the extremities results in death of tissues and initial symptoms include peeling off of tissues and loss of sensation in the affected areas.

Many outbreaks of acute human mycotoxicoses have occurred, particularly in Asia. The symptoms usually reported are nausea, vomiting, gastrointestinal upset, dizziness, diarrhoea and headache (see Table 5.2).

Fumonisins have been implicated in a fatal disease in horses known as leucoencephalomalacia (highly fatal neurological disease, also referred as to 'hole in the head syndrome'). In humans, high prevalence of oesophageal cancer has been observed in maize-eating population of various parts of Africa, Central America and Asia. As Fumonisin B1 reduces uptake of folate by the body, it has also been linked with neural tube defects in human babies, which are a result of folate deficiency during pregnancy. Alimentary toxic aleukia is characterised by a decrease in the number of leukocytes along with the other gastrointestinal symptoms. It is believed to be caused by the T2 toxin produced by the *Fusarium* spp.

Ochratoxin A has been implicated in progressive kidney disease referred to as the 'endemic Balkan nephropathy' in populations who live in areas bordering the Danube river in parts of Romania, Bulgaria and the former Yugoslavia. Ochratoxin was detected more in the food and serum samples of the affected population than others in the same area who were free from

Table 5.2: Some Outbreaks of Mycotoxicosis in Humans Reported across the World

Toxin	*Fungus*	*Food/Feed implicated*	*Adverse effect seen*
Fumonisins	*Fusarium* spp.	Maize and sorghum	In India, an acute episode of borborygmy (intestinal rumbling sound), abdominal pain and diarrhoea
		Maize	In rural populations of South Africa and northern China, a high incidence of neural tube defects (as seen in folate deficiency)
		Maize	Oesophageal cancer in regions of Transkei
Aflatoxins	*Aspergillus* spp.	Maize	Toxic hepatitis, jaundice and death in humans in Kenya, India and Malaysia
		Maize	In 1974, more than 150 villages in Rajasthan and Gujarat affected with high fever, rapid progressive jaundice, oedema of the limbs, pain, vomiting and swollen livers; about 106 people died
		Maize	In 1982, in Kenya, symptoms indicating liver damage seen in people. Mortality was 60 per cent of the affected individuals
Ergot alkaloids	*Claviceps purpurea*	*Bajra* (pearl millet)	Outbreaks in Maharashtra, Gujarat and Rajasthan. People affected had symptoms of nausea, vomiting, giddiness and drowsiness
Deoxynivalenol trichothecene	*Fusarium* spp.	Wheat and bread	In 1987, in the Kashmir valley, people who consumed contaminated wheat flour developed symptoms of abdominal pain and vomiting.
Trichothecene T-2 Toxin	*F. sporitrichoides and F. poae*	Cereal grains	Alimentary toxic aleukia in humans in Russia from 1932–47. Symptoms included mucous membrane hyperaemia, oesophageal pain, laryngitis, asphyxiation, gastroenteritis and vertigo

Source: Adapted by Author from Lewis et al. 2005; Bennett and Klitch 2003; Marasas et al. 2004; Bhat et al. 1997; and Bhat et al. 1989.

the disease. However, a cause-and-effect link has not been clearly established in humans as has been shown in several animal species.

Deoxynivalenol causes nausea, vomiting and diarrhoea in farm animals when ingested in high doses; and at lower doses, symptoms of weight loss and food refusal are seen. That is why the toxin is also referred to as 'vomitoxin' or 'food refusal factor'.

Mycotoxins have been detected not only in our food or animal feed samples, but also in human blood samples. This highlights the fact that populations across the world are ingesting potent toxins which, on continuous exposure, may lead to adverse effects which are very difficult to pin to a particular mycotoxin. Hence, it is vital that suitable regulatory and public health measures are taken to reduce our exposure to these health hazards.

PREVENTION AND CONTROL MEASURES

The world over, mycotoxin contamination of foods and feeds has led to significant health and economic impacts—loss of human life, cost of healthcare and, in addition, the losses incurred when farm animals or livestock are affected. This is especially a problem in India, where farmers can lose their source of livelihood if their cattle or other livestock succumb to the toxic effects of mycotoxin-contaminated feeds. Most studies in India have shown high levels of contamination at the farm level, and attribute it to poor animal-rearing and agricultural practices. In addition, the country has had to deal with huge financial losses due to the **rejection of shipments of foods** by importing nations due to high levels of mycotoxins.

The **economic impact** of mycotoxin-contaminated food and feeds includes the **cost of human healthcare** and **veterinary care**, the losses in production as well as the cost of discarding food/feed found to be contaminated. A lot of research time and other resources of the scientific community are diverted towards tackling the menace of mycotoxin-related adverse effects and effort put in towards controlling the problem.

National and international organisations dealing with food safety have issued guidelines to reduce man's exposure to these toxins. All countries have set maximum permissible limits for different mycotoxins in food. You may wonder why foods containing even small amounts of these toxins are not rejected. This is because it is not always economically feasible to reject mycotoxin-containing foods. If the levels are low enough, they cause us no harm even if consumed over a long period of time. These levels, however, need to be monitored regularly to ensure that they do not exceed safe levels. **Spread of awareness** regarding the harmful effects of mycotoxins, and ways to prevent and reduce their levels in food and feed are very important. The **FSSAI**, in India, puts the limit for aflatoxin in different foods for human consumption at 10–15 ppb. For Ochratoxin A, the limit is 20 ppb in wheat, rye and barley, 50 ppb for Patulin in apple juice and 1,000 ppb for DON in wheat. The European Union has the strictest maximum acceptable limit in the world (of 4 ppb) for aflatoxins in food for human consumption.

Some **processing conditions** are known to reduce the level of mycotoxins in food. For example, milling and cooking processes reduce aflatoxin levels in foods. However, studies in India have shown that processing and pasteurisation of milk do not destroy the aflatoxin completely. Binding agents like bentonite and aluminosilicate clays are added to feeds to bind and hence reduce the bioavailability of aflatoxin. However, preventing the growth of the fungi seems to be the more logical way of reducing the mycotoxin content of foods.

The role of dietary factors in potentially reducing the adverse effects of mycotoxins is also being explored. Some of the food components which have been studied are antioxidants like selenium, vitamins A, E and C, fructose, phenolic compounds, chlorophyll and coumarins. **Dietary interventions** like broccoli sprouts and green tea can increase an animal's detoxification processes (Kensler et al. 2004). **Enterosorption** is another technique used to decrease absorption of mycotoxins in the gastrointestinal tract by ingesting special clays or compounds which can adsorb the toxin and prevent its absorption. However, there is a risk that these non-specific adsorption agents may also prevent the absorption of useful micronutrients from food.

Aflatoxins are considered unavoidable contaminants of food and feed, even where good manufacturing practices have been followed. To reduce the amount of the mycotoxin in our food, simple measures like **separating visibly mouldy grains** or seeds from healthy ones before consuming or processing them into food products, can go a long way. The **refining process** for groundnut oil also destroys aflatoxin. Thus, consuming refined oil is safer than unrefined oil. Even the process of filtering the unrefined oil reduces the aflatoxin content. If aflatoxin levels in animal feed are controlled, levels in milk will automatically reduce.

DON is thermally stable so once formed, it is likely to persist through storage and processing. However, as it is water soluble, a significant proportion can be removed by **washing** the grain. It is important to get rid of DON as it is sometimes found in very high concentrations in foods commonly eaten as a staple. Fumonisins are also quite stable and are not destroyed by moderate heat. About 40–90 per cent of Ochratoxin is destroyed during **roasting of coffee beans**.

In whole fruits and vegetables, it is easy to identify and reject the ones which are damaged and contaminated with fungus. This is not possible in the case of juices and other processed products. If contaminated fruits are used for the production of these, then the mycotoxin levels can be quite high. When **sulphur dioxide** is used as a preservative in fruit juices or other foods, mycotoxins like patulin are broken down. Patulin exposure can be successfully managed by following **good agricultural practices** such as removing mould, washing and not using rotten or damaged apples for baking, canning or juice production.

Figure 5.3: Preventing Mycotoxin Contamination in Foods

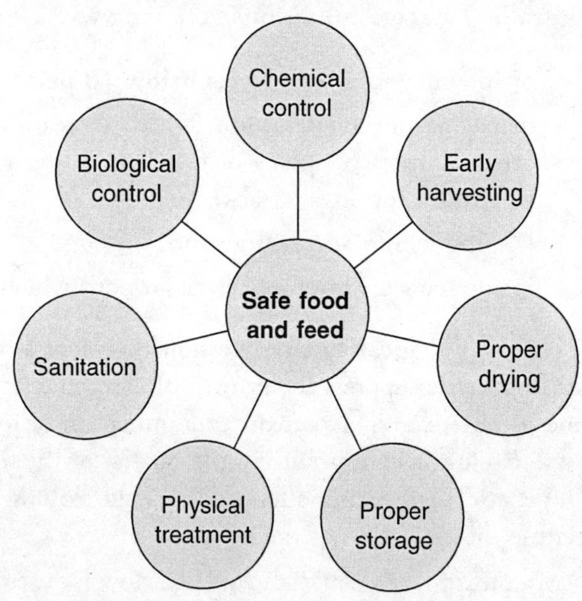

Source: Adapted by Author from Zain 2011.

Figure 5.3 highlights the steps that can be taken to prevent or, at least, reduce the fungal contamination of food or feed material. Good agricultural practices go a long way in protecting the crop from fungal infestation in the field. For instance, harvesting the crop early is known to protect the crop from fungus which is known to attack standing ready crop, especially if the weather is unpredictable. The crop, once harvested, needs to be dried sufficiently and rapidly as low moisture levels will further discourage the fungi from growing. Physically removing infected grains from the rest by **sorting**, **winnowing**, **washing**, **crushing** combined with **de-hulling** of grains like maize or peanuts are effective in reducing mycotoxin levels. This, however, is possible only when a small fraction of the grains is infested and physically removing them significantly gets rid of the fungus. To clean seeds and grains, a **flotation method** is used in which salt water or a solution of approximately 30 per cent potassium chloride is poured over the seeds and stirred. The ergot-stage grain is buoyant and will float to the top and can be skimmed off. The good seeds sink to the bottom. **Hand picking** and **sieving** can also be used to remove the ergoty grains.

To minimise the amount of ergot formation after grains have been harvested, the field can be deeply ploughed so that the ergot will not germinate. A different crop, not susceptible to ergot, can be planted the following year so that whatever ergot was left in the field would die out a natural death due to lack of a host plant. Farmers and scientists have also been successful in identifying and developing crop varieties that are resistant to fungi.

Maintaining absolute **cleanliness** and **sanitation** of the storage area—the bins/bags in which the food or feed is stored—is of prime importance in decreasing the possibility of the food getting infected with the spores of fungi from the last stock. It is important to also get rid of stalks and other leftover debris from the last crop lying in the field as it may transfer the fungi to the fresh crop in the field.

Controlling storage conditions go a long way in reducing contamination levels by:

- maintaining **moisture levels below 10 per cent**;
- managing insect infestation (which increases moisture levels due to respiration and also acts as carriers of spores of fungi, infecting grains by damaging them and making them susceptible to fungal attack);
- keeping **temperatures low**; and
- maintaining an **inert gas environment** which discourages fungal growth.

Use of **biological agents** like non-toxigenic strains of fungi, yeasts or bacteria to compete with and hence suppress the growth of toxigenic strains of fungi has been experimented with as a means of reducing mycotoxin contamination of foods and feed. This should not, of course, in any way result in compromising the quality of the final commodity. **Selective breeding** of crops and **genetic engineering** offer scope for developing crops which are resistant to fungal attack or decrease the formation of the mycotoxin.

Mycotoxin levels could also be kept low by use of **chemicals** to control growth of fungi and insect infestation. A number of **fungicides** are used by the agricultural sector, although there are several concerns with regard to pesticide residues in feeds and food, and damage to the environment. This is discussed in detail in chapter 6 of this volume.

SUMMARY

- Mycotoxins are toxic substances produced by fungi (moulds) growing on feed or food, in the field or in storage.
- Not all fungi produce mycotoxins.
- To produce mycotoxins, fungi require suitable conditions of nutrition, moisture and temperature.
- Mycotoxins have been found in many types of food for human consumption, particularly cereal grains and nuts.
- Some of these toxins which are of concern to human health are aflatoxins, ergot alkaloids, ochratoxin A, fumonisins, trichothecenes, deoxynivalenol, patulin and zearalenone.
- Aflatoxin is a potent liver toxin and carcinogenic. It is produced by the fungi *Aspergillus flavus* and *Aspergillus parasiticus*.
- Ergot is a plant disease that is caused by the fungus *Claviceps purpurea*. The ergot contains several alkaloids (mycotoxins) that are poisonous.
- Besides being a health hazard, mycotoxins lead to huge economic losses as well. It is thus imperative to reduce our exposure to all types of mycotoxins and this can be achieved by making storage and processing conditions unfavourable for fungal growth.
- By keeping storage temperatures low, humidity under check and moisture content of the foods low, fungal growth can be checked.
- Processing can be used to destroy fungi and some mycotoxins; for instance, aflatoxin in unrefined groundnut oil is destroyed during the refining process.
- Separating good grains and fruit from ones with fungus either by sieving, hand picking, flotation method, etc. also helps in reducing the level of mycotoxin in the final food product.

KEY WORDS

Acute toxicity: Rapid onset toxic response.

Borborygmi: Rumbling or gurgling sound caused by the movement of gas in the intestines.

Carcinogenic: Cancer causing.

Chronic toxicity: Characterised by low-dose exposure over a long time period, resulting in cancers and other generally irreversible effects.

Convulsion: Fits or sudden violent movement of the body caused by involuntary contractions of muscles.

Delusion: A false belief or impression.

Disorientation: Confusion as to one's whereabouts or bearings.

Gangrene: Death and decomposition of a part of the body tissue usually resulting from obstructed circulation.

Haemorrhage: Escape of blood from a ruptured blood vessel.

Hyperaemia: Excess of blood in vessels supplying blood to an organ/tissue.

Oedema: Swelling of part of the body due to accumulation of fluids in the intercellular tissue spaces.

Overt: Not concealed.

Muscle spasm: Sudden involuntary muscular contraction.

Psychedelic drug: A drug which produces hallucinations.

Teratogen: Agent which causes malformation in developing embryo.

Wry neck: Twisting of the neck.

EXERCISES

1. What is a mycotoxin? Explain by giving examples of fungi which produce different mycotoxins.
2. What are the toxic effects of consuming food contaminated with aflatoxins? How can exposure to aflatoxins be reduced?
3. Name the mycotoxin commonly found in apple juice.
4. Which food was implicated in a gastrointestinal disease outbreak in the Kashmir valley? Which mycotoxin was found to be responsible?
5. List some measures to control the problem of fungal contamination of foods.
6. Which fungus is implicated in the disease ergotism? What are the typical symptoms of ergotism?

REFERENCES

Bennett J. W., and M. Klich, 'Mycotoxins', *Clinical Microbiology Reviews* 16(3), 2003, pp. 497–516.

Bhat, R. V., P. H. Shetty, R. P. Amruth, and R. V. Sudershan, 'A Foodborne Disease Outbreak due to the Consumption of Moldy Sorghum and Maize Containing Fumonisin Mycotoxins', *Clin. Toxicol.* 35(3), 1997, pp. 249–55.

Bhat, R. V., S. R. Beedu, Y. Ramakrishna, K. L. Munshi, 'Outbreak of Trichothecene Mycotoxicosis Associated with Consumption of Mould-damaged Wheat Production in Kashmir Valley, India', *Lancet* 1(8628), 7 January 1989, pp. 35–37.

Kensler, T. W., P. A. Egner, J. B. Wang, Y. R. Zhu, B. C. Zhang, P. X. Lu, J. G. Chen, G. S. Qian, S. Y. Kuang, P. E. Jackson, S. J. Gange, L. P. Jacobson, A. Munoz, J. D. Groopman, 'Chemoprevention of Hepatocellular Carcinoma in Aflatoxin Endemic Areas', *Gastroenterology* 127(5), 2004, pp. 310–18.

Lewis, L., M. Onsongo, H. Njapau, H. Schurz-Rogers, G. Luber, S. Kieszak, J. Nyamongo, L. Backer, A. M. Dahiye, A. Misore, K. Decoct, C. Rubin, 'Aflatoxin Contamination of Commercial Maize Products during an Outbreak of Acute Aflatoxicosis in Eastern and Central Kenya', *Environ Health Perspect.* 113(12), 2005, pp. 1763–67.

Marasas, W. F. O., R. T. Riley, K. A. Hendricks, V. L. Stevens, T. W. Sadler, J. Gelineau-van Waes, S. A. Missmer, J. Cabrera, O. Torres, W. C. A. Gelderblom, J. Allegood, C. Martinez, J. Maddox, J. D. Miller, L. Starr, M. C. Sullards, A. Roman, K. A. Voss, E. Wang, A. H. Merrill, 'Fumonisins Disrupts Phingolipid Metabolism, Folate Transport, and Neural Tube Development in Embryo Culture and In Vivo: A Potential Risk Factor for Human Neural Tube Defects among Populations Consuming Fumonisin Contaminated Maize', *J. Nutr.* 134(4), 2004, pp. 711–16.

Zain, M. E., 'Impact of Mycotoxins on Humans and Animals', *Journal of Saudi Chemical Society* 15(2), 2011, pp. 129–44.

ONLINE SOURCES

T. Kuiper-Goodman, *Approaches to the Risk Analysis of Mycotoxins in the Food Supply*, Available at http://www.fao.org/docrep/x2100t/x2100t03.htm (accessed 13 April 2018).

Mycotoxins in Grain, FAO Corporate Document Repository, Available at http://www.fao.org/wairdocs/x5008e/x5008e01.htm (accessed 13 April 2018).

Video on Aflatoxins in Groundnuts by ICRISAT, Available at https://www.youtube.com/watch?v=9QBO4Y1gtZc (accessed 13 April 2018).

Video on Ergot Disease of Sorghum by ICRISAT, Available at https://www.youtube.com/watch?v=P5UEv_PDRLQ (accessed 13 April 2018).

6

CHEMICAL CONTAMINANTS: PESTICIDE RESIDUES

HIGHLIGHTS

- Types of pesticides
- Sources of contamination
- Impact on health
- Prevention and control measures

Pesticides are chemicals used to protect food from pests such as insects, rodents, weeds, mould and bacteria. These may also be used to sanitise public areas to prevent outbreaks of diseases caused by pests and controlling vectors—like mosquitoes and flies—of tropical diseases such as dengue, malaria, leishmaniasis, filariasis and Japanese encephalitis. Pesticides have been in use for thousands of years. The first known pesticide was probably elemental sulphur dust, used in Sumeria about 4,500 years ago. Nicotine sulphate obtained from tobacco leaves has been used as an insecticide. Pyrethrum derived from chrysanthemums and rotenone derived from the roots of tropical vegetables are other examples of natural compounds used. Use of dried *neem* leaves as an insect repellent for storage of woollens was common in several homes before the introduction of chemicals in the form of naphthalene balls.

With increase in agriculture, the use of pesticides has increased several-fold in India and it is likely to increase further in the coming years. Pesticides are potentially toxic to humans and research evidence on their harmful effects is mounting. In 1939, Paul Muller discovered dichlorodiphenyltrichloroethane (DDT), which was widely used for several years before its harmful effects on the environment and humans was realised. In India, the use of DDT for the control of malaria and benzene hexachloride (BHC) for locusts did a lot in controlling these pests but at the same time, gravely damaged the environment. Studies have shown that certain pesticides are carcinogenic, while some others affect various organ systems like the reproductive, immune and nervous systems. This chapter highlights the different kinds of pesticides that are used, how their residues contaminate our food or enter our bodies, the adverse health effects attributed to these pesticides, and the basic measures to control the growing menace of food and water being contaminated with pesticides. The regulatory provisions in place for monitoring contamination are also discussed.

TYPES OF PESTICIDES

Pesticides may be **classified according to the pest** they are used to control; for instance, there are:

- insecticides to control insects
- rodenticides to control rodents (such as rats, mice, moles)
- herbicides to control weeds
- fungicides to control moulds and fungi
- antimicrobials to control bacteria

Acaricide (for acarids like ticks and mites), aphicide (for aphids), miticide (for mites), ixodicide (for ticks), larvicide (for larval life stage of an insect), molluscicide (for molluscs like snails) and nematocides (for nematodes) are names given to pesticides used to kill specific pests, as indicated.

Pesticides are also **classified based on their chemical nature** as:

- organochlorine pesticides
- organophosphates and carbamates
- pyrethrins and pyrethroids

> The common mosquito repellent creams and sprays we use for our bodies mostly have DEET (diethylbenzamide) as the active ingredient. DEET is classified by WHO under category III (slightly hazardous) for acute toxicity. Some others have citronella oil, which is obtained from the leaves and stem of different species of the lemongrass plant. The United States Environmental Protection Agency (EPA) considers oil of citronella as a biopesticide with a non-toxic mode of action. It also has strong antifungal properties. Transfluthurin, a pyrethroid classified under the U category by WHO, is the active ingredient in most mosquito repellent vaporisers. Allethrin (WHO category II) and Resmethrin (WHO category III) are used in combination in household insectide sprays by most companies. These are pyrethroids.

In addition, a large number of inorganic pesticides is also in use. WHO (2010) has classified pesticides on the basis of their acute toxicity. **Acute toxicity** refers to the harmful effects seen when there is a single exposure or multiple exposures to the pesticide within a short span of time. The classification is based primarily on the acute oral and dermal (skin) toxicity to rats, since in toxicology, it is standard procedure to use the rat as a model. The LD_{50} (the lethal dose that will kill 50 per cent of the animals to whom the dose is administered) is estimated for each pesticide. The dose will vary depending upon the formulation of the pesticide and whether it is in solid or liquid form. It will also vary with the kind of exposure, that is, dermal or oral. Thus, WHO has classified the pesticides into categories:

- Ia (extremely hazardous)
- Ib (highly hazardous)
- II (moderately hazardous)
- III (slightly hazardous) and
- U (unlikely to present acute hazard)

Table 6.1 gives some examples of commonly used pesticides. Pesticides are available as various formulations like liquid, gel, paste, chalk, powder, granules, pellets and baits containing 2–80 per cent of active ingredient. The toxicity depends on the type of formulation (the characteristics of the solvent or other substances contained in it), the concentration of the active ingredient and even on whether it is a solid or liquid product.

Table 6.1: Some Commonly Used Pesticides

Action	*Chemical categories/types*	*Examples*	*Toxicity category (WHO)*
Insecticides	Organophosphates	Mevinphos, Parathion	Ia
		Dichlorvos, Azinphos, Coumaphos	Ib
		Cyanophos, Fenthion	II
		Malathion, Temephos	III
	Organochlorines	Chlordane, DDT, Endosulfan	II
		Methoxychlor	U
	Carbamates	Adicarb	Ia
		Carbofuran	Ib
		Fenobucarb	II
	Pyrethrins and pyrethroids	Cyfluthrin, Zeta-Cypermethrin	Ib
		Bifenthrin, Bioallethrin, Allethrin	II
		Empenthrin, Fluvalinate, Resmethrin	III
		Bioresmethrin, Phenothrin, Transfluthrin	U
Herbicide	Nitrophenol derivative	Dinoterb	Ib
	Bipyridylium derivative	Paraquat and diquat	II
	–	Bromoxynil	II
	Organophosphate	Fosamine	III
	–	Acetochlor	III
Fungicide	Organochlorines	Hexachlorobenzene	Ia
		Dichlorophen	II
	–	Blasticidin	Ib
	–	Biphenyl, Borax	III
	–	Chlorothalonil, Carbendazim	U
	Copper	Copper sulphate, Copper hydroxide	II
Molluscicides	–	Metaldehyde	II
	–	Niclosaminde	U

(*Contd*)

(*Contd*)

Action	*Chemical categories/types*	*Examples*	*Toxicity category (WHO)*
Rodenticide	–	Bromethalin	Ia
	Coumarin derivative	Difenacoum	Ia
	–	Strychnine, Zinc phosphide	Ib
	Coumarin derivative	Warfarin	Ib
Insect repellents	–	Diethyltoluamide/Diethylbenzamide (DEET)	III
	–	Dimethyl phthalate	U

Source: Adapted by Author from WHO 2010.

SOURCES OF CONTAMINATION

People can be exposed to pesticides intentionally or unintentionally. **Intentional exposure** is when people try to commit suicide by consuming pesticides or try to poison and kill someone else (homicide). **Unintentional exposure** can be from several sources as shown in Table 6.2. The water, air or food can get contaminated in each case, resulting in ingesting, inhaling or at least having dermal contact with the pesticide. Accidental poisoning has been seen in a number of reported cases where:

- pesticides had been stored in an old medicine/water/soft drink bottle or when its container resembles either of these;
- pesticide containers are reused for storing food or drinks;
- pesticide containers are stored along with food/medicine containers and the formulation resembles a food ingredient like flour or salt; or
- pesticide has been sprayed into the air or on food kept in the area while trying to get rid of pests

Thus, a lot of precautions need to be taken when pesticides are used for sanitation/pest control in homes, schools, offices, hospitals and other institutions. Baits are especially dangerous if there are children or pets in homes as they may just consume these, mistaking them for a food item.

Table 6.2: Types of Unintentional Exposure to Pesticides

Occupational Exposure	*Non-occupational Exposure*
Persons working in pesticide manufacturing plants	Handling or applying pesticide at home without taking adequate precautions
Farmers applying the pesticide in their fields without adequate protective gear	Accidental mixing of pesticide with food because of storage in close proximity
Health workers spraying or applying pesticide on the roads/drains/vector breeding grounds, etc.	Consumption of contaminated food and water

Source: Compiled by Author.

Pesticides are generally used at home to keep away mosquitoes, cockroaches, moths, ants, termites or rodents. In gardens, it may be used to get rid of weeds or aphids and other plant pests. They are also used to treat humans, household pets and farm animals infested with lice, fleas, ticks, scabies, etc. Any such product should be carefully applied, taking care not to contaminate the surroundings and making sure the pesticide is not ingested by the animal by licking in case of dermal applications, or by getting mixed into the water or feed. After application, the pesticide may contaminate the environment by settling on plants. Animals and insects which were not the target for the pesticide may also get contaminated by consuming contaminated plants or by simply coming in contact with the pesticide lying on the surface of plants, soil, rocks and other things in the environment. Residues of organophosphorus insecticides sprayed in indoor environments have been reported to occur on floors, carpets, children's toys, furniture, bed covers and in dust. Volatile pesticides might vaporise and pollute the air for days after their application on surfaces.

Figure 6.1: Hazardous Ways of Applying Pesticides

6.1A: Crop Duster

Source: 'Spraying pesticide in California' by USDA (CC0 1.0; Wikimedia Commons).

6.1B: Without Protective Gear

Source: 'Blausig, Kartoffelkäferbekämpfung', by Krueger (CC BY-SA 3.0; Wikimedia Commons).

Farmers or health workers may be at great risk, especially if they are spraying pesticides without using protective gear which covers their nose and exposed body parts (see Figure 6.1B). When large-scale application of pesticide is done by airplanes called 'crop dusters,' the pesticide tends to settle on everything else in the vicinity as well (see Figure 6.1A). Seeds which have been treated with pesticides to preserve them till the next growing season should not be consumed by man and animals. Pesticides are primarily used in the agricultural sector for preserving seeds and protecting crops from pests. When it is applied on a crop, the entire area around the crop is affected. The plants, soil, organisms living in the soil, birds and small animals which live in the field or come to feed, and the humans working in the field or living adjacent to the field can imbibe the pesticide. From the soil, the pesticides can even contaminate groundwater as they travel down different layers of the soil along with irrigation or rain water. A significant amount of the pesticides used in agriculture leach into the rivers (especially from farms bordering river banks) and other water bodies. Pesticides in water bodies may go into aquatic organisms and then enter our food chain as we feed on fish, shell fish, sea weeds, etc. Figure 6.2 illustrates the routes followed by an agricultural chemical, presenting a risk to applicators, bystanders and wildlife.

Figure 6.2: How Pesticides Contaminate the Food Supply and Reach Man

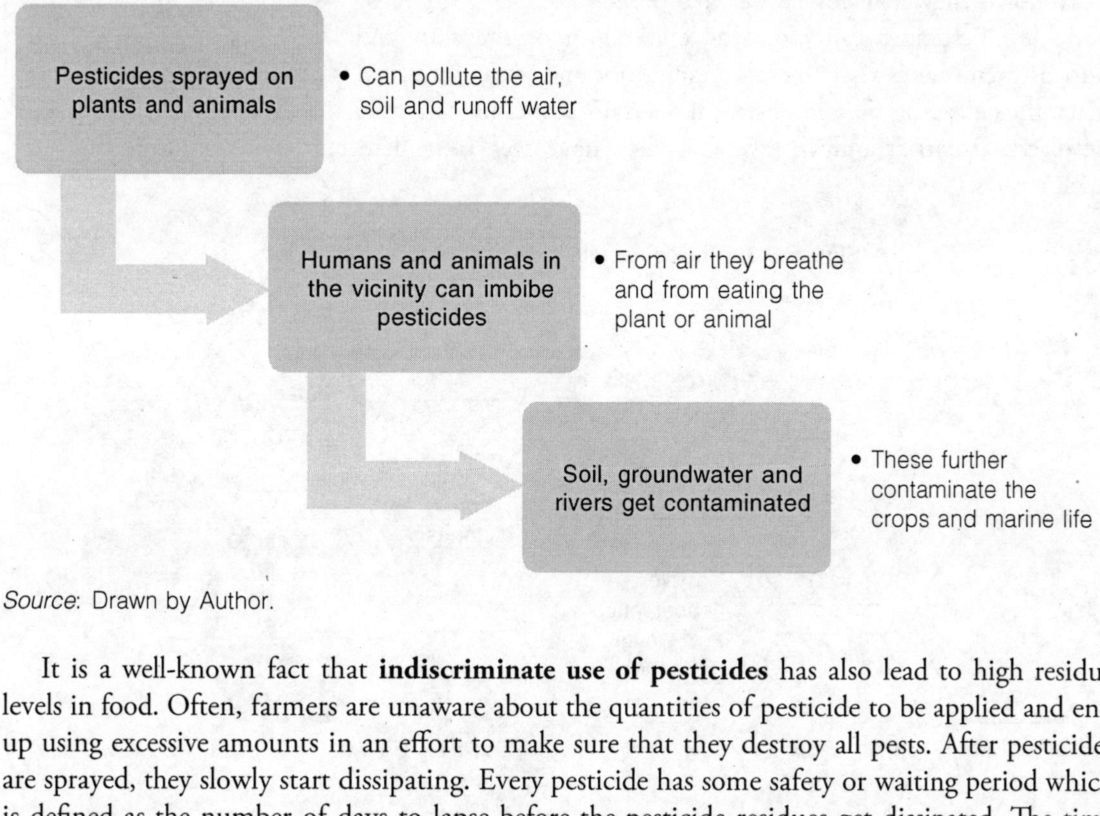

Pesticides sprayed on plants and animals

- Can pollute the air, soil and runoff water

Humans and animals in the vicinity can imbibe pesticides

- From air they breathe and from eating the plant or animal

Soil, groundwater and rivers get contaminated

- These further contaminate the crops and marine life

Source: Drawn by Author.

It is a well-known fact that **indiscriminate use of pesticides** has also lead to high residue levels in food. Often, farmers are unaware about the quantities of pesticide to be applied and end up using excessive amounts in an effort to make sure that they destroy all pests. After pesticides are sprayed, they slowly start dissipating. Every pesticide has some safety or waiting period which is defined as the number of days to lapse before the pesticide residues get dissipated. The time varies from pesticide to pesticide and also from one crop to another. Food products become safe for consumption only after the waiting period has lapsed. If fruits and vegetables are harvested before completion of the waiting period, they are likely to have higher levels of residue, which are hazardous to health.

Pesticides have different distribution and **persistence patterns in the environment**. They can contaminate the soil, water or air. How much of the pesticide stays in the environment and for how long determines the acute and chronic exposure. Climate characteristics also play a role in persistence. Studies in the Arctic have shown that insecticides and herbicides persist three to eight times longer in cold climates than in temperate ones. The most persistent pesticides are termed '**persistent organic pollutants**' (POPs). These have low solubility in water but are lypophilic and hence tend to accumulate in the food chain. They can **biomagnify** (concentrate) in marine and land animals as well as humans, residing chiefly in the adipose tissue, leading to toxic effects in the long run on the endocrine system and development in general. Examples of POPs include pesticides (mainly organochlorine), namely aldrin, endrin, dieldrin, clordane, DDT, heptachlor, mirex, toxaphene, chlordecone, hexachlorocyclohexane, endosulfan, lindane, pentachlorobenzene and hexachlorobenzene, among other industrial chemicals and by-products. People working in industrial units manufacturing pesticides are also at a great risk of both acute and chronic exposure. If they do not take adequate precautions, they may inhale or have dermal contact with these pesticides. Pesticides can cross the epithelium of the skin and mucous membranes that line the respiratory and gastrointestinal tracts, thus entering the blood stream. Certain pesticides can cross the placental barrier and, in several studies, have even been detected in the amniotic fluid and foetal tissues.

> Residues of organochlorine pesticides and POPs have been detected in breast milk (including DDT, HCB and HCH isomers).

Figure 6.3: Indiscriminate Use of Chemical Pesticides

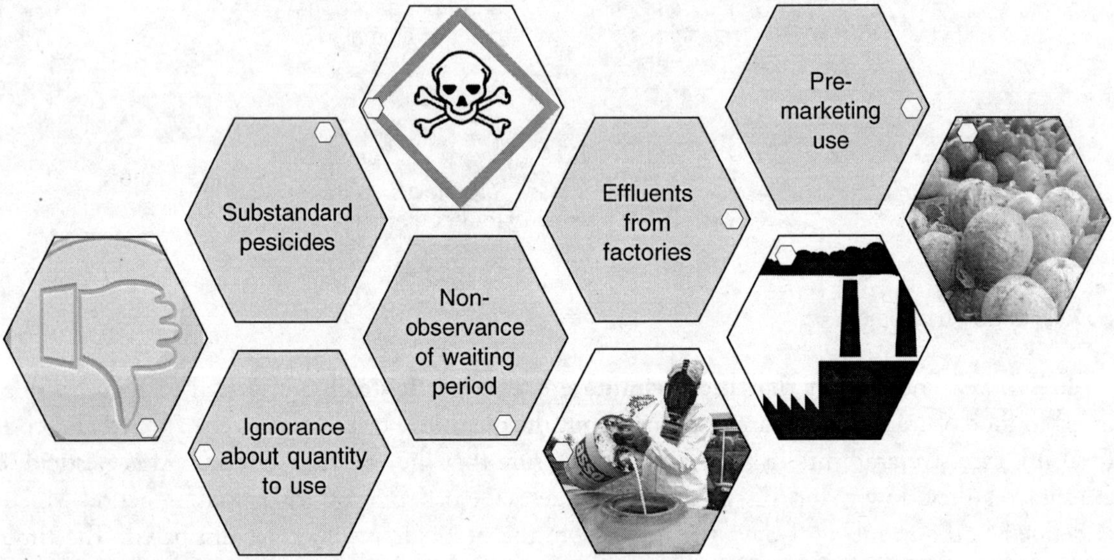

Substandard pesicides

Pre-marketing use

Effluents from factories

Non-observance of waiting period

Ignorance about quantity to use

Source: Drawn by Author.

Images: Danger Sign: 'GHS-pictogram-skull' by Perhelion (CC0 1.0; Wikimedia Commons).
Factory: 'factory silhouette' (CC0 1.0; Wpclipart).
Thumb-down Icon: 'coin thumbs down' (CC0 1.0; Wpclipart).
Pouring Pesticide: 'Hazardous pesticide' (CC0 1.0; Wikimedia Commons).
Fruits: Author.

Indiscriminate use of pesticides—as illustrated in Figure 6.3—is resulting in an increase in levels of contamination of our environment and our food supply. This is mainly due to ignorance about good agricultural practices and non-observance of prescribed waiting periods. People applying the pesticide are not aware of concentrations to use, frequency with which to apply, sometimes feeling that the more they use, the better protected their crops will be. They also lack the knowledge about the safest pesticide to use and end up purchasing substandard pesticides which they must apply more of to get the desired effect. Alternately, they may purchase the more toxic varieties even though safer and more effective substitutes are readily available. In developing nations, where monitoring and regulation are not very strong, banned pesticides are still in use. Effluents from pesticide manufacturing units add to pollution levels along with people disposing of leftover pesticides irresponsibly. Another reason for high residue levels in foods is the treatment of grains, fruits and vegetables after harvest, before they are marketed. This is mainly done to prevent spoilage due to insects and microbes.

Several studies have indicated pesticide contamination of foods in India. ICMR's (1993) multi-centric study shed light on the widespread contamination of foodstuffs with pesticides. Other studies by Bhanti and Taneja (2007) and Bhushan (2006), among others, have also revealed that fruits, vegetables, milk, and even processed foods and beverages have pesticide residues more than the maximum residue limits (MRLs) set by the FSSAI.

An analysis of the health risk posed by use of organophosphorus pesticides on vegetables in northern India indicated that chlorpyriphos and malathion did not pose a direct hazard; however, exposure to methyl parathion definitely posed some risk to human health (Bhanti and Taneja 2007).

IMPACT ON HEALTH

The mode of action of pesticides is usually by targeting systems/enzymes in the pests, which may be identical or very similar to systems/enzymes in human beings. Therefore, these chemicals pose a risk to human health and the environment. Toxicity of a specific pesticide depends on its chemical characteristics and formulation. Inside the body, the pesticide may undergo chemical reactions producing metabolic products, which may be less or more toxic than the original compound. Both the dose and the time for which exposure to the pesticide occurs will determine the type of toxicity—acute or chronic. In acute toxicity, the harmful effects appear usually within 24 hours of ingestion. Pesticides with a high acute toxicity are considered deadly as even small amounts can lead to severe adverse effects. In chronic toxicity, the adverse effects become apparent after exposure for a relatively longer period of time. Pesticides with high chronic toxicity lead to very serious consequences when consumed for an extended period of time. These pesticides may or may not have high acute toxicity. The adverse effects can be local or systemic. Local effects occur at the point of contact like the skin of the hand which touched the pesticide or the mucous membranes of the respiratory tract when the pesticide was inhaled. Systemic effects occur away from the point of contact and usually affect the entire system/body.

> Punjab is one of the largest users of pesticides in the country. It is now a hotspot of cancer in India with several studies linking cancer to excessive exposure to pesticides.

Even small quantities of these residues eaten daily can lead to high levels in the body. This is because it is difficult for the body to throw out the pesticides and so, they keep getting accumulated, mostly in the adipose or fatty tissue (**bioaccumulation**). Elimination is mostly via urinary, biliary and faecal routes. Residues of pesticides have been found in almost all kinds of foods, that is, milk and milk products, edible oils and fats, food grains, vegetables and fruits. A study estimated that 50–70 per cent of all vegetables grown and sold around the country were contaminated with insecticide residues, some of them well beyond permissible levels. We use the term 'permissible levels' here even though pesticide residues are undesirable contaminants in our food. This is because it is sometimes economically not feasible to totally remove these residues from the food. So levels which will not cause us harm are permissible in most foods by law. Studies in India have shown the presence of pesticides like DDT and BHC in the breast milk of some women. Residues have also been detected in human blood and fat. The organochlorine pesticides were banned in most technologically advanced countries as far back as the 1960s. A number of other pesticides which are banned in several countries of the world arc still used in India!

The first report of poisoning due to pesticides in India was from Kerala in 1958, where over 100 people died after consuming wheat flour contaminated with parathion. This is an incidence of acute toxicity. The effects of chronic or long-term exposure to pesticides do not appear immediately after first exposure and may take years to produce signs and symptoms. Examples of **chronic poisoning** effects may include:

- Carcinogenicity: ability to produce cancer
- Mutagenicity: ability to cause genetic changes
- Teratogenicity: ability to cause birth defects
- Oncogenicity: ability to induce tumour growth (not necessarily cancers)
- Liver damage: death of liver cells, jaundice (yellowing of the skin), fibrosis and cirrhosis
- Endocrine disruption: hormonal disorders
- Reproductive disorders: such as reduced sperm count, sterility and miscarriage
- Neurotoxicity: nerve damage
- Development of allergies to pesticides or chemicals used in formulation of pesticides

Exposure of either parent to pesticides before conception or of the mother during pregnancy has been associated with increased risk of foetal death, spontaneous abortion and early childhood cancers. Exposure within the womb is also associated with increased risk of growth retardation, low birth weight and congenital anomalies. The toxicity caused by different types of pesticides is given in Table 6.3, while commonly used pesticides which are either carcinogenic or endocrine disruptors are shown in Table 6.4.

PREVENTION AND CONTROL MEASURES

FAO and WHO jointly work towards assessing the risk associated with pesticide residues. The risk assessment is conducted by the Joint FAO/WHO Meeting on Pesticide Residues (JMPR)

Table 6.3: Toxicity Symptoms of Some Pesticides

Pesticide	*Toxic symptoms*
Organochlorines	Toxic to the central nervous system (CNS); gastrointestinal and respiratory symptoms
Organophosphates	Vomiting, nausea, constriction of the pupil, excessive salivation, blurred vision and CNS manifestations such as giddiness, headache, disturbances in consciousness; cardiac manifestations such as tachycardia or bradycardia
Carbamates	Similar symptoms as organophosphate poisoning
Paraquat	Severe inflammation of throat, corrosive injury to gastrointestinal tract, renal tubular necrosis, hepatic necrosis and pulmonary fibrosis
Thallium (rodenticide)	Alopecia
Warfarins	Prolonged bleeding time
Barium carbonate	Severe hypokalaemia, respiratory muscle paralysis
Aluminium phosphide	Pulmonary and cardiac toxicity, death
Pyrethroids and insect repellents like diethyltoluamide	Relatively harmless but may harm the lungs or CNS on chronic exposure. Acute toxicity symptoms include salivation, vomiting, diarrhoea and abdominal pain
Ethylene dibromide (fumigant)	Highly toxic, causes oral ulcerations, followed by liver and renal toxicity, death

Source: Adapted by Author from Bradberry et al. 2005 and www.merckmanuals.com (accessed 14 January 2017).

Table 6.4: Carcinogenic and Endocrine-disrupting Pesticides Commonly Used in Foods

Suspected carcinogen	*Suspected endocrine-disrupting chemical*
Aldicarb	Aldicarb
Bifenthrin	Bifenthrin
Captan	Carbaryl
Carbaryl	Carbendazim
Carbendazim	Chlordane
Chlordane	Chlorfenvinphos
Cypermethrin	Cypermethrin
DDT	DDT
Dicofol	Dicofol
Dieldrin	Dieldrin
Difenoconazole	Dimethoate
Dimethoate	Endosulfan
Fenvalerate	Fenvalerate
Glyphosate	Iprodione
Hexachlorobenzene	Malathion
Iprodione	Procymidone

(*Contd*)

(*Contd*)

Suspected carcinogen	*Suspected endocrine-disrupting chemical*
Malathion	Triadimenol
Phosmet	Trifluralin
Pyrimethanil	Vinclozolin
Thiabendazole	
Triadimenol	
Trifluralin	
Vinclozolin	

Source: Adapted by Author from Craig 2010.

In April 2011, the use of endosulfan was banned globally under the Stockholm Convention. It is one of the most toxic pesticides. It can act as an endocrine disruptor and cause developmental and reproductive damage. The use of DDT was also banned in most countries except a handful, where it is used for malaria control. DDT is a suspected carcinogen—it affects fertility, has been linked to developmental delays, miscarriages, low birth weight and damage to the liver and nervous system. India is the only country still producing DDT! The worldwide ban deadline has been set for 2020.

and a safe level of intake is established called Acceptable Daily Intakes (ADIs). Exposure at this intake level is not likely to cause harm even if the individual consumes this amount of the pesticide throughout their life. JMPR was established in 1963 and meets annually to conduct scientific evaluations of different pesticide residues in foods. These values are of use to governments of different countries and also to international risk managers such as the Codex Alimentarius Commission (CAC), who establish maximum residue limits (MRLs) for each of the pesticides in foods. JMPR has a WHO Core Assessment Group and the FAO Panel of Experts on Pesticide Residues in Food and the Environment. The WHO Core Assessment Group is responsible for reviewing pesticide toxicological data and estimating ADI, while the FAO Panel is responsible for reviewing pesticide residue data and for estimating MRLs. The MRLs are recommended to the Codex Committee on Pesticide Residues (CCPR) for consideration to be adopted by the CAC.

In India, the Insecticide Act, promulgated in 1968 and enforced on 1 August 1971, regulates the import, manufacture, sale, transport, distribution and use of insecticides, with a view to prevent risks to human beings and animals. The Central Insecticides Board and Registration Committee (CIBRC) registers the pesticides in India and recommends them for use in various crops. In all, 234 pesticides have been registered. The FSSAI prescribes MRLs for different pesticides which have been registered by the CIBRC (see Table 6.5).

A huge debate was generated when the Centre for Science and Environment, New Delhi reported pesticide residues in soft drinks. The residues were traced to contaminated groundwater which was being used for the manufacture of soft drinks.

Household or industrial level processing may either increase or decrease the level of pesticides in foods.

- Washing and peeling, for instance, have been shown to remove pesticides adhering to surfaces and hence reducing contaminant levels. Washing should be done using clean potable water. A scrubbing action also helps to remove adhering pesticide residues.

- Fruits and vegetables which are consumed along with skin may be soaked in vinegar diluted with water for five to 10 minutes. These vegetables and fruits can also be washed with a 2 per cent common salt solution or a mix of lemon juice and baking soda according to a public notice by the Department of Food Safety, government of Delhi.
- Dipping in ozonated water has also been shown to reduce the level of pesticides.
- Cooking further reduces the levels.
- Hulling and polishing of rice also reduce the concentration of pesticides.
- Milling and storage of wheat reduce pesticide levels.
- Juicing and canning also tend to lower residue levels.

Drying and concentration may, however, increase the levels of pesticides and certain other processes may actually increase the toxicity because of formation of metabolites, which are more toxic. In butter making, the pesticides of the milk get concentrated in the butter because of their affinity for fat.

Table 6.5: Pesticides and their Tolerance Limits (in ppm) given by the FSSAI for Some Food Products

Food grains	*Fruits and vegetables*	*Milk and milk products (on a fat basis)*	*Meat*	*Fish*
Aldrin, dieldrin (0.01)	Aldrin, dieldrin (0.1)	Aldrin, dieldrin (0.15)	Aldrin, dieldrin (0.2)	–
Carbaryl (1.5)	Carbaryl (5.0 for most vegetables)	–	–	Carbaryl (0.2)
–	DDT (3.5)	DDT (1.25)	DDT (7.0)	DDT (7.0)
Dichlorvos (1.0)	Dichlorvos (0.1/0.15)	–	–	–
–	Endosulfan (2.0)	–	–	Endosulfan (0.2)
Fenitrothion (0.02)	Fenitrothion (0.5/0.3)	Fenitrothion (0.05)	Fenitrothion (0.03)	
Malathion (4.0)	Malathion (4.0/3.0)	–	–	–
Pyrethrins (nil)	Pyrethrins (1.0)	–	–	–
Monocrotophos (0.025)	Monocrotophos (0.05–1.0)	Monocrotophos (0.02)	Monocrotophos (0.02)	–
Carbendazim (0.5)	Carbendazim (0.5–5.0)	Carbendazim (0.1)	Carbendazim (0.1)	–

Note: Figures in parentheses are the tolerance limits in ppm.
Source: Adapted by Author from FSSAI Regulations 2011.

A constant monitoring is required, especially of the population at risk, namely agricultural and industrial workers. Levels of pesticide residues in different foods also need to be regularly monitored to identify regions from where the contaminated food is being supplied. Water and air levels near farm lands and industries need to be constantly monitored. Surveillance cells need to be incorporated into the healthcare system to document any incidence of pesticide poisoning. Health of industrial and agricultural workers should also be monitored through periodic checkups. Also, notification of pesticide poisoning should be made obligatory by all hospitals and medical practitioners to the National Informatics Centre for proper storage and retrieval of information. It is also important to regularly review the ADI and MRL for all pesticides in use in the country. Farmers and industrial workers need to be made aware about the precautions to be observed while handling pesticides, and good agricultural practices (GAP) while using these to protect their crops. Research on and promotion of natural pesticides and less harmful alternatives is the need of the hour. Many otrganisations besides FAO and WHO, such as the Intergovernmental Forum for Chemical Safety (IFCS) and the International Labour Organization (ILO), work towards monitoring the use of pesticides and also promote alternative safer ones. Figure 6.4 summarises the steps that are recommended towards decreasing the menace of pesticide residues in our food supply.

Figure 6.4: Recommendations for Reducing Exposure to Pesticides in the Future

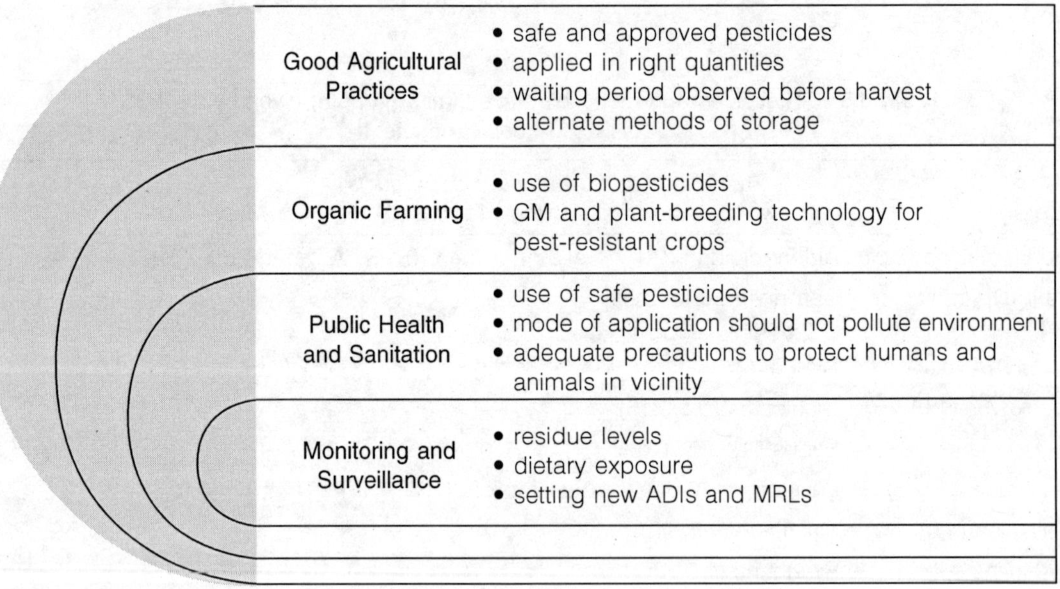

Good Agricultural Practices
- safe and approved pesticides
- applied in right quantities
- waiting period observed before harvest
- alternate methods of storage

Organic Farming
- use of biopesticides
- GM and plant-breeding technology for pest-resistant crops

Public Health and Sanitation
- use of safe pesticides
- mode of application should not pollute environment
- adequate precautions to protect humans and animals in vicinity

Monitoring and Surveillance
- residue levels
- dietary exposure
- setting new ADIs and MRLs

Source: Drawn by Author.

There has been a constant effort to increase environment-friendly forms of pest control and there is increasing engagement in non-pesticide dependent agriculture and integrated pest management (IPM). The UN's Food and Agriculture Organization defines IPM as,

> [T]he careful consideration of all available pest control techniques and subsequent integration of appropriate measures that discourage the development of pest populations and keep pesticides and other interventions to levels that are economically justified and reduce or minimise risks to human

Stockholm Convention on Persistent Organic Pollutants was put into practice on 22 May 2001 by the United Nations Environment Programme (UNEP). It was decided to regulate the use of POPs across the world in order to protect the environment and human health. Most countries in the world have ratified the Convention.

Prague Declaration on Endocrine Disruption, May 2005

International experts and scientists representing different disciplines and countries came together in Prague for a workshop on chemicals which could interfere with the hormone systems. These chemicals are referred to as 'endocrine disruptors'. Some of these chemicals are pesticides. These substances alter the function of hormonal systems, causing adverse effects by mimicking the effect of natural hormones or affecting their function and metabolism. The declaration included ways and means to regulate the use of these chemicals and better protect human life and wildlife in Europe and beyond.

health and the environment. IPM emphasises the growth of a healthy crop with the least possible disruption to agro-ecosystems and encourages natural pest control mechanisms.

Biopesticides: The Natural Way of Controlling Pests

Biopesticides are natural materials like animals, plants, bacteria and certain minerals or biochemicals which can be used for pest management. Microbes like fungi have been used to control weeds and also insects. Strains of *Bacillus thuringiensis* (Bt) have been used to control insect larvae. Certain genetically modified plants may have the ability to produce proteins which are pesticidal. Biopesticides are less toxic than conventional pesticides. They do not affect the environment adversely as they do not persist in the environment and also do not affect other organisms. Beneficial nematodes have also been used to control insect and slug pests. Animals can exercise a predatory control over other animals or insects.

SUMMARY

- Pesticides are chemicals used to protect food from pests such as insects, rodents, weeds, mould and bacteria.
- Pesticides are potentially toxic to humans and research evidence on their harmful effects is mounting.
- Pesticides may be classified according to the pest they are used to control—insecticides to control insects; rodenticides to control rodents (such as rats, mice, moles); herbicides to control weeds; fungicides to control mould and fungus; and antimicrobials to control bacteria.
- Pesticides are also classified based on their chemical nature as—organochlorine pesticides; organophosphates and carbamates; pyrethrins and pyrethroids. In addition, many inorganic pesticides are also in use.
- WHO has classified the pesticides into categories according to their toxicity.
- Pesticides are available in various formulations like liquid, gel, paste, chalk, powder, granules, pellets and baits containing 2–80 per cent of active ingredient.
- People can be exposed to pesticides intentionally or unintentionally. Intentional exposure is when people try to commit suicide by consuming pesticides or try to poison and kill someone else (homicide).
- Unintentional exposure can be from several sources—water, air or food getting contaminated and each case resulting in ingesting, inhaling or at least having dermal (skin) contact with the pesticide.

- Indiscriminate use of pesticides has also led to high residue levels in food.
- Every pesticide has some safety or waiting period which is defined as the number of days to lapse before the pesticide residues get dissipated. Food products become safe for consumption only after the waiting period has lapsed.
- The most persistent pesticides are termed 'persistent organic pollutants' (POPs). These have low solubility in water but are lypophilic, and hence tend to accumulate in the food chain.
- Chronic toxicity due to exposure to pesticides has led to cancer, genetic mutation, birth defects, liver damage, endocrine disruption, nerve damage, reduced sperm count and sterility.
- FAO and WHO jointly work towards assessing the risk associated with pesticide residues. The risk assessment is conducted by the Joint FAO/WHO Meeting on Pesticide Residues (JMPR).
- In India, FSSAI prescribes MRLs for different pesticides which have been registered by the CIBRC.
- Processing may either decrease or increase pesticide levels in foods.
- Levels of pesticide residues in different foods need to be regularly monitored. Health of industrial and agricultural workers should also be monitored through periodic checkups.
- In addition, good agricultural practices, organic farming, and safe use in public health and sanitation can help to reduce the pesticide residues in our food supply.
- Biopesticides are natural materials like animals, plants, bacteria and certain minerals or biochemicals which can be used for pest management. Integrated pest management is increasingly being opted for.

KEY WORDS

Acute toxicity: The harmful effects seen when there is a single exposure or multiple exposures to the pesticide within a short span of time.

Biomagnification: The increasing concentration of a substance—such as a toxic chemical—in the tissues of organisms at successively higher levels in a food chain.

Biopesticides: Natural materials like animals, plants, bacteria and certain minerals or biochemicals which can be used for pest management.

Carcinogenic: Cancer causing.

Chronic toxicity: Adverse effects becoming apparent after exposure for a relatively longer period of time.

Dermal: Skin.

Endocrine disruptors: Those which adversely affect the normal functioning of hormones in the body.

Integrated pest management (IPM): Emphasises the growth of a healthy crop with the least possible disruption to agro-ecosystems and encourages natural pest control mechanisms.

LD_{50}: The lethal dose which will kill 50 per cent of the animals to whom the dose is administered.

Persistent organic pollutants (POPs): Organic compounds that are resistant to environmental degradation through chemical, biological and photolytic processes; hence, they tend to persistent in and pollute the environment.

EXERCISES

1. How will you classify pesticides based on their chemical nature?
2. What are some of the harmful effects of pesticide residues?
3. How does a pesticide enter the food chain?

4. What can be done to reduce our exposure to pesticides?
5. What do you understand by 'IPM'?
6. What are 'biopesticides'? Give a few examples.

REFERENCES

Bhanti, M., and A. Taneja, 'Contamination of Vegetables of Different Seasons with Organophosphorous Pesticides and Related Health Risk Assessment in Northern India', *Chemosphere* 69(1), 2007, pp. 63–68.

Bhushan, C., *Regulation of Pesticides in India*, New Delhi: Centre for Science and Environment, 2006.

Bradberry, S. M., S. A. Cage, A. T. Proudfoot, and J. A. Vale, 'Poisoning due to Pyrethroids', *Toxicol Rev.* 24(2), 2005, pp. 93–106.

Craig, A., 'Your Daily Poison: The Second UK Pesticide Exposure Report', in A. Chakraborty (ed.), *Pesticides in Food-Issues and Perspectives*, Hyderabad: The ICFAI University Press, 2010, pp. 127–41.

Department of Food Safety, Government of Delhi, 'Ways to Minimize Pesticide Residues in Fruits and Vegetables before Eating-Cooking', Available at http://www.delhi.gov.in/wps/wcm/connect/DoIT_PFA/pfa/home/citizen+charter/english_minimize+pesticide (accessed 22 October 2017).

Goel, A., and P. Agarwal, 'Pesticide Poisoning', *The National Medical Journal of India* 20(4), 2007, pp. 182–91.

ICMR, 'Pesticide Pollution: Trends and Perspectives', *ICMR Bulletin* 31(9), New Delhi: ICMR, 2001.

ICMR Task Force Study, 'Surveillance of Food Contaminants in India. Report of an ICMR Task Force Study (Part 1)', eds G. S. Toteja, J. Dasgupta, B. N. Saxena, and R. L. Kalra. New Delhi: Indian Council of Medical Research, 1993, p. x.

John, P. J., N. Bakore, and P. Bhatnagar, 'Assessment of Organochlorine Pesticide Residue Levels in Dairy Milk and Buffalo Milk from Jaipur City, Rajasthan, India', *Environment International* 26(4), 2001, pp. 231–36.

Karunakaran, C. O., 'The Kerala Food Poisoning', *J Indian Med Assoc* 31(5), 1958, p. 204.

Kumari, B., R. Kumar, V. K. Madan, R. Singh, J. Singh, and T. S. Kathpal, 'Magnitude of Pesticidal Contamination in Winter Vegetables from Hisar, Haryana', *Environ Monit Assess* 87(3), 2003, pp. 311–18.

Reddy, J., B. N. Rao, M. A. Sultan, and K. N. Reddy, 'Pesticide Residues in Farmgate Vegetables', *J.Res. ANGRAU* 26(3–4), 1998, pp. 6–10.

'The Insecticide Act 1968', Lucknow: Eastern Book Agency, 1988, p. 1.

WHO, *The WHO Recommended Classification of Pesticides by Hazard and Guidelines to Classification: 2009*, Geneva: WHO, 2010.

ONLINE SOURCES

Pesticide Action Network, UK, Available at http://www.pan-uk.org/ (accessed 13 April 2018).

Toxic Effects of Pesticides, Available at https://www.merckmanuals.com/professional/injuries-poisoning/poisoning/organophosphate-poisoning-and-carbamate-poisoning (accessed 13 April 2018).

Video on Bioaccumulation and Biomagnification of Pesticides, Available at https://www.youtube.com/watch?v=J9i6a_NRahg (accessed 13 April 2018).

7

CHEMICAL CONTAMINANTS: VETERINARY DRUG RESIDUES

HIGHLIGHTS

- Types of veterinary drugs
- Impact on health
- Prevention and control measures

Just like there have been significant advances in medical science for humans, the advances in the field of veterinary science and animal husbandry have introduced a number of drugs for tackling diseases and for promotion of growth in animals. Residues of these drugs find their way into the food chain. The milk, eggs and flesh of animals become contaminated with the residues of these drugs when they are fed antibiotics and other growth-stimulating medicines and hormones. Usually, these drugs remain in the body of the animal for a few days. It is not advisable to milk the animal or consume its meat during the period immediately after administration of the drugs. Ignorance and non-compliance with safety norms can, however, result in these compounds entering the food chain. It is, hence, vital to understand the impact of these drug residues on our health and the concerted efforts which need to be made to prevent such contamination.

TYPES OF VETERINARY DRUGS

Widespread protein energy malnutrition the world over probably triggered the intensive production of animal proteins. Profit margins drove people raising livestock and veterinarians to use drugs not only for treating diseases in these animals, but also for improving feed efficiency and growth performance, breeding performance, and controlling reproduction. Various types of drugs are used for animals, fowl and insects like bees, which provide us with food. Some are injected into the animal while some others are given orally—mixed in the feed or added as feed additives. Some chemicals which are sprayed or applied on the animals or where they are being kept can find their way into the animal. Certain

> Antibiotics are used in bee keeping to tackle infections of bees reared in hives. As a consequence, residues of these antibiotics have been detected in honey.

unintentional residues of mycotoxins or pesticides/insecticides may also find their way into the meat, milk and eggs of animals from contaminated feed or surroundings. Figure 7.1 shows the different ways in which veterinary drugs enter the food chain. These drugs then find their way into the meat, milk, eggs and honey produced by them.

Figure 7.1: How Veterinary Drug Residues Enter the Food Chain

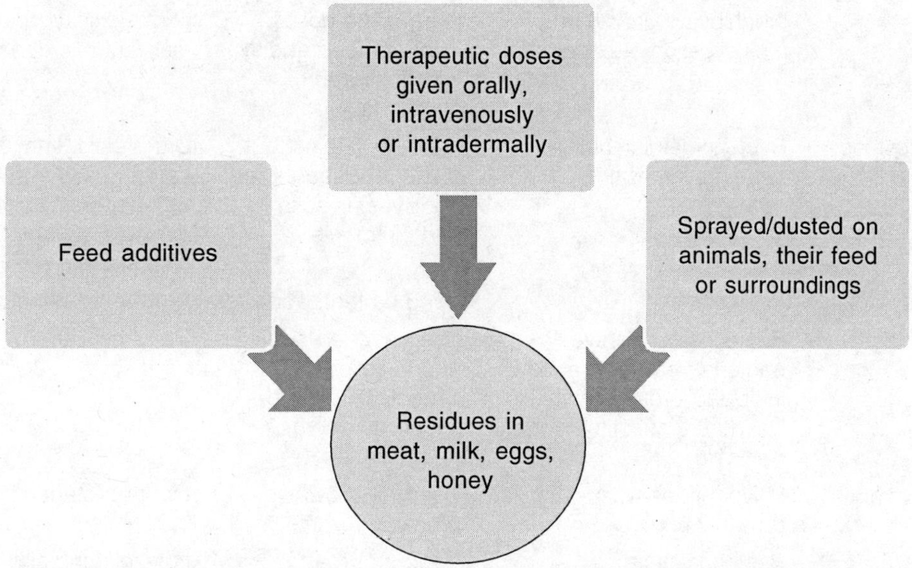

Therapeutic doses given orally, intravenously or intradermally

Feed additives

Sprayed/dusted on animals, their feed or surroundings

Residues in meat, milk, eggs, honey

Source: Drawn by Author.

The different types of drugs are:

- Antibiotics
- Anticoccidial
- Ectoparasiticides
- Anthelmintics
- Antifungal agents
- Hormones

Antimicrobials act in several ways to kill microbes or to slow down their growth and multiplication. Some of these drugs interfere with the synthesis of the bacterial cell wall, or that of nucleic acids or proteins. Some others may affect the permeability of the cell membrane causing vital substances to come out of the cell, while others may interfere with crucial metabolic processes of the microbes.

Antibiotics are usually prescribed to tackle infections in animals being reared. Some of these drugs also have growth-promoting effects, especially at low concentrations. These are then added to the feed of the animals. Some classes of antibiotic drugs used are given in Table 7.1.

Table 7.1: Types of Antibiotics Used in Veterinary Medicine

Type of drug	*Action*	*Uses*	*Adverse effects*
Penicillins and Cephalosporins (β lactam antibiotics)	Bactericidal to cell wall synthesis	For controlling animal diseases including mastitis	Acute allergic/ hypersensitivity reactions, drug resistant microbes
Tetracyclines	Bacteriostatic (capable of inhibiting growth or multiplication of bacteria)	Broad spectrum at therapeutic doses. Used as feed additives, injections and ointments	Immunodepression and photo-toxicity, drug resistant microbes
Aminoglycosides	Bactericidal; inhibits protein synthesis	Effective against gut bacteria. Used as feed additives, injections and ointments	Drug-resistant microbes. Large doses associated with nephrotoxicity (kidney damage) and ototoxicity (hearing loss)
Macrolides	Bacteriostatic	Used as feed additives	Drug-resistant microbes
Lincosamides	Bacteriostatic; prevents bacteria from replicating by inhibiting protein synthesis. Used as a substitute for penicillin	Used as feed additives and injections, especially to treat infections in pigs	Drug-resistant microbes
Verginiamycin and Bacitracin	Polypeptides which stimulate growth	Used for growth promotion	Drug-resistant microbes
Nitrofurans	Bacteriostatic	Used as broad spectrum antibiotic	Furazolidone and nitrofurantoin banned for use in food-producing animals due to carcinogenicity
Quinolones	Prevent bacterial DNA from unwinding and duplicating	Used against respiratory infections in animals and in culturing fish. Some used as feed additives and some in ointments to treat mastitis	Drug-resistant microbes
Sulfonamides	Bacteriostatic; inhibits enzymes	Used as feed additives, oral powders, injections and ointments	Hypersensitivity reactions. Can induce thyroid adenoma and hyperplasia in laboratory animals. Drug resistance in microbes

Source: Adapted by Author from Lee et al. 2001.

Anticoccidial drugs are those which are used to treat parasitic intestinal infections in animals and birds. Coccidiosis is caused by coccidian protozoa and the primary symptom is diarrhoea. These infections spread from animal to animal when they come in contact with infected faeces or infected tissue. Polyether antibiotics (salinomycin, rasalocid, monensin, etc.) are used as feed additives to promote growth and prevent coccidial infections. These drugs can induce resistance. A number of other drugs like nicarbazine, arprinocid, etc. are also used against coccidial infections and are usually added as feed additives.

Ectoparasiticides are chemicals used in the treatment of ectoparasitic infestations (to kill the parasites that live on the body surface like lice, keds, mites, ticks, etc.). These parasites cause a lot of losses in livestock production as they also act as vectors of diseases. Most of these chemicals are neurotoxins exerting their effect on the nervous system of the parasite. Permethrin, sulfur, lindane, dicophane, benzyl benzoate, ivermectin and crotamiton are well known ectoparasiticides. The chemicals may also be classified according to their nature as organochlorines, organophosphates, carbamates, pyrethrins, macrocyclic lactones, etc. Products are available for parenteral administration or for topical application by various methods, including dips, sprays, pour-ons, spot-ons, dusting powders and ear tags. Insect repellents and insect growth regulators are also sometimes used in addition to pesticides. Some of these chemicals, especially the organochlorines (DDT, BHC), have been discontinued due to concerns regarding their persistence in the environment and consequent toxicity to man and animals. Parasites have also developed resistance to some of these chemicals over time.

Anthelmintic drugs are antiparasitic drugs used against parasitic worms (helminths) and other internal parasites which infect animals. These drugs work by stunning (vermifuges) or killing the parasites (vermicides) and then expelling them from the body of the host. Some examples of these drugs are phenothiazine, piperazine, benzimidazoles, imidazothiazoles, tetrahydropyrimidines and organophosphates. There is a danger of inducing resistance in the helminths. Parasites which become resistant survive treatments with anthelmintics and pass on their resistance genes to the next generation. When a number of resistant varieties accumulate, the infected animal does not respond to treatment with the particular anthelmintic.

Antifungal agents are used against pathogenic fungi infecting animals. These can be filamentous moulds or intracellular yeasts. Fungal infections are mostly superficial, affecting the skin or hide. These are at most irritating for the animal. Systemic infections, on the other hand, can be life-threatening. Discontinuing therapy after clinical signs have resolved but before infection is eradicated leads to therapeutic failure. Therapy can fail especially if it is long in duration, or due to host toxicity. As a class, antifungal drugs tend to be more toxic than antibacterial drugs. Fluconazole, ketoconazole, itraconazole, griseofulvin, iodine, copper or sulphur preparations are some antifungal drugs commonly used in veterinary medicine. Resistance to many antifungal drugs is common.

Hormones are generally used to promote growth performance and lactational performance in animals. These have been shown to improve growth rate, nitrogen retention and feed conversion efficiency (how efficiently the feed protein is converted into body tissues of the animal) in veal calves and beef cattle. In the production of meat for human consumption, a hormonally-induced increase in growth rate of the order of 10 per cent has major economic implications. These hormones are usually mixed with the feed of the animal, but in recent years, there has been an increase in the use of injectibles and implants. Use of hormones is regulated differently in various countries. Many countries do not permit the use of hormones in livestock production. Diethyl stilbestrol (DES) was earlier used to promote growth in the beef and poultry industries. Its use has now been banned in food-producing animals as it was found to be a strong carcinogen. The use of anabolic steroids is strictly regulated for use in food-producing animals. Oestrogens, progesterone and testosterone are the common steroid hormones used either in their natural or synthetic form. If used properly the amount of residue in meat and milk, cream, butter is in very low concentration. The problem usually comes when these hormones are misused. Oxytocin is often used for the letdown of milk. Its abuse in the dairy industry, and instances of fruit and vegetable farmers using the hormone to increase the size of their produce have led to its sale being restricted in India. Very few studies in India are available on the presence of veterinary drug residues in foods (see Table 7.2).

Table 7.2: Veterinary Drug Residues Detected in Foods in India

Drugs	*Foods*	*Proportion testing positive*	*City*	*Reference*
Oxytetracycline, chlortetracycline and doxycycline (class tetracyclines); enrofloxacin and ciprofloxacin (class fluoroquinolones) and neomycin, an aminoglycoside	Chicken (n = 70)	40 per cent samples contaminated (concentrations of 3.37–131.75 μg/kg)	Delhi-NCR	Paliwal and Singh 2014
Unidentified antimicrobial	Milk (n = 65)	6 per cent samples	Delhi	Jain and Mathur 2013
Unidentified antimicrobial	Milk (n = 120)	23.3 per cent	Guwahati	Dinki and Balcha 2011
Oxytetracycline, chloramphenicol, ampicillin, enrofloxacin, ciprofloxacin, erythromycin	Honey (n = 12)	11/12 samples contaminated (concentrations of 10.1–614.2 μg/kg)	Delhi	CSE 2012
Gentamicin	Milk (n = 158)	One brand from Hyderabad (40–80 μg/ml)	Delhi-NCR, Kolkata, Hyderabad	Mathur 2000
Oxytetracycline	Milk (n = 205)	9 per cent market samples and 73 per cent individual animal samples found contaminated (0.2–6.7 μg/ml)	Hyderabad	Sudershan and Bhat 1995
Streptomycin	Milk	3.9 per cent samples	NDRI, Karnal	Ramakrishna and Singh 1985

Source: Compiled by Author from References given in Table.

IMPACT ON HEALTH

All drugs have a side effect, especially if given in higher than recommended doses or if given for a prolonged period of time. Hence, drugs should be used only under the supervision of a veterinarian and dosage prescriptions should be followed. Misuse of drugs can prove to be harmful for livestock and leave residues in farm products, which can adversely affect human health.

Acute poisoning outbreaks attributed to veterinary drugs have been described in literature. People in Lyons, France developed symptoms of tremor, headaches, abnormally rapid heart rate and dizziness 1–3 hours after eating veal liver. On investigation, this was revealed to be a case of poisoning by clenbuterol residues in the veal liver in the concentration of 0.375 and 0.500 micrograms/g (Pulce et al. 1991). Similar acute outbreaks were seen in 1996 in Caserta, Italy and in 1992 in Catalonia, Spain which affected 113 people.

Among the different drug residues, **antibiotic residues** are of special concern because of their possible adverse effects on persons **allergic** to certain antibiotics like penicillins and aminoglycosides. Antibiotic residues may also cause a potential **build-up of antibiotic resistant organisms** in humans. What is more harmful is the use of sub-therapeutic doses of antimicrobials which induce resistance among microbes and make the treatment of the disease more difficult. It also promotes abuse of other medication which may then be prescribed in an effort to treat the disease.

Sometimes, antimicrobials are added as feed additives to enhance production of livestock. The concentrations are below the minimum inhibition concentration (MIC) and hence, too small to control microorganisms. A recent study in poultry farms of Punjab detected multidrug resistance among birds fed antimicrobials in sub-therapeutic concentrations (Brower et al. 2017).

Chloramphenicol has been shown to induce **aplastic anaemia** in sensitive individuals. Nitrofurans and some sulpha drugs have shown the potential to cause **cancer** in experiments conducted on laboratory animals. These drugs have been mostly banned for use in food-producing animals. When the microflora of our gut is exposed to low doses of antibiotics in the form of residues in the food that we eat (such as meat, milk and eggs of contaminated animals), it starts changing. This **alteration of gut microflora** may lead to diseases and the development of resistant strains which cause failure of antibiotic therapy in case of an infection.

Hormones have been used by the beef and meat industry for several years to improve an animal's ability to more efficiently utilise nutrients for promoting its growth or increasing the milk yield. There have been serious concerns about **environmental contamination**, particularly of drinking water, from faecal and urinary excretion of hormones by millions of cattle. There is increased risk of residues of hormones in meat and milk products, causing **disruption of the endocrine system** of humans. Hormones in food have been linked to increased risk of breast cancer and have been associated with girls reaching puberty earlier than usual. Diethyl stilbesterol (DES), as has been discussed earlier, was used to promote growth of cattle. It is now banned as it was found to be a potent carcinogen.

Animals and livestock are infected by a number of parasites like flies, lice, fleas and other bugs, causing intense irritation and skin disease. These may result in major economic losses in production of livestock. After application of an ectoparasiticide on an animal, some time should be given to allow the chemical to dissipate before milking or slaughtering. Otherwise, residues of ectoparasiticides applied on the bodies of cattle, sheep, goats and chicken may find their way into the milk and meat of these animals, especially if proper precautions are not taken during milking or slaughtering.

> Organ meats like liver are likely to have higher levels of drug residues as the liver is the major detoxifying organ of the body.

The use of anthelmintics to get rid of worms like tapeworms has been increasing rapidly in recent years. They cause a serious ecological problem with their residues being detected in the soil where cattle on these drugs had grazed. Antifungal medicines, similarly, leave residues not just in milk and meat, but also present a threat to the environment.

Concerns over food residues are not limited to public health. They can have serious **economic consequences** as well. Antibiotic residues present in milk intended for the production of cheese, or for preparing milk products requiring the use of bacterial or yeast cultures, may result in killing of these cultures. This results in subsequent economic losses to the food industry. Every year, several consignments of seafood, honey and other foods are rejected due to the detection of antibiotic residues by the USA and the European Union.

PREVENTION AND CONTROL MEASURES

Drugs have become a necessity for the efficient production of milk, meat and eggs. However, they should not be considered a substitute for **good hygiene** and maintaining **sanitary conditions** in farms. The responsibility for residue control is not solely that of the government. The responsibility should be shared by producers, marketing co-operatives, veterinarians, scientists and all those involved in the industry.

> Buying milk from bulk suppliers decreases the risk of drug residues being present as the milk is sourced from multiple animals from different farms and hence, even if milk from a few farms was contaminated, by dilution, the risk to you decreases significantly.

Numerous scientific bodies and regulatory agencies have looked at the issue of residues of these hormones coming into the milk and meat meant for human consumption. Most of them have concluded that the use of hormones is safe as long as good veterinary practices are followed. Similarly, if care is taken for other veterinary drugs as well, drug residues would not pose a significant risk to health. **Good veterinary practices** mean that the veterinarian is consulted before these drugs are administered to the animals, over-medication is avoided, and appropriate time gap is given between administering

> Processing of food by washing, freezing and cooking can reduce the amount of veterinary drug residue in our food products.

the drug and milking or slaughtering the animal to avoid high residue levels in the food products. This time gap is referred to as the **withdrawal time** or period during which the drug gets metabolised in the animal's body and the residues are excreted from the body so that these do not linger in the meat, milk or eggs of the animal when slaughtered for consumption. It is the time period between the last administration of the drug and the treated animal being ready for slaughter with residue levels below tolerance limits set by the law. Withdrawal times vary with type of drug, dosage, route of administration of drug and the target animal. Drug manufacturers are required to provide tissue residue and depletion rate data for all new drugs. They also need to provide a method to detect the residues in tissues.

Codex Committee on Residues of Veterinary Drugs in Foods (CCRVDF) is the risk management body and the Joint FAO/WHO Committee on Food Additives (JECFA) is the risk assessment body. The latter establishes tolerance limits for veterinary drug residues in foods. The tolerance is the tissue concentration below which a marker residue for the drug or chemical must fall in the target tissue before that animal's edible tissues are considered safe for human consumption. **Tolerances** are established based on extensive toxicological studies of potential hazards of consumption to humans. Acceptable daily intake (ADI) is the maximum amount of the drug residue, which when ingested daily over the lifetime of an individual, appears to be without appreciable risk to health, according to toxicological data available at that point of time.

A **maximum residue limit** is the maximum allowable concentration of a chemical in the feed or food at a specified time of slaughter or harvesting, processing, storage or marketing, up to time of consumption by animal or human.

In India, the Food Safety and Standards (Contaminants, Toxins and Residues) Regulations, which came in to force on 5 August 2011, deals with compliance to standards set for various contaminants, toxins (microbial and naturally occurring) and residues (of pesticides, veterinary drugs and other pharmacologically active substances) in food.

The FSSAI specifies the tolerance limits for antibiotic residues in sea foods like shrimps, prawns, fish and fishery products (see Table 7.3).

Use of other pharmacologically active substances and the following antibiotics is prohibited in seafood-processing units—all nitrofurans, chloramphenicol, neomycin, nalidixic acid, sulphamethoxazole, chloroform, chloropromazine, cholchicine, dapsone, nitromidazoles, clenbuterol, DES, sulfanonamide drugs, fluoroquinolones and glycopeptides—due to safety concerns.

Though the Indian regulations (till early 2016) are limited to seafood and honey, the FSSAI has issued an advisory on restricted use of antibiotics in feeds and treatment of meat- and milk-producing animals and poultry.

The USFDA gives the residue limits of veterinary drugs according to the animal/fowl (cattle, sheep, goat, swine, poultry, etc.) and the part consumed like the muscle, kidney, liver or entire edible tissue. Regulatory authorities around the world are involved in the assessment of the effects of antimicrobial drug residues from food of animal origin on the human intestinal microbiota.

Table 7.3: Tolerance Limits for Antibiotics in Foods Prescribed by the FSSAI

Food	*Name of antibiotic*	*Tolerance limit*
Seafood	Tetracycline	0.1 mg/kg
	Oxytetracycline	0.1 mg/kg
	Trimethoprim	0.05 mg/kg
	Oxolinic acid	0.3 mg/kg
Honey	Chloramphenicol	0.3 µg/kg
	Nitrofurans and its metabolites	0.5 µg/kg
	Sulphonamides and its metabolites	5.0 µg/kg
	Streptomycin	5.0 µg/kg
	Tetracycline	5.0 µg/kg
	Ampicillin	5.0 µg/kg
	Ciprofloxacin	5.0 µg/kg
	Enrofloxacin	5.0 µg/kg
	Erythromycin	5.0 µg/kg
	Tylosin	5.0 µg/kg

Source: Adapted by Author from FSSAI and FSIS Data. Available at http://www.fsis.usda.gov/OPHS/red98/appendix1c.pdf http://www.fssai.gov.in/Portals/0/Pdf/Food%20safety%20and%20 standards%20(contaminats,%20toxins%20and%20residues)%20 regulation,%202011.pdf (accessed 20 March 2018).

These include Food and Drug Administration (FDA), Joint Expert Committee on Food Additives (JECFA), European Medicines Evaluation Agency (EMA/CVMP), Veterinary International Cooperation on Harmonization (VICH), Codex Alimentarius Commission (CAC) and other National Regulatory Authorities (like Health Canada).

If use of antibiotics or any other drug is necessary for prevention and treatment of animal diseases, or from an economic point of view for improving production, then a withholding period must be observed until the residues are negligible or no longer detected.

Educating the livestock producers, sensitising veterinarians and enforcing regulations with regard to drug sale and use can go a long way in keeping our food safe. Quality assurance procedures need to be in place from farm to fork to ensure that these drugs do not cause harm to humans or the animals on which they are used.

SUMMARY

- Residues of veterinary drugs find their way into the food chain. The milk, eggs and flesh of animals become contaminated with the residues of these drugs when the animals are treated with antibiotics and other growth-stimulating medicines and hormones.

- Ignorance and non-compliance with safety norms can, however, result in these compounds entering the food chain.
- The different types of drugs are—antibiotics, anticoccidial, ectoparasiticides, anthelmintics, antifungal agents and hormones.
- Drugs should be used only under the supervision of a veterinarian and dosage prescriptions followed. Misuse of drugs can prove to be harmful for livestock, and leave residues in farm products, which can adversely affect human health.
- Antibiotic residues are of special concern because of their possible adverse effects on persons allergic to certain antibiotics like penicillins and aminoglycosides. They may also cause a potential build-up of antibiotic-resistant organisms in humans.
- Antibiotics may also interfere in the production of foods requiring the use of bacterial or yeast cultures.
- Drugs have become a necessity for the efficient production of milk, meat and eggs. However, they should not be considered a substitute for good hygiene and maintaining sanitary conditions in farms.
- Codex Committee on Residues of Veterinary Drugs in Foods (CCRVDF) is the risk management body and the Joint FAO/WHO Committee on Food Additives (JECFA) is the risk assessment body.
- Quality assurance procedures need to be in place from farm to fork to ensure that veterinary drugs do not cause harm to humans or the animals on which they are used.
- In India, the Food Safety and Standards (Contaminants, Toxins and Residues) Regulations, which came into force on 5 August 2011, deals with compliance to standards set for various contaminants, toxins (microbial and naturally occurring) and residues (of pesticides, veterinary drugs and other pharmacologically active substances) in food.

KEY WORDS

Acceptable daily intake (ADI): The maximum amount of drug residue which when ingested daily over the lifetime of an individual appears to be without appreciable risk to health according to toxicological data available at that point of time.

Anticoccidial drugs: Drugs used to treat parasitic intestinal infections in animals and birds.

Anthelmintic drugs: Antiparasitic drugs used against parasitic worms (helminths).

Ectoparasiticides: Drugs used in the treatment of ectoparasitic infestations (to kill the parasites that live on the body surface like lice, keds, mites, ticks, etc.

Gut microflora: Refers to the microbes living in the digestive tract.

Maximum residue limit (MRL): The maximum allowable concentration of a chemical in the feed or food at a specified time of slaughter or harvesting, processing, storage or marketing up to time of consumption by animals or humans.

Neurotoxin: Toxins that affect the nerve tissue.

Tolerance: The tissue concentration below which a marker residue for the drug or chemical must fall in the target tissue before that animal's edible tissues are considered safe for human consumption.

Withdrawal time: Period during which the drug gets metabolised in the animal's body and the residues are excreted from the body.

EXERCISES

1. List the different types of veterinary drugs that are in use.
2. Why are hormones used in animal husbandry? How can residues of these hormones in our food affect our health?
3. Discuss in detail the consequences of consuming food contaminated with veterinary antibiotic residues.
4. Describe good practices which need to be followed to avoid residues of veterinary drugs in our food supply.

REFERENCES

Aeillo, S. E., and M. A. Moses (eds), 'The Merck Veterinary Manual', Available at http://www.merckvetmanual.com/mvm/pharmacology/ (accessed 10 March 2016).

Brambilla, G., A. Loizzo, L. Fontana, M. Strozzi, A. Guarino, and V. Soprano, 'Food Poisoning Following Consumption of Clenbuterol-treated Veal in Italy', *JAMA* 278(8), 1997, p. 635.

Brower, C. H., S. Mandal, S. Hayer, M. Sran, A. Zehra, S. J. Patel, R. Kaur, L. Chatterjee, S. Mishra, B. R. Das, P. Singh, R. Singh, J. P. S. Gill, and R. Laxminarayan, 'The Prevalence of Extended-Spectrum Beta-Lactamase-Producing Multidrug-Resistant Escherichia Coli in Poultry Chickens and Variation According to Farming Practices in Punjab, India', *Environ Health Perspect.* 125(7), 2017.

CSE, 'Antibiotics in Food–Honey', in *Food as Toxin – Regulating for Good Food and Good Health*, New Delhi: Centre for Science and Environment, 2012.

Dinki, N., and E. Balcha, 'Detection of Antibiotic Residues and Determination of Microbial Quality of Raw Milk from Milk Collection Centres', *Adv. Anim. Vet. Sci.* 1(3), 2011, pp. 80–83.

Jain, J., and P. Mathur, 'Evaluation of the Safety Aspects of Milk Available in Delhi', Dissertation submitted to University of Delhi, New Delhi in partial fulfilment of the requirements for the degree of Master of Science in Food and Nutrition, 2013, pp. 49–52.

Lee, M. H., H. J. Lee, and P. D. Ryu, 'Public Health Risks for Drugs and Antibiotic Residues', *Asian Aust. J Anim Sci.* 14(3), 2001, pp. 402–13.

Mathur, P., 'Risk Analysis of Food Adulterants', PhD Thesis submitted to University of Delhi, New Delhi, 2000, pp. 114–15.

Paliwal, A., and J. Singh, 'Hatching Superbugs', *Down to Earth*, Fortnightly Magazine of the Centre for Science and Environment, New Delhi, 15 August 2014, Available at http://www.downtoearth.org.in/coverage/hatching-superbugs-45547 (accessed 13 April 2018).

Pulce, C., D. Lamaison, G. Keck, C. Bostvironnois, J. Nicolas, and J. Descotes, 'Collective Human Food Poisonings by Clenbuterol Residues in Veal Liver', *Vet Hum Toxicol.* 33(5), 1991, pp. 480–81.

Ramakrishna, Y., and R. S. Singh, 'Residual Streptomycin in Milk—A Survey', *Ind. J. Dairy Sci.* 38(2), 1985, pp. 148–49.

Salleras, L., A. Domínguez, E. Mata, J. L. Taberner, I. Moro, and P. Salvà, 'Epidemiologic Study of an Outbreak of Clenbuterol Poisoning in Catalonia, Spain', *Public Health Rep.* 110(3), 1995, pp. 338–42.

Sudershan, R. V., and R. V. Bhat, 'A Survey on Veterinary Drug Use and Residues in Milk in Hyderabad', *Food Additives and Contaminants* 12(5), 1995, pp. 645–50.

Velle, W., 'The Use of Hormones in Animal Production', Agriculture and Consumer Protection, FAO Corporate Document Repository, Available at http://www.fao.org/docrep/004/x6533e/x6533e01.htm (accessed 10 March 2016).

WHO, 'Evaluation of Certain Veterinary Drug Residues in Food: Seventy-eighth Report of the Joint FAO/WHO Expert Committee on Food Additives', *WHO Technical Report Series*, no. 988, 2014.

ONLINE SOURCES

Centre for Science and Environment, Available at https://www.cseindia.org/international-workshop-on-national-action-plan-on-antimicrobial-resistance-for-developing-countries-6651 (accessed 14 April 2018).

Food Safety Updates, Available at https://foodsafetyupdate.wordpress.com/ (accessed 14 April 2018).

8

CHEMICAL CONTAMINANTS: HEAVY METALS

HIGHLIGHTS

- Definition
- Sources of contamination
- Impact on health
- Prevention and control measures

Metals are integral parts of our body and our environment. They have been used for centuries and are still used in manufacturing several items like electronics, batteries, paints and pigments, jewellery, fertilisers, pesticides and herbicides (see Box 8.1). They are also used for electroplating and making metal works and utensils/decoration pieces. However, some of these metals, especially the heavy metals, can prove to be very harmful if they find their way into our food.

Box 8.1: Use of Heavy Metals in Ancient Times and Now

Lead: as building material, in pigments for glazing ceramics, water pipes, lead acetate as an additive for wine (used by ancient Romans), cosmetics, tetraethyl lead as a petrol additive

Mercury: cinnabar (HgS) used as red colouring in pre-historic cave paintings, used to alleviate teething pain in infants (by ancient Romans), as a remedy for syphilis, for gold mining, cosmetics (in ancient Greece), amalgam for filling teeth, methyl mercury as a fungicide, in diuretics, in thermometers, barometers and sphygmomanometers

Cadmium: used in paints by some artists like Monet, stabilisers in PVC products, several alloys, re-chargeable nickel-cadmium batteries, as an anticorrosion agent

Arsenic: treatment of syphilis, treatment of protozoan and helminthic infestations in ancient times, as a wood preservative, pesticides, homeopathic medicine, treatment of leukaemia

DEFINITION

Heavy metals are typically those also known as transition and post-transition metals. Quantitative criteria used to define heavy metals have included density, atomic weight and atomic number.

Typically, metals with specific density greater than 5g/cm^3 are classified as heavy metals. Other definitions include metals having an atomic weight greater than that of sodium as heavy metals, while some others consider heavy metals as those having atomic weights greater than 40.

Heavy metals regarded as essential for human health in small quantities include vanadium, manganese, iron, cobalt, copper, zinc and molybdenum. Iron is an essential component of haemoglobin and myoglobin. Copper, cobalt, chromium, zinc and selenium are essential for our body and mostly function as co-enzymes (facilitating the function of enzymes in our body). Lead, cadmium, mercury and arsenic are considered threats to human health. Arsenic is actually a metalloid but is usually classified as a heavy metal. The commonly used heavy metals are listed in Table 8.1.

Table 8.1: Heavy Metals with their Atomic Numbers and Symbols

Name of Metal	*Atomic Number*	*Symbol*
Beryllium	4	Be
Aluminium	13	Al
Chrome	24	Cr
Manganese	25	Mn
Iron	26	Fe
Cobalt	27	Co
Nickel	28	Ni
Copper	29	Cu
Zinc	30	Zn
Arsenic	33	As
Selenium	34	Se
Molybdenum	42	Mo
Silver	47	Ag
Cadmium	48	Cd
Tin	50	Sn
Antimony	51	Sb
Barium	56	Ba
Mercury	80	Hg
Thallium	81	Ti
Lead	82	Pb

Source: Compiled by Author.

SOURCES OF CONTAMINATION

In the previous section, you have seen how these metals are used for multiple purposes. They can contaminate our foods when **factories** throw their **waste products** into the seas and rivers or bury their wastes before appropriately treating them. **Smoke** from industries, and **exhaust fumes** from vehicles and machinery pollute the atmosphere. Thus, metals enter our bodies through the water we drink, the air we breathe and the food that is grown in such contaminated soil (see Figure 8.1).

Emissions into the air tend to be of the greatest concern in terms of human health, both because of the quantities involved and the widespread dispersion and hence, the potential for exposure. Lead emissions are from road transport, cadmium emissions are mainly from fuel combustion and metallurgical operations, and mercury emissions are related to coal consumption.

Metals may also enter food from **metallic cans** in which the food is packaged. Acidic foods may cause the inner lining of cans to dissolve and mix with the food. Aluminium containers and **utensils** which slowly dissolve under acidic conditions are more rapidly

The tobacco plant naturally accumulates relatively high concentrations of cadmium in its leaves. Cigarette paper also has cadmium to make it burn slowly. Cigarette smoking can cause significant increases in the concentrations of cadmium in the kidney, the main target organ for cadmium toxicity.

corroded under alkaline conditions. Another source of metal contaminants is vessels and utensils used in cooking and storage of prepared foods and beverages. **Vessels** made of brass are usually tinned from inside. Poor-quality tin coating or improper tinning of the vessels can result in tin and copper leaching into the food cooked or stored in the vessel.

Fish consumption strongly predicts mercury levels in the body. Large fish typically have had a longer time to accumulate heavy metals from polluted waters and eating contaminated smaller fish. Similarly, green leafy vegetables with large leaves tend to accumulate more heavy metals than the ones with smaller leaves.

Plants have been found to pick up heavy metals from the **soil** in which they grow. The heavy metals in soil tend to contaminate the **ground water** as well. **Raw sewage water and sludge** used for irrigation in farms can lead to a build-up of heavy metals in the soil and consequently the plants. **Vehicular exhaust**, at one point of time, had high levels of lead. Ever since the introduction of unleaded petrol, heavy metal contamination of air and crops growing in fields near busy roads has decreased. Food sold by roadside vendors was also at risk of contamination due to vehicular exhaust.

Figure 8.1: Sources of Heavy Metal Contamination

Industries
- Effluent released into water bodies
- Smoke released into air
- Waste buried in soil

Vehicles
- Leaded fuel (petrol) releases lead into air
- Exhaust contaminates plants growing near roads

Utensils and Containers
- Cooking utensils made of or coated with heavy metals
- Cans used for packaging
- Pipes/tanks carrying/storing water

Untreated Sewage/Sludge
- Used for irrigation
- Released into water bodies

Source: Drawn by Author.

Cadmium exposure mainly occurs from the consumption of contaminated food, inhalation in an industry and active and passive inhalation of tobacco. The metal readily accumulates in many organisms, specially molluscs and crustaceans, and not so much in foods of plant origin. Cadmium compounds are used in rechargeable nickel-cadmium batteries. Cadmium-containing products are usually not recycled but are disposed with other waste, thus contaminating the soil.

Heavy metals can cause a lot of damage to human health. These metals are not readily excreted from our bodies and so keep getting deposited in different tissues and organs of the body. Concentrations of these heavy metals in blood, hair, nails and urine have been used as biomarkers of exposure. For instance, arsenic excretion in urine is used as a measure of arsenic exposure from cigarette smoke. Cigarette smoking may be a substantial source of exposure to many heavy metals not only to the smoker but also, through passive smoking, to non-smokers. Of special concern is the exposure of unborn children in the womb and little children to the second-hand smoke of their parents. Let us look at how these metals can affect our health.

IMPACT ON HEALTH

Heavy metals like lead, cadmium, mercury and arsenic have been extensively studied and their effect on health is regularly reviewed by the WHO. Others like chromium and **thallium** are potentially hazardous due to their toxicity in combined or elemental forms. Hexavalent **chromium**, for example, is highly toxic. These elements have a strong affinity for sulphur and in the human body they usually bind, via sulfhydryl groups (–SH), to enzymes thus inhibiting their action. Other heavy metals noted for their potential toxicity include nickel, copper, zinc, silver, tin and antimony (see Table 8.2).

Figure 8.2: Symptoms of Arsenic Poisoning

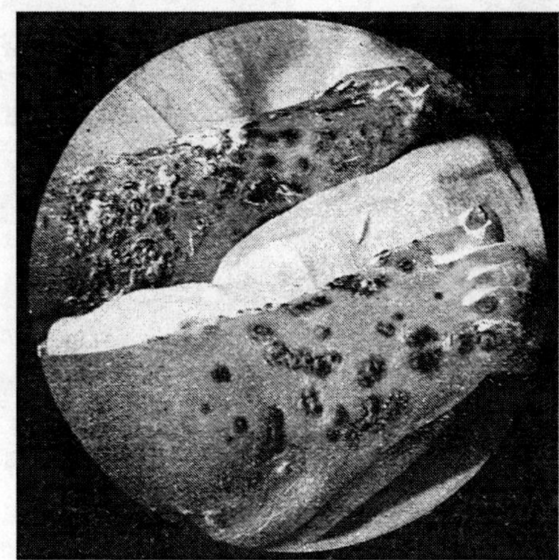

Source: Untitled by The British Journal of Dermatology (CC0 1.0; Flickr).

Contamination of drinking water with inorganic **arsenic** is a major problem in some parts of India, especially states like West Bengal. Argentina, USA, Vietnam, Thailand, China, Chile and Bangladesh are other countries of the world where this is a problem. Fish have been found to be contaminated with organic arsenic compounds. Several

Table 8.2: Sources and Toxicity of Some Heavy Metals

Metal	*Source*	*Acute toxicity*	*Chronic toxicity*
Aluminium	food additives, adulterants, food containers and cooking utensils	Rare	Alzheimer's disease, bone disease
Antimony	gray enamelware and antimony-containing utensils	Vomiting, abdominal pain and diarrhoea	Respiratory irritation, spots on the skin, gastrointestinal symptoms, possibly carcinogenic
Arsenic	contaminated ground water, by-product of smelting for copper, lead and zinc, burning fossil fuels, manufacture of pesticides	Constriction of throat, difficulty in swallowing, garlic taste, intestinal pain, vomiting, diarrhoea, muscle cramps, cardiac arrhythmias, coma and death	Garlic odour on breath, general muscular weakness, nerve damage and inflammation, a burning sensation ('needles and pins') in hands and feet, loss of appetite, birth defects, hepatomegaly, roughness of the palms and soles of the feet (hyperkeratosis) together with increased pigmentation of the skin

(*Contd*)

(*Contd*)

Metal	*Source*	*Acute toxicity*	*Chronic toxicity*
			(hyperpigmentation), particularly in areas not exposed to the sun. Arsenic poisoning may lead to nodular keratosis, kidney, bladder, lung and skin cancers
Cadmium	industrial wastes, utensils, batteries, cigarette smoke	nausea, vomiting, abdominal cramps, diarrhoea and shock; acute pulmonary effects if fumes inhaled	Lung disease, renal disease, and fragile bones. Other symptoms include hair loss, anaemia, arthritis, learning disorders, migraines, growth impairment, osteoporosis, loss of taste and smell, poor appetite, and cardiovascular disease, linked to cancer of prostrate, kidney and lungs.
Copper	mines, metallurgic industry, brass or copper utensils, pipes, fertilisers and pesticides	Metallic taste, nausea, vomiting (green vomitus) and abdominal pain, renal necrosis, hemolytic anaemia, coma, death	Rare, except Wilson's disease, which is a genetic disorder
Lead	exhaust from vehicles, industrial wastes, paints, ceramic glazes, cosmetics, toys, hair colour	tiredness, abdominal discomfort, headache, irritability	birth defects, diminished intellectual capacity, mental retardation, allergies, hyperactivity, weight loss, shaky hands, muscular weakness, anaemia and paralysis, possible carcinogen (lung and stomach cancers)
Mercury	coal-fired power plants, industries, water, fish, dental amalgam	neurological problems such as speech and hearing impairment, loss of coordination and a tingling sensation in the limbs, lung damage	nerve toxin, loss of appetite, weight loss, tiredness, tremor, restlessness, anxiety, sleep disturbances and developed kidney failure
Nickel	stainless steel utensils	–	fatigue, headaches, respiratory illness and heart conditions
Tin	paint and plastic industries, pesticides	headache, stomach ache, sickness, dizziness, severe sweating, breathlessness and urination problems	depression, liver damage, malfunctioning of immune systems, chromosomal damage, shortage of red blood cells and brain damage (causing anger, sleeping disorders, forgetfulness and headaches)
Thallium	rodenticide, electronics, pigments	anorexia, vomiting, gastrointestinal bleed, abdominal pain, seizures, fatigue, renal failure, skin erythema, dysfunction, coma, delirium, hallucinations, cardiotoxicity with arrhythmias, potentially fatal	tiredness, headaches, depression, hallucinations, psychosis, dementia, poor appetite, leg pains, hair loss and disturbances of vision

Source: Adapted by Author from Järup 2003 and WHO 2011.

surveys in India have detected high levels of **lead** in different foodstuffs, in drinking water and in seafood. Storing high-acid foods in lead-containing vessels, storing lead-containing pesticides in the same area as food, using canned high-acid foods with faulty seams can all contaminate the food with this metal. Emissions from industries, smelters, mines and battery plants can pollute the air. The gastrointestinal uptake of lead from food is high. Also, lead can easily cross the blood–brain barrier in children, thus resulting in neurotoxic effects. There may be a link between heavy metals and autism, according to current research indicating the role of lead, mercury and arsenic due to their neurotoxic effects. Zinc and copper levels have also been found to be abnormal in autistic children.

Heavy Metal Poisoning Outbreaks in History

In Japan, the *Minamata* disease outbreak in the 1950s was attributed to people consuming fish contaminated with methyl mercury. In the 1970s, almost 10,000 people were affected by mercury poisoning in Iraq after consuming bread baked with contaminated grain.

One example of cadmium toxicity was *Itai-Itai* (ouch-ouch) disease in Japan, first reported in the 1950s. This disease had symptoms which were a combination of osteomalacia and osteoporosis. The affected people had been consuming rice which had been irrigated with cadmium-contaminated water.

In a province of Taiwan, exposure to arsenic via drinking water has been shown to cause a severe disease of the blood vessels, which leads to gangrene, known as 'black foot disease'. This disease has not been observed in other parts of the world, and it is possible that malnutrition contributes to its development.

Arsenic poisoning has played havoc in West Bengal and Bangladesh for several decades. The ground water in this region is contaminated with arsenic. Skin lesions were a common sight in some areas. Government efforts towards decontamination of ground water have decreased the incidence of arsenic poisoning.

The general population which does not eat fish may not face any significant health risk from **methyl mercury**; however, people with high fish consumption may be at risk of neurological damage if they have been consuming fish from contaminated waters. These fish have a longer life span, are higher in the food chain and hence, tend to accumulate more mercury. Mercury from coal-fired power plants and other sources travels through the atmosphere and water. Some of the inorganic mercury changes to methyl mercury. This, when released into the water, enters the food chain. Plankton tend to accumulate the mercury. Several plankton are eaten by small fish and then several small fish are eaten by large fish. Mercury thus gets concentrated at each step (see Figure 8.3). This process is known as biomagnification. Pregnant women need to be extra careful and avoid a high intake of certain fish such as shark, swordfish, tuna, pike, walleye and bass. Methyl mercury can easily pass through the placental barrier and harm the foetus. The safety of dental amalgams is also under the scanner, with claims that mercury used in the amalgam may cause a variety of diseases. Experimental studies have shown that mercury-based amalgams release mercury vapour and that the quantity released increases during chewing.

Storing high-acid foods in **copper** utensils or using copper pipes for dispensing high-acid beverages, and faulty back-flow prevention valves in vending machines may lead to copper leaching

Figure 8.3: How Mercury Enters the Food Chain

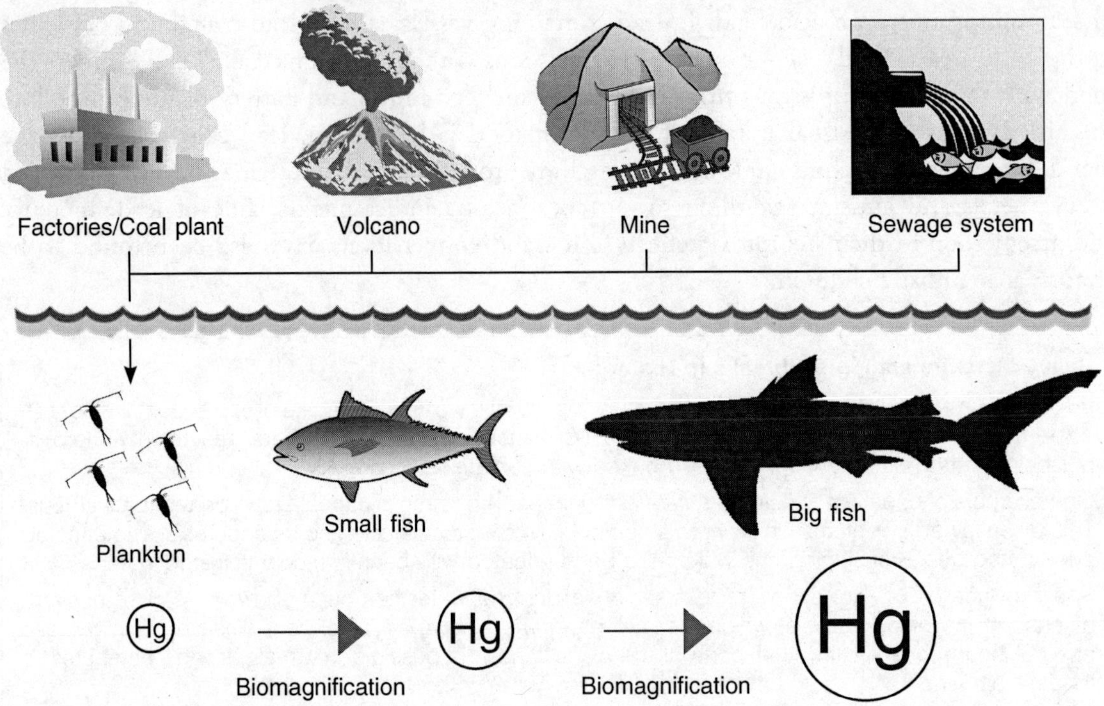

Source: Drawn by Author; Image Sources:
'Factory' by Gabrielle Nowicki (CC0 1.0; Openclipart).
'Erupting volcano' by Juhele (CC0 1.0; Openclipart).
'RPG map symbols: mine' by nicubunu (CC0 1.0; Openclipart).
'Water pollution' by Moini (CC0 1.0; Openclipart).
'Zooplankton silhouette' by dear_theophilus (CC0 1.0; Openclipart).
'Thunfish' by hextrust (CC0 1.0; Openclipart).
'Shark silhouette' by Firkin (CC0 1.0; Openclipart).

into the food or beverage. Copper is also a component of several fertilisers and consequently can end up as a soil or water contaminant.

Nickel is used as a catalyst in the manufacture of hydrogenated vegetable oil. If good manufacturing practices are not followed, it can end up as a contaminant in the oil. Cheap-quality stainless steel utensils containing nickel can also release this metal into the food stored or cooked in them, especially high-acid foods.

PREVENTION AND CONTROL MEASURES

Unlike organic pollutants, heavy metals do not decay and thus, pose a different kind of challenge. Extensive research has shown that certain **plants** (such as *Pelargonium*, *Brassicanapus* and *Brassica juncea*, yellow poplar, etc.) or **microorganisms** (such as fungi of the genera *Penicillium*, *Aspergillus* and *Rhizopus*, and *Saccharomyces cerevisiae*, *Pseudomonas* spp.) can be used to remove some heavy metals such as mercury. These plants can hyper-accumulate the heavy metals from soils by concentrating them in their bio matter.

Use of lead in petrol has decreased over the last few decades; **phasing out** of the remaining uses of **lead additives** in motor fuels should be encouraged. Similarly, use of lead in paints, food containers and glazings should be banned to reduce exposure to this toxic heavy metal.

Exposure to arsenic is mainly through food and water intake. **Folic acid supplementation** may reduce the risk of arsenic-related health outcomes, according to a study (Gamble et al. 2006). Folic acid helps in the methylation of arsenic and decreases excretion of the inorganic form, which has been linked to skin and bladder cancers and peripheral vascular disease. Lack of various B vitamins, antioxidants and the amino acid cysteine has been shown to adversely affect the metabolism of arsenic. In fact, a study in Bangladesh (Freeman 2009) has indicated that improved nutritional status could constitute a key strategy for reducing the risk of arsenic-related diseases, especially in children. The *Itai-Itai* disease, in which cadmium accumulates in the bones, is also seen more in people who, in addition to being exposed to excessive cadmium, consume a diet low in calcium and have poor vitamin D status. Thus, having a **nutritious diet** can protect us from the toxic effects of heavy metals.

Avoiding farm produce grown in contaminated soil, choosing smaller fish to consume and green leafy vegetables with small leaves can also help to **reduce our exposure**. Utensils made of only good-quality alloys should be used. Cheap alloys may leach out more metals when in contact with food materials being stored or cooked in it. Other measures of reducing exposure would include a crackdown on polluting industries, treatment of sewage/sludge to decrease the load of heavy metals, safe and responsible disposal of electronics and batteries, etc., which have heavy metal components, and vigilance in monitoring heavy metal levels in the food and water of the population. Contaminated ground water should be treated before consumption. Scientists have been working on low-cost technologies to decontaminate water at the household level, especially in rural areas.

SUMMARY

- Metals are integral parts of our body and our environment. They have been used for centuries and are still used for the manufacture of several items like electronics, batteries, paints and pigments, jewellery, utensils, pipes, machinery parts, fertilisers, pesticides, herbicides, etc.
- Some of these are essential for our body as nutrients (such as vanadium, manganese, iron, cobalt, copper, zinc and molybdenum) while others (such as lead, cadmium, mercury and arsenic) can lead to harmful effects if they enter our body.
- By definition, metals with specific density greater than $5 g/cm^3$ or those having atomic weights greater than 40 are classified as heavy metals.
- Heavy metals enter our body through the water we drink, the air we breathe and food that is grown in contaminated soil.

- Storing or cooking food in utensils made from these metals can cause the metal to leach into the food or beverage.
- Plants have been found to pick up heavy metals from the soil in which they grow. The heavy metals in soil tend to contaminate the ground water as well.
- Raw sewage water and sludge used for irrigation, vehicular exhaust, effluents from factories and household electronic waste can all lead to contamination of the air, soil and water, and consequently of our food.
- Heavy metals can cause a lot of damage to human health. These metals are not readily excreted from our bodies and so, keep getting deposited in different tissues and organs of the body. Concentrations of these heavy metals in blood, hair, nails and urine have been used as biomarkers of exposure.
- Heavy metals are known to cause several adverse health effects—inhibition of enzymes, neurotoxicity, kidney damage, dermal lesions, cardiac and liver damage, and birth defects, among others.
- Unlike organic pollutants, heavy metals do not decay and thus pose a different kind of challenge. Hence, steps need to be taken to prevent contamination of our air, soil and water with these heavy metals. Low-cost technologies also need to be developed to decrease contamination levels.
- Studies have shown that a good nutritional status and a nutritious diet can decrease the severity of harmful effects in the population.

KEY WORDS

Arrhythmias: Irregular or abnormal heart beat.

Biomarker: Characteristic biological properties or molecules that can be detected or measured in blood or tissue and are used to indicate normal or diseased processes in the body.

Blood–brain barrier: A highly selective semipermeable membrane barrier that separates the circulating blood from the brain extracellular fluid.

Dementia: Mental disorder marked by memory disorders, personality changes and impaired reasoning.

Fatal: Resulting in death.

Hallucination: Seeing or perceiving something which is not there; delusion.

Hemolytic anaemia: Condition in which there is breakdown of red blood cells.

Hepatomegaly: Enlarged liver.

Hyperkeratosis: Roughness of the palms and soles of the feet.

Nodular keratosis: Thick, scaly or crusty skin which forms nodules (lumps).

Osteomalacia: Bone softening, resulting in bending of bones.

Osteoporosis: Brittle, porous bones which break easily.

Passive smoking: The involuntary inhaling of smoke from other people's cigarettes.

Psychosis: Severe mental disorder in which one loses touch with reality.

Seizures: Convulsions, fits.

Skin erythema: Reddening of skin.

Wilson's disease: Genetic disorder in which copper builds up in the body, producing adverse effects in the brain and liver.

EXERCISES

1. List the ways in which toxic metals enter our food chain.
2. Match the metal to the disease it can cause:

a) cadmium	a) Alzheimer's
b) mercury	b) *Itai-Itai*
c) aluminium	c) *Minamata*

3. Why are children more susceptible to lead poisoning?
4. How does mercury enter the food chain? Explain why certain fish have more concentration of mercury than others.
5. How can our exposure to heavy metals be reduced?

REFERENCES

Freeman, K., 'Nutrient Protection against Arsenic Toxicity: Folate, Cysteine Support Methylation in Children', *Environmental Health Perspectives* 117(5), 2009, p. A211.

Gamble, M. W., Xinhua Liu, Habibul Ahsan, J. Richard Pilsner, Vesna Ilievski, Vesna Slavkovich, Faruque Parvez, Yu Chen, Diane Levy, Pam Factor-Litvak, and Joseph H. Graziano, 'Folate and Arsenic Metabolism: A Double-blind Placebo Controlled Folic Acid Supplementation Trial in Bangladesh', *Am J ClinNutr.* 84(5), 2006, pp. 1093–101.

Järup, L., 'Hazards of Heavy Metal Contamination', *British Medical Bulletin* 68, 2003, pp. 167–82.

Tchounwou, P. B., C. G. Yedjou, A. K. Patlolla, and D. J. Sutton, 'Heavy Metals Toxicity and the Environment', *EXS* 101, 2012, pp. 133–64.

WHO, 'Adverse Health Effects of Heavy Metals in Children', *Children's Health and the Environment, WHO Training Package for the Health Sector*, Geneva: World Health Organization, 2011.

ONLINE SOURCES

Video on Bioaccumulation and Biomagnification, Available at https://www.youtube.com/watch?v=85I7oPWUuak (accessed 14 April 2018).

WHO 10 Chemicals of Major Public Health Concern, Available at www.who.int/ipcs/features/10chemicals_en.pdf (accessed 14 April 2018).

9

OTHER HAZARDS

HIGHLIGHTS

- Naturally occurring toxicants of animal and plant origin
- Anti-nutritional factors in food
- Chemicals present in packaging/equipment or produced during processing
- Safety measures

Several chemical substances may be present in our food as unintentional contaminants or naturally occurring toxic substances (toxicants), which can lead to adverse health effects varying in severity and sometimes leading to death. Humans have, by experience over the ages, identified and learnt to avoid some of these naturally occurring toxicants. In several cases, humans have tried to develop methods to process the food to remove the toxic compounds. Foods also contain a wide range of natural chemical compounds which may act as anti-nutritional factors, interfering with the way our body utilises nutrients. These may be harmful, resulting in serious illness if consumed in large quantities.

Several chemicals have been introduced by man into his food supply as a result of his lifestyle-related activities. Industrial effluents, untreated sewage, household chemical wastes (detergents, soaps, pesticides, discarded batteries, etc.), packaging material, equipment and the actual method of food processing may all result in residues in the environment (air, water and soil) and food. Plants get contaminated as they draw water from contaminated soils, and take in polluted air. Animals may directly pick up contaminants from soil, water and air or when they consume contaminated plants. Animals eating plants containing natural toxins may not be affected by them; however, other animals or man feeding on them may exhibit toxicity symptoms. Since man is on top of the food chain, consuming both contaminated plants as well as animals, he is worst affected. In fact, one of the oldest accounts of poisoning is mentioned in the Bible. It is said that the Hebrews were poisoned after consuming quails. Normally, quail flesh can safely be eaten. However, in this case it was suggested that the toxicity resulted from the quails having earlier eaten hemlock seeds, which are poisonous, resulting in paralysis.

This chapter looks at the different types of chemical contaminants that can enter the food chain and how they can affect the quality of the food and our health. Reducing exposure to these harmful chemicals has always been a research priority. Issues related to safe disposal and environment protection are also important to address.

NATURALLY OCCURRING TOXICANTS OF ANIMAL AND PLANT ORIGIN

Certain chemical substances present in plants and animals protect them from predators and pests. Others are normal constituents of their bodies or produced as a result of natural metabolic reactions. Although these chemicals are beneficial for the plant or animal, they may prove to be harmful for other animals who feed on them. Figure 9.1 gives the different types of chemicals which have been identified either as toxins or as substances which interfere in the utilisation of nutrients.

Figure 9.1: Naturally Occurring Toxicants and Antinutritional Factors in Foods

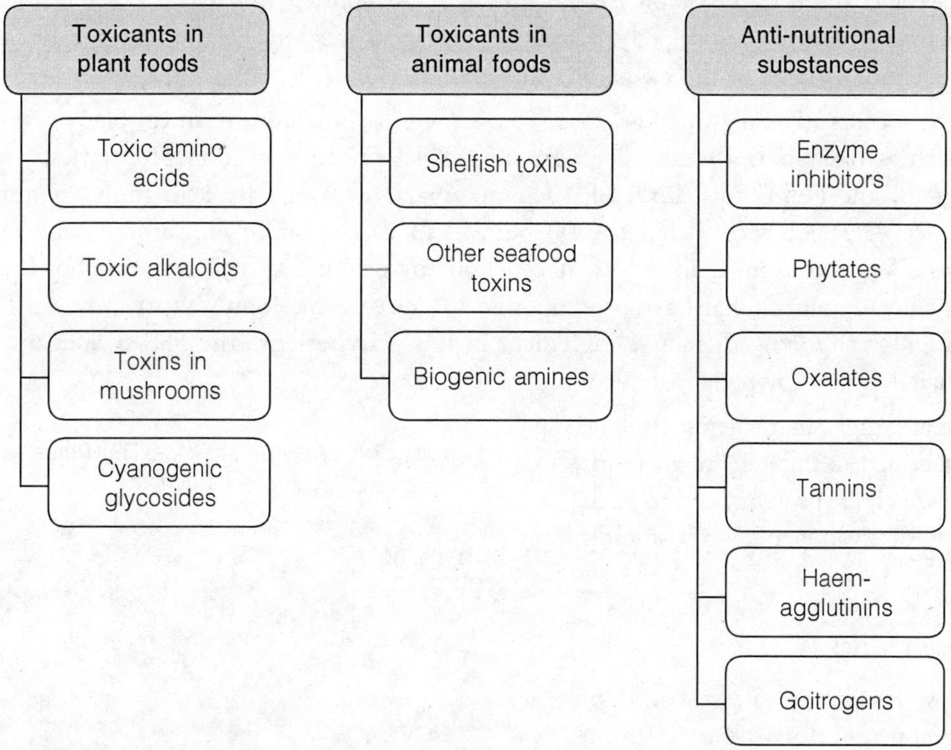

Source: Adapted by Author from Dolan et al. 2010, FAO, and Tang 2007.

Toxicants in Plant Foods

Some of the commonly consumed plant foods may have compounds in them which can cause adverse health effects in man. Fava beans, which are a major protein source in parts of Asia and North Africa, are a hazard for those individuals who have a deficiency of the enzyme glucose-6-phosphate dehydrogenase. Initial symptoms of the disease ***favism*** caused by eating these beans include headache, nausea, vomiting, pain and fever. This is followed by haemoglobin in the urine, resulting from a rapid breakdown of red blood cells, jaundice and death. ***Gossypol***, another toxicant, is present in cotton seed and may come into cotton seed oil if it is not treated properly. ***Erucic acid***, which has been linked to heart disease, is found in mustard and rapeseed oil. Consumption of bitter cucumber, bitter squash, zucchini, bottle gourd and other cucurbits has resulted in symptoms of severe cramps, diarrhoea and collapse. This is because of increased levels of the toxin ***cucurbitacins*** in the bitter cucurbits. Bitter cucurbits should, therefore, not be eaten. A case of a man dying after consumption of bitter bottle gourd (*lauki*) juice in Delhi and two others in Uttar Pradesh highlighted the danger of consuming vegetables of this family in juice form as one can ingest a large amount of the toxin. The presence of other ingredients usually masks the bitter taste. Twenty-six others were admitted to various hospitals of the country—National Capital Region (16), Madhya Pradesh (7), Gujarat (2) and Uttarakhand (1)—on complaint of abdominal pain and vomiting following consumption of freshly prepared bottle gourd juice. Diarrhoea and vomiting of blood (haematemesis) was reported in 18 (69.2 per cent) and 19 (73.1 per cent) patients respectively. Excessive ulceration was seen in the oesophagus, stomach and duodenum in most of the cases (Sharma et al. 2012).

Safrole occurs naturally in a variety of spices such as cinnamon, nutmeg, black pepper, and herbs such as basil. It is a weak hepatocarcinogen. Its presence in food preparations has been restricted by the FSSAI to a limit of 10 ppm. **Agaric acid**, a fatty acid found in fungi like *Laricifomes officinalis*, is restricted to 100 ppm in foods containing mushrooms and alcoholic beverages. When consumed in excess, it can lead to vomiting and diarrhoea. Photosensitivity is often seen in animals that have been allowed to graze on St. John's Wort, a flowering plant (*Hypericum perforatum*). The active ingredient in this is **hypericin**. The FSSAI does not permit more than 1 ppm of hypericin in alcoholic beverages.

Several other such chemicals have been identified in different plant foods, some of which are proteins, amino acids, alkaloids or cyanogenic glycosides in nature.

Figure 9.2: *Lathyrus sativus*—The Pulse which Causes Lathyrism

Source: 'chickling pea' by Andrew Butko (CC BY-SA 3.0; Wikimedia Commons).

Toxic Amino Acids

The most researched disease condition due to consumption of toxic amino acids is *Lathyrism*. It is attributed to consumption of the pulse *Lathyrus sativus* (*khesari dal* or grass pea) as a major part of the diet (see Figure 9.2). Toxic effects were seen only when a person's consumption of the *dal* was about 30 per cent of daily calories for several months.

This pulse contains a toxic amino acid called ***β*-oxalyl-L-*α*, *β*-diaminopropionic acid (ODAP)** or *β*-N-oxalyl-amino-L-alanine (BOAA), which is a nerve toxin. Victims of this disease have a typical scissored gait (a way of walking in which the legs criss-cross). The legs first develop a muscle rigidity and spasticity, forcing people to walk by crossing one limb in front of the other. This is painful and the person experiences weakness. As the disease progresses, the legs may get locked in a fixed position. Painful spasms in the calf muscles, heaviness, pain in the knee and ankle joints, and difficulty in walking are the typical symptoms of this disease. The disease has been seen especially in areas of Madhya Pradesh where this pulse was grown and consumed in large quantities because of poverty. The pulse is also used to adulterate the more expensive *arhar dal* and *chana dal* and their flour. It was also cultivated in Bihar, West Bengal and some districts of Andhra Pradesh, Karnataka and Maharashtra. Men in the 18–40 age bracket have proved most vulnerable to lathyrism and thus, families lose their earning members to this crippling disease. Steeping the pulse in water and then cooking after discarding the water seems to decrease the toxicity. Local methods of processing which are akin to parboiling of paddy are also employed to decrease the toxicity. A lot of research has also been done on developing varieties with low amounts of the toxic amino acid.

Amino acids, which are not a part of proteins, are found in a variety of plants. Alfalfa (*Medicago sativa*) seeds and sprouts contain **canavanine**, which has been linked to lupus-like symptoms (intense tiredness, muscle aches and joint pain) and other auto-immune diseases in primates, including humans. The problem is reversed once the person stops consumption.

Trogia venenata is a species of mushroom which has been implicated in the deaths of hundreds of people in China. Researchers have isolated three toxic amino acids from the mushroom: 2R-amino-4S -hydroxy-5-hexynoic acid, 2R-amino-5-hexynoic acid and -guanidinobutyric acid.

Vicia sativa, also known as the vetch, is a fodder crop for ruminant animals. The seeds have a very high protein content and resemble the red lentil (*masoor dal*). However, their use as a human food is questionable because of their known toxicity to monogastric animals (animals with a single-chambered stomach) such as rats which have exhibited reduced growth, and poultry which have died on diets containing 50 per cent vetch. The toxin **gamma-glutamyl-beta-cyanoalanine** can be reduced by leaching and can be inactivated by food acids. This pulse was imported from Australia at one time point and sold as *masoor dal* until the regulatory authorities caught up with the unscrupulous traders.

Hypoglycin A is a naturally occurring amino acid derivative found in the unripened fruit of the Ackee tree (*Blighia sapida*). The fruit is safe to eat only when it is allowed to fully open and expose the large black seeds while on the tree. If eaten before that, it leads to what is popularly known as the 'Jamaican vomiting sickness' with symptoms

> There was a massive outbreak of epidemic dropsy in 1998 at New Delhi, in which over 60 persons died and more than 3,000 were hospitalised. This was followed by epidemics in Gwalior (2000), Kannauj (2002) and Lucknow (2005) cities of India. The regulatory authorities stepped in to ban sale of loose oil and made it mandatory for all edible oil companies to declare on their labels that the product was free of argemone oil.

of abdominal discomfort and vomiting. The toxin present in the unripe fruit has been identified as hypoglycin A. Dehydration, seizures, coma and death have been seen in serious cases, especially in children.

Mimosine or leucenol is a toxic alkaloid, β-3-hydroxy-4 pyridone amino propionic acid, a non-protein amino acid. It occurs in *Mimosa spp.* and members of the closely related genus *Leucaena. Leucaena leucocephala* (known as *subabul* in India) is used in animal feed and as food for humans in Central America, Indonesia and Thailand. Toxic effects like alopecia (hair loss), growth retardation, cataract, goitre, decreased fertility and mortality have been seen in non-ruminants. Washing, soaking, boiling, drying and fermenting followed in traditional preparations reduce the toxin. In Indonesia, where *L. leucocephala* is consumed, from time to time groups of children and adults developed alopecia involving the scalp and eyebrows. Localised oedema of the scalp has also been observed. Hence, extensive consumption is not recommended.

Toxic Alkaloids

Contamination of food products may also occur when certain toxic plants may be harvested or mixed with the edible species unintentionally. For instance, the seed of *Argemone mexicana* (a seed with toxic alkaloid compounds like ***sanguinarine***) resembles the seed of mustard which is widely consumed in India as a seasoning and for production of mustard oil (see Figure 9.3). It is also wilfully used as an adulterant of mustard seeds and oil. The condition resulting from sanguinarine toxicity is known as **epidemic dropsy**. Common symptoms include oedema (see Figure 9.4), breathlessness and cardiac failure.

There are several other examples of food being contaminated with toxic weeds and resulting in serious ailments. **Veno-occlusive disease (VOD)** of the liver is a well-known form of liver injury produced by pyrrolizidine group of alkaloids. In one such outbreak in the tribal areas

Figure 9.3: Argemone Seeds and Mustard Seeds

9.3A: Argemone Seeds

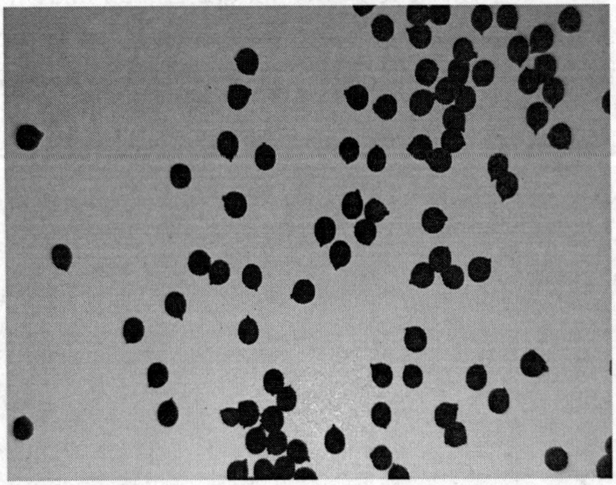

Source: Author.

9.3B: Mustard Seeds

Source: Author.

of Madhya Pradesh, a millet called *gondhli* consumed by the tribals got contaminated with the toxic weed seeds of *Crotalaria nanaburn*. The symptoms included pain in the stomach along with fluid accumulation (ascites). The poisoning was fatal in many cases. Such cases highlight the importance of keeping standing crops free of weeds. It is also important to check and remove foreign seeds after harvesting by winnowing or sorting.

Figure 9.4: Bilateral Pitting Oedema of Epidemic Dropsy (Indicated by Arrows)

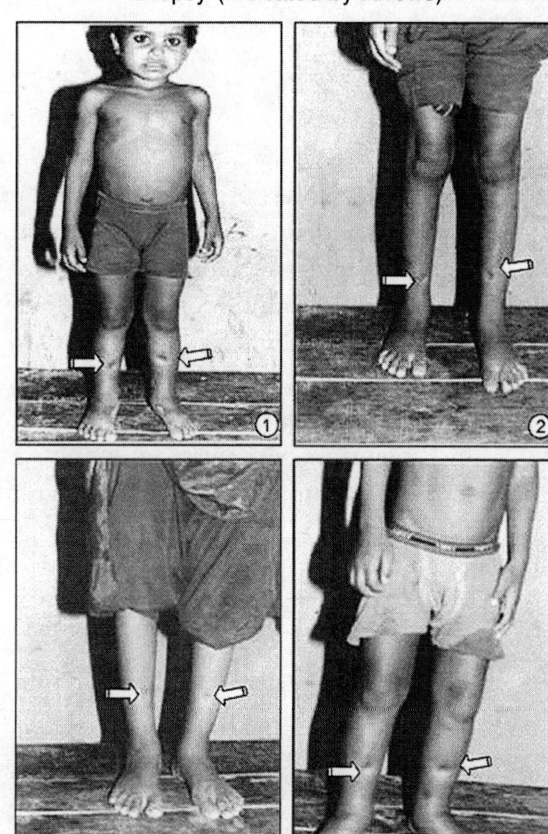

Source: Untitled by Naveen Reddy (CC BY-SA 3.0; Wikimedia Commons).

You may have noticed that some **potatoes** have green portions which we do not consume. These green portions and the peel of the potato have toxic compounds known as glycoalkaloids, such as **solanine**. They impart a bitter taste to the potatoes. Symptoms of toxicity include apathy, restlessness, drowsiness and visual disturbance.

Cyanogenic Glycosides

Linamarin is a cyanogenic glycoside which is converted to toxic **hydrocyanic acid or prussic acid** when it comes into contact with linamarase, an enzyme that is released when the cells of cassava roots are ruptured. Ingested linamarin can liberate cyanide in the gut during digestion. Acute poisoning symptoms include vertigo, vomiting, collapse and, in some cases, death within one or two hours. Long-term exposure to small levels of cyanide results in the production of thiocyanate in the body which interferes with the uptake of iodine by the thyroid gland. This increases the risk of iodine deficiency disorders like goitre and cretinism. It also results in neuropathies (diseases of the nervous system), sometimes resulting in uncoordinated gait called ataxia and spastic paraparesis. **Cassava** (its starch is also known as tapioca or arrowroot in some places) is consumed in large quantities in countries of South-east Asia, Africa and South America. In India, it is widely cultivated and consumed in Tamil Nadu, Andhra Pradesh, Kerala and Assam. Traditional processing and cooking methods for cassava can, if efficiently carried out, reduce the cyanide content to non-toxic levels. The FSSAI does not permit more than 5 ppm of hydrocyanic acid in foods and beverages.

Lima beans (*Vicia faba/Phaseolus Lunatus*, also known as broad bean, fava bean, butter bean or *sem phali* in Hindi) also contain a high concentration of cyanide precursors, as do

bitter almonds and **apple seeds**. The beans should be thoroughly cooked before eating and preferably by open pan cooking to allow the poisonous gaseous compounds to escape. The water used for boiling should also be discarded.

Mushroom Poisoning

Mushrooms are a type of fungus which is widely consumed all over the world. Mushroom poisoning, also known as *mycetism*, can result from consumption of mushrooms either raw or cooked. The kind of toxin present varies with the type of mushroom. The symptoms of poisoning can range from mild gastrointestinal disturbance (nausea, vomiting, diarrhoea, abdominal pain) to death. In fact, mushrooms are also referred to as toadstools coming from the German word *Todesstuhl*, meaning death's stool. Other symptoms include hallucinations, sweating and shortness of breath. Only some varieties of wild mushrooms are poisonous and death has resulted only in instances when, due to close physical resemblance, a poisonous mushroom like the Jack-o-Lantern has been mistaken for an edible variety like the Chanterelle (see Figure 9.5). Moreover, most mushrooms that cause human poisoning cannot be made non-toxic by cooking, canning, freezing or any other means of processing. Thus, people gathering and consuming mushrooms growing wild should be knowledgeable about mushroom varieties and be careful in selection.

Figure 9.5: Jack-O-Lantern and Chanterelle Mushrooms

9.5A: Jack-O-Lantern, a Poisonous Mushroom

Source: 'Omphalotus olearius, Mallorca' by Thomas Schoch (CC BY-SA 3.0; Wikimedia Commons).

9.5B: Chanterelle, an Edible Mushroom

Source: 'Cantharellus cibarius Chanterelle' by Bf5man (CC0 1.0; Wikimedia Commons).

> According to some unsubstantiated accounts, the Buddha died after eating some poisonous mushroom (Stamets 2000). Roman emperor Claudius was allegedly murdered by being fed a poisonous mushroom (Marmion and Wiedemann 2002).

Toxicants in Animal Foods

Just like plants can have certain substances which are harmful for us, animals too may have toxins which can adversely affect our health. These toxins are, in most cases, substances which protect the animals from pests or predators.

Seafood has most commonly been implicated in food poisoning outbreaks due to a variety of toxins which can be found in them. **Shellfish poisoning** is the most common. Shellfish include oysters, scallops, clams, shrimps, lobsters and mussels, among others (see Figure 9.6). Shellfish are

Figure 9.6: Types of Shellfish

9.6A: Prawns

Source: 'Garnelen im Verkauf' by Frank C. Müller (CC0 1.0; Wikimedia Commons).

9.6B: Red Shrimp

Source: 'Red shrimps at market in Valencia' by Melimama (CC BY-SA 2.0; Wikimedia Commons).

9.6C: Mussels

Source: 'Cooked mussels' by David Monniaux (CC BY-SA 1.0; Wikimedia Commons).

9.6D: Lobster

Source: 'Lobster' by US National Oceanic and Atmospheric Administration (CC0 1.0; Wikimedia Commons).

also known to cause food allergies. They tend to spoil very fast and may result in food poisoning due to the presence of pathogenic bacteria.

Described here are only the types of poisoning which are associated with the presence of a toxin in seafood. Shellfish like oysters, mussels, clams and scallops are filter feeders (filter the sea water through their body and feed on things like algae which come in with the water). They hence accumulate toxins produced by these microscopic algae. Shellfish poisoning can be categorised into four groups:

- ***Paralytic shellfish poisoning*** (***PSP***), which causes the most severe symptoms of all the shellfish poisonings. This is due to the presence of a toxin known as saxitoxin.. Within half an hour of consumption, the initial symptoms of numbness and tingling in the extremities appear which soon spread to the whole body. There is a loss of coordination and inability to move, speech defects, nausea and vomiting. If the respiratory system is affected, it may lead to death.

Harmful algal blooms (**HABs**) are algal bloom events involving toxic or harmful phytoplankton such as dinoflagellates (A) or diatoms (B), a type of algae. Such blooms often take on a red or brown hue and are sometimes referred to as red tides. Filter feeders bioaccumulate the toxins of these algae and plankton. Humans consuming such seafood fall prey to poisoning.

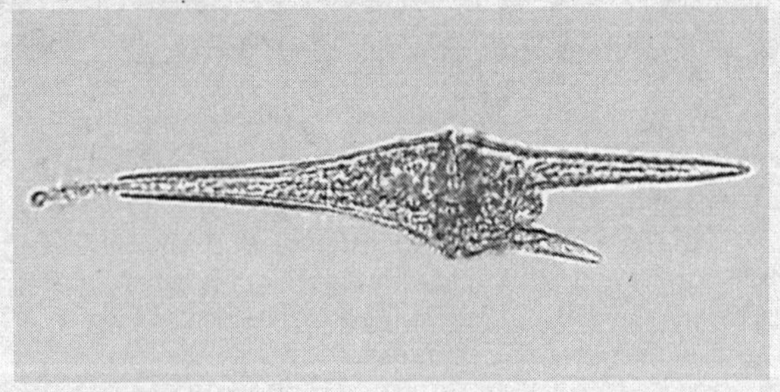

A

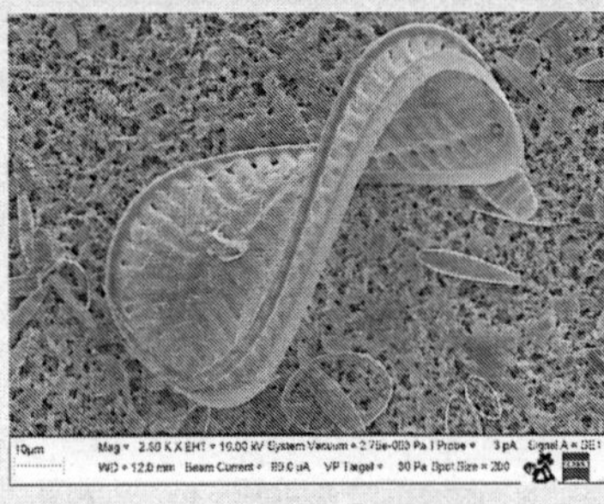

B

Image Sources: 'Ceratium furca' by Minami Himemiya (CC BY-SA 3.0; Wikimedia Commons). 'Electron scanning microscope image of the diatom Surirella Spiralis' by Nicola Angeli/MUSE (CC BY-SA 3.0; Wikimedia Commons).

- ***Amnesic shellfish poisoning*** (***ASP***) is caused by consumption of *domoic acid* which is produced naturally by marine diatoms. The name signifies that the major symptom is short-term memory loss (amnesia). These diatoms are consumed and accumulated by shellfish in their bodies. When humans consume the contaminated shellfish, they exhibit signs of poisoning. Domoic acid is a neurotoxin which causes headache, dizziness, disorientation, vision disturbances, brain damage and permanent short-term memory loss. It can also lead to unstable blood pressure, cardiac arrhythmia, coma and death. Gastrointestinal symptoms include nausea, vomiting, diarrhoea, bleeding and abdominal cramps. The toxin is heat resistant and hence cooking or freezing would not lessen the toxicity.

- ***Neurotoxic shellfish poisoning* (*NSP*)** is caused by the consumption of shellfish contaminated by *breve-toxins* which result in gastrointestinal symptoms (like vomiting and nausea) as well as neurological symptoms (like slurring of speech). This is usually not life threatening.
- ***Diarrhoetic shellfish poisoning* (*DSP*)**, as the name suggests, is characterised by symptoms of diarrhoea along with nausea, vomiting and abdominal cramps. The toxin associated with this type of poisoning is *okadaic acid* which makes the cells more permeable to water, resulting in diarrhoea and consequent dehydration. This is usually not life threatening.

Scombroid poisoning can be caused by ingestion of improperly stored or decayed seafood. The toxin scombroid is produced by the bacteria growing in the flesh. This toxin is a combination of histamine-like chemicals. Histidine, an amino acid naturally found in fish, gets converted into **biogenic amines** such as histamine at temperatures greater than 16°C. Symptoms of this poisoning resemble a typical allergic reaction because histamine is the compound naturally released by the body in response to an allergen. The person may experience flushing, sweating, nausea, vomiting, abdominal cramps, dizziness, headache, blurry vision, rash, swelling of tongue, generalised oedema, rapid heart rate and respiratory distress. Cooking destroys the bacteria, but not the toxin.

Ciguatera Fish Poisoning is caused by the ciguatera toxin which is produced by dinoflagellates. Small fish feed on these and big fish feed on small fish, thus bio-concentrating the toxin. Ciguatera, being lipid soluble, is deposited in the flesh, fatty tissue, and organs of the larger fish. The toxin is odourless and tasteless, and so the contaminated fish taste normal. The toxin is heat stable and thus, may affect people even if the fish are cooked properly. Although death due to this poisoning is rare, the symptoms can range from gastrointestinal—nausea, vomiting, abdominal pain—to rashes, itching, shortness of breath, tingling sensation, numbness, burning sensation in contact with cold surface, vertigo, irregular heartbeat, paralysis and coma.

Pufferfish poisoning or blowfish poisoning or fugu is caused by *Tetrodotoxin*. Pufferfish or blowfish (see Figure 9.7) is considered to be a delicacy in Asian countries like Japan, despite the danger of the toxin being present in the fish. Tetrodotoxin is a neurotoxin and one of the most poisonous substances found in nature. Its consumption can result in death in as little time as 20 minutes of ingestion. The toxin tends to concentrate in the organ meats and gonads of the fish. The symptoms appear within minutes of consumption and include numbness and tingling sensation around the mouth, nausea, vomiting, loss of consciousness, respiratory failure, paralysis and death.

Hallucinogenic fish poisoning can occur by eating fish which have fed on certain algae and plankton. *Indole compounds*, with hallucinogenic effects similar to drugs like lysergic acid diethylamide (LSD), are believed to be the toxic compounds produced by macroalgae which cause this poisoning. Hallucinations are the main symptoms seen in this type of poisoning, accompanied by loss of balance and coordination, delirium, nausea, vomiting, abdominal pain and hyperventilation. This type of poisoning affects the central nervous system. Ciguatera poisoning, which has many similar clinical symptoms, affects the peripheral nervous system.

Figure 9.7: Pufferfish Normal and Puffed Up

Source: 'Arothron meleagris' by US National Park Service (CC0 1.0; Wikimedia Commons).

Source: 'Arothron meleagris' by US National Park Service (CC0 1.0; Wikimedia Commons).

ANTI-NUTRITIONAL FACTORS IN FOOD

In addition to substances which are toxic, plant- and animal-based foods may contain anti-nutritional factors which affect the utilisation or absorption of the nutrients present in food by the human body. For instance, **avidin**, a protein present in raw eggs, binds to the vitamin biotin, making it unavailable to us. Some of the other anti-nutritional factors are trypsin inhibitors, phytates, oxalates, tannins, lectins and goitrogens.

Enzyme inhibitors like trypsin inhibitors, chymotrypsin inhibitors and protease inhibitors are found in a number of legumes and some cereals in our diet. They interfere with the functioning of protein-digesting enzymes, thus decreasing digestion, absorption and utilisation. These inhibitors are heat labile and so, for better digestibility and utilisation of the proteins, these foods need to be thoroughly cooked before consumption.

Thiaminase is an **enzyme** found in fish, crab, clams and in some fruits and vegetables such as blueberries, black currants, red beets, brussels sprouts and red cabbage. It renders the vitamin thiamine biologically inactive. Cooking destroys this enzyme.

Anti-metals like *phytates and oxalates* are widely distributed in plants. Phytates are present mostly in unrefined cereal and millet grains

Biogenic amines are natural anti-nutritional and toxic factors formed by the action of living organisms. They are mainly formed from microbial decarboxylation of amino acids. The common biogenic amines, which have had a role to play in several food poisoning episodes, are histamine, putrescine, cadaverine, tyramine, tryptamine, β-phenylethylamine, spermine and spermidine. These may be considered as carcinogens because of their ability to react with nitrites to form potentially carcinogenic nitrosamines. They are found in cheese, fish and meat products, eggs, mushrooms, foods prepared by a fermentative process, such as alcoholic beverages like beer; sauerkraut; and soybean products.

while oxalates are found primarily in vegetables, especially green leafy vegetables like spinach. Phytates and oxalates bind to metals and decrease their absorption. So even though our diet may have enough of nutritionally important minerals like iron, zinc, magnesium and calcium, their bioavailability is poor. Phytates have also been shown to inhibit digestive enzymes. Ingestion of foods containing high concentrations of oxalates may cause decreased bone growth, kidney stones, renal toxicity, vomiting, diarrhoea and impaired blood clotting.

Soaking the grains overnight in water helps the dietary iron to break free from the phytate. Germination and fermentation of grains also reduces the phytate content considerably because of breakdown of the phytate by enzymes (phytases). This improves the availability of minerals in the grains.

Tannins are another class of compounds which interfere with the absorption of minerals like iron and reduce the availability of proteins by binding to them. These are widely distributed in the plant kingdom and are present in high amounts in the seed coat of most legumes, spices, tamarind, turmeric, in certain vegetables, fruits and tea. Millets like *bajra*, *ragi*, *sorghum* also contain a fair amount of tannin. A typical Indian diet based on cereals, legumes, vegetables and spices may contain as much as 2–3 g of tannin. Removal of seed coat of legumes, exclusion of tamarind and avoiding tea with meals may improve iron absorption from the diet by reducing the tannin content of the diet.

Goitrogens/anti-thyroid substances present in certain plant foods have been found to interfere with the uptake of iodine by the thyroid gland in the body. This can contribute to the development of iodine deficiency disorders when iodine intakes are low. Thiocyanates, isothiocyanates and their derivatives are the chief goitrogens which occur in leaves and vegetables belonging to the Brassica genus and family Cruciferae, like radish, cabbage, cauliflower, rapeseed-mustard, broccoli, brussels sprouts, turnips, etc. Soybean and other legumes, *bajra*, peanut and lentils also contain goitrogens. These compounds are fortunately heat labile and also water soluble. They are destroyed during cooking and can also be leached away in water during processing.

Haemagglutinins are found in seeds of plants like double bean, broad bean (*sem*), common bean, kidney bean (*rajmah*), field bean, white bean (*Pisum* sp.), etc. These have the property of agglutinating (sticking) red blood cells. They also affect the permeability of cell membranes and transport of protein. They are known to bind to mucosal cells and interfere with nutrient absorption from the intestine. Consumption of improperly processed beans has been reported to result in nausea, vomiting and diarrhoea. On a long-term basis, the consumption of these agglutinins has been shown to reduce food intake and growth of laboratory animals.

> Legumes contain a wide range of biologically active substances in addition to anti-nutritional factors. These include oestrogenic isoflavones and coumestans (linked with reproductive disturbance in mammals), and oligosaccharides (which cause excessive intestinal gas production and flatulence). Legumes are a rich source of proteins and minerals for humans, especially vegetarians. To be eaten safely, these need to be thoroughly cooked as heat destroys most of the anti-nutritional factors.

CHEMICALS PRESENT IN PACKAGING/EQUIPMENT OR PRODUCED DURING PROCESSING

Several toxic chemicals, which are not naturally found in foodstuff, may be introduced in them because of how we process and package them. Cooking normally destroys or decreases the amount of toxicants in the food. However, in some cases, it may introduce new chemicals which are harmful to our health. Some of these have been discussed here, highlighting the need to reduce human exposure to these toxic chemicals which can be carcinogenic.

Advanced Glycation End Products (***AGEs***) are proteins or lipids that become glycated on exposure to sugars. The most significant sources of AGEs are from the food we ingest, and cigarette smoking. Animal fats cooked at high temperatures, and even plant foods cooked to the point of browning or crisping are likely to contain AGEs. Animal-derived foods that are high in fat and protein are generally AGE-rich. The amount of AGEs further increases during cooking. These have been implicated in atherosclerosis and ageing of the skin (formation of wrinkles). They are known to contribute to increased oxidative stress and inflammation, which increase the risk of diabetes and cardiovascular disease. Hence, avoiding smoking and consumption of foods cooked at high temperatures (such as by frying, grilling and baking) and refraining from eating foods that are cooked to a crisp, charred or blackened, may reduce exposure to this harmful chemical product.

Acrylamide is formed whenever foods that contain the amino acid asparagine and any reactive carbohydrate are heated at temperatures greater than 120°C. Starch-based foods like potato, bread, bakery products and breakfast cereal, cocoa-based products and coffee are especially likely to contain acrylamide. Acrylamide causes DNA damage, neurological and reproductive damage, and is a probable carcinogen. Cooking foods at lower temperatures (boiling, steaming temperatures) or eating some vegetables in the raw form will reduce exposure.

> A large serving of French fries may contain 82 micrograms, more than 683 times the acceptable level, of acrylamide. This is due to the high content of asparagine in potatoes and the high temperatures attained during deep fat frying. To reduce the acrylamide content, potato slices can be soaked before cooking, deep frying should be avoided, and the fries can be cooked at a lower temperature and to a lighter colour. Similarly, bread should also be toasted to a lighter colour.

Heterocyclic Amines are formed from the pyrolysis of amino acids and proteins at high temperature or when creatine and amino acids present in muscle tissues of animals are heated to high temperatures during cooking of meat. They may also be formed during the maillard reaction in which amino acids react with carbohydrates. These are mutagenic and carcinogenic. These may also be formed in plant-based foods when they are browned or charred. Cooking at low temperatures (as in stewing) instead of grilling can reduce exposure to these food toxins.

Nitrosamines are formed when nitrates or nitrites combine with amino acids on exposure to high temperatures during cooking (for instance, grilling or frying). Nitrites and nitrates are used as preservatives in processed meat products like sausages, bacon, ham, salami, etc. and hence, it is undesirable to eat these foods as a part of the regular diet. Nitrosamines have also been detected in alcoholic beverages like beer, cheese, soybean oil and canned fruit. Drying, kilning, salting, smoking and curing of food also promote formation of nitrosamines. Nitrosamines have been shown to produce cancer in experimental animals.

Polycyclic Aromatic Hydrocarbons (***PAHs***) are formed during grilling or charring of food, especially meats. Food exposed to fumes of cooking oil or to smoke from the fossil fuels (wood, coal and oil) used for cooking may also contain these toxins. Of course, one could also be exposed to these through exhaust from vehicles, cigarette smoke or fumes from cooking fires. Foods found with the highest concentration of PAHs include grilled/smoked meat or fish, smoked or cured cheese, tea (especially if dried over burning fuel) and roasted coffee. Cooking directly in contact with the flame also increases the PAH content. Benzo(a)pyrene is a PAH found in smoked, grilled or barbecued meat. The FSSAI has prescribed a limit of 5 ppb in smoked fishery products. Health effects from long-term or chronic exposure to PAHs may include decreased immune function, kidney and liver damage. Some of the PAHs are considered to be carcinogenic.

> **Concentrations of PAHs** in meat in the decreasing order are:
>
> charcoal grilling > smoking > roasting > steaming. The estimated safe levels of intake of the benchmark PAH benzo[a]pyrene is 100 μg /kg bw/day.

Toxic chemicals may also migrate from the **packaging/holding container** to the food. Hence, it is very important that the best quality materials be used for cooking, storing and packaging food. So, for instance, all types of plastic cannot be used for packaging or storing food. Food-grade plastic is made specially to ensure that it does not affect the colour, odour and taste of food, and does not react with the food material. Tin, aluminium, iron/steel cans and containers may also leach metals into foods stored in them. Acidic foods generally react with metals and tend to become contaminated. Inks used on the packaging for branding, writing all the label information and bar-coding may also leach out into the food product. Sterilisation while food is there in the packaging using gamma radiation, steam or ethylene oxide treatments can introduce leachables. Gamma radiation can break the carbon–chlorine bonds found in PVC plastics and some additives, forming breakdown products that can then percolate into food. Some of these chemicals which are considered health hazards have been discussed here.

Plastics have replaced glass and metal in the manufacture of food-processing equipment, utensils and as packaging material. **Plastics** are synthetic polymers requiring the addition of chemicals for achieving certain desirable properties. Additives like *plasticisers*, antioxidants, catalysts, suspension and emulsifying agents, stabilisers and polymerisation inhibitors, pigments, fillers, etc. are regularly used in the manufacture of different types of plastics. The polymerisation process may also leave trace quantities of residual monomer or low-molecular-mass polymer in the plastic. It is, therefore, very important to use food-grade plastic, which at least ensures that harmful chemicals have not been used in its manufacture and that good practices have been followed to ensure a safe product. The extent to which migration of contaminants into foods occurs depends upon the contact area, the rate of transfer, the type of plastic material, the temperature and the contact time. The migration of substances from plastic into food is also related to the type of food packaged.

Alcoholic beverages, edible fats and oils, and acidic foods tend to extract substances more readily than dry food such as cereals and pulses. The United Nations warned about the presence of **microplastics** in fish in their *Environment Project* report for 2016. These tiny bits of plastic land up in the rivers and oceans due to poor waste disposal methods. They are ingested by marine life, which is food for man, thus increasing the risk of human exposure to chemicals present in plastics.

Bisphenol A (***BPA***), a component of polycarbonate used to make plastic bottles and also the epoxy-resin lining of metal cans, is a chemical which has been detected even in plain water stored in plastic bottles. BPA is an endocrine disruptor and its use has been banned in many countries, especially in baby bottles and sipper-cups for children.

Phthalates, which make plastics more supple and bendable, have also been known to leach out into food and beverages in contact with plastics. Food packaging material, tubing and other parts of processing equipment may all have phthalates which can leach out into the food products. That is why highly processed foods are likely to contain higher amounts of these chemicals. Various studies have detected the presence of metabolites of phthalates in urine. NHANES data from USA indicates that higher the consumption of fast foods by participants, the higher is the concentration of phthalate metabolites in their urine. Phthalates have also been identified as potential carcinogens and endocrine disruptors.

> The first evidence of mass poisoning by PCB was in 1968 in Japan in which 1,600 people were affected. The PCBs, used in the heat transfer units for processing of rice bran oil, disintegrated due to heat, contaminating the oil in the process. The number of still-births in women who consumed this oil increased, as did the number of children born with varied health problems. The illness was known as '***Yusho***', the rice oil disease.

Polychlorinated biphenyls (PCBs) are still used in lubricants, coatings, plasticisers and inks, although their manufacture has been considerably scaled down due to their toxicity. These are fat-soluble compounds and hence, tend to concentrate in the adipose tissue of animals. Foods containing animal fat like meat, fish, eggs and milk tend to have high levels of PCBs. High levels of PCB in the blood have been linked to reduced mental development and suppressed immune reactions, especially in children exposed to PCB in the womb. Recent studies suggest that PCB can also cause short-term memory loss and learning problems in adults and children. The Food and Drug Administration (FDA) of USA requires that milk, eggs, other dairy products, poultry fat, fish, shellfish and infant foods should contain no more than 0.2–3 ppm of PCB. The FSSAI mandates that PCB levels in inland and migratory fish should not be more than 2 ppm and in marine fish, crustaceans and molluscs not more than 0.5 ppm.

Dioxins are a group of chemicals which are considered as persistent organic pollutants (POPs). They are polychlorinated aromatic compounds formed as a by-product of industrial processes. Some 419 types of dioxin-related compounds have been identified, but only about 30 of these are considered to have significant toxicity, with 2, 3, 7, 8-tetrachlorodibenzo para dioxin (TCDD) being the most toxic. Dioxins are fat-soluble and hence, tend to accumulate in the body and persist in the food chain. Apart from atmospheric deposition, soils may be polluted by sewage sludge or composts, spills and erosion from nearby contaminated areas. More than 90 per cent of human exposure is through food, mainly meat and dairy products, fish and shellfish. In most of the cases, dioxin content was traced back to animal feeds which had been contaminated by industrial wastes. Dioxins have a broad series of toxic effects and some of them are known to cause cancer in humans. They have also been linked to severe effects on the brain, and the reproductive and immune systems.

SAFETY MEASURES

As we have seen in this chapter, a number of chemical hazards lurk in our food supply. Some of these are naturally found in the foods we eat, while some others are introduced by the processing equipment or packaging. Let us see what steps are possible in order to reduce our exposure to these chemicals.

Most anti-nutritional factors present in food can be destroyed by **cooking**, such as enzyme inhibitors. **Germination** and **fermentation** of grains (see Figure 9.8) reduces the phytate content, removing the seed coat of legumes and decreasing the intake of tea and tamarind can easily decrease the intake of tannins. Only excessive intake of foods containing goitrogens, in the face of marginal intake of iodine from foods and water, may lead to precipitation of iodine deficiency disorders. Goitrogen content of foods can be reduced by cooking. They have also been shown to be lost by **leaching** into the cooking water.

Figure 9.8: Decreasing Anti-nutritional Factors and Toxins in Cereal and Pulse Grains

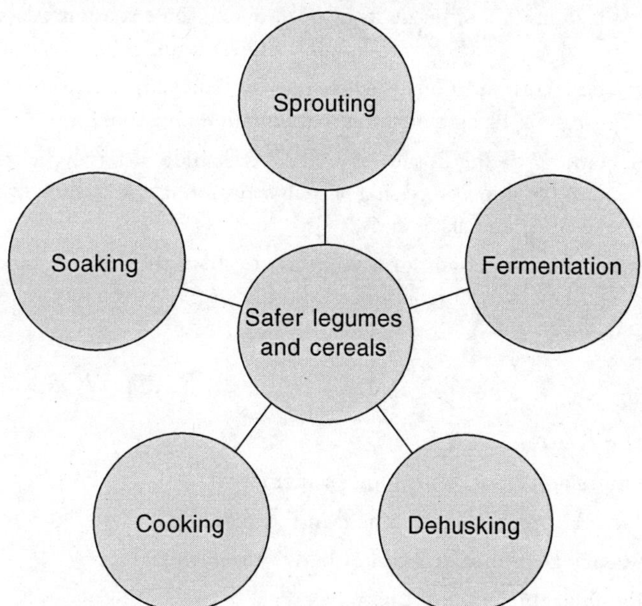

Source: Adapted by Author from Dolan et al. 2010, FAO, Soetan and Oyewole 2009, and Tang 2007.

Food should not, however, be cooked at very high temperatures. Grilling, deep fat frying and even pan roasting lead to formation of harmful chemicals. Smoking, burning and charring food also makes it a hazard to consume. Pressure cooking, boiling, blanching and steaming are the other types of cooking methods which make food safer and more nutritious to eat.

Eating small fish as compared to larger fish is advisable as the big fish would have bio-accumulated a greater quantity of toxin by feeding on small fish. Consuming fish and other seafood during algal bloom seasons is also not advisable as these algae are the source of many toxins.

Materials used for the manufacture of food-processing equipment need to follow strict quality control guidelines to ensure that no substandard material is used which can leach toxins into the food products. The food packaging material also needs to be of good quality to ensure that it does not react with the food or beverage.

SUMMARY

- Naturally occurring toxicants in some plant and animal foods pose a health hazard. Seafood, especially shellfish, have been a posing a major hazard.
- Shellfish poisoning generally occurs because the shellfish may have fed on toxic plankton or algae.
- Toxic amino acids, alkaloids and cyanogenic glycosides are some of the toxicants present in foods derived from plant sources. Lathyrism is one such crippling disease caused by the toxic amino acid (BOAA) present in the lathyrus pulse.
- Mushroom poisoning is caused by the consumption of poisonous species of mushrooms and it can be fatal.
- Anti-nutritional substances like tannins, phytates, oxalates, enzyme inhibitors, goitrogens, etc. interfere with the utilisation of nutrients by our bodies. These substances are present in foods which are an important part of our diet, such as cereal grains, pulses, legumes and vegetables.
- These anti-nutritional factors can be removed, inactivated or reduced in quantity by simple household processing like germination, fermentation and cooking.
- Harmful chemicals such as AGEs, acrylamide, heterocyclic amines, nitrosamines and PAHs may be formed during cooking/processing or may be introduced into food from packaging material or processing equipment like BPA, phthalates and PCBs.
- It is very important for us to be aware about the different kinds of toxicants that can be present in our foods and how we can reduce our exposure to these toxicants.

KEY WORDS

Alopecia: Hair loss.

Amnesia: Partial or total loss of memory.

Ascites: Accumulation of fluid in the abdominal cavity.

Ataxia: Loss of full control of body movements.

Carcinogenic: Cancer causing.

Diatom: Single-celled alga.

Endocrine disruptor: A chemical which interferes with the normal functioning of hormones in the body.

Haematemesis: Vomiting of blood.

Leachables: Trace amounts of chemicals which leach into food from packaging, equipment or containers.

Lupus: Autoimmune disease in which the body's immune system attacks its own healthy tissue, resulting in intense fatigue, joint and muscle pain, among other symptoms.

Neuropathy: Any diseased condition of the nervous system.

Paraparesis: Partial paralysis affecting the lower limbs.

Scissored gait: A way of walking in which the legs criss-cross.

Spasticity: Condition in which individual has muscle spasms (painful involuntary contractions).

Vertigo: Dizziness or giddiness.

EXERCISES

1. What are anti-nutritional compounds? Give some examples.
2. How can the availability of iron be improved from grains?
3. Why should you avoid drinking tea or coffee with your meals?
4. Name the toxins present in the following foods:
   a. *Lathyrus sativus* b. *Argemone mexicana*
   c. Potato d. Cucumber
   e. Pufferfish f. Lima beans
5. What are the different types of shellfish poisonings?
6. Why should only food-grade plastic materials be used for packaging and storing foodstuffs?
7. How do dioxins enter our food supply?
8. Suggest measures to reduce our exposure to chemical contaminants.

REFERENCES

FAO, 'Roots, Tubers, Plantains and Bananas in Human Nutrition. Toxic Substances and Antinutritional Factors. Agriculture and Consumer Protection', *FAO Corporate Document Repository*, Available at http://www.fao.org/docrep/t0207e/t0207e08.htm (accessed 15 April 2018).

Dolan, L. C., R. A. Matulka, and G. A. Burdock, 'Naturally Occurring Food Toxins', *Toxins (Basel)* 2(9), 2010, pp. 2289–332.

Marmion, V. J., and T. E. J. Wiedemann, 'The Death of Claudius', *J R Soc Med* 95(5), 2002, pp. 260–61.

Nunn, P. B., E. A. Bell, A. A. Watson, and R. J. Nash, 'Toxicity of Non-protein Amino Acids to Humans and Domestic Animals', *Nat Prod Commun.* 5(3), 2010, pp. 485–504.

Sethi, P., and P. R. Kulkarni, 'Leucaena Leucocephala A Nutrition Profile', Available at http://archive.unu.edu/unupress/food/8F163e/8F163E08.htm (accessed 20 June 2016).

Sharma, S. K., R. Puri, A. Jain, M. P. Sharma, A. Sharma, S. Bohra, Y. K. Gupta, A. Saraya, S. Dwivedi, K. C. Gupta, M. Prasad, J. Pandey, N. P. Dohroo, N. Tandon, B. Sesikeran, A. K. Dorle, N. Tandon, S. S. Handa, G. S. Toteja, S. Rao, K. Satyanarayana, and V. M. Katoch, 'Assessment of Effects on Health due to Consumption of Bitter Bottle Gourd (*Lagenaria siceraria*) Juice', *Indian J Med Res.* 135(1), 2012, pp. 49–55.

Soetan, K. O., and O. E. Oyewole, 'The Need for Adequate Processing to Reduce the Antinutritional Factors in Plants used as Human Foods and Animal Feeds: A Review', *African Journal of Food Science* 3(9), 2009, pp. 223–32.

Stamets, P., *Growing Gourmet and Medicinal Mushrooms*, Berkeley: Random House, 2000, p. 1.

Tang, A. S. P., 'Natural Toxic Substances in Seafood', *Food Safety Focus* (12th Issue, July 2007)—Food Safety Platform, Centre for Food Safety, Hong Kong. Available at http://www.cfs.gov.hk/english/multimedia/multimedia_pub/multimedia_pub_fsf_12_02.html (accessed 21 June 2016).

Zota, A. R., C. A. Phillips, and S. D. Mitro, 'Recent Fast Food Consumption and Bisphenol A and Phthalates Exposures among the U.S. Population in NHANES, 2003–2010', *Environ Health Perspect* 124 (10), 2016, pp. 1521–28.

ONLINE SOURCES

Are Microplastics in Our Water Becoming a Macroproblem? National Geographic, Available at https://www.youtube.com/watch?v=ZHCgA-n5wRw (accessed 15 April 2018).

Food Standards Agency, UK Video on Acrylamide, Available at https://www.youtube.com/watch?v=CWEXJkxBO4w (accessed 15 April 2018).

Video on Biodegradable Edible Packaging by American Chemical Society, Available at https://www.youtube.com/watch?v=wt32GgQGTcI (accessed 15 April 2018).

10

FOOD ADDITIVES

HIGHLIGHTS

- Classification of additives
- Functional role
- Labelling requirements
- Safety issues

The diets of Indians are undergoing a transition. Increasingly, people are turning to processed foods and including these in their daily diets. Although most foods undergo primary processing before landing up in our kitchens, a large variety of ultra-processed products are now commercially prepared and available as easy-to-cook and ready-to-eat foods. As these are more convenient to use and require less time to prepare than traditional home-cooked foods, they are increasingly being opted for. Very few families now make their own jams, sauces and pickles. It is easier to buy a jar of the same from the nearest retail store. But have you ever wondered how some of these processed foods available in the market stay good for so many days/months without getting spoiled while the same would spoil in a few days if made at home? Also, can you guess how mango ice cream can be made without the use of even one mango or how packaged mayonnaise can stay without refrigeration for six months on the shelf? These achievements have been made possible with the help of **food additives**.

Food additives are chemicals required for the formulation of food products. They help to ensure that the products are consistent, such that each batch tastes and looks the same. Additives are important for maintaining the flavour and palatability, sometimes imparting a desired new taste or flavour that is not there in the original ingredients used. They have been used to control product characteristics such as texture, determining how much the biscuit dough should rise, or what the acidity level in tomato sauce should be. Additives also help to keep food products wholesome and safe for a longer period of time. Without the use of food additives, most of the food products you see on a supermarket shelf would not be possible. Additives have enabled food products to be sold in places far away from the place of manufacture and even across international boundaries. You can easily enjoy ice cream or mayonnaise made in Australia or the UK and cheese spread from Denmark, while sitting in India.

According to the FSSAI, a food additive is,

> [A]ny substance not normally consumed as a food by itself and not normally used as a typical ingredient of the food, whether or not it has nutritive value, the intentional addition of which to food for a technological (including organoleptic) purpose in the manufacture, processing, preparation, treatment, packing, packaging, transport or holding of such food results, or may be reasonably expected to result (directly or indirectly), in it or its by-products becoming a component of or otherwise affecting the characteristics of such foods. The term does not include contaminants or substances added to food for maintaining or improving nutritional qualities.

Simply put, an additive is an ingredient which you add to a food product to obtain a desired characteristic in the final product. It may be a colour or flavour to improve the appearance and taste of the product or it may be something which improves the texture, or simply increases the shelf life of the product. However, it does not include chance contaminants which might come into the food like pesticide residues or plasticisers which leach into the food from the storage container or even nutrients, which may have been added to maintain or improve nutritional quality of the food. The Codex Alimentarius Commission gives a similar definition of a food additive.

CLASSIFICATION OF FOOD ADDITIVES

A few thousand additives are currently in use by the food industry. These have different roles to play in various types of food products. Based on their functional role in foods, additives have been broadly classified as colouring matter, artificial sweeteners, preservatives, antioxidants, emulsifiers and stabilisers, anti-caking agents, antifoaming agents, sequestering and buffering agents (see Table 10.1).

Table 10.1: Different Types of Food Additives and Foods in which they are Permitted

Food Additive	*Examples of additive permitted for use in India*	*Foods in which it is permitted**
Colouring matter	*Natural colouring matter* (carotenoids, chlorophyll, riboflavin, caramel, annatto, saffron, curcumin)	Any article of food except otherwise specified in the regulations
	Inorganic colouring matter or pigment (only titanium dioxide allowed)	Chewing gum
	Synthetic food colours: ponceau 4R, carmoisine, erythrosine (red), tartrazine, sunset yellow FCF (yellow), indigo carmine, brilliant blue FCF (blue) and fast green FCF (green)	Ice creams, frozen desserts, flavoured milk, biscuits, confectionery, cakes, pastries, sweets, candy, some savouries, non-alcoholic beverages, canned peas, strawberries and cherries, custard, jelly, jams and marmalade

(*Contd*)

(*Contd*)

Food Additive	Examples of additive permitted for use in India	Foods in which it is permitted*
Artificial sweeteners	Saccharin sodium, aspartame, acesulfame potassium, sucralose and neotame	Non-alcoholic beverages, sweets, biscuits, jams, jellies, chocolate, confectionery, bread, cake, pastries, ice cream, frozen desserts, flavoured milk, yoghurt, ready-to-eat cereals, chewing gum
	Polyols like isomalt, erythritol, maltitol/maltitol syrup	Non-alcoholic beverages, ice cream, yoghurt, flavoured milk, cake, cookies, pastries, candies, chocolates, bakery products, jams, jellies, marmalades, Indian sweets and sweet mixes
	Polydextrose	Ice cream, frozen desserts, cake, biscuit, yoghurt, confectionery, jam and traditional sweets
Preservatives	*Class I*: common salt, sugar, dextrose, glucose syrup, spices, vinegar, honey, edible vegetable oil	Any food except otherwise specified in the regulations
	Class II: benzoic acid, sulphurous acid and their salts,# nitrates, nitrites, sorbic acid, propionates, lactic acid and its salts, acid calcium phosphate, nisin, sodium diacetate	Sausages, canned or pickled meat, fruit pulp, fruit juice and concentrate, dried fruits, non-alcoholic beverages, jams and preserves, sugar, corn flour, beer, wine, pickles, chutneys, sauces, dehydrated vegetables, cheese, flour confectionery, soups and mixes, paneer, fruits, vegetables flakes and powder, fat spread
Antioxidants	Lecithin, ascorbic acid and tocopherol	Any food except otherwise specified in the regulations
	Ethyl gallate, propyl gallate, octyl gallate, dodecyl gallate, ascorbyl palmitate, butylated hydroxyanisole (BHA), citric acid, tartaric acid, gallic acid, resin guaiace, tertiary butyl hydroquinone (TBHQ)	Edible oils and fats except *ghee* and butter (BHA may be added to ready-to-eat dry breakfast cereal, chewing gum, dry mixes of rasogollas and vadas, *ghee* and butter. BHA and TBHQ may be added to fat spread. Ascorbyl palmitate and lecithin may be added to ready-to-drink infant milk substitute)
Emulsifying and stabilising agents	Agar, alginic acid, alginates, carrageen, edible gums, gelatin, modified starches, pectin, sorbitol, dextrins and many others	Each of these can be used in a limited number of foods like ice creams, frozen desserts, salad dressing, pudding, snacks, sauces, soups, gravies, bread and cakes, etc.
Anticaking agent	Carbonates and phosphates of calcium and magnesium, silicates of calcium, magnesium, aluminium or sodium, silicon dioxide, myristates, palmitates or stearates of aluminium, ammonium, calcium, potassium or sodium	Table salt, onion powder, garlic powder, fruit powder and soup powder Calcium, potassium or sodium ferrocyanide may be used as crystal modifiers and anti-caking agents in iodised, iron fortified or common salt

(*Contd*)

(*Contd*)

Food Additive	*Examples of additive permitted for use in India*	*Foods in which it is permitted**
Antifoaming agent	Dimethyl polysiloxane	Edible oil and fat for deep frying
Sequestering and buffering agents	Acetic acid, adipic acid, calcium gluconate, calcium carbonate, calcium oxide, citric acid, malic acid, lactic acid, phosphoric acid, polyphosphate, tartaric acid, fumaric acid, ethylene diamine tetra acetate	Each of these can be used in limited number of foods like soft drinks, other beverages, processed cheese, bread, cake mixes, salad dressings, sandwich spread, fat spread and miscellaneous other foods

Note: * All additives in a category may not be permitted in all foods listed.
Only specific salts permitted. See original document for details.

Source: Adapted by Author from FSSAI 2011.

Direct and Indirect Food Additives

Additives may also be classified as direct or indirect (or carry-over) additives. If an additive is added during the formulation or packing of a food product to serve a specific role, it is referred to as a *direct additive.* For example, sulphites may be used for bleaching during the manufacture of sugar. Many direct additives are identified as ingredients on the packaging label of foods.

Indirect food additives are those that become part of the food in trace amounts due to some ingredient which had been treated with an additive, or the additive is added to one or more of the ingredients used in the formulation of that food product. For instance, sugar used to make soft drinks or beverage concentrates may contribute to the sulphite levels of these drinks even though the additive wasn't directly added to the beverage. Similarly, antioxidants used in edible oils (direct additives) may be found in chips or any food item prepared with this oil (indirect additives). This is known as the 'carry-over' principle.

FUNCTIONAL ROLE

So why do we need to add so many chemicals to our food? Why can the food items not be prepared the way we cook at home? The answer is simple. Commercial cooking is very different from household cooking. For instance, when we make bread or biscuits at home, does the product turn out exactly the same each time? How long does the product stay fresh? When food products are prepared in bulk and the finished products are to be transported across great distances, companies cannot afford to have any variations in quality. Moreover, the bread and biscuits across batches should be of the same texture, taste and appearance. This is why additives are added to food. Additives perform a variety of useful functions in foods. Additives like preservatives and antioxidants help to keep food wholesome and appealing through their journey to markets which are sometimes thousands of miles away from where it is grown or manufactured. Additives can also be used to make food more appealing by improving the taste, texture, consistency or colour.

We can understand this better by looking at the additives which go into producing good-quality biscuits (see Figure 10.1). Each additional component has a positive impact on making the product more desirable for the consumer.

Figure 10.1: Additives Required for Making Good-quality Biscuits

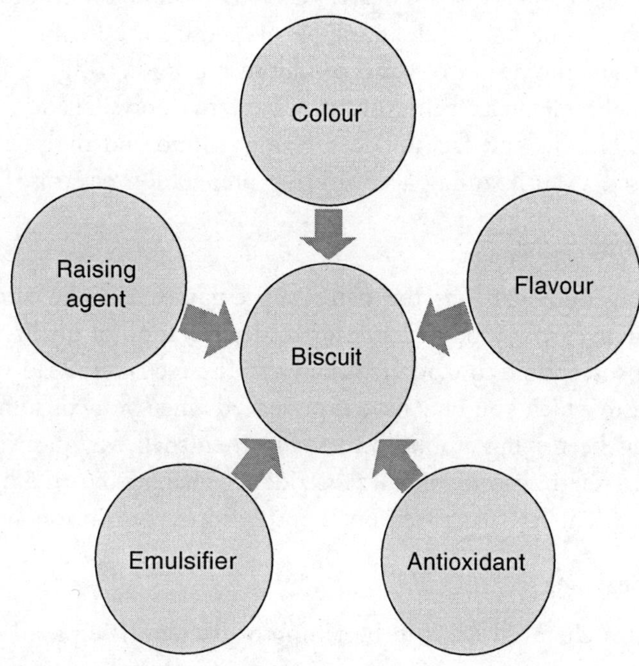

Source: Drawn by Author.

Different brands and types of biscuits may have five or more chemical food additives. Although Figure 10.1 lists just the basic additives which are needed to make a biscuit, companies may choose to put more than one kind of emulsifier or raising agent in a product to achieve specific characteristics. The antioxidant, for instance, would prevent the fat used in the biscuit preparation from going rancid. The emulsifier would help in stabilising the emulsion and improving the quality of the biscuit dough, the raising/leavening agent would help the dough rise thus giving the biscuit a good texture, while the colour and flavour would improve the sensory qualities of the biscuit. Let us examine the role of each type of food additive in detail.

Acidity Regulator/Acidifying Agents/Buffering Agent

Acidifying agents are primarily used to increase the acidity of a food product. Acidity regulators, on the other hand, control or even alter the pH of the food. This may include use of acidic, alkaline substances or what are known as buffering agents. These allow the pH to be maintained within a certain range in the product during processing or storage, thus maintaining the flavour and improving the stability of foods.

Anti-caking agents

While pouring salt from a shaker or dry powder mixes from their container, have you faced the difficulty of the substance sticking together in the container and not coming out? Many products are hygroscopic (those which readily absorb moisture), and so, on being exposed to moisture in the air, start caking. To keep the product free-flowing, anti-caking agents are added. They are also sometimes referred to as anti-sticking, drying agents or dusting agents as they prevent substances from sticking to each other.

Antifoaming Agents

When certain oils are heated, there is production of a foam-like substance, which is undesirable while cooking. Antifoaming agents reduce the foaming properties of the oils, which essentially means the height of foam produced during heating. It also helps to retard deteriorative changes in the oil or fat being heated. Dimethyl polysiloxane may be used as an antifoaming agent in edible oils and fats for deep frying. Mono and diglycerides of fatty acids of edible oil may be used as antifoaming agent during preparation of jams, jellies and marmalades.

Antioxidant

An antioxidant, as the name suggests, refers to an additive which will prevent the oxidative changes in a food which leads to deterioration of quality. Usually, it is the fat component which is susceptible to oxidative changes. These changes lead to the production of off-odours and off-taste which you may have experienced when you consume a biscuit or any bakery product which has been lying around on your kitchen shelf way past its best-before date. These changes in fat are referred to as rancidity. Oxidative changes also reduce the nutrient content of foods as some nutrients are destroyed on exposure to oxygen in the air.

Bleaching Agent

This chemical helps in bleaching or decolourising food or some of its ingredients. These agents may be used to whiten—for instance, table sugar or refined flour (*maida*)—simply because the manufacturer would find it difficult to sell *maida* and sugar which looks cream or off-white.

Bulking Agent or a Filler

This is an additive which increases the weight of a food. It does not, however, affect the taste of the food. Bulking agents are used in bakery products, sauces, seasonings, condiments and soups, confectionery products, spreads, mayonnaise and salad dressings. Examples include starch and soluble fibres like guar gum.

Carbonating Agent

An additive which helps to provide carbonation in a food is referred to as a carbonating agent. In soda water and 'fizzy' or carbonated drinks, carbon dioxide is dissolved under pressure in the beverage. When you uncork the bottle, the pressure is released and so is the gas, which is weakly soluble in water, producing effervescence. Carbonation is also used for alcoholic beverages like beer and sparkling wine. These carbonating agents may also be added to dry beverage mixes which are effervescent when rehydrated with water.

Carrier

A food additive used to dissolve, dilute, disperse or otherwise physically modify a food additive or nutrient without altering its function is called a carrier. It may also be an encapsulating agent. Addition of sodium hexa metaphosphate (SHMP) in double fortified salt helps in preventing iodine from reacting with iron and with other salt components. The carrier does not exert any chemical effect by itself. It just tries to facilitate the handling, application or use of the other food additive or nutrient.

Colour

Sometimes, during processing operations of food like drying, canning, roasting and frying, the natural colour of the food ingredients may become dull or be lost or reduced. To improve the visual appeal of the food, colouring matter may be added. Colour additives are also used in foods to correct natural variations in food colour. For instance, a manufacturer would want every batch of his mixed fruit jam to be of the same shade of red. As a consumer, you also expect a certain colour in your food and beverages. While having strawberry milkshake or ice cream, you expect to see pink colour and the *boondi ladoo*s or *jalebi*s to be orange or yellow in colour. You would reject canned fruit that has become dark in colour or green vegetables that have lost their bright green and become olive green due to the heat involved in processing. These colours may be either natural or synthetic. The law permits the use of synthetic colouring matter as given in Table 10.1 to be added to certain food items up to 100 ppm. Colour retention agents may also be added to stabilise, retain or intensify the colour of a food.

> Have you ever wondered why carbonated soft drinks as well as alcoholic drinks like beer taste better when chilled? It is because the solubility of CO_2 increases with decrease in temperature; hence, more CO_2 goes into the solution. This gives a better mouthfeel and taste when consumed.

Emulsifiers

Emulsifiers give products a consistent texture and prevent ingredients from separating. They help in forming a uniform emulsion of two or more phases in a food. For instance, you would not buy a bottle of ketchup if the ingredients had separated out—the pulp had settled at the bottom with the liquid floating on top! Emulsifiers may perform the role of dispersing agents, surface active agents, crystallisation inhibitors, density adjustment agent (for example, flavouring oils in beverages), suspension agents and clouding agent. **Stabilisers** and **thickeners** also give smooth uniform texture to foods like sauces and pastes. Stabilising agents help to stabilise emulsions, foams and colloids. Such substances are widely used in the commercial production of bread, confectionery, ice cream, chocolate and soft drinks. **Thickening agents** increase the viscosity and also function as binders, bodying agents and texturising agents. Modified starches are being used by the food processing industry as thickeners, binders and stabilisers. These starches contribute in making our sauces thick in consistency, potato chips crisp and giving that special smooth texture to puddings.

Flavouring Agents

These impart flavour to the food in which they are added. Have you ever wondered how strawberry jelly tastes of strawberry even when the fruit has not been added to it? This is because of flavouring agents which can impart flavours which resemble naturally occurring foods or something different altogether. Flavouring agents may be of three types—natural flavours, nature-identical flavouring substances and artificial flavouring substances. *Natural flavours* are those exclusively obtained by physical processes from plant, sometimes animal, raw materials. *Nature-identical flavouring substances* are substances chemically isolated from raw materials or synthesised. They are chemically identical to the substances present in natural products. On the other hand, *artificial flavouring substances* are those which have not been identified in natural products and are chemically synthesised. Flavour enhancers may improve the flavour or odour of a food. Monosodium glutamate (also popularly known as *ajinomoto*) is a flavour enhancer added to many processed foods as well as in Chinese cooking. Vanillin, spices and herbs are a few natural flavouring agents. Synthetic flavours like esters impart a fruity flavour, while terpenoids add a citrus flavour.

Flour Treatment Agent

This is generally added to flour or dough to improve its appearance or baking quality. It may also serve the purpose of a bleaching agent, flour improver, dough conditioner or dough strengthening agent. Examples include ascorbic acid, sodium bisulfite and amylases.

> Colour plays a crucial role in taste and perception of food. In 1993, the two major cola giants Pepsi and Coke launched cola drinks which were clear and without colour called 'Crystal Pepsi 'and 'Tab Clear' respectively in the USA. Both the beverages were a flop as people perceived colas to be a dark beverage, not realising that they are dark because manufacturers put colouring in them.

Foaming Agent

This makes it possible to form or maintain a uniform dispersion of a gaseous phase in a liquid or solid food. This additive is used as an aerating agent or whipping agent to give a good mouthfeel to beverages and food products. Examples include quillaja extract, lecithin and xanthan gum.

Gelling Agents

These help in gel formation and provide texture to food products. They find use in food products like jams, jellies, marmalades, desserts and confectionery. Gums, starches, pectin, agar-agar and gelatin are common gelling agents.

Glazing Agents

Glazing agents add a shine to the external surface of a food product. They may also help to provide a protective coating, preventing loss or gain of moisture as well as protection from pests. They can also be used as sealing agents, surface-finishing agents, polishing agents and film-forming agents. Examples include beeswax, shellac and petroleum jelly.

Humectant

This is also referred to as a moisture retention agent or wetting agent and this prevents food from drying out by counteracting the effect of a dry atmosphere. Examples include sorbitol and glycerine.

Leavening Agents

Leavening agents that release acids when heated can react with baking soda to help cakes, biscuits and other baked goods rise during baking. Leavening agents, also referred to as **raising agents**, are what make fluffy pastries, spongy cakes and breads and crisp biscuits possible. The term leavening refers to introduction of a gas (generally carbon dioxide) in the batter or dough which enables it to expand in volume. Yeast was traditionally used as a leavening agent. The principle disadvantage in its use was that the fermentation process was slightly difficult to control and at times could lead to undesirable flavours. Chemical leavening agents like baking soda (sodium bicarbonate) do not have this problem. Most of the chemical leavening systems are based on the reaction of an acid with sodium bicarbonate to release carbon dioxide. There are several acids which might be used and they differ in the speed at which they release the leavening gas. Examples include cream of tartar (rapid release), sodium aluminium phosphate or sulphate (slow release) and anhydrous monocalcium phosphate (for an intermediate speed of release).

Packaging Gas

This is considered as a food additive by the FSSAI as the gas can be introduced in a food container before, during or after filling it with the food product. Gases like carbon dioxide and nitrogen protect the food from spoilage by oxidation and even restricts the growth of microbes which can deteriorate food quality.

Preservatives

Preservatives are substances which, when added to food, retard, inhibit or arrest the activity of microorganisms. Hence, they prolong the shelf life of a food product. These are also known as antimicrobial substances, antimycotic agents, bacteriophage control agents, fungistatic agents, anti-mould and anti-rope agents or antimicrobial synergists. Microbes spoil food by processes such as fermentation (for example, *dosa* batter becoming very sour on keeping), acidification (for example, milk splitting when heated due to excessive acid production) and decomposition of foods (for example, fungus spoiling grains). In India, preservatives have been grouped into two classes: I and II. Included under **Class I preservatives** are common food ingredients such as salt, sugar, glucose, honey, spices, vinegar, oil, etc., which we use for preserving pickles, jams, etc. There is no restriction on the use of these preservatives in foods. However, **Class II preservatives** are chemicals (see Table 10.1 for details) which can be added to only specific foods in a specified quantity. This is because consumption of more than the acceptable quantity of the additive can result in toxicity.

Sulphites, as a source of sulphur dioxide, have been used as preservatives in several foods like jam, jelly, marmalade, fruit, fruit pulp and juices, syrups and sherbets, alcoholic beverages, confectionery and dry fruits. They are also used as bleaching agents in the refining of sugar and to control browning reactions in dehydrated fruits and vegetables.

Nitrates and *nitrites* are added as preservatives to particular meat products like ham, bacon and pickled meat. They are especially effective against bacteria like *Clostridium botulinum* and

Staphylococcus aureus which have a long history of causing lethal food poisoning. Nitrates are more effective when they are used in combination with common salt. The presence of nitrites imparts the characteristic pink colour to meat apart from protecting its flavour. Nitrates and nitrites are not, however, permitted to be added to any infant food.

> **Gums** derived from plants and seaweeds have been traditionally used in India for preparation of several food items. Gums are obtained from various sources. Gum arabica, karaya and ghatti are tree exudates; guar gum, cassia gum and konjac mannan are seed and root gums; pectin is obtained from the peel of fruits; sodium carboxymethyl cellulose are obtained from cellulose pulp; gellan gum and xanthan gums are microbial gums; whereas agar, alginate are seaweed extracts. They are used as a thickening agent in jams, gravies and sauces; as a gelling agent in pudding desserts; and as an encapsulating agent to stabilise flavours.

Benzoic acid and salts are mainly used to protect foods against yeasts and moulds. They are not very effective against bacteria and have to be used in combination with sulphur dioxide in foods which get spoiled by bacteria. Benzoic acid is used in squashes, fruit syrups, cordials, juices, jams, marmalades, preserves, sweetened ready-to-serve beverages, pickles, *chutneys*, sauces, tomato pureé and paste, and fat spread.

Sorbic acid and its salts are effective against moulds, yeasts and many bacteria. It is more effective as a preservative than propionates and benzoates at higher pH values and therefore, it is widely used for bakery and confectionery products like cakes, fillings for chocolates and various types of cheese, cheese spreads and fat spreads, *paneer* and ready-to-eat preserved *chapatis*.

Sequestrants

These additives control the availability of cations, improving the stability and quality of foods. They can form chelates with metal ions like copper, iron, cobalt and nickel, which are powerful catalysts in the auto-oxidation processes. Binding the metals in a chelate helps to slow down the oxidative changes in foods which would otherwise result in decolourisation, rancidity and production of an off-taste in the food product. Addition of sequestering agents is permitted in a specified list of foods only. Some examples of commonly used sequestering agents are citric acid, phosphoric acid, tartaric acid, ethylene diamine tetra acetate (EDTA), etc. in foods, thus preventing spoilage due to oxidation of fats.

Sweeteners

These include additives that impart a sweet taste to food. They may or may not provide calories. Mono and disaccharide sugars like cane sugar, glucose syrup, jaggery, honey, khandsari sugar, dextrose, invert sugar or golden syrup, and icing sugar have been used as ingredients in several food products and beverages. They also provide calories to the body, roughly 4 kcal per gram sugar and so are also referred to as caloric sweeteners.

Non-caloric sweeteners do not provide any calories and are usually high-intensity sweeteners many times sweeter than table sugar. Both aspartame and acesulfame K are about 200 times sweeter than sucrose, while saccharin is 300 times sweeter. Acesulfame K is heat resistant and, therefore, suitable for use in food which requires cooking. Sucralose is derived from ordinary sugar by selective treatment resulting in a product which is 600 times sweeter than sugar. Sucralose does not break down in the body and is poorly absorbed in humans. Saccharine, on the other hand, is absorbed by the body and then excreted unchanged by the kidneys. Another sweetener permitted by the FSSAI is neotame in soft drinks. It is 7,000–13,000 times sweeter than sucrose. Steviol glycosides obtained from the leaves of the plant *Stevia rebaudiana* are also used widely as a natural sweetener. Sugar alcohols like sorbitol, mannitol, xylitol, etc. are low-calorie sweeteners providing around 2 kcal/g. Their use is, however, limited as they may not be sweeter than sucrose. Consuming large amounts of these sweeteners can have a laxative effect.

Box 10.1: *The Chemicals We Eat Daily*

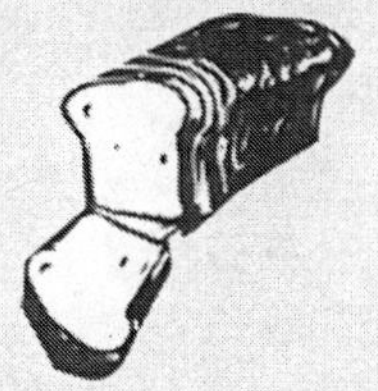

Have you ever looked at the list of ingredients on the label of the bread that you consume? In addition to the food ingredients, you may see food additives like preservatives (to increase shelf life), emulsifiers (to stabilise the emulsion), improvers (improve baking quality), acidity regulators (alter or control the pH) and flour treatment agent (to improve the strength and workability of the dough).

A bottle of tomato ketchup, besides having the basic ingredients of tomato paste, water, sugar, spices and salt, may also have an acidifying agent (to increase the acidity), thickening agent (to thicken the sauce and give smooth uniform texture) and a preservative (to increase shelf life).

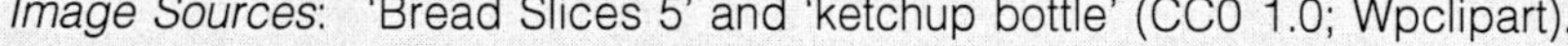

Image Sources: 'Bread Slices 5' and 'ketchup bottle' (CC0 1.0; Wpclipart).

LABELLING REQUIREMENTS

According to the FSSAI, it is mandatory that addition of additives to a food product be declared on the label. These are to be listed along with the list of ingredients, as the class title (such as antioxidant, acidity regulator, emulsifier, etc.) together with the specific name of the additive or the INS/E number of the additive. Table 10.2 presents the International Numbering System (INS) numbers used for some of the common additives of interest. These can enable a consumer to identify the chemical additives which are present in the packaged food they are consuming. But why would a consumer want to know exactly which chemical has been added? Is it not sufficient to know that a preservative or an artificial colour has been added? In the next section, you will be introduced to the toxicity of some of the additives. Certain people may be sensitive to particular additives. They would benefit by avoiding foods which contain the additive they are allergic to.

Table 10.2: Identification of the Additive Present in your Food by Reading the Food Label

Category of Additive	*Additive*	*INS number*
Antioxidants	Ascorbic Acid	300
	Tocopherols	306, 307, 308, 309
	Propyl, octyl, dodecyl, ethyl gallates	310, 311, 312, 313
	Tertiary Butylhydroquinone (TBHQ)	319
	Butylated hydroxyanisole (BHA)	320
	Butylated hydroxytoluene (BHT)	321
	Lecithins	322
	Citric Acid	330
	L-Tartaric Acid	334
Colouring matter	Turmeric extract	100
	Tartrazine	102
	Sunset yellow FCF	110
	Carmoisine	120
	Ponceau 4R (Cochineal red A)	124
	Erythrosine	127
	Allura red AC	129
	Indigotine (Indigo carmine)	132
	Brilliant blue FCF	133
	Fast green FCF	143
	Caramel	150
	Annatto	160b
	Titanium dioxide	171
Preservative	Sorbic acid including its sodium, potassium and calcium salts	200, 201, 202, 203
	Benzoic acid and its sodium, potassium and calcium salts	210, 211, 212, 213
	Sulphur dioxide	220
	Sodium sulphite	221
	Sodium hydrogen sulphite	222
	Sodium metabisulphite	223
	Potassium metabisulphite	224
	Nisin	234
	Potassium and sodium nitrite	249, 250
	Sodium and potassium nitrate	251, 252
	Propionic acid, sodium propionate, calcium propionate, singly or in combination, expressed as propionic acid	280, 281, 282, 283

(*Contd*)

(*Contd*)

Category of Additive	*Additive*	*INS number*
Sweetener	Acesulfame potassium	950
	Aspartame	951
	Saccharin (and Na, K, Ca Salts)	954
	Sucralose (Trichlorogalactosucrose)	955
	Alitame	956
	Steviol glycosides	960
	Aspartame-Acesulfame salt	962
	Maltitol and Maltitol Syrup	965

Note: The E numbers given by the European Union are the same as the INS numbers
Source: Adapted by Author from Codex data.

Further, there are regulations regarding declaration of the presence of some additives. The following statements are to be displayed in capital letters just beneath the list of ingredients on the label of foods which have extraneous colouring matter added to them:

CONTAINS PERMITTED NATURAL COLOURS (S)

or

CONTAINS PERMITTED SYNTHETIC FOOD COLOUR (S)

or

CONTAINS PERMITTED NATURAL AND SYNTHETIC FOOD COLOUR (S)

Similarly, addition of extraneous flavouring agents also needs to be written below the list of ingredients in capitals as 'CONTAINS ADDED FLAVOUR'. In addition, the particular type of flavouring agent needs to be specified according to the regulations, that is, Natural Flavours and Natural Flavouring Substances, Nature-Identical Flavouring Substances or Artificial Flavouring Substances, along with the common name of the flavour, such as chocolate, vanilla, etc. In case of natural and nature-identical flavouring substances, however, only the class name of flavours needs to be indicated.

Every packet of *maida* which has been treated with improver or bleaching agent should carry the following declaration on its label:

WHEAT FLOUR TREATED WITH IMPROVER/BLEACHING AGENTS, TO BE USED BY BAKERIES ONLY

Every advertisement for and/or package of food containing added monosodium glutamate should declare the following on its label:

(This package of......................(name of food) contains added MONOSODIUM GLUTAMATE) NOT RECOMMENDED FOR INFANTS BELOW 12 MONTHS

Addition of artificial sweeteners to foods has to be declared on the label as follows:

Contains..........................(name of artificial sweetener) Not recommended for children Quantity of sugar added.................g/100g or, No sugar added in the product (whichever is applicable) Not for Phenylketonurics (if aspartame has been added)

Packages of aspartame marketed as table-top sweeteners and every package of food containing aspartame have to carry that warning on their labels. This is because aspartame breaks down into its constituent amino acids—aspartic acid and phenylalanine—in our body. Phenylketonuria is a hereditary disease which affects the way in which the body metabolises phenylalanine, resulting in the accumulation of toxic breakdown products, which, in turn, may lead to brain damage. Hence, it is dangerous for people suffering from this disease to consume this sweetener. Therefore, the fact that it is unsuitable for people with this disease—the words, 'Not for Phenylketonurics'—has to be mentioned on the packet of table-top sweeteners, products containing aspartame, and in advertisements of the same.

Every label and advertisement of food products which contain artificial sweeteners need to declare the name of the sweetener used as well as the fact that it is 'not recommended for children'. In addition, they also need to state on the label:

CONTAINS ARTIFICIAL SWEETENER AND FOR CALORIE CONSCIOUS

Every container or package of table salt, whether iodised or iron fortified which contains permitted anti-caking agents, needs to bear the following label:

IODIZED SALT/IRON FORTIFIED COMMON SALT CONTAINS PERMITTED ANTI-CAKING AGENT

In addition to the above regulations, the FSSAI also mandates that if, for instance, hard cheese has been surface treated with the antimicrobial Natamycin, the same be declared on the label. Similarly, if fresh fruits have been coated with wax, they need to carry a label which declares, 'Coated with wax' with the name of the wax used. Every package of food to which polyols or polydextrose have been added needs to declare, 'Polyols/ Polydextrose may have a laxative effect', as the case may be.

SAFETY ISSUES

> The Delaney Clause introduced by the Food and Drug Administration of the US states that any chemical additive found to induce cancer in man, or in animals would not be permitted to be added to any article of food.

Eating natural, organic food has always been recommended by nutritionists and health professionals. Food additives are, after all, chemicals which we are introducing into our food. Our daily diet contains a variety of processed foods which are likely to contain these chemicals. The addition of these chemicals is important from the technological point of view for a product to look and taste better. However, at the back of one's mind, we may be wondering whether it is safe to consume so many chemicals daily.

In India, the FSSAI regulates the additives which can be used, the foods to which they can be added and the quantity in which they can be added. When regulatory authorities permit the use of chemicals as food additives, they first look at the toxicological profile of the chemical and its **Acceptable Daily Intake** (**ADI**). *ADI is the amount of a food additive, expressed on a body weight basis, that can be ingested daily over a lifetime without appreciable health risk.* Many substances in use today as food additives are '**generally recognised as safe**' or **GRAS substances**. GRAS substances are those whose use is generally recognised as safe by experts, based on their extensive history of use in food or based on published scientific evidence. Based on this data, the maximum permissible levels of the additive in a food are also defined. The primary objective is to ensure that the ADI is not exceeded, even when people consume all foods which may contain the additive. The additive should present no appreciable health risk to consumers at the use levels proposed. The FAO/WHO Joint Expert Committee on Food Additives (JECFA) evaluates the toxicological profile of different food additives and assigns an ADI/GRAS status.

The use of a food additive is justified only when it serves to fulfil a technological function which cannot practically be achieved by other means keeping cost and technological feasibility in mind. The use of the additive should not be misleading to the consumer or pose appreciable health risk.

Although most food additives are without any potential adverse effects, there have been problems concerning the safety of some of these chemicals (see Table 10.3). However, most of these toxic effects are at very high levels of intake, the kind not likely to be seen among the normal population. Most of these toxic effects have been documented in animal studies only and

Table 10.3: Toxic Effects Attributed to the Consumption of Some Common Food Additives

Food Additive	*Toxic effects*
Antioxidants	
BHA	Carcinogenic in rodents, affecting the stomach
BHT	In rats elevated serum cholesterol levels, fatty liver, and hepatocellular carcinomas
Colours	
Erythrosine	Thyroid tumours
Ponceau 4R	Hepatic cirrhosis and renal problems in rats
Sunset yellow FCF	Body weight reduction and diarrhoea
Tartrazine	Allergic reactions, irritability, restlessness and sleep disturbance
Preservatives	
Benzoates	Urticaria and angioedema
Nitrites	Form cancer-causing nitrosamines, cause allergic reactions, anaphylactic shock
Sulphites	In rats, irritation of stomach and intestinal lining, vomiting reflexes and haemorrhages; while in humans, adverse reactions like urticaria, angioedema and aggravation of asthmatic symptoms
Sweeteners	
Aspartame	Neurobehavioral effects like irritable moods and depression
Polyols	Laxative effect in humans
Saccharin	Swelling of renal glomeruli, growth depression and carcinoma in rats (although the carcinogenicity has been strongly debated)
Sucralose	Alteration in glucose, insulin and glucagon-like peptide-1 levels, mutagenic, shown to alter intestinal microflora
Others	
Monosodium glutamate	Allergic reactions: flushing of face, itching

Source: Adapted by Author from Jain and Mathur 2015.

hence, one can never be sure whether the same effects would be seen in humans as well. Hence, it is important to constantly monitor intake levels of additives in a population and to document any adverse event which is reported.

The suggestion, therefore, is that one should chose foods which have a minimum number of additives. Foods with artificial or synthetic colours and

Natural vs Artificial

Are natural colours and other additives then safe for use? Natural occurring chemicals also have an ADI. Sometimes allergic reactions to natural ingredients can also be seen in people. Natural colours like annatto and carmine have been known to evoke allergic reactions in sensitive individuals. So, the general belief that all that is natural is safe is not true!

class II preservatives should specially be avoided. If you have to choose between two juices, one which has added colour and/or added preservatives and one which does not, you would be wise to select the latter. The label of the food product declares the presence of the additives used in the product. Hence, only properly labelled foods should be selected.

It is important to make sure that each additive is safe at its intended levels of use before it may be added to foods. Although most additives are generally regarded as safe for consumption, some of them (especially food colours and class II preservatives) may cause problems, especially in sensitive individuals. Hence, in general, consumers should try to choose food products with a minimum number of additives. This can be achieved by reading the label of a processed food item before consuming it.

SUMMARY

- A number of food additives are used in food products we consume each day.
- They are added to preserve flavour, blend, thicken, colour foods and give them desirable texture and to increase shelf life.
- Food additives are classified based on their function in food, that is, the purpose for which the additive has been incorporated in the food.
- The various classes of food additives can thus be listed as: antioxidants, preservatives, food colours, food flavours, emulsifiers and stabilisers, sweeteners, anti-caking agents, sequestrants, acid, bases and buffers, antifoaming agents and raising/leavening agents.
- In India, the FSSAI regulates the additives which can be used, the foods to which they can be added and the quantity in which they can be added.
- The additives present in a food have to be declared on the label of foods. They can be identified by an International Numbering System number (INS number).
- Additives can have toxic effects if consumed in excess and hence they should be added only if they are technologically essential.
- Consumers should select foods which have a minimum number of additives and be aware about their allergies or adverse reactions to certain additives.

KEY WORDS

Angioedema: Swelling that occurs just beneath the surface of the skin or mucous membranes.

Carcinogenic: Cancer causing.

Chelate: Heterocyclic compound having a central metallic ion attached by covalent bonds to two or more non-metallic atoms in the same molecule.

Deterioration: Spoilage, decrease in quality.

Hepatocellular carcinomas: A cancer arising from liver cells.

Hepatic cirrhosis: Degenerative disease in which the liver cells are damaged and replaced by scar tissue.

Intestinal microflora: The microorganisms residing in our intestines.

Mutagenic: Causing mutation in genes.

Urticaria: Rash, hives.

EXERCISES

1. Define food additives. Why are these added to foods?
2. What do you understand by INS number? Why are additives given this number?
3. What are antioxidants? Name any two antioxidants that can be added to edible oil in India.
4. Separate the following into class I and II of preservatives: salt, propionates, nitrites, sugar, spices, sodium benzoate, vinegar and sulphur dioxide.
5. Select two brands of table-top intense sweeteners sold in India and identify which artificial sweetener they contain.
6. Which food additive can be added to salt to make it 'free flowing'?
7. Why should a consumer try to select food products with a minimum number of additives?
8. Name three additives which may pose a threat to your health. Elaborate on the toxic effects which have been attributed to them.

ACTIVITY

Visit your local grocery store or supermarket and note down, from the label, the ingredients present in processed food items like jam, tomato sauce, biscuits, bread, soup powder, health drinks (like Bournvita, Horlicks, etc.), cheese, cheese spread, butter, breakfast cereals, sherbets, squashes, pickles, chocolates and canned fruits, vegetables and meat products. Make a table of items which are ingredients and those which are additives. Try to identify the type of additives using the INS numbers.

REFERENCES

Burrows, A., 'Palette of Our Palates: A Brief History of Food Coloring and Its Regulation', *Comprehensive Reviews in Food Science and Food Safety* 8 (4), 2009, pp. 394–408.

Codex, 'General Standard for Food Additives', CODEX STAN 192-1995, Codex Alimentarius International Food Standards, FAO/WHO, Available at http://www.fao.org/fao-who-codexalimentarius/standards/gsfa/en/ (accessed 16 June 2016).

FSSAI, 'Notice for Operationalization of Standards of Food Additives for Use in Various Food Categories', 2015, Available at http://www.fssai.gov.in/Portals/0/Pdf/Notice_Operationalization_Food_Additives_standards.pdf (accessed 12 May 2016).

Jain, A., and P. Mathur, 'Evaluating Hazards Posed by Additives in Food: A Review of Studies Adopting a Risk Assessment Approach', *Current Research in Nutrition and Food Science* 3 (3), 2015, pp. 243–55.

Mahindru, S. N., *Food Additives—Characteristics, Detection and Estimation*, New Delhi: APH Publishing Corporation, 2008.

ONLINE SOURCES

Combined Compendium of Food Additive Specifications, JECFA, FAO. This database provides the most recent specifications for food additives evaluated by JECFA. Each food additive can be searched for by name or INS number. Available at http://www.fao.org/food/food-safety-quality/scientific-advice/jecfa/jecfa-additives/en/ (accessed 15 June 2016).

Comprehensive Listing of Food Additives in Ascending Order of E Number, Available at https://www.food.gov.uk/science/additives/enumberlist (accessed 15 April 2018).

Comprehensive Listing of Food Additives in Ascending Order of INS Number, Available at http://www.fao.org/tempref/codex/Meetings/CCFAC/CCFAC31/INS_e.pdf (accessed 15 April 2018).

What are Food Additives? European Food Information Council, Available at https://www.youtube.com/watch?v=Hy3-QHhzvPE (accessed 15 April 2018).

11

FOOD ADULTERATION

HIGHLIGHTS

- Definition and extent of problem
- Common adulterants
- Harmful effects of adulterants
- Methods for detection
- Prevention and control

Wholesome food is important for providing nourishment to the body and for the maintenance of good health. Food of poor quality, on the other hand, may do more harm than good. Adulteration of food has been prevalent in society ever since food has been commercially traded. Unscrupulous traders increased their profit margins by intentionally adding cheap filler materials to increase the bulk of the produce or by artificially masking poor quality with the help of chemical colourants and preservatives. So, for instance, the colour of a not so bright red chilli powder would be enhanced with the addition of an artificial dye or the shelf life of a perishable commodity like milk would be extended by adding a neutraliser of acidity or a preservative. The problem of adulteration exists even today in spite of better facilities for storage and transport, and advanced food preservation and processing technology. In India, it is a persistent problem which often makes news headlines.

This chapter describes in detail the profile of food adulteration, especially in India, foods commonly adulterated, the commonly used adulterants as well as newer forms of adulteration. The harmful effects of various adulterants on human health and on the economy have been discussed to understand the implications of consuming adulterated food. Ways and means of controlling the problem of adulteration and some simple tests which can be performed for the detection of common adulterants have been outlined.

DEFINITION AND EXTENT OF PROBLEM

Under the earlier Prevention of Food Adulteration Act of 1955, food adulteration was defined as 'not only the intentional addition or substitution or abstraction of substances which adversely affect the nature, substance and quality of foods, but also their incidental contamination during the period of growth, harvesting, storage, processing, transportation and distribution'. So, intentionally adding things to a food which were not supposed to be added (like water to milk), or substituting ingredients with something inferior (like coloured starch instead of turmeric powder), or abstracting, that is, removing something from a food (like cream from milk or essential oil from spices) were all considered adulteration. Unintentional contamination was also considered to be adulteration. The definition has undergone change in the new Act of 2006 with different components being spelt out separately (see Box 11.1). Earlier, it was all included under the broad umbrella term of 'adulteration' and now adulterants, contaminants and extraneous matter are being defined separately to bring out the subtle differences.

Box 11.1: Definitions of Terms related to Unsafe Food

According to the Food Safety and Standards Act, 2006 the terms related to the problem of adulteration and unsafe food have been defined as follows:

An **adulterant** is defined as 'any material which is or could be employed for making the food unsafe or sub-standard or misbranded or containing extraneous matter'.

A **contaminant** means 'any substance, whether or not added to food, but which is present in such food as a result of the production (including operations carried out in crop husbandry, animal husbandry or veterinary medicine), manufacture, processing, preparation, treatment, packing, packaging, transport or holding of such food or as a result of environmental contamination and does not include insect fragments, rodent hairs and other extraneous matter'.

Extraneous matter, on the other hand, means 'any matter contained in an article of food which may be carried from the raw materials, packaging materials or process systems used for its manufacture or which is added to it, but such matter does not render such article of food unsafe'.

Misbranding of food has been separately spelt as any article of food which:

- has misleading or deceptive claims on its label, advertisement; for example, a product claims to be high in fibre but has very little fibre;
- is being sold under a name which belongs to another food; for instance, hydrogenated vegetable fat being sold as ghee;
- is being sold under the name of a fictitious company or individual, which is mostly done when the producer does not want to get caught in case he is breaking the law;
- is being sold as a product of a place or country when it actually is not from there; for instance, olive oil made from olives grown in India is being claimed as olive oil from Italy;
- is an imitation of or substitute for another similar article of food under the name of which it is being sold, and resembles that food in a manner which is likely to deceive the consumers. In such cases, usually the labelling on the packet is similar to the packaging of a known brand so that the consumer is fooled into picking up this product mistaking it for the original product of better quality.. One may come across a number of these products in

markets of small towns or those catering to the low-income group where the manufacturer is confident that the consumer will not be very vigilant in reading labels carefully. Packets of salt labelled 'Toto' written in a style which resembles 'Tata' or wheat flour (*atta*) labelled 'Captain Cool' instead of 'Captain Cook' have been seen in such markets.

- is being sold with false or misleading claims on the label regarding the presence of certain ingredients or substances in the food, like 'this product has pistachios' and actually only an artificial flavour of pistachios has been added instead of real pistachios.
- has any food additive like artificial flavouring, colouring or chemical preservative without declaring it on the label in a manner stipulated under the FSSAI. For instance, one of the leading brands of instant noodles had been hauled up to court for not declaring on their label that their product contained monosodium glutamate (MSG), a flavour enhancer.
- has been offered for sale as a product for special dietary uses, but does not provide on its label the information for the consumer about its special dietary properties or content of special nutrients which make the product suitable for the special dietary use. Even if the product does contain the nutrients or special substances within the limits as specified under the Act, it would be considered misbranding.

Unsafe food, on the other hand, has been defined as 'an article of food whose nature, substance or quality is so affected as to render it injurious to health'. This would include foods which:

- contain any poisonous or deleterious substance in the packaging or food itself, like harmful chemicals leaching into the food from plastic packaging;
- contain any filthy, putrid, rotten, decomposed or diseased animal substance or vegetable substance;
- have been processed unhygienically and hence, or otherwise, may contain any harmful substance, like bacterial or fungal toxins;
- have been substituted wholly or in part with inferior or cheaper substances, like husk, starch or saw dust added to spice powders or starch to milk powder;
- contain substances which have been added to the food directly or as ingredients which are not permitted, like preservatives to milk;
- have had any of the natural constituents abstracted completely or in part; for instance, fat removed from milk or essential oils removed from spices;
- have been flavoured, coloured, processed (like powdered or polished or coated) so as to conceal the true quality in an attempt to make the food appear better than it actually is, like vegetables, spice powders with artificial colour;
- contain colouring matter or preservatives other than that specified. There is a list of permitted artificial colours and preservatives which can be added to specified foods. If any unpermitted colour or preservative is added, the food becomes unsafe for consumption;

- are infected or infested with worms, weevils or insects, often seen in cereals and pulse grains and flour;
- have been prepared, packed or kept under insanitary conditions, and hence, have microbial counts higher than permissible or have pathogenic microbes;
- are misbranded or sub-standard or contain extraneous matter;
- contain pesticides or other contaminants in excess of quantities specified by regulations.

Extent of the Problem

Adulteration is not a problem unique to India. Poor quality, substandard, misbranded food is sold all over the world. The difference lies in the fact that the regulation of laws and the monitoring is much more effective in developed nations than in developing economies.

In India, the data on country-wide adulteration is available from the food testing laboratories of the FSSAI, which were earlier under the Prevention of Food Adulteration Act (PFA). According to these official reports, the overall extent of food adulteration in India has been gradually diminishing from 31 per cent in the 1960s to around 10 per cent in the 1990s. However, the FSSAI annual report (2014–15) pegged adulteration at around 19 per cent. That means nearly one out of five food samples failed quality tests in India.

Adulteration in India is widespread, covering all states. The FSSAI data helps us to see how the extent and type of adulteration varies across different states. The foods likely to be adulterated more may also depend on the region. Filler substances and cheaper alternatives which are readily available in the region are usually the most common type of adulterant. So, the more expensive oils of a particular area, like safflower, rice bran or groundnut oil will be adulterated with oils which are cheap and readily available in that area, like castor oil or cottonseed oil. Madhya Pradesh, Maharashtra, Uttar Pradesh and Tamil Nadu were found to have the largest samples of food items violating safety standard norms.

Figure 11.1: Foods Most Likely to be Adulterated

- Foods which are expensive, like edible oils, spices, etc.
- Foods which sell more, like wheat flour, oil, etc.
- Foods which are perishable, like milk and milk products
- Foods sold loose, like milk, spices, etc.
- Foods in which it is easy to mix adulterant, like those in the form of powder, paste or mince

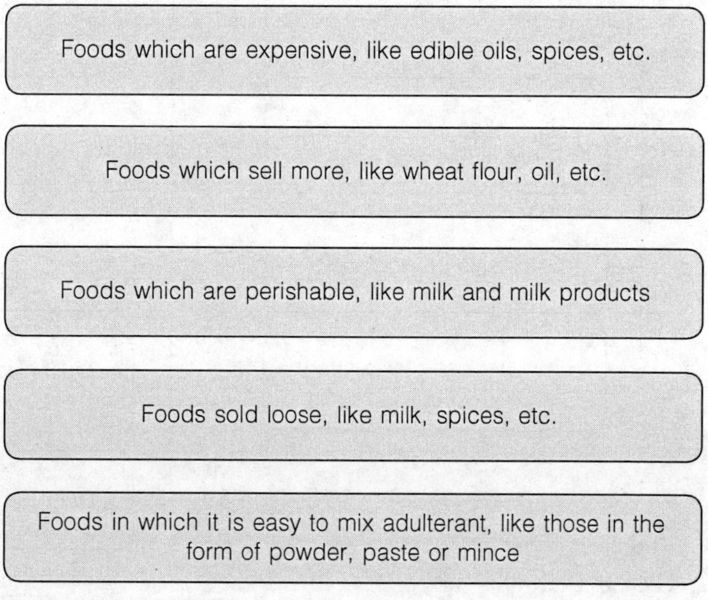

Source: Drawn by Author.

Any commodity that is either expensive or sells more is a target for adulteration (see Figure 11.1). Surveys on the current trends in food adulteration reveal that adulteration of milk and milk products, edible oils and fats and spices is most common. This is because these foods are expensive and easy to adulterate. Foods which are in a powder, minced or paste form are also more likely to be adulterated, as it is more difficult for the naked eye to detect adulteration in these foodstuffs. For instance, when buying minced mutton, it is difficult to tell whether the goat meat has been mixed with meat from other animals, or similarly whether sawdust dyed green has been added to coriander powder.

Adulteration of foods sold loose by the retailer is also more common as compared to packaged foods. This is simply because packages carry the name and address of the manufacturer or distributor and they can easily be traced if the regulatory authorities find their foodstuff to be substandard. On the other hand, a trader selling foodstuff like oil, wheat flour, sugar, spices and tea in loose form can easily adulterate them and, if caught, shift the blame on the manufacturer or distributor. Manufacturers should discourage their products from being sold loose and their packaging should also be tamper-proof. Consumers, on the other hand, should avoid buying foodstuff sold loose even though these are cheaper.

Besides intentional addition of sub-standard or harmful substances, food can also become unsafe if good agricultural or animal husbandry practices are not followed (see Figure 11.2). As discussed in earlier chapters, food can become contaminated with pesticide residues, veterinary

Figure 11.2: How Food Gets Contaminated or Becomes Unsafe for Consumption

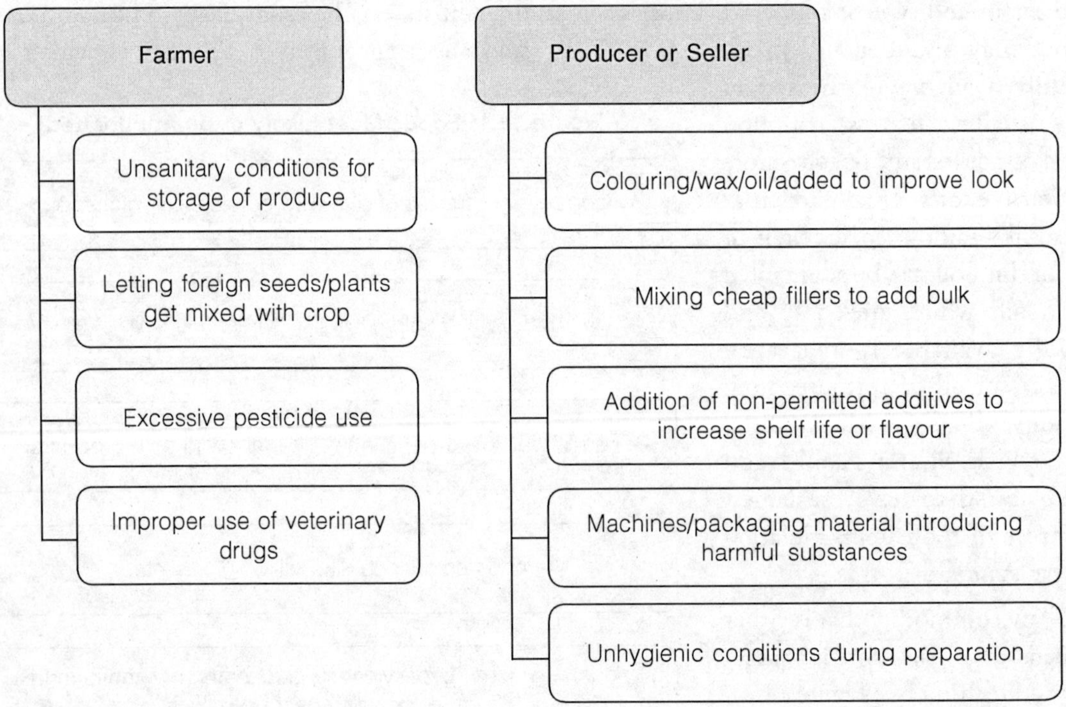

Source: Drawn by Author.

drug residues and other chemicals depending upon the processing as well as storage and transport conditions. In some cases, farmers may accidently harvest toxic weeds and other plants which look like the crop, a mistake often made while harvesting mustard. Argemone seeds grow like a weed alongside and resemble mustard seeds. Insanitary conditions during handling and processing of food can also lead to microbial contamination and the food becoming unfit for human consumption. Machines can also introduce foreign substances in food; for example, the presence of iron fillings from iron rollers in tea is a common physical hazard introduced during processing.

Inappropriate storage and transportation conditions may also contaminate the food; for instance, commodities like milk and milk products, frozen foods, etc. need to be stored and transported at low temperatures. If the cold chain is broken at any time from the producer to the consumer, the food is likely to get spoiled. In addition, the foodstuff also needs to be protected from pests like rats and insects and hence, need to be packaged properly.

COMMON ADULTERANTS

Adulterants have been detected in almost all kinds of foods—food grains and pulses, edible oils and fats, spices, milk and milk products, meat and meat products, beverages (both alcoholic and non-alcoholic), tea, coffee, sweetening agents like sugar, honey, jaggery and items made from these like *mithai*. As the main motive behind adulteration is economic gain, the adulterant used would have to be cheap and readily available. Sometimes, because of ignorance, the trader may not realise that the adulterant he is using could be injurious to the health of consumers. However, sometimes, greed simply wins over any concern that one human being should have for another.

It cannot be denied that many cases of adulteration occur simply due to the negligence and lack of awareness on the part of manufacturers, distributors or retailers. As such, grain lying exposed to rodents and insects in warehouses can get contaminated by faeces and insect eggs/larvae merely due to negligence, rather than any profiteering motive. Similarly, if the ambient moisture level is not controlled, the food grain may absorb excess moisture, making conditions ideal for fungal growth. These unintentional contaminants make food unsafe. Even if the foods do not have any toxic substance in them, just by not meeting any of the quality standards set down by regulatory authorities like the FSSAI, AGMARK or BIS, the product can be declared unfit for consumption. So, for instance, poor processing, packaging and/or storage may result in the product picking up moisture. High moisture levels may encourage growth of microbes and hence spoilage.

Table 11.1 presents the kinds of adulterants which have been detected in different food groups. The table has been compiled using the various surveys which have been carried out in various parts of India and also in other countries of the world. However, this is not to say that these are the only adulterants which can be used. It has been seen that with time, the type of adulterants has also changed. Newer adulterants keep getting added to the list with better availability of chemicals and also ingenuity on the part of the adulterator.

Table 11.1: Variety of Adulterants which have been Detected in Foods

Food group	*Food item*	*Intentionally added adulterant*	*Unintentional contaminant/ extraneous matter*
Cereals and Pulses and their products	Rice, wheat	Stones, grit, straw	Pesticide residues, fungal toxins, dirt, pest droppings and hair, insect infestation
	Flour (*atta, maida*)	Foreign starch, chalk powder	Pesticide residues, fungal toxins, dirt, pest droppings and hair, insect infestation
	Semolina (*suji*)	Sand	Iron filings, dirt, pest droppings and hair, insect infestation
	Pulses	Foreign pulses like *Lathyrus sativus* (*kesari dal*), *Vicia sativa, Lens esculenta*, artificial colours, stones, oil, talc	Pesticide residues, fungal toxins, dirt, pest droppings and hair, insect infestation
	Besan, flour of other pulses, products made from these like *mithai* or *namkeen* (savouries)	Foreign starch, flour of foreign pulses especially *kesari dal*, non-permitted colours, permitted colour more than prescribed limit, aluminium foil	Pesticide residues, fungal toxins, dirt, pest droppings and hair, insect infestation
Milk and milk products	Milk	Water, formalin, boric acid, neutralisers like sodium bicarbonate, caustic soda, urea, water, sugar, starch, foreign fat, removal of fat	Antibiotic residues, pesticide residues
	Milk powder	sugar, starch, removal of fat	Pesticide residues
	Ghee	Hydrogenated vegetable oil (*Vanaspati*), animal body fat, yellow colour	Pesticide residues
	Butter	Artificial non-permitted colours	Pesticide residues
	Mithai	Starch, non-permitted colours, permitted colours more than prescribed limit, aluminium foil	Microbes and their toxins
Edible oils and fats	Vegetable oils	Cheaper edible (cotton seed, castor) or inedible oils (mineral oil, argemone oil), colour	Pesticide residues, fungal toxins (aflatoxin)
	Hydrogenated fat	Colour, cheaper oils, animal body fat	Nickel

(*Contd*)

(*Contd*)

Food group	*Food item*	*Intentionally added adulterant*	*Unintentional contaminant/ extraneous matter*
Spices (whole and powdered)	Whole spices like cardamom, cloves	Essential oil abstracted, artificial colour	Pesticide residues
	Black pepper	Papaya seeds, mineral oil coating	Pesticide residues
	Asafoetida (*hing*)	Foreign resin	–
	Spice powders	Artificial colours (metanil yellow, lead chromate, Sudan dyes, etc.), starch, powdered husk/bran	Pesticide residues, heavy metals
Beverages	Tea leaves/powder	Foreign leaves, exhausted leaves, husk, straw, artificial colours	Iron filings
	Coffee powder	Chicory, date or tamarind seed powder, starch, artificial colours	Fungal toxin (ochratoxin)
	Soft drinks	Saccharin, dulcin, brominated vegetable oils, non-permitted colours, excess permitted colours	Pesticide residues
Sweetening agents	Sugar	Starch, pebbles	Dirt
	Honey	Sugar	Antibiotic and pesticide residues

Source: Drawn by Author.

In **milk**, the most widely used adulterant is water. Milk being sold loose by vendors is most easily adulterated in this manner. However, there have also been several reports of delivery personnel removing part of the milk from plastic pouches of known brands and then making up the volume with water and resealing the pack. Such addition of water is very easily detected by measuring the specific gravity or relative density of the milk. However, to avoid detection, the vendors increase the specific gravity of diluted milk by adding sugar, starch or urea. Addition of preservatives like formalin, boric acid, hydrogen peroxide and neutralisers like sodium bicarbonate and caustic soda is also prevalent to increase the shelf life of the milk. This is especially done in summer months, when milk spoils easily, and by vendors who have to transport the milk over long distances. In recent years, there have been media reports of production of synthetic milk using a combination of washing detergent, urea, vegetable oil and then adulteration of milk by addition of this synthetic milk. Contaminants usually found in milk are pesticide residues (from pesticides sprayed in cattle sheds), antibiotic residues (from medications given to the cattle) and aflatoxin (from aflatoxin-contaminated feed given to the cattle).

Expensive **edible oils** are usually adulterated with cheaper options of edible or inedible oils like castor oil, mineral oil, argemone oil, palmolein and cottonseed oil. *Ghee* is usually adulterated with *vanaspati* or hydrogenated oils. *Argemone mexicana* grows wild and can be seen in fields of mustard. If harvested together, they may accidently contaminate the mustard oil. However, intentional adulteration has also been reported. Lard, a cheaply available animal body fat, may also be added. Contaminants which have been detected in oils are pesticide residues (from the pesticides which had been sprayed on the oilseed crops before harvesting) and aflatoxin, especially in unrefined groundnut oil (from use of poor quality, fungus-infested groundnuts). The process of refining the oil destroys the aflatoxin and hence, it is safer to consume refined oils.

Cheaper agricultural produce like wheat starch, *jowar*, rice, corn and arrowroot starch are used in a number of expensive foods like ground **spices** (red chilli powder, turmeric, coriander powder, *garam masala* etc.). The starch, which is white in colour, is usually dyed to the colour of the spice to which it is being added. Sometimes, essential oils are extracted from expensive spices like cloves and the exhausted spice is sold as such. Cinnamon bark may be mixed with the bark of another similar looking tree, asafoetida may be mixed with a foreign resin, seeds of black pepper may be mixed with papaya seeds and mustard seeds may be mixed with argemone seeds, which look similar.

Colour seems to be an adulterant which is added to a large variety of foods such as non-alcoholic beverages, confectionery, sweets and savouries, and even to fresh fruits and vegetables to improve their appeal to the consumer. Colours other than the ones prescribed by law are referred to as non-permitted colours. The most commonly used non-permitted synthetic colours detected in various surveys are Orange II, Sudan dyes, Metanil Yellow, Auramine, Malachite Green and Rhodamine B. **Aluminium foils** may be used instead of silver foils in several products like sweets (*mithai*) and *paan*. In addition, **extraneous matter** like sand, husk, sawdust, wood pieces, stones, straw, etc. have also been used as adulterants, especially in cereals and pulses to increase the bulk. Similar-looking foreign **pulse** grains may be used to adulterate popular, but expensive *toor* or *arhar dal*. **Metal** adulterants include iron filings (in *suji* coming from the grinders and in tea coming from the rollers) and nickel (added as a catalyst during production of *vanaspati*), which are present mainly as a result of poor processing techniques. Intense or **artificial sweeteners** may be added in excess to non-alcoholic beverages or to foods in which they are not permitted, like confectionery and sweets. Non-permitted sweeteners like dulcin and several other chemicals like urea, acetic acid, sodium hydroxide and sodium bicarbonate continue to be problematic.

Why is Milk the Most Adulterated Commodity?

Milk is consumed daily by most families and hence, the volume traded and profit margins are high for traders who adulterate. Water is miscible in milk and hence, to increase the volume of this commodity, the cheapest and easiest option is to add water. You may have observed at home that if milk is not boiled and refrigerated, it tends to spoil faster. This is because milk normally has some bacteria in it. When milk is at room temperature, these bacteria multiply, producing acid in the process. When too much acid accumulates, the milk curdles on heating. Milk vendors very commonly add chemicals like sodium bicarbonate to neutralise this developed acidity in the milk and thus increase its shelf life.

Adulteration was earlier done at a small scale by individuals who wanted to make a quick buck or simply wanted to fool the customer by masking the poor quality of their produce. Adding water to milk was, perhaps, the simplest form of adulteration, where the milk vendor wanted to increase the quantity of milk he had available to sell. Newer types of adulterants are being used today and the techniques used for adulteration are also becoming more complex, indicating the involvement of an organised network. Use of ultramarine blue, a fabric whitener, to mask insect infestation in dry ginger was detected in Hyderabad. Urea is added to improve the texture of puffed rice, and fresh fruits are being coloured and sweetened artificially to improve their sale. Growth promoters being injected into plants to produce oversized vegetables has also been reported, though not substantiated. Addition of melamine to milk and infant milk formula in China is another example of an adulterant never used before. This scandal sent shockwaves throughout the world in 2008. The manufacturers were trying to mask the dilution of milk by adding melamine which gave the impression of a higher protein value when tested. Thousands of babies were reportedly hospitalised, with some of them developing kidney stones.

> 'Pesticides in your soft drink bottle', ran the headlines in all national dailies in 2003. The Centre for Science and Environment reported the presence of pesticides beyond permissible levels in popular soft drinks brands. The source for the contamination was identified to be the water used for the production of the soft drink. It was negligence on the part of the manufacturer, who failed to ensure that all ingredients used were contaminant-free.

Focus is also now more on unintentional contaminants like pesticide and veterinary drug residues which are increasingly being detected because of the sophisticated analytical equipment available. Also, a number of private food-testing laboratories and non-government organisations working in the field of food safety and quality control have highlighted the new hazards lurking in our foods.

HARMFUL EFFECTS OF ADULTERANTS

In a developing country like ours, food-borne diseases continue to be an important cause of illness and death. The hazards posed by biological (microbial) and chemical contaminants (pesticides, veterinary drug residues, heavy metals, etc.) in food have been discussed in earlier chapters. So what are the harmful effects of some of the intentionally added adulterants?

Water added as an adulterant to foods like milk may not present a hazard to health unless the water used is contaminated. However, it decreases the nutritive value of milk and products made from it due to the dilution. So, one glass of diluted milk will not give as much of protein, calcium and vitamins as a glass of pure milk.

> An outbreak of **Epidemic dropsy** was first documented in Calcutta in 1877 and attributed to the consumption of mustard oil adulterated with argemone oil. Outbreaks of epidemic dropsy have been reported from Itarsi, Madhya Pradesh, Delhi, Rajasthan and Andhra Pradesh. A massive outbreak of the disease was reported in Delhi in 1998, which resulted in several deaths. It resulted in the authorities clamping down on loosely sold oil.

Excess moisture content of food decreases shelf life and hence, can be a problem. Similarly, **filler adulterants** like starch, powdered husk/bran, chalk powder may not pose a serious hazard except for decrease in nutritional value of the food. However, if these have been artificially coloured using **non-permitted colours** or permitted colours in excess, they can pose a serious health hazard (see Table 11.2). Chemicals like urea, sodium carbonate (washing soda, soda), sodium hydroxide (caustic soda), formaldehyde and hydrogen peroxide added to increase the shelf life of milk can damage the intestinal lining by irritating it.

Use of the pulse *Lathyrus sativus* (***khesari dal***) to adulterate lentils (*masoor*) or *toor dal* or *besan* can prove to be harmful. This pulse has a toxic factor (β oxalyl diamino propionic acid), which if consumed in large amounts, causes the crippling disease lathyrism. The disease begins with stiffness and pain in the legs, knee and ankle joints. The patient gradually becomes crippled, with paralysis of the lower limbs setting in. Toxic weeds being inadvertently mixed with the food grains can also result in serious problems. Mustard and other vegetable oils have been found to be adulterated with argemone oil, which is very toxic and has often led to widespread poisoning outbreaks. *Argemonemexicana* seeds resemble mustard seeds but have toxic alkaloids like sanguinarine and dihydrosanguinarine. The resulting condition is characterised by oedema, gastrointestinal disturbances, increased permeability of blood vessels, glaucoma, respiratory symptoms and congestive heart failure. Mineral oil (liquid paraffin) and castor oil, **cheap inedible oils** used as adulterants, may have a laxative effect with nausea and vomiting. They may damage the intestine if consumed in excessive amounts or for a long period of time. Prolonged intake may also interfere with the absorption of fat-soluble vitamins like vitamins A, D, E and K. **Tricresyl phosphate** (TCP) is a chemical used as a plasticiser in various industries as well as like an additive to turbine engine oil. It is a neurotoxin. In 1959, it was used as an adulterant in cooking oil in Morocco and in 1969 in Fiji, with disastrous consequences. Outbreaks of tricresyl phosphate poisoning have also been reported in India from Kolkata in which about 600 people were affected with paralysis of the hands and feet due to consumption of rapeseed oil adulterated with tricresyl phosphate. Apparently the tanker used to transport the cooking oil had earlier been used to transport engine oil containing TCP. Outbreaks have also been reported from other parts of West Bengal and Raipur, Chhattisgarh.

> In May 1982, the infamous Toxic Oil Syndrome (TOS) in Spain resulted in 25,000 people reporting ill and nearly 2.5 per cent of them dying. The cause of the outbreak was identified as ingestion of adulterated oil containing various proportions of rapeseed oil denatured with aniline. Pentachlorophenol was also detected in the oils which, along with anilides, contributed to the toxic effect seen.

Colouring matter used in foods can be harmful if used in excess. Even permitted food colours have a safe limit beyond which they should not be consumed. People indulging in adulteration are usually illiterate or ignorant. Hence, they do not understand that adding too much colour is neither necessary nor desirable from the consumers' point of view as well. Bright orange jalebis are, after all, not more appetising than a light shade of orange! Sometimes, they may use industrial dyes like malachite green, metanil yellow, orange II, auramine, rhodamine B and Sudan dyes also for colouring foods as these are readily available in cheap bulk packs. They do not realise that these can be very toxic. Metanil yellow has been reported to cause symptoms of giddiness, weakness, vomiting and cyanosis. The people who developed these symptoms had eaten *laddoo* coloured with this dye. In another incident, *biryani* coloured with metanil yellow caused similar symptoms two to four hours after consumption. Lead chromate added as a colourant to chilli powder caused lead poisoning among Gurkha soldiers with symptoms of stomach ache, nausea, constipation and anaemia.

Harmful effects of different adulterants have been elaborated in Table 11.3. The hazards of consuming food laced with contaminants or additives added in excess have already been discussed in previous chapters.

Table 11.2: Toxic Effects of Some Intentionally Added Adulterants

Food stuff	*Adulterant*	*Toxicity*
Milk	Formalin, hydrogen peroxide, neutralisers	Irritation and corrosion of the gastrointestinal tract lining
Edible oil	Mineral oil, castor oil	Laxative action, damage to gastrointestinal lining, decreased absorption of fat-soluble vitamins, nausea, vomiting
	Machine or engine oil	Nerve damage, paralysis, death
	Argemone oil	Epidemic dropsy
	Hydrogenated fat	The trans fatty acids have been implicated in increasing the risk of heart disease
Pulses and their products	*Kesari dal*	Nerve damage
Processed foods and beverages, spices	Non-permitted colours	Can be mutagenic and cancer-causing
	Orange II	Retardation of growth, affects the proper functioning of vital organs like the liver, kidney, heart, spleen, lungs, bones and the immune system
	Metanil yellow	Injurious to the stomach, ileum, rectum, liver, kidney, ovary and testis
	Lead chromate	Ingestion can lead to abdominal pain and spasms, nausea, vomiting and headaches, and even death

Source: Drawn by Author.

Economic Loss

Although the trader indulges in adulteration for economic gain, he does not realise the implications of adulteration on the economy of the country and on trade. In the long run, everyone loses. The trader, if caught, may face imprisonment and a fine depending on the degree of harm caused to the consumer. He loses face in the market—the consumer will find it hard to trust his products again. Big companies have been known to lose a huge market share if the media gets hold of any report of their product being sub-standard in any way. You may recall the case of a multinational company which suffered huge financial losses because their instant noodles were detected with lead levels beyond permissible limits and a flavour enhancer, monosodium glutamate, which according to the label, had not been added. Noodles worth millions of rupees had to be recalled, their sale was banned and the company had to work very hard to re-launch the product and win consumer confidence. In these times of open markets and trade liberalisation, it is important to understand that there is no place for substandard products, especially if they can be a threat to human health. Traders can be blacklisted and lose their livelihood if found to be indulging in adulteration.

Economic loss due to rejection of export-oriented food products not only damages the trader's reputation but also that of the exporting country. Every year, millions of rupees worth of fruit, spices, meat, shellfish, fish and their products are returned by the importing countries because they do not match up to the rigorous quality standards these countries demand. By the time the food produce comes back to India, most of it is unfit for human consumption because of spoilage. The rest finds its way into local markets sometimes after repackaging!

As we have seen, consuming unsafe food leads to illness, disability and even death. So, the losses involve not just the value of the food rendered unfit for consumption as a result of the adulteration, but also the cost of treating people who have fallen sick or been disabled after consuming the adulterated food. Providing good-quality food is thus of considerable importance not just for public health, but also for the national economy. Spreading awareness among manufacturers and traders about the serious health consequences of adulteration, and among consumers about the importance of being vigilant, is essential for rooting out the menace of adulteration.

METHODS FOR DETECTION

After learning about the different types of adulterants that may be present in our foods and their ill-effects on our health, as a consumer we should be aware of what to do in order to detect if these adulterants are present in the food we purchase daily. In fact, the FSSAI has come out with a manual to help the consumer check for adulterants. Presented here are some tests which can be done at home without the use of chemicals (see Table 11.3). Some others need simple chemicals which are available in the form of commercial kits prepared by various NGOs. Some others can easily be performed in a simple school or college laboratory (see Table 11.4).

The state food authorities under the FSSAI pick up samples for analysis in their laboratories. There is a provision for the public to submit food products for testing at these laboratories. As a consumer, you can also send samples to private laboratories for testing. However, this kind of testing has a fee attached to it.

PREVENTION AND CONTROL

Regulatory provisions are in place in the country to tackle the problem of adulteration. Over the years, although the extent of adulteration has gone down, consumers do encounter adulterated

Table 11.3: Simple Tests for Adulteration which do not Require Chemicals

Food	*Adulterant*	*Procedure*	*Observation*
Milk	Water	Immerse a lactometer in milk kept in a deep vessel to measure the specific gravity	Values lower than 1.028–1.032 indicate added water.
	Spoilt milk with developed acidity	Place a test tube containing 5 ml of the milk sample in a boiling water bath and hold for about five minutes. Remove the tube and rotate in an almost horizontal position.	Formation of clots is indicative of developed acidity in the milk due to microbial spoilage. Such milk is unsuitable for consumption.
Tea, *suji*	Iron filings	Move a magnet over the tea/ *suji* spread out on a paper	Magnet attracts the iron filings and they stick to the magnet.
Tea	Artificial colour	Put the tea leaves on a moistened blotting paper.	Artificially dyed tea will impart colour to the moistened blotting paper immediately.
Coffee	Chicory	Sprinkle coffee powder on the surface of water in a glass.	Coffee floats while chicory starts sinking, leaving a trail of colour, due to large amount of caramel.
Pulses, whole and split	*Khesari dal*	Examine the grains of the pulse carefully.	*Khesari dal* is wedge shaped, with a slant on one side and a square face on the other side.
Mustard seeds	Argemone seeds	Examine the seeds under a magnifying glass. Press to crack the seeds.	Argemone seeds have a rough surface with a little tail at one end. Mustard seeds are smooth. Upon pressing, mustard seeds are yellow inside while argemone seeds are white.
Black pepper whole	Papaya seed	Examine the seeds carefully.	Papaya seeds are comparatively shrunken, oval and greenish brown to brownish-black in colour.
Honey	Sugar solution	Dip a cotton wick in the honey and light it.	If the honey is pure, it will burn smoothly. If sugar dissolved in water has been added, then the wick will burn with a crackling sound.

Source: Adapted by Author from FSSAI 2012.

Table 11.4: Simple Tests Requiring Chemicals to Detect Adulteration

Adulterant	*Food*	*Procedure*	*Observation*
Starch	Powdered spices, milk, milk powder, paneer, milk-based *mithai*	Mix food sample in test tube with water, add a few drops of iodine solution.	Blue-black colour indicates the presence of starch.

(*Contd*)

(*Contd*)

Adulterant	*Food*	*Procedure*	*Observation*
Neutralisers like carbonates	Milk, milk powder	To about 5 ml of milk in a test tube, add 5 ml of alcohol and a few drops of rosalic acid solution and mix the contents of the test tube.	A rose-red colour is obtained in the presence of a carbonate whereas pure milk shows only a brownish colouration.
Hydrogenated fat (*Vanaspati*)	*Ghee*, butter	To one teaspoon-full of completely melted sample, add 5 ml concentrated hydrochloric acid. Shake for 5 minutes, add a pinch of sugar or furfural.	Appearance of pink colour in the acid layer indicates added *vanaspati*.
Khesari dal	Pulse, *besan* and its products	Put the powdered sample in dilute hydrochloric acid.	Pink colour develops, indicating the presence of *khesari dal*.
Metanil yellow	Sweetmeats, ice cream and beverages, rice preparations, pulses, spices	Extract colour with lukewarm water from food samples and add a few drops of concentrated hydrochloric acid.	A magenta colour indicates the presence of metanil yellow.
Aluminium foil	Silver foil	To metal foil, add two drops of concentrated nitric acid in a test tube.	The silver foil will completely dissolve, whereas the aluminium foil remains undissolved.

Source: Adapted by Author from FSSAI 2012.

food samples. Have you ever seen vegetables or fruits which have been artificially dyed? If not, then you may have overheard your family elders complain about how milk being delivered to your home by the milk vendor is too diluted. The common consumer in India still has to be careful about which food product to buy for the fear of it being a substandard or unsafe product. What then can be done to bring assurance to the minds of the people of this country that the food they eat is safe and wholesome?

The regulatory authorities need to implement the laws which safeguard the quality of foods more effectively. The unscrupulous trader should not feel that he can get away with putting the lives of people at risk. The government should declare zero tolerance for the sale of unsafe food. For this, consumer groups and NGOs working in this area as well as associations of food service providers should join hands and work together towards improving the food safety scenario.

Food fraud costs the global food industry up to $40 billion every year! Hence, different ways of ensuring food traceability are increasingly being used by big food companies. **Blockchain traceability** is a way that is currently in vogue. Blockchain enables food retailers to obtain data from a single receipt, including suppliers, details on how and where food was grown, and who inspected it. All transactions are recorded digitally in a ledger which is accessible, yet secure and tamper-proof.

Food traceability (see Box 11.2) is becoming vital for better managing risks related to food hazards. The European Union's desire to protect and/or to promote production of food and agricultural products from specific regions (such as those with a reputation for high quality) have prompted food labelling policies such as protected designation of origin (PDO), protected geographical indication (PGI) and country-of-origin labelling (COOL). This is important when dealing with misbranding and claiming that a food item is from a particular place when actually it is not. Incidences of food-borne disease outbreaks like bovine spongiform encephalopathy (BSE), threats of bioterrorism and concerns regarding other issues of food safety, trade policy and access to the export market have prompted many countries to consider traceability as a part of regulatory legislation.

Box 11.2: Importance of Food Traceability

'Being able to ascertain the origin of products, ingredients and their attributes, from the farm through food processing to retail, food service and the consumer' is called food traceability. At a time when the global food supply chain is growing, traceability of foods has become increasingly important, especially from the point of view of ensuring food safety and building consumer confidence. Traceability enables corrective action to be implemented quickly and effectively when something goes wrong. In case of a problem with any food product, it becomes easier to recall the product from the market by using special coding or markers. This ensures easy identification of where all the defective products have been sent for sale, enabling easier recall. It is one of the best risk management methods in use today. To explain with the help of an example, if a food like frozen nuggets of chicken were found to have a pathogenic strain of bacteria, it would necessitate the recall of all nuggets of that batch. It would also be important to track which farms the chickens came from. If all the chicken on the supply farms were contaminated and had been used for making other food products as well, then the food-borne disease outbreak would affect more number of consumers. So, it would be vital to be able to track the source of each ingredient going into formulating a food product, to check the spread of infection/food-borne hazard.

Education may play a key role in making producers, traders and consumers more aware about hazards lurking in foods and consequences of mishandling or adulterating foods. Capacity building would also help decrease the need for adulteration; for instance, if the milk delivery personnel was empowered to chill his milk and transport it in containers which do not heat up, he would not be tempted to add preservatives and neutralisers. Technology transfer from the lab to the farm needs to take place to enable the producers to follow good agricultural, animal rearing and manufacturing practices.

Consumers have a really important role to play. Not only do they have to be vigilant about detecting different forms of adulteration, they should also report to the authorities any type of adulterated food they come across. The FSSAI has launched a mobile application called 'Food Safety Voice' for consumers to raise their food safety concerns. The app has videos and tips on how to keep food safe. It also enables consumers to check details of food business operators and report food safety violations in food service establishments and packaged foods.

Consumers also need to make it very clear to the people selling food of substandard quality that they will not tolerate unsafe food and they would take their business elsewhere if the seller does not improve the quality of his products. If the consumer refuses highly coloured *mithai*, why will the seller want to add so much colour?

SUMMARY

- Adulterants lower the quality of the food we eat and also sometimes endanger our health.
- A number of foods of different types have been found to be adulterated in country-wide surveys. Milk and milk products, edible oils and fats, and spices are the foods most commonly found adulterated.
- Foods sold loose or without proper packaging are easy to adulterate. Also, foods sold in powder, paste or mince form are more likely to be adulterated.
- Various types of adulterants can be intentionally added to foods and several others can be present as unintentional contaminants due to negligence on the part of the food producers or traders.
- Colour seems to be an adulterant which is added to a large variety of foods to improve their appeal to the consumer. Newer forms and types of adulteration are also emerging.
- Pesticide residues, veterinary drug residues and fungal toxins present as a result of poor production or storage practices result in food which is unsafe for human consumption.
- While the consumption of some of the adulterants has resulted in minor health problems like diarrhoea, vomiting and abdominal pain, others have even resulted in the deaths of a large number of people.
- Adulteration can lead to great economic loss to a nation in terms of money spent on treating diseases or disabilities as a result of eating adulterated food as well as money lost in product recalls, legal cases and loss of product credibility.
- A few adulterants can be detected by simple tests at home while others require detailed laboratory analysis.
- Consumers need to be vigilant regarding the quality of food purchased by them.

KEY WORDS

Abstraction: Removal.

Acute toxic reaction: Toxic reaction which occurs after single exposure to toxic substance or multiple exposures over a short period of time.

Cyanosis: A bluish discolouration of the skin due to the presence of oxygen-deficient blood.

Exhausted spices: Spices from which essential oils and flavours have been extracted.

Extraneous: Of external origin.

Laxative effect: Stimulating or facilitating evacuation of bowels.

Nausea: A feeling of sickness with an inclination to vomit.

Oedema: A condition characterised by an excess of watery fluid collecting in the cavities or tissues of the body.

Putrid: Rotten, foul.

Wholesome: Conducive to good health.

EXERCISES

1. Define food adulteration.
2. Which foods are more likely to be adulterated? List some foods which are commonly found adulterated.
1. Name a few adulterants which are commonly added to:
   a) milk b) cooking oil c) ground spices
4. Name the adulterant associated with the following health hazards:
   a) epidemic dropsy b) cyanosis
5. Discuss in a few lines how adulteration can have a negative impact on the economy.
6. How would you detect the presence of the following adulterants:
   a) artificial colour in coriander powder
   b) metanil yellow in *boondi laddoo*
   c) iron filings in tea leaves
7. How can we distinguish mustard seeds from argemone seeds?
8. Write a short note on what can be done to reduce the menace of adulteration in our country.

REFERENCES

FSSAI, 'Quick Tests for Some Adulterants in Food', Instruction Manual-Part II (Methods for Detection of Adulterants), Food Safety and Standards Authority of India, 2012.

——, 'Annual Report 2014–15', 2015, Food Safety and Standards Authority of India, Available at http://www.old.fssai.gov.in/Portals/0/Pdf/Annual_Report_2014_15_Eng_Hindi.pdf (accessed 18 January 2017).

IARC, 'Monographs on the Evaluation of the Carcinogenic Risk of Chemicals to Man', Geneva: World Health Organization, International Agency for Research on Cancer, V73, Available at http://monographs.iarc.fr/ENG/Monographs/vol73/mono73-17.pdf (accessed 15 April 2018).

Mehta, R. S., I. P. Dixit, and S. J. Khakharia, 'Toxic Neuropathy in Raipur due to Triorthocresylphosphate (TOCP)', *J. Assoc. Physicians India* 23 (2), 1975, pp. 133–38.

'Melamine and Cyanuric Aacid: Toxicity, Preliminary Risk Assessment and Guidance on Levels in Food', World Health Organisation, 25 September 2008, Available at https://web.archive.org/web/20081006051717/http://www.who.int/foodsafety/fs_management/Melamine.pdf (accessed 9 June 2016).

Regattieri, A., M. Gamberi, R. Manzini, 'Traceability of Food Products: General Framework and Experimental Evidence', *Journal of Food Engineering* 81 (2), 2007, pp. 347–56.

Sarkar, J. K., 'Outbreaks of Paralytic Disease in West Bengal due to Tricresyl Phosphate Poisoning', *J. Indian Med. Assoc.* 63 (11), 1974, pp. 359–61.

Smith, H. V., and J. M. Spalding, 'Outbreak of Paralysis in Morocco due to Ortho-cresyl Phosphate Poisoning', *Lancet* 2 (7110), 1959, pp. 1019–21.

Sorokin, M., 'Orthocresyl Phosphate Neuropathy: Report of an Outbreak in Fiji', *Med. J. Aust.* 1 (10), 1969, pp. 506–08.

Srivastava, A. K., M. Das, and S. K. Khanna, 'An Outbreak of Tricresyl Phosphate Poisoning in Calcutta, India', *Food Chem. Toxicol.* 28 (4), 1990, pp. 303–04.

ONLINE SOURCES

FSSAI Mobile App, Available at http://foodsafetyhelpline.com/mobile-app/ (accessed 15 April 2018).

Tests for Detection of Adulterants, Available at http://www.fssai.gov.in/Portals/0/Pdf/Final_Test_kit_Manual_II(16-08-2012).pdf (accessed 30 May 2016).

Video on Detection of Adulterants in Common Foods, Available at https://www.youtube.com/watch?v=U99dNaGcKos (accessed 15 April 2018).

12

FOOD LAWS AND REGULATIONS

HIGHLIGHTS

- The Food Safety and Standards Authority of India
- Quality Standards: BIS, AGMARK
- Consumer Protection Act
- Codex Alimentarius Commission
- International Standards and Agreements

The earlier chapters have described the different types of hazards which can make our food unsafe for consumption. Keeping food safe at home is in our hands, but how can one ensure that the food we consume outside our home or food ingredients which we purchase for our homes are contamination-free? How does a food manufacturer know how much of colour or a preservative can be safely added to a food product? The government needs to step in with certain rules and regulations and ensure that these are followed by food manufacturers and food service providers in the country. But what about foods which are imported from other countries? For smooth and fair trade between countries, there are international trade agreements and an international regulatory body. Countries wanting to trade in food become members of or signatories to treaties and agreements, which are then governed by international laws. In this chapter, you will learn about the various national and international food regulatory bodies and how they ensure safe and wholesome food for all consumers. You will also be introduced to the various laws and regulations pertaining to the quality of food, which protect the consumers.

THE FOOD SAFETY AND STANDARDS AUTHORITY OF INDIA

The Food Safety and Standards Authority of India (FSSAI) was established under the Food Safety and Standards Act (FSSA) of 2006 and has its headquarters in New Delhi. Before this Act came into being, there were several different Acts and Orders pertaining to food-related issues. These came under different ministries and departments of the government, and it was felt that consolidating them under one body would streamline the regulatory process and be beneficial for all—the regulatory authorities, the industry and the consumer. There was also an urgent need to harmonise the laws of the country pertaining to food quality and standards with internationally accepted norms. Worldwide, the emphasis is now on developing science-based standards to ensure safe and wholesome food for consumers. Manufacturers of food products must comply with these standards which regulate how these products should be manufactured, stored, distributed and sold.

Figure 12.1 shows the Acts and Orders which were repealed with the enforcement of the Food Safety and Standards Act of 2006. Other Orders pertaining to food under the Essential Commodities (EC) Act, 1955 were also repealed. The EC Act basically controls the production, distribution and supply of essential commodities like rice, edible oils and seeds, *vanaspati*, sugarcane and its products, pulses, etc. and ensures that they are equitably distributed and available at reasonable prices.

Figure 12.1: Act and Orders Repealed after Enforcement of the FSSA in 2006

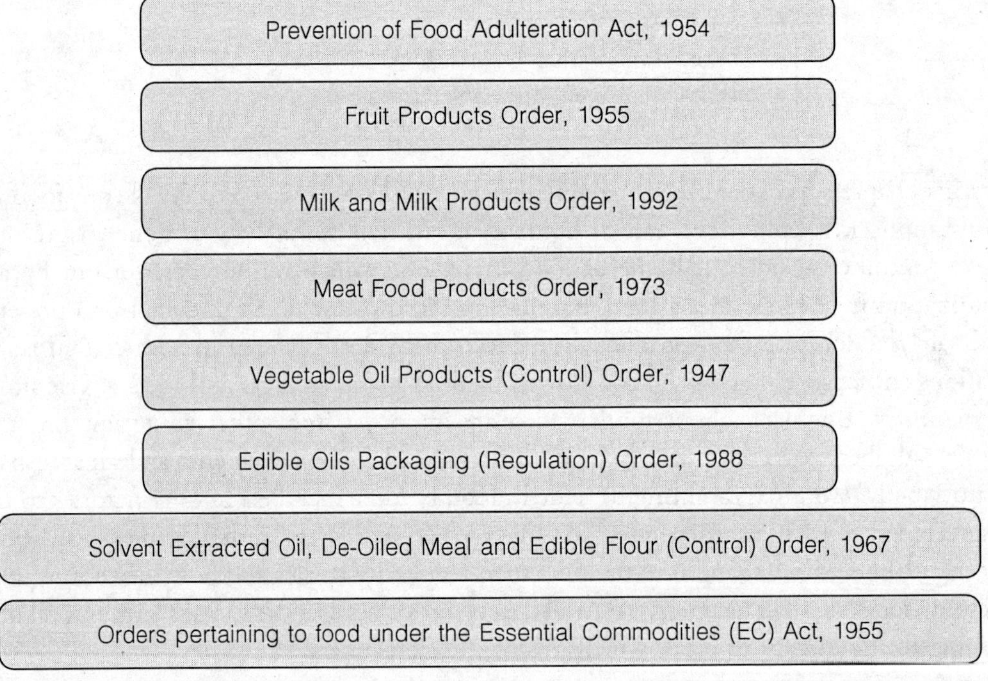

Source: Drawn by Author on the basis of information in the Food Safety and Standards Act (FSSA), 2006, Available at http://www.fssai.gov.in/home/about-us/introduction.html (accessed 26 March 2018).

The administration of the FSS Act is under the Ministry of Health and Family Welfare, Government of India. The FSSAI has a chairperson (in the rank of secretary to government of India) and a Chief Executive Officer (CEO). Under them are directors of different departments, under whom are directors of different regional offices. The Central Advisory Committee of the FSSAI consists of the CEO, state commissioners as well as representatives from consumer bodies, the food industry, agriculture sector, research bodies and food laboratories. In addition, there are scientific committees and panels to look into different issues and products. The FSSAI and State Food Authorities are jointly responsible for implementation and enforcement of FSSA, 2006. Enforcement is undertaken on the basis of surveillance, monitoring, inspection and random sampling of food products carried out by the officials of food safety departments. At the state level, there is a Commissioner of food safety. Under the Commissioner are other officials including Food Safety Officers and Food Analysts in the State Food Laboratories. The enforcement is primarily undertaken by all Food Safety Commissioners of states/union territories along with designated officers and Food Safety Officers. If any Food Business Operator (FBO) does not comply with the regulations, he may be served an 'Improvement notice.' If he still does not comply, his license may be suspended.

The mandate of the FSSAI is to:

- frame regulations and lay down standards for different foods. It also specifies the system for enforcing the various standards;
- ensure safety of foods which are imported;
- frame guidelines and lay down mechanisms for accrediting bodies which certify the food safety management system of food businesses;
- promote safe food management practices in processing, transportation, storage and distribution;
- decide what goes onto a food label and conditions for making health and nutrition claims;
- specify the guidelines and procedure for laboratories to get accredited and notification of the accredited laboratories;
- provide technical support and scientific advice to the government both at the central and state levels in framing rules and policies pertaining to food safety and nutrition. For instance, fortification of foods to mitigate malnutrition and controlling obesity by regulating high fat, salty and sugary foods (HFSS foods);
- monitor hazards in the food supply by collecting and collating data on intake, incidence and prevalence of food poisoning, presence of contaminants and their residues in foods and identifying emerging risks. The body also needs to introduce a rapid alert system for the hazards and the adverse effects they can cause;
- promote general awareness about food safety and food standards;
- enhance consumer choice and build consumer engagement through effective complaint redressal;
- create an information network throughout the country to communicate reliable information related to food safety to consumers in both urban and rural areas;
- train people involved in or wanting to start a food business;
- play a role in the development of international standards for food.

The FSS Act specifies standards for several foods, beverages and food additives. Under the provisions of this Act, sale of substandard food or food that is injurious to health is a punishable offence. When caught, the trader can be prosecuted and if found guilty has to pay a fine and can also be imprisoned depending on the seriousness of the offence and injury caused to consumers. His license can be cancelled, the food recalled from the market, his property or establishment can be forfeited especially in cases of grievous injury or death of consumer. This monitoring of the safety of food products was earlier done under the Prevention of Food Adulteration Act of 1954 (see Box 12.1), which has now been repealed.

Box 12.1: Prevention of Food Adulteration Act, 1954 and Rules, 1955

The Prevention of Food Adulteration Act of 1954 and Rules, 1955 was essentially meant to protect the interests and health of the consumer and improve the safety of food available. It was meant to clamp down on the fraudulent practice of adulterating food and sale of substandard and contaminated food. It aimed at protecting the consumer from falsely labelled and unsafe food. The Central Committee of Food Standards under the Ministry of Health and Family Welfare had the power to amend the laws in the interest of consumer protection. The responsibility of implementation of the PFA Act and Rules rested with the state governments and union territories. Samples of food were regularly picked up by food inspectors and analysed in the food laboratories. If the food was found to be substandard or adulterated, the vendors were prosecuted under the Act.

The Fruit Products Order, 1955 made it obligatory to obtain a license for the manufacture of fruit products. It laid down hygienic and sanitary requirements for setting up factories that manufacture fruit products, such as suitable location, adequate storage space, minimum fly-proof area for manufacture, maintenance of factory premises, worker amenities and their personal hygiene. Minimum specifications for various types of fruit products were also laid down in the Order. There were packing, labelling and marking requirements to be fulfilled and provision of a laboratory for quality control purposes.

There are several regulations under the FSSA (Box 12.2) pertaining to licensing and registration of food business operators, standards for food products and use of food additives, analysis, packaging and labelling, presence of contaminants and restriction of sale.

Box 12.2: Regulations under the Food Safety and Standards Act

- Food Safety and Standards (Licensing and Registration of Food Businesses) Regulation, 2011
- Food Safety and Standards (Food Product Standards and Food Additives) Regulation, 2011 (part I)
- Food Safety and Standards (Food Product Standards and Food Additives) Regulation, 2011 (part II)
- Food Safety and Standards (Prohibition and Restriction on Sales) Regulation, 2011
- Food Safety and Standards (Packaging and Labelling) Regulation, 2011
- Food Safety and Standards (Contaminants, Toxins and Residues) Regulation, 2011
- Food Safety and Standards (Laboratory and Sampling Analysis) Regulation, 2011

To commemorate a decade of the formulation of the FSS Act, in 2016, the FSSAI launched the Ten@Ten Initiatives—10 new initiatives to assure safe and nutritious food for the citizens of the country. These are:

1. Safe and Nutritious @ Home
2. Safe and Nutritious @ School
3. Safe and Nutritious @ Workplace
4. Serve Safe
5. Corporates for Safe and Nutritious Food (C4SNF)
6. Connect to Citizens
7. Diet4Life
8. Food Safety Training and Certification
9. Integrated Food Standards—Quick Access System
10. Strengthening of Food Testing Laboratories

As most people in India eat home-cooked food, the first initiative deals with educating people about eating safe and nutritious food at home. The second initiative is to inculcate safe food habits among school children while the third is for ensuring hygiene and safety of the food served in workplaces like offices and factories. The fourth initiative addresses safe food being served in all food service establishments like restaurants, hotels, canteens and by street food vendors. Ensuring food safety is a shared responsibility and all stakeholders need to be involved in the process. The C4SNF programme is an initiative to collaborate with businesses engaged in the food sector, towards creating awareness about food safety and nutrition among all stakeholders, including consumers. To connect to consumers, the FSSAI has developed Food Safety Display Boards (FSDBs) for all food businesses to prominently display in their premises. The FSDB will indicate the registration/license number of the business operator, whether he runs a milk booth, fruit or vegetable shop, a retail outlet or a restaurant/street food stall. It will educate the consumers about the basics of hygiene. It also provides a toll-free number to call or the numbers to send an SMS or WhatsApp message. A mobile app has also been launched for consumers to give their feedback. The seventh initiative is for children with metabolic disorders and addressing their food needs. The eighth initiative is about training and certifying food business operators. For easy and effective monitoring of the implementation of the food safety standards, the FSSAI plans to take concrete steps. It will integrate laws and standards to make the process simpler, so that there is better compliance from food businesses. The tenth initiative is aimed at strengthening the food-testing infrastructure in the country for monitoring the safety of food.

Export Inspection Council (EIC) of India

The Export Inspection Council of India, under the Union Ministry of Commerce and Industries, has been entrusted with the task of checking quality of exports. It was set up under the Export (Quality Control and Inspection) Act, 1963 to ensure development of export trade of India through quality control and inspection. Through Export Inspection Agencies, it certifies the quality of export commodities through installation of quality assurance systems and food safety management systems. It also issues certificates of origin (which, as the name suggests, establishes where the product has originated), health certificates (for establishments processing seafood, peanuts, animal casings etc.), authenticity certificates (for instance, the European Commission demands a certificate to establish the authenticity of every consignment of basmati rice imported by them), etc. The EIC also offers laboratory testing facilities, training and technical assistance to the industry to set up quality and safety management systems based on the principles of Hazard Analysis Critical Control Point (HACCP).

QUALITY STANDARDS

The FSS Act is binding on all food products and food business operators. There are other standards as well like BIS and AGMARK, which are not mandatory for manufacturers to adopt. However, they may choose to adopt them as they are marks of quality and would help instil confidence in consumers regarding the safety and goodness of the product.

Bureau of Indian Standards (BIS)

The Indian Standards Institute (ISI) was set up on 6 January 1947 for the formulation of Indian standards. It started operating the Certification Marks Scheme under the Indian Standards Institution (Certification Marks) Act, 1952. The scheme, which was formally launched by ISI in 1955–56, enabled it to grant licences to manufacturers producing goods in conformity with Indian standards and to apply the ISI Mark on their products. BIS replaced ISI as the national standards body of India and was established under the BIS Act of 1986 with additional scope and powers. BIS works under the aegis of the Ministry of Consumer Affairs, Food and Public Distribution, Government of India. Besides standards formulation and product certification, the BIS is involved in other activities like laboratory services and laboratory certification scheme, consumer affairs activities, promotional, information and training activities. It also runs the Hallmarking Scheme (for precious metals like gold and silver) and the Foreign Manufacturers' Certification Scheme. Relevant guidelines of the International Organization for Standardization (ISO) were followed for the standards formulation activity of BIS to ensure harmonisation as much as possible.

> Since 1991, the BIS has been operating **Management Systems Certification Schemes**. Some pertaining to the food industry are:
>
> - Quality Management System Certification (IS/ISO 9001)
> - Environmental Management System Certification (IS/ISO 14001) since 1997
> - Hazards Analysis and Critical Control Point Certification (IS 15000) since 1998
> - Food Safety Management System (IS/ISO 22000) since 2006

BIS has its headquarters at New Delhi and has five regional offices at Kolkata (Eastern), Chennai (Southern), Mumbai (Western), Chandigarh (Northern) and Delhi (Central). Under the regional offices are branch offices which offer certification services to the industry and serve as effective links between state governments, industries, technical institutions, consumer organisation, etc. of the respective region.

Manufacturers complying with standards laid down by BIS can use the ISI mark on the package of their products. Although the ISI mark certification is voluntary, for some food products, it is mandatory; for instance, formula milk, milk powder, infant weaning/complementary foods, food colours, packaged drinking water and condensed milk. BIS has testing laboratories and has certified some others as well to perform the testing of products. It has a consumer affairs department at the headquarters in New Delhi and public grievance officers at the regional and branch offices for speedy redressal of public grievances against products.

AGMARK

The Agricultural Produce (Grading and Marking) Act, 1937 provides for the grading and marking of agricultural and other allied commodities with the objective of making available only quality agricultural produce to the consumers. It is operated by the Directorate of Marketing and Inspection, Government of India. This includes horticulture, forest and livestock produce. The logo of AGMARK on a package of a food item assures the consumer that the product is of a good quality. More than 200 foods are covered in the Act, including vegetable oils, *ghee*, butter, eggs, cereals, pulses, fruits, vegetables, jaggery, honey, spices and sugar. It is not a mandatory standard. Under the provisions of this Act, the central government is authorised to:

- formulate rules and standards for fixing grades indicating quality of food products;
- designate bodies to undertake the grading process;
- specify conditions of packing, sealing and marking;
- confiscate produce which has not been marked per the provisions of the Act.

AGMARK laboratories act as testing and certifying centres. The Central AGMARK Laboratory (CAL) is in Nagpur. There are around 11 regional AGMARK laboratories (RALs) as well, in different cities across the country. The complaints and grievances of the consumers against products having AGMARK grade but not having the stipulated quality can be sent to the agricultural marketing advisor, who is empowered to order free replacement of the product. Failure to conform to standards can result in downgrading or removal of the mark from the package of the product.

CONSUMER PROTECTION ACT

The Consumer Protection Act, 1986 is aimed at providing expedited justice to consumers who were aggrieved by defects in goods purchased from a trader or manufacturer, or deficiency in services;

for instance, from hotels, restaurants or any other food service provider. The objective was to provide justice in an informal and inexpensive manner. To achieve this, there was establishment of consumer councils and other authorities for the settlement of disputes. A consumer could also approach consumer redressal agencies like the district forum, state commission and national commission based on the amount of compensation claimed. The rights of consumers under this Act have been listed in Figure 12.2.

Figure 12.2: Rights Given to Consumers under the Consumer Protection Act

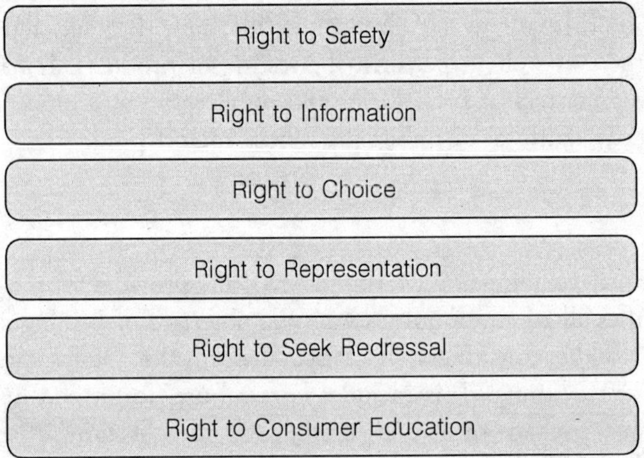

Source: Drawn by Author on the basis of information available at http://www.yourarticlelibrary.com/consumers/consumer-rights-under-the-consumer-protection-act-india/8786/ (accessed 5 January 2017).

National Consumer Helpline (**NCH**) is a project of the Union Ministry of Consumer Affairs. It provides a national toll-free number (1800-11-4000) to seek information or guidance for redressal of their complaints. An SMS can also be sent to +918130009809 mentioning the name and city. Besides this, there is a 'Jago Grahak Jago' consumer awareness programme. You may have come across several public-oriented messages on food safety and quality under this initiative.

The right to safety refers to protection against goods and services which are hazardous. The consumer also has the right to know about the quality, quantity, purity, standard and price of goods or services. The consumer should also be given assurance of availability, ability to access a variety of products and services at competitive prices. The retailer or producer should not force the consumer to buy one brand only. The consumer also has the right to be heard in case of any grievance regarding quality of goods or services. Companies are required to have complaint cells to address problems faced by consumers. The consumer also has the right to seek redressal and compensation in case he has been exploited or is a victim of unfair trade practices. The government is also making special effort using media, and schools and colleges for enhancing the knowledge and skills of consumers regarding their rights and about how to protect themselves against unfair trade practices.

INTERNATIONAL STANDARDS: CODEX ALIMENTARIUS COMMISSION

International food trade is a 200-billion-dollar a year industry with billions of tonnes of food produced, marketed and transported. Not only is there a need to ensure fair trade practices, but also to ensure the safety of consumers across nations. The Codex Alimentarius was established by the FAO and WHO in 1963. Standards, guidelines, codes of practice and recommendations constitute the Codex Alimentarius. The Codex Alimentarius Commission (CAC) is the body responsible for compiling these.

The Codex Alimentarius, or the 'Food Code', is a global reference point. Codex standards have been scientifically formulated by international experts and are the best available standards. Although they are voluntary standards, many countries have adopted them as a part of their national legislation. Also, being an active member of Codex enables countries to actively participate in the process of formulation of standards and to compete in the world market, that is, exporting countries will be aware of what the importing countries are demanding. Countries are also protected from substandard or unsafe food being dumped in their markets through the CAC.

The Codex Alimentarius includes standards for all foods, whether processed, semi-processed or raw. It also includes provisions in respect of food hygiene, food additives, residues of pesticides and veterinary drugs, contaminants, labelling and presentation, methods of analysis and sampling, and import and export inspection and certification. The Codex has a number of committees which formulate standards for different aspects of food safety like pesticide residues in food, veterinary drug residues in food, and regulations for food labelling, maintaining food hygiene, etc. (see Box 12.3). The FAO/WHO Coordinating Committee for Asia (CCASIA) was established by the Codex Alimentarius Commission in 1978, with the objective of facilitating communication among member countries. It also aimed to develop regional standards for specific

Box 12.3: Different Committees of Codex

CCCF: Codex Committee on Contaminants in Foods
CCFA: Codex Committee on Food Additives
CCFH: Codex Committee on Food Hygiene
CCFICS: Codex Committee on Food Import and Export Inspection and Certification Systems
CCFL: Codex Committee on Food Labelling
CCGP: Codex Committee on General Principles
CCMAS: Codex Committee on Methods of Analysis and Sampling
CCNFSDU: Codex Committee on Nutrition and Foods for Special Dietary Uses
CCPR: Codex Committee on Pesticide Residues
CCRVDF: Codex Committee on Residues of Veterinary Drugs in Foods

food products and ensure fair trade practices. India was elected as the Regional Co-ordinator for Asia in July 2015.

INTERNATIONAL AGREEMENTS

As trade between nations of the world grew, a need was felt to have a global international organisation which formulates the rules of trade between different countries of the world. A multilateral agreement regulating international trade called **General Agreement on Trades and Tariffs** (**GATT**) was signed by 23 nations of the world on 30 October 1947 in Geneva. The **World Trade Organization** (**WTO**) was established on 1 January 1995, replacing the GATT. The primary purpose of the WTO is to ensure open trade and protect producers of goods and services. Providing equal opportunities for all nations of the world to trade, reducing obstacles and ensuring fair trading practices, the WTO provides a forum for negotiating trade agreements between nations. It is like an institution which provides the legal framework for the implementation and monitoring of agreements as well as settling of disputes. The WTO also assists in capacity building in international trade matters of government officials from developing countries. It conducts economic research and collects and disseminates trade data to support its other activities. The Secretariat of the WTO is in Geneva, Switzerland.

> International standards tend to be stricter as compared to domestic standards of most countries. Hence, if a country has more stringent standards, it needs to demonstrate how the international standard would not give the adequate protection to the consumers of that country.

The Agreement on Technical Barriers to Trade (TBT Agreement)

The TBT Agreement is an international treaty administered by the WTO, which came into force along with the creation of WTO in 1995. It strives to ensure that technical regulations, standards, testing and certification procedures followed by different countries do not create barriers for trade. It promotes the use of international standards, although it also protects legitimate interests of individual nations wanting to safeguard their environment, human and animal health. Under the treaty, nations are obliged to aid each other in drafting technical regulations. Procedures for settlements of disputes between nations have been set out under the Agreement. It encourages transparency in procedures so that a predictable trading environment can be created.

Technical standards and regulations are important. However, trade can become very complicated for producers and exporters if every country follows different regulations and has different technical standards. Standards need to be based on science and not be arbitrary in nature. The TBT helps countries to challenge rigid technical specifications and subjects them to scientific scrutiny.

According to the agreement, the procedures adopted to decide whether a food product conforms to the standards should be fair and equitable so that domestically produced goods do not have an unfair advantage over those imported from other countries. Countries are encouraged to recognise each other's procedures so that products do not have to be tested twice, first by the exporting country and then by the importing country. The TBT Agreement is binding on all members of the WTO.

The Agreement on Application of Sanitary and Phytosanitary Measures (SPS Agreement)

The SPS Agreement also came into force along with the establishment of the WTO in 1995. It pertains to animal and plant health standards, and regulations and the basic rules for food safety. 'Sanitary' refers to human and animal health, whereas 'phytosanitary' refers to plant health. Although countries can have their own standards, these should be based on science and should not discriminate between countries where identical or similar conditions prevail. Member countries are encouraged to use international standards, guidelines and recommendations where they exist. Countries wanting to set higher standards should base them on risk assessment and give appropriate scientific justification.

According to the agreement, member countries need to ensure safety of food for consumers and prevent the spread of pests and diseases among animals and plants. This would mean that the food products should come from a disease-free area. They may be subject to inspection, treatment or processing. Maximum levels of pesticide residues, use of food additives are all in the ambit of the agreement. Governments may sometimes be under pressure to shield domestic producers from external competition and may set very high standards for imported foods. This is referred to as '*protectionism*'. For instance, earlier, some countries would set up very stringent standards like very low maximum residue limits for pesticides to discourage import of food from developing nations. It was not cost effective for producers in these countries to achieve such low residue levels.

The agreement, therefore, covers all aspects of food safety, protecting human and animal life from:

- contaminants, additives, toxins, disease-causing organisms in food
- pests, diseases or disease-causing organisms
- diseases carried by plants and animals

The agreement also covers protection of a country from entry, establishment or spread of pests, as well as measures taken to protect the health of the wild flora, fauna, fish and forests.

The agreement requires that sanitary and phytosanitary measures be applied only to ensure food safety and animal and plant health, considering certain factors while assessing risk involved. The SPS Agreement encourages governments to establish national SPS measures consistent with international standards, guidelines and recommendations so that there is 'harmonisation'. However, due to differences in climate, kinds of pests and/or diseases existing in the countries, and due to the food safety conditions, it may not be always possible to impose the same requirements on products coming from different countries.

The WTO relies on other international bodies like the CAC to develop standards. It does not develop its own standards. An acceptable level of risk can be arrived at keeping in consideration technological and economic feasibility as well as health protection. The level should not be restrictive for trade and should allow healthy economic competition. The use of risk assessment approach in setting standards is encouraged among member nations.

The scopes of the two agreements—TBT and SPS—are different (See Figure 12.3). The SPS Agreement covers all measures whose purpose is to protect humans or animals from food-borne risks like microbes, their toxins, contaminants and additives; humans from diseases which are carried by animals or plants; and animals and plants from pests and diseases. The TBT covers all technical specifications except those covered by SPS. In terms of food, it covers aspects of food quality, nutritional claims and concerns, labelling and packaging regulations, etc.

Figure 12.3: Differences in the Scope of the TBT and SPS Agreements

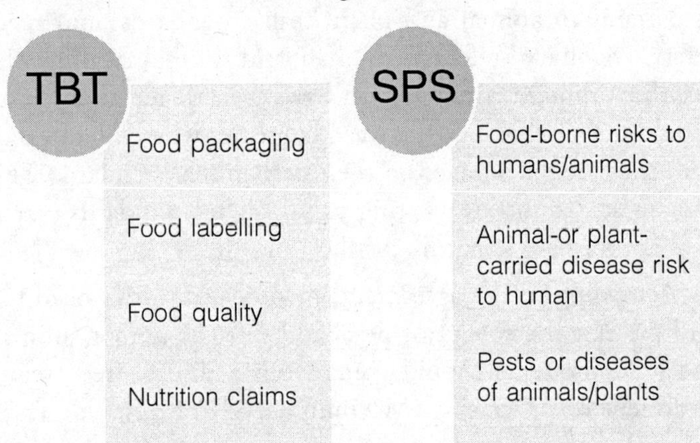

Source: Adapted by Author from WTO 2010, 2014.

Box 12.4: Other Organisations Responsible for Food Standards and Safety

USA:	U.S. Food and Drug Administration (FDA)
European Union:	European Food Safety Authority (EFSA)
UK:	Food Standards Agency (FSA)
Canada:	Canadian Food Inspection Agency (CFIA)
Australia and New Zealand:	Food Standards Australia New Zealand (FSANZ)

International Organization for Standardization (ISO)

The ISO is a network of national standards institutes of 163 countries (as of 2015). It began operations on 23 February 1947 with the objective of facilitating international coordination and unification of industrial standards. The secretariat for ISO is in Geneva in Switzerland. It has technical bodies responsible for formulation of standards. The ISO has developed voluntary global standards for products and services to ensure their safety and quality. It works closely with other global organisations like the CAC, FAO, WHO and the Global Food Safety Initiative. With greater number of countries opening movement of food products across borders, the need for global standards has grown.

Out of more than 21,000 ISO international standards, around 1,000 are specifically related to food, dealing with diverse subjects such as agricultural machinery, transportation, manufacturing, labelling, packing, storage, taste, hygiene, traceability, limits on additives, contaminants, specifications for food products, etc. ISO brings all stakeholders (producers, retailers, regulatory authorities and consumers) on board to share the best practices.

Some of these are:

- ISO 9000 Quality management
- ISO 14000 Environmental management
- ISO 31000 Risk management
- ISO 22000 Food safety management

> ISO also has standards for how to make a perfect cup of tea (ISO 3103) and for how long to cook spaghetti (ISO 7304)!

Global Food Safety Initiative (GFSI)

The GFSI is a global collaboration launched in May 2000 to advance food safety. It is an industry-driven initiative providing guidance on food safety management systems which provide safety along the supply chain. Its scope is limited to that of food safety. It does not provide certification or training, nor does it own any food safety schemes or standards.

The International Food Safety Authorities Network (INFOSAN)

This is a global network of national food safety authorities, managed jointly by FAO and WHO with the secretariat in WHO. National authorities of 186 member states are part of the network, as of 2018. WHO helps member nations in managing food safety risks. It encourages sharing of information, especially under emergencies. This helps in stemming the spread of contaminated food from one country to another.

SUMMARY

- To ensure safe and wholesome food for all consumers, various laws and regulations are in place in our country and internationally. Some of these are trade agreements which facilitate fair trade practices between nations.
- The Food Safety and Standards Authority of India (FSSAI) was established under the Food Safety and Standards Act of 2006 with its headquarters in New Delhi. This Act consolidated several Acts and Orders pertaining to food-related issues, thus streamlining the regulatory process for all concerned—the regulatory authorities, the industry and the consumer.
- The Act also attempted to harmonise the laws of the country pertaining to food quality and standards with internationally accepted norms.
- The FSS Act specifies standards for several foods, beverages and food additives. Under the provisions of this Act, sale of substandard food or food that is injurious to health is a punishable offence.
- In 2016, the FSSAI launched the Ten@Ten Initiatives, 10 new initiatives to assure safe and nutritious food for the citizens of the country.
- The Export Inspection Council of India, under the Union Ministry of Commerce and Industries, has been entrusted with the task of checking quality of exports. It was set up under the Export (Quality Control

and Inspection) Act, 1963 to ensure development of export trade of India through quality control and inspection.

- The FSS Act is binding on all food products and food business operators. It ensures the basic quality and safety of the food served or manufactured. ISI and AGMARK are quality marks which assure the consumer of a certain quality of food product. These are voluntary standards.
- The Bureau of Indian Standards replaced ISI as the national standards body of India and was established under the BIS Act of 1986 with additional scope and powers. Besides standards formulation and product certification, the BIS is involved in other activities like laboratory services and laboratory certification scheme, consumer affairs activities, promotional, information and training activities.
- The Agricultural Produce (Grading and Marking) Act, 1937 (AGMARK) provides for the grading and marking of agricultural and other allied commodities with the objective of making available only quality agricultural produce to the consumers. It is operated by the Directorate of Marketing and Inspection, government of India. This includes horticulture, forest and livestock produce.
- The Consumer Protection Act, 1986 aimed at providing expedited justice to consumers who were aggrieved by defects in food products (among other goods) purchased from a trader or manufacturer, or deficiency in services, for instance, from hotels, restaurants or any other food service provider.
- The Codex Alimentarius (or the Food Code) was established by the FAO and WHO in 1963. Standards, guidelines, codes of practice and recommendations constitute the Codex Alimentarius. The Codex Alimentarius Commission (CAC) is the body responsible for compiling these.
- A multilateral agreement regulating international trade called General Agreement on Trades and Tariffs (GATT) was signed by 23 nations of the world on 30 October 1947 in Geneva.
- The World Trade Organization (WTO) was established on 1 January 1995, replacing the GATT. The primary purpose of the WTO is to ensure open trade and protect producers of goods and services.
- The TBT Agreement is an international treaty administered by the WTO, which came into force along with the creation of the WTO in 1995. It strives to ensure that technical regulations, standards, testing and certification procedures followed by different countries do not create barriers for trade.
- The Agreement on Application of Sanitary and Phytosanitary Measures (SPS Agreement) also came into force along with the establishment of the WTO in 1995. It pertains to animal and plant health standards, and regulations and the basic rules for food safety.
- The International Organization for Standardization (ISO) began operations on 23 February 1947 with the objective of facilitating international coordination and unification of industrial standards. The secretariat for ISO is in Geneva in Switzerland. It has technical bodies responsible for formulation of standards.
- Out of more than 21,000 ISO International Standards, around 1,000 are specifically related to food; ISO 22000 pertains to food safety management.
- The Global Food Safety Initiative is an industry-driven initiative providing guidance on food safety management systems which provide safety along the supply chain.
- INFOSAN is a global network of national food safety authorities managed by FAO/WHO.

KEY WORDS

Act: A law passed by Parliament or any legislature.

Harmonisation: Adjustment of differences and inconsistencies among different specifications.

Order: (here) Lays down quality standards and is issued by a government body or ministry.

Protectionism: To shield domestic producers from external competition by setting very high standards for imported foods.

Standard: A reference established by law, used as basis for comparing quality.

Regulation: Issued by a government authority and has to be followed by those functioning under the control of the authority.

Rule: An established standard or guide which determines conduct, procedure or action. It typically clarifies the operational details of an Act. This is also passed by the legislature.

Tariffs: List of items with corresponding rates of tax, such as import duties levied on food items imported into a country.

EXERCISES

1. Why were the existing Orders and PFA Act and Rules repealed and a consolidated FSS Act formulated?
2. What are the salient features of the FSS Act?
3. Distinguish between mandatory and voluntary standards giving examples.
4. What is the role of Codex Alimentarius?
5. What is the difference between TBT and SPS Agreements?
6. What do you know about the ISO? Which standard pertains to food safety management system?
7. Visit the local grocery shop and supermarket and search the labels of food products for quality marks. Write down the names of at least two products on which you saw each of the following marks:
   - FSSAI logo
   - ISI mark (hint: look for infant milk formulae, milk powders, permitted food colour packets)
   - AGMARK (hint: this will be present only on agricultural products)
   - HACCP
   - ISO 22000 certification

REFERENCES

Bhat, R. V., 'Achieving Food Safety from Farm to Table: Global Requirements and the Indian Scenario', *NFI Bulletin* 34 (4), 2013, pp. 1–8.

FAO/WHO, *Infosan Activity Report 2014–2015*, Geneva: International Food Safety Authorities Network, 2016.

ISO, *ISO and Food: Quality and Safety from Farm to Fork*, 2012, Geneva, Available at http://www.iso.org/iso/iso_and_food.pdf (accessed 30 December 2016).

Rights of Consumers, 'Consumer Protection Act', Available at http://www.yourarticlelibrary.com/consumers/consumer-rights-under-the-consumer-protection-act-india/8786/ (accessed 5 January 2017).

WTO, *Sanitary and Phytosanitary Measures*, The WTO Agreements Series, Geneva: World Trade Organization, 2010.

———, *Technical Barriers to Trade*, The WTO Agreements Series, Geneva: World Trade Organization, 2010.

ONLINE SOURCES

About the Codex Alimentarius, Available at http://www.fao.org/fao-who-codexalimentarius/en/ (accessed 15 April 2018).

Bureau of Indian Standards, Online Complaint Registration on BIS website at www.bis.org.in or mobile application or by email at complaints@bis.gov.in (accessed 15 April 2018).

Mobile App for FSSAI Compliance Needs, Available at http://foodsafetyhelpline.com/mobile-app/ (accessed 15 April 2018).

World Trade Organization, Available at https://www.wto.org/english/thewto_e/whatis_e/whatis_e.htm (accessed 15 April 2018).

13

RISK ANALYSIS

HIGHLIGHTS

- Concept
- Risk assessment
- Toxicological analysis
- Risk management
- Risk communication
- Roles and responsibilities

Food quality control programmes form an integral part of government health programmes. The Government of India has enacted several laws and regulations to ensure a safe food supply to the nation. Risk analysis is a discipline widely recognised as fundamental in food safety evaluation and the setting of safety standards. It is based on sound scientific principles. The development of processes, procedures and regulations for keeping food safe in a country requires that the available scientific knowledge is utilised in a rational way. Risk analysis is seen primarily as a method of systematically organising scientific and technical information to answer specific questions about health risks. It requires evaluation of relevant information to be used in drawing inferences (FAO/WHO 1995).

The role of risk analysis is vital in the work of the World Trade Organization (WTO) and related agreements on the Application of Sanitary and Phytosanitary Measures (SPS Agreement) and Technical Barriers to Trade (TBT). The primary goal of these is to limit the use of measures that may restrict trade to those justified to provide the necessary level of health protection. The science of risk analysis forms the basis of these measures. This chapter highlights the basic principles and components of the process of risk analysis and explains how these are used to evolve standards for foods and regulations for ensuring food safety.

CONCEPT

Public health officials attempting to identify, evaluate and control hazards in the food supply depend on the process of risk analysis. Not only do they need to assess the quantum of risk the hazard can pose to human health (risk assessment), they also need to work out procedures to manage the risk by controlling the hazard (risk management). Equally vital is a third process—risk communication. The risk evaluator needs to communicate his findings and recommendations to the risk manager who then needs to involve all stakeholders in the effort to control the hazard. Involving the consumers by making them more aware about the presence of the hazard, the adverse health effects it can lead to, and ways and means of reducing/avoiding the hazard in their diet can go a long way in reducing risks. Figure 13.1 depicts the three components of the process of risk analysis which are risk assessment, risk management and risk communication.

Figure 13.1: Components of Risk Analysis

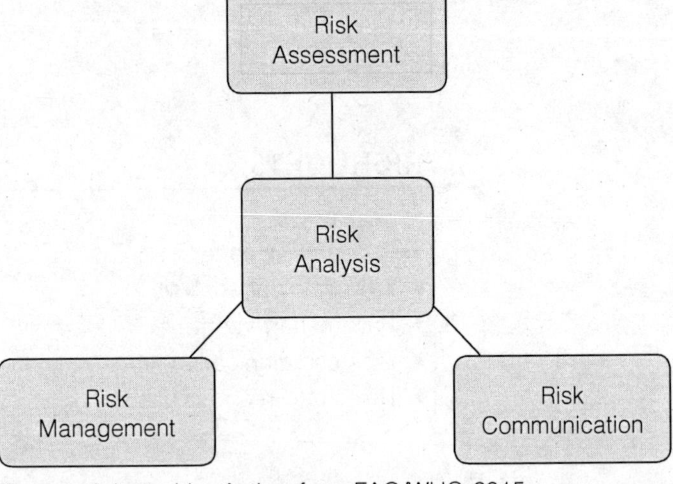

Source: Adapted by Author from FAO/WHO 2015.

An adverse effect is defined as 'any change in the morphology, physiology, growth, development, reproduction or life span of an organism, system, or (sub) population that results in an impairment of functional capacity, an impairment of the capacity to compensate for additional stress, or an increase in susceptibility to other influences' (FAO/WHO 2015). In simple words, an adverse effect is the harmful effect a substance has on the health of the consumer. The risk assessment process evaluates the likelihood of an adverse effect occurring at the level of exposure through food. Table 13.1 provides some definitions of terms related to the process of risk analysis.

Table 13.1: Definitions of Risk Analysis Terms Related to Food Safety

Hazard	A biological, chemical, or physical agent in food or a property of food that may have an adverse health effect
Risk	A function of the probability of an adverse effect occurring, and the magnitude of that effect, as a result of a hazard(s) in food
Risk Analysis	A process consisting of three components: risk assessment, risk management and risk communication
Risk Assessment	The scientific evaluation of known or potential adverse health effects resulting from human exposure to food-borne hazards. The process consists of the following steps: (i) hazard identification; (ii) hazard characterisation; (iii) exposure assessment; and (iv) risk characterisation. The evaluation should take note of inherent uncertainties in the process.

(*Contd*)

(*Contd*)

Hazard Identification	The identification of known or potential health effects associated with a particular agent
Hazard Characterisation	The qualitative and/or quantitative evaluation of the nature of the adverse effects associated with biological, chemical and physical agents which may be present in food. For chemical agents, a dose-response assessment should be performed. For biological or physical agents a dose-response assessment should be performed if the data is obtainable.
Exposure Assessment	The qualitative and/or quantitative evaluation of the degree of intake likely to occur
Risk Characterisation	Integration of hazard identification, hazard characterisation and exposure assessment into an estimation of the adverse effects likely to occur in a given population, including attendant uncertainties
Risk Management	The process of weighing policy alternatives to accept, minimise or reduce assessed risks and to select and implement appropriate options
Risk Communication	An interactive process of exchange of information and opinion on risk among risk assessors, risk managers and other interested parties

Source: Adapted by Author from FAO/WHO 1995, 2015.

RISK ASSESSMENT

The process of risk assessment consists of four steps as shown in Figure 13.2.

Figure 13.2: Components of Risk Assessment

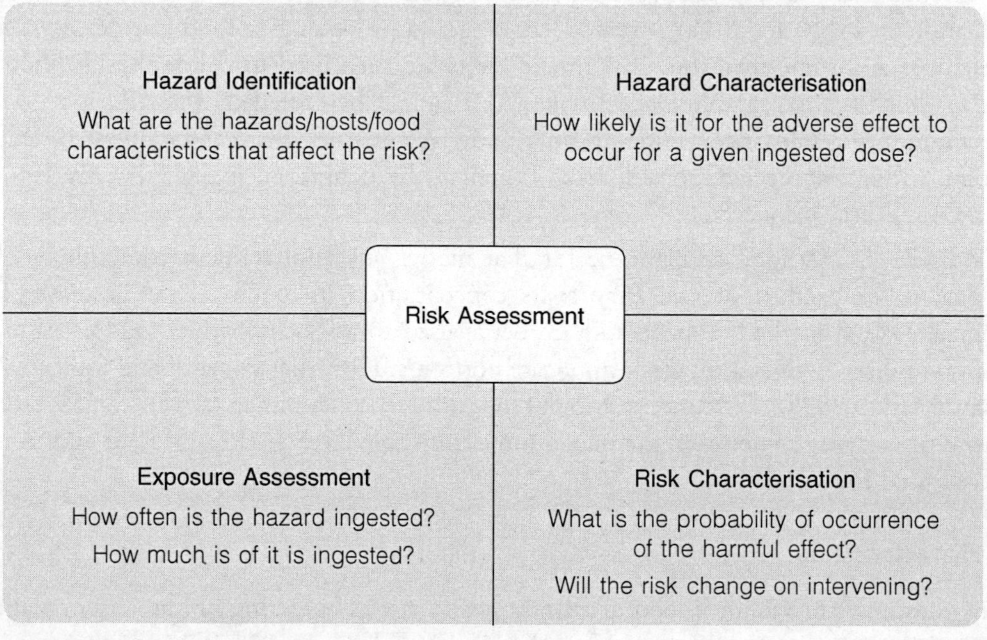

Hazard Identification
What are the hazards/hosts/food characteristics that affect the risk?

Hazard Characterisation
How likely is it for the adverse effect to occur for a given ingested dose?

Risk Assessment

Exposure Assessment
How often is the hazard ingested?
How much is of it is ingested?

Risk Characterisation
What is the probability of occurrence of the harmful effect?
Will the risk change on intervening?

Source: Adapted by Author from FAO/WHO 1995.

Hazard Identification

The goal of hazard identification is to identify potential adverse health effects in humans associated with exposure to a chemical and the host/hazard/food characteristics which are likely to affect the likelihood of such effects occurring. It requires an adequate and documented review of relevant scientific information obtained from appropriate databases, peer-reviewed literature and, if available, unpublished studies from other sources such as industry. More emphasis is given to studies which document the adverse effects in humans followed by toxicological studies on animals.

Hazard Characterisation

The Organisation for Economic Co-operation and Development (OECD) has set guidelines for toxicity testing. These are valid for micro-ingredients in food, such as food additives, processing aids, contaminants, etc., which are present in amounts less than 1 per cent of the food. The guidelines recommend that foods and food ingredients should be tested at those levels comparable with probable human exposure levels and one or two multiples beyond that. This step evaluates the likelihood of adverse effect occurring at different dosages.

Exposure Assessment

To assess whether food additives or contaminants pose a hazard to our health, an estimation of our exposure to these through food needs to be made. Exposure assessment should include the entire farm-to-fork pathway to estimate the extent of possible contamination, whether intentional or unintentional. Many factors and processes along the pathway can increase or decrease the amount of contaminant in the food. For instance, cooking and processing of food can destroy/decrease the microbes and some toxicants. The intake levels are then used to define the likelihood and extent to which the Acceptable Daily Intake (ADI) might be exceeded. The ADI is an estimate of the amount of a substance, expressed on a body weight basis, that can be ingested daily over a lifetime without appreciable health risk. Therefore, by definition, intakes that are below the ADI are not a health concern.

The intake of any food additive, or for that matter any adulterant or contaminant, by an individual is the product of two factors: its concentration in food and the amount of food consumed. Several methods can be and are being used to assess individual food consumption, such as food diary (weighed intakes), duplicate portion studies, dietary recall and food frequency (Jain and Mathur 2015). The concentration of the additive, contaminant or adulterant is estimated by chemical analysis. Sometimes, the maximum permissible levels (MPLs) of food additives have also been used for calculation.

Risk Characterisation

This is an estimate of the likelihood of adverse health effects occurring in human populations as a consequence of people being exposed to the chemical through food. The risk characterisation is performed by taking into consideration the results of the hazard identification, hazard characterisation and exposure assessment. For *threshold acting agents*, that is, chemicals which show toxic effects only after a certain quantity has been consumed, the population risk is characterised by comparison of the ADI with exposure. In this case, the likelihood of adverse health effects is notionally zero when exposure is less than the ADI. For non-threshold acting agents, population risk is the product of exposure to the chemical and potency of the chemical.

Risk assessment, as an approach for ensuring food safety, has several benefits (see Box 13.1). Risk assessment has been used to evaluate several food-borne hazards. In a study on dietary lead exposure, distribution of intake, lead levels in dietary and non-dietary sources and lead absorption were used to predict blood lead levels in populations of concern. Risk of exposure to lead was estimated from each source (Carrington et al. 1996). A risk assessment study of the consumption of *Crotalaria brevidens*, an indigenous Tanzanian vegetable containing a toxic alkaloid, was carried out. It was found that given the very low amounts of toxic alkaloids detected in this leafy vegetable, it is likely that under normal circumstances, the nutritional and medicinal benefits from eating it outweigh the detrimental effects. When consumption is increased because other foods are not available to the people, the harmful effects might outweigh the benefits, especially for undernourished individuals like children and the elderly (Uiso and Johns 1995).

Box 13.1: Benefits of Risk Assessment for Ensuring Food Safety

- Integrates information in an objective, structured, systematic, transparent way
- Increases understanding of how the hazard interacts with the host via the food vehicle
- Facilitates application of science for formulation of policy
- Predicts relative effectiveness of prevention and control practices

While assessing the risk of any hazard, one can face several **challenges**. The first challenge is the type of data available. Is the data available sufficient to characterise risk? Is it of reasonably good quality to withstand scientific scrutiny? Is it relevant to the hazard being evaluated? There is always a certain amount of uncertainty associated with interpreting data from animal studies to human beings and in predicting doses at which one is likely to see adverse health effects. The resources available for the work involved in assessing the risk faced by a population also have to be considered. Developing, low-income countries may not have enough people who are sufficiently trained to conduct risk assessment studies. They may also lack sufficient funding to conduct large-scale surveys for assessing exposure of their population to various hazards.

Although a safety factor of 100 is applied to the NOAEL (no-observed-adverse-effect level) to arrive at the ADI of a food additive, it is theoretically possible that some individuals are even more sensitive than provided for by the safety factor.

TOXICOLOGICAL ANALYSIS

Toxicologists use the **Lethal Dose (LD_{50})** to characterise the toxic potency of a compound. This is the dose which produces a 50 per cent mortality in a given population. So, for instance, if rats are the test animals, then the dose at which half the rats taken for the experiment die is taken as the LD_{50}. It is used to compare the relative lethality of several toxins.

According to Paracelsus (c. 1493–1541), a Swiss physician and alchemist, 'All substances are poisons; there is none which is not a poison. The right dose differentiates a poison and a remedy.' (Rodricks 1992).

The process of risk assessment requires adequate information on the toxicological profile of the chemical/toxin present in food. This profile is generated using a standardised testing protocol accepted by the international community (for example, OECD, EPA, JECFA, etc.) and should follow Good Laboratory Practices (GLP) and standardised quality assurance/quality control procedures. For ethical reasons, this kind of testing cannot be done directly on humans. Hence, most toxicological data is generated using laboratory animals like rats, mice, hamsters, guinea pigs and monkeys. The animal model is chosen keeping in mind the one that will best predict the human response to the chemical. Data from human clinical studies or epidemiological studies is, of course, given preference in risk assessment studies, but such data is limited. Dose-response assessment determines the relationship between the magnitude of intake of or exposure to a chemical (the dose) and the severity and/or frequency of associated adverse health effects (response). To generate a dose-response relationship for a chemical hazard, one needs to conduct meticulously planned animal studies. An intra-species conversion factor helps to ascertain the toxic effects that may be seen at doses humans are likely to be exposed to.

The animal studies can be of short duration to examine **acute toxicity** or of a longer term to study the effects of **chronic** exposure. These studies facilitate the identification of the range of adverse effects which are likely to occur at different intake levels such as cancer, reproductive effects, effects on the development of the animal, neurotoxic effects, immunotoxic effects and the organs which get damaged. The animal toxicological study should be designed in such a way that it identifies the '**no-observed-adverse-effect level**' or **NOAEL**, a benchmark dose at which no adverse effect is seen. Using data from toxicological studies, the lowest observed adverse effect level (LOAEL) is also determined, that is, the lowest dose at which the adverse effects have been seen in humans or animals. These figures are used to derive a safe level of intake or an ADI by applying appropriate safety factors. A safety factor of 100 is used by JECFA, for instance, for arriving at the ADI for food additives. For example, erythrosine a food colour, has a NOAEL of 1 mg/kg body weight from studies on humans. The LOAEL is 200 mg/kg/day. The ADI has hence been set at 0.1 mg/kg body weight. So one would have to consume 2,000 times the ADI for any adverse health effects to be seen.

RISK MANAGEMENT

The role of risk analysis in food safety evaluation and setting of safety standards is considered to be vital. Safety standards need to be developed to specify the level of acceptable risk which can be adopted by risk managers. Such safety standards can be at several levels, as shown in Table 13.2.

Table 13.2: Type of Standards and Associated Level of Risk

Types of Standards	*Defined Levels/Risk*
Zero-risk standards	ADI levels
As Low As Reasonably Achievable (ALARA) or 'balancing' standards	Those looking at cost-benefit, cost effectiveness
Threshold standards	Where a non-zero level of risk is stipulated as acceptable
Procedural standards	Where the acceptable risk level is determined by an agreed process such as negotiation and referendum

Source: Adapted by Author from FAO/WHO 1997.

Balancing standards which look at the cost effectiveness of a level set as a regulatory standard are important as very strict standards may result in great economic loss without much of appreciable increase in the availability of safe food. According to W. F. O. Marasas, of the South African group responsible for the discovery of fumonisin mycotoxin, if the safety standards are too low, the economic consequences may be disastrous; for example, levels less than 1,000 mg/g may result in 34.5 per cent of the commercial corn products for human consumption in the USA being declared illegal. If they are too high, human and animal health may be endangered; for example, levels more than 8,000 mg/g may result in leukoencephalomalacia in horses (Marasas et al. 1993).

Risk managers need to understand where to look for hazards. They need to set priorities and accordingly allocate the often limited resources so that the worst hazards can be tackled first. They need to identify the major risk-contributing events in the farm-to-fork continuum. Risk managers also need to evaluate effectiveness of interventions and decide on potential control measures, proposed standards and compliance by food producers and food business operators. Some general principles of food safety risk management are presented in Figure 13.3.

It is also important to monitor and review the risk management decisions. If certain controls have been put in place to lower population exposure to a chemical, these controls should be monitored and their outcomes studied to see if they have indeed been effective.

RISK COMMUNICATION

Risk communication is more than a dialogue among stakeholders. It is a multidimensional process involving an exchange of risk information. It includes community outreach activities, briefings

> In case a hazard is detected in a food product—for instance, a high level of pesticide/a pathogenic microbe in a beverage or food product—the company recalls the food product from the market and communicates to the consumer through mass media channels like newspapers or television that they should not consume their product of a particular batch number. This is a process of risk communication very common in developed countries.

Figure 13.3: General Principles of Food Safety Risk Management

Risk management should follow a structured approach

Protection of human health should be the primary consideration in decisions

Decisions and practices should be transparent

Risk assessment policy should be determined

Risk management should be functionally separate from risk assessment to maintain the scientific integrity of the latter

Management decisions should factor in uncertainty in results of risk assessment

It should include a clear, interactive communication with stakeholders

It should be a continuing process which reviews decisions in light of newly generated data

Source: Adapted by Author from FAO/WHO 1997.

to lawmakers, regulatory enforcement communications, food safety education of consumers and labels on food products, among other efforts to convey relevant information to all stakeholders concerned. Risk communicators have the task of developing communication/outreach messages which are suitable for the target population. The first step, however, is to identify the groups in the population who are at an increased risk. For instance, it may be the children in a community who are more at risk due to their food habits like eating candy which has a certain food additive (like food colour) in high concentration. The children are thus at risk of exceeding the ADI and suffering from adverse effects. Similarly, if we are looking at reducing the risk of consuming heavy metals in our diet, people residing near the river Yamuna are at an increased risk, as they are probably consuming contaminated vegetables grown on the banks of the river.

Barriers to Effective Risk Communication

The interpretation of risk information is strongly influenced by:

- people's beliefs
- technical knowledge
- familiarity with the hazard, and
- control over the risk and its avoidance.

How different stakeholders perceive the risk and their value systems often determine whether the communication process is effective or not. Even if one stakeholder in the group does not perceive the hazard to be a real threat to health, it can derail the whole process. For instance, if antibiotic residues have been consistently found in the milk sold in a city, the regulatory authorities need to first perceive the risk to health. Once the government is convinced that the threat is real, it needs to take certain measures to manage the risk. The milk producers are the other set of stakeholders who also need to recognise the adverse effects arbitrary use of antibiotics in animal husbandry can cause. Lastly, if the consumer does not adequately perceive the threat, he will not change his source of supply or heed to the suggestions put forward by the government to reduce risk. Sometimes, language may be a barrier in communication. With only a fraction of the population fluent in the English language, warnings on labels in English (like 'refrigerate after opening'; 'not safe for consumption by children') are not understood by most of the population. Since a good number of consumers in India are probably illiterate/semi-literate, reading the label is a problem anyway. Do we then need to communicate through pictures? Information to the consumer which is laden with scientific jargon and statistical data is not very well understood by the consumer. These need to be presented in a simplified and engaging manner.

Value systems of risk managers as well as food producers/handlers will also determine how the communicated risk is perceived, such as what priority consumer health has over the profit margins that the producer would have to forgo in recalling his product or re-processing it to decrease contaminant levels. In all cases, for this reason, the risks have to be balanced against the costs for controlling them.

Another challenge is to determine how the public emotionally perceives the risk, and hence, how it reacts to measures taken to control the risk. For this purpose, it is important to ensure the participation of all stakeholders at each step of risk analysis. There has to be transparency in decision-making and the consumer needs to be provided with all the information about the risk that say, a traditional food or food served at a religious place poses.

Thus, **food safety education** of all stakeholders is very important. Sensitisation to issues of food safety of the officials of the regulatory machinery, personnel working in food industries/food service establishments, especially food handlers, and, of course, the consumers will help them to understand the consequences of unsafe food. Sources of contamination and how to keep food safe is basic knowledge that everyone should possess. The FSSAI has launched major initiatives to spread awareness about keeping food safe. One of the mandates of the FSSAI is training food safety supervisors who will ensure safety of food in all kinds of catering establishments (cafeterias in schools, colleges, offices, food service operations in places of worship, mid-day meal programme and even street foods). This training will be offered through training partners of the FSSAI, such as universities, colleges, NGOs and other institutes. School and college curricula should incorporate basic food safety information. The FSSAI has developed training books for the same, which the teachers can use. These documents are available on their website. Mass media play a crucial role in the dissemination of information. Basic food hygiene and personal hygiene-related messages can be periodically communicated using different popular media like television, radio and newspapers to reach people in all corners of the country.

ROLES AND RESPONSIBILITIES

Ensuring safe food for the citizens of a nation is the responsibility of the government. In most countries, the government plays the role of the regulator, monitoring compliance to food safety standards spelt out under local or national law. However, the responsibility of providing safe and wholesome food is also that of every food business operator, every producer—the farmer who grows the food and the manufacturer who processes the food ingredients and makes different food products (see Figure 13.4). In India, the responsibility of ensuring food safety lies with the FSSAI. The Food Safety and Standards Act and Rules have specified guidelines and regulations which all food business operators need to follow. There are various expert committees with scientists and industry representatives which aid the FSSAI in formulating food safety standards. These standards are developed based on the scientific principles of risk assessment. However, the science itself is in its infancy in our country with risk management and communication picking up on a national scale only in the last few years.

ISO standards and HACCP are being adopted voluntarily by private manufacturers. The emphasis has now shifted from ensuring food safety by end-product testing for compliance to standards, to ensuring that the process of manufacture is so good that the end product is safe. More on these laws, regulations and standards has been discussed in other chapters. The

Figure 13.4: Roles and Responsibilities of Different Stakeholders in the Process of Risk Analysis

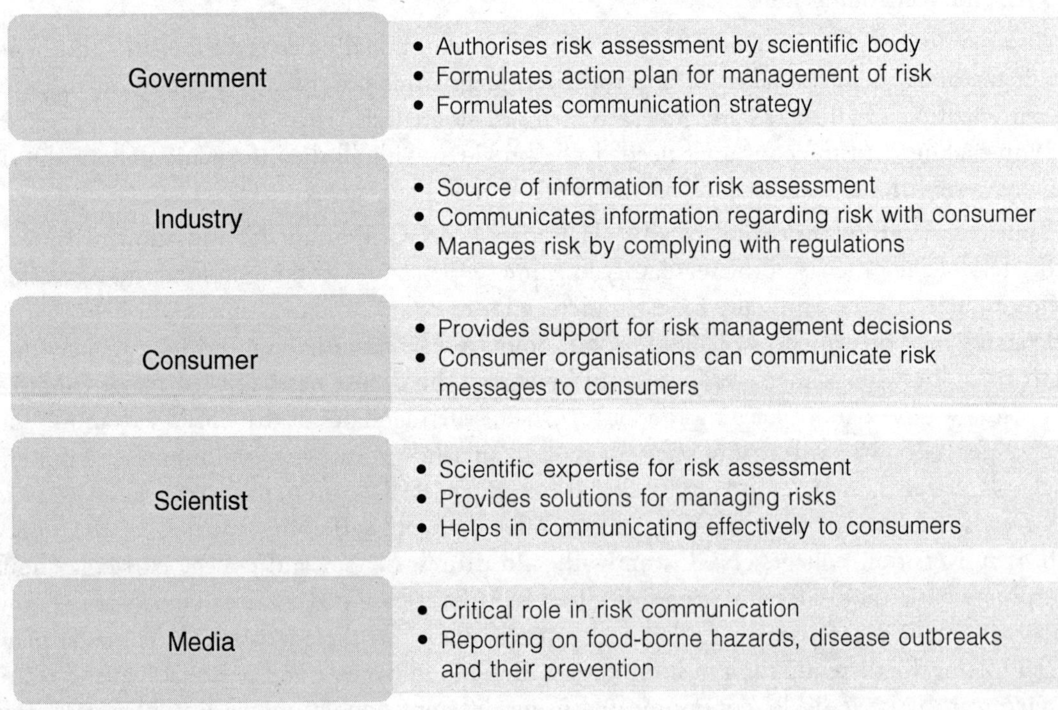

Source: Drawn by Author.

consumer is also an important stakeholder whose participation is vital in risk management. Consumer organisations can also play an important role in risk communication and also alerting the authorities about potential hazards in the food supply. Similarly, the media can also help by promptly reporting the threat of a food-borne hazard or an outbreak of a food-borne disease to the concerned authorities. This can trigger the process of risk assessment if the hazard is relatively new, or risk management, if the spread of infection has to be controlled as soon as possible. The media also has the responsibility of effectively communicating to the consumer about the hazard and how to protect oneself from adverse effects.

Internationally, the Codex Committee on Contaminants in Foods (CCCF) is primarily responsible for recommending risk management proposals for adoption by the Codex Alimentarius Committee (CAC). The Joint FAO/WHO Expert Committee on Food Additives (JECFA) is primarily responsible for performing the risk assessments, upon which the CCCF and, ultimately, the CAC base their risk management recommendations.

SUMMARY

- Risk analysis is a discipline widely recognised as fundamental in food safety evaluation and the setting of safety standards. It is based on sound scientific principles.
- Risk analysis is seen primarily as a method of systematically organising scientific and technical information to answer specific questions about health risks.
- The three components of the process of risk analysis are risk assessment, risk management and risk communication.
- The risk assessment process evaluates the likelihood of an adverse effect occurring at the level of exposure through food in the population.
- Risk assessment consists of four steps—hazard identification, which spells out the adverse health effects likely to occur; hazard characterisation, which describes the toxicity seen at different doses of the substance; exposure assessment, which estimates the amount of the chemical substance being ingested from all food sources; and risk characterisation, which collates the data to work out the risk to the population at the current levels of exposure.
- Risk management involves working out and directing the implementation of the strategy to reduce or minimise the risk while evaluating various alternatives.
- Risk communication is an interactive process of exchanging information between risk assessors, managers, consumers and other interested parties/stakeholders.
- It is the responsibility of all stakeholders—the government, the food business operators, the consumer, scientists and the media—to ensure smooth functioning of regulations and keep food safe from the farm to the fork.

KEY WORDS

Acceptable Daily Intake (ADI): An estimate of the amount of a substance, expressed on a body weight basis, that can be ingested daily over a lifetime without appreciable health risk

Acute toxicity: Adverse effects resulting from a single exposure or multiple exposure to a substance within a short period of time (usually within 14 days)

Adverse effects: Undesirable harmful effect

Chronic toxicity: Adverse effects resulting from repeated exposure to a substance over an extended period of time (usually months or years)

Dietary Recall: Tool to estimate the daily intake of food by an individual in which the person reports all the food and beverage items consumed the previous day (24 hours) in terms of household measures like cups, bowls and spoons.

Duplicate Portion Studies: Study to estimate the daily intake of food by an individual in which the individual is asked to provide a duplicate portion of whatever he eats or drinks in a day. The composite sample is then chemically analysed for nutrients, additives or contaminants depending on the objective of the survey.

Food Diary: Tool to estimate the daily intake of food by an individual. The individual is asked to maintain a diary in which he notes down all the food items and beverages consumed in a day either in terms of household measures (like bowls, spoons and glasses) or in terms of weight (so many grams of cooked vegetables, etc).

Food Frequency Questionnaire: Tool to estimate the daily intake of food by an individual in which the person is asked to report the frequency with which he eats a food item in a week, also sometimes reporting typical portion sizes; for example, he drinks a glass of milk daily or eats half a bowl of spinach twice a week. The list of foods in a food frequency questionnaire is made according to the objective of the survey.

Lethal Dose (LD_{50}): To characterise the toxic potency of a compound. This is the dose which produces 50 per cent mortality in a given population

Leukoencephalomalacia: A disease of the central nervous system that affects horses and mules

LOAEL: Lowest dose at which an adverse effect is observed

NOAEL: No-observed-adverse-effect level or a benchmark dose at which no adverse effect is seen

Stakeholders: Interested parties or those affected by a certain policy or regulation

Toxicant: Toxic substance

EXERCISES

1. What are the three components of a risk analysis study? Discuss what each component includes.
2. What are the different steps of risk assessment? Describe each in detail.
3. Discuss the significance of toxicological testing in hazard identification and hazard characterisation.
4. What are some of the barriers to the process of risk communication? Discuss giving examples.

REFERENCES

Carrington, C. D., Bolger, P. M., Scheuplein, R. J., 'Risk Analysis of Dietary Lead Exposure', *Food Additives and Contaminants* 13 (1), 1996, pp. 61–76.

FAO/WHO, 'Application of Risk Analysis to Food Standards Issues', Report of the Joint FAO/WHO Expert Consultation, 13–17 March 1995, WHO/FNU/FOS/95.3, Geneva: World Health Organization, 1995.

———, 'Risk Management and Food Safety', FAO Food and Nutrition Paper 65, Report of a Joint FAO/WHO Consultation Rome, Italy, 27–31 January 1997, World Health Organization and Food and Agriculture Organization of the United Nations, Rome, 1997.

———. 'Food Safety Risk Analysis—A Guide for National Food Safety Authorities', FAO Food and Nutrition Paper 87, World Health Organization and Food and Agriculture Organization of the United Nations, Rome, 2006.

FAO/WHO, *Codex Alimentarius Commission Procedural Manual*, 24th edition, Joint FAO/WHO Food Standards Programme, FAO, Rome, 2015.

'FDA Guidelines for Toxicity Testing', Available at http://www.fda.gov/downloads/Food/GuidanceRegulation/GuidanceDocumentsRegulatoryInformation/IngredientsAdditivesGRASPackaging/UCM078734.pdf (accessed 10 January 2017).

Jain, A., and P. Mathur, 'Estimation of Food Additive Intake—Overview of the Methodology', *Food Reviews International* 31 (4), 2015, pp. 355–84.

Marasas, W. F. O., G. S. Shephard, E. W. Sydenham, P. G. Thiel, 'Worldwide Contamination of Maize with Fumonisins. Food-borne Carcinogens Produced by Fusarium Moniliforme', in J. R. N. Taylor, P. D. Randall and J. H. Viljoen (eds), *Cerea Science and Technology—Impact on a Changing Africa*, Pretoria: CSIR, 1993, pp. 791–805.

OECD Guidelines for Testing of Chemicals, Available at https://ntp.niehs.nih.gov/iccvam/suppdocs/feddocs/oecd/oecd_gl423.pdf (accessed 10 January 2017).

Rodricks, J. V., *Calculated Risks—Understanding the Toxicity and Human Health Risks of Chemicals in our Environment*, UK: Cambridge University Press, 1992, pp. 38–48.

Uiso, F. C., and T. Johns, 'Risk Assessment of the Consumption of a Pyrrolizidine Alkaloid Containing Indigenous Vegetable *Crotalaria Brevidens (Mitoo)*', *Ecol. Food Nutr.* 35, 1995, pp. 111–119.

WHO, *Principles and Methods for the Risk Assessment of Chemicals in Food*, Environmental Health Criteria, 240, Geneva: World Health Organization, 2009.

ONLINE SOURCE

The Poison is the Dose, eToxicPennState's Channel—Video on Toxicology, Available at https://www.youtube.com/watch?v=THr7roac0cA (accessed 15 April 2018).

14

FOOD SAFETY IN FOOD SERVICE ESTABLISHMENTS

HIGHLIGHTS

- Importance of food safety for different types of establishments
- Sources of contamination and indicator organisms
- Water quality
- Hygiene and sanitation of premises
- Personnel hygiene
- Cleaning and sanitising agents
- Waste disposal
- Pest management

With an increase in the number of people choosing to eat meals prepared outside their homes, the need to look at the safety of the food served by these establishments is increasing. Changes in lifestyle have encouraged people to travel for work and pleasure. Food, as a consequence, is being served on 'wheels, wings and waves,' that is, on trains, buses, aeroplanes and ships. In addition, there is a wide range of food service establishments, from hotels, restaurants, canteens of offices, schools, colleges, hostels, hospitals, to small kiosks and street food vendors. Whatever be the type of establishment, people have the right to expect that the food served to them is wholesome and safe to eat. This chapter covers essential aspects to ensure that food served by any establishment is safe to consume. The chapter covers the ways by which food can get contaminated, how to assess if food is spoilt, and how to improve the hygiene of the premises and the food handler. It also covers essential aspects of cleaning and sanitisation, disposing waste generated in these establishments, controlling pests and maintaining water quality.

IMPORTANCE OF FOOD SAFETY FOR DIFFERENT TYPES OF ESTABLISHMENTS

Irrespective of the size of the operations of any food business, the principles of ensuring safe food remain more or less the same. Effective hygiene control is vital to avoid the adverse health effects of food-borne illnesses. The economic consequences—money lost in food spoilage, food recalls, treatment for food-borne diseases—are also to be reckoned with.

Food hygiene comprises '*conditions and measures necessary for the production, processing, storage and distribution of food designed to ensure a safe, sound, wholesome product fit for human consumption.*' (FAO/WHO 2015). The **Codex** has outlined the essential principles of food hygiene applicable throughout the food chain and has indicated how these principles should be implemented to ensure safety of food from the farm to the table.

To ensure food safety in an establishment, one needs to consider various features, starting with the selection of the site where the unit will be set up, to the design of the premises. In the premises, the design of the kitchen is of primary importance—the layout of the kitchen, that is, the area where the food will be stored, prepared and served, the drainage and waste disposal facility, and also provisions for protection from pests.

> Under the 'Serve Safe in Restaurants' Initiative, the FSSAI has proposed that a **Safe and Hygienic Food (SAHF) Rating** be developed, which will inform consumers of the quality of a restaurant. Two types of ratings will be provided to each catering establishment: one will be provided on the basis of audit scores and the second on the basis of a consumer feedback system.

Although the primary function of all food service establishments is to prepare and serve food, there are vast differences in the operations of the different types of establishments. The discussion in this chapter excludes food prepared and served at home, as well as food processing industries and retail stores. A separate chapter has been dedicated to street foods.

Food service establishments can be temporary/mobile units or those which are fixed and so, more or less permanent. A ***mobile food service establishment*** like a van, pushcart or even a movable stand, is a self-contained food unit which prepares and serves food to consumers. Street food vendors come under this category—the *chola-kulcha* seller on his movable stand, the Chinese food mobile van or the mobile handcart selling *chat*. A ***fixed food service establishment***, on the other hand, operates at a specific location and probably has all the basic facilities like water supply, electricity, waste disposal system, etc. In contrast, these facilities are mostly not available in mobile units. Fixed establishments include canteens, restaurants, cafes, and food served in institutions like hostels, hospitals, etc. A *temporary food service establishment* is usually one which sets up operation for a fixed number of days at a location—usually at a fair, or gathering for a festival, exhibition, or any other celebration/event. These units may be supplied with the basic amenities (water, electricity, waste disposal) during the event, so that they can function smoothly.

> **Restaurant Grading to Help Consumers Identify Safe Places to Eat**
>
> Food service establishments in several cities of the world are graded based on how they follow Food Safety Guidelines. This helps the consumer choose where he would like to eat. Some places like Dubai and Alameda County, USA use coloured cards (such as green, yellow and red) to grade, while others like New York use letter grades (such as A, B and C). Some are even known to use emojis (such as happy, sad and sour)! This concept is being introduced in different parts of the world and is not mandatory as yet in most places.

Food safety on Wheels, Wings and Waves

With a surge in the number of people travelling for business or pleasure, there is a focus on providing them with safe food during their long journeys by bus or train (wheels), airlines (wings) and ships (waves). Some of these journeys may last a few days. Contaminated food can lead to serious food poisoning, affecting several people at the same time. Can you imagine what impact a food poisoning outbreak would have on the business of a luxury cruise liner or an airline?

For railway and airplane journeys, the food is generally prepared in advance. Care needs to be taken that this preparation is not too much in advance. Food should be fresh when loaded on trains or airplanes. Sometimes, the food is served within a few hours of the journey; however, in some long-distance flights, the food may be served 10–12 hours later. If trains or flights are delayed, the freshness of the food is further compromised. To ensure that the food remains safe, adequate cool and hot storage facilities should be available on board. The food should be kept safely packaged and unexposed to contaminants and pests. Usually, the packaging available now is single-use only. The food is mostly served in its original package, eliminating the problem of ensuring clean service utensils. Spoons, forks and knives are usually packed along with the food after sterilisation. Only safe packaging material should be used, which does not introduce chemical contaminants into the food. Also, safe potable water should be served. Maximum care has to be taken for the quality of ice, which should be prepared using potable water and handled carefully (never using bare hands).

Journeys on ships may last much longer—a few days to a few weeks. It is not possible for all food to be cooked in advance; hence, ships have proper fully functional kitchens like any other hotel or restaurant. They need to follow the same principles of hygiene and sanitation as other food service establishments with proper storage facilities, food processing areas, cleaning areas and well-trained personnel.

SOURCES OF CONTAMINATION AND INDICATOR ORGANISMS

As several food-borne disease outbreaks have been linked to food served in establishments, it is important to understand how food gets contaminated and factors which contribute to the outbreak (see Figure 14.1).

The problem could start with the use of **raw ingredients** which are heavily contaminated. Cooking may not always destroy all the microbes. In large-scale catering establishments, washing, cleaning and sorting of raw ingredients is a difficult job, especially when ingredients include items like green leafy vegetables. **Inadequate cleaning** may result in a high microbial load to start with. Further, if the food to be prepared does not require major cooking, then the final product is likely to be contaminated and unsafe for consumption. That is why you may have been advised not to eat uncooked items like salads and *chat* preparations at weddings or from street food vendors. Ingredients may also have chemical contaminants like pesticide residues, veterinary drug residues or heavy metals. If they are not screened for quality at entry points, these foods or ingredients could contaminate other foods to which they are added.

Figure 14.1: Factors Increasing the Risk of Food-borne Disease Outbreaks

Preparation	Storage	Service
• Contaminated raw ingedients and water • Unclean utensils and equipment • Handling by infected or unclean persons	• Cross-contamination from raw to cooked food • Improper cooling • Improper holding temperature • Food left at room temperature	• Inadequate reheating • Unclean utensils for service • Handling by infected or unclean persons

Source: Drawn by Author.

The **water** used for cooking and cleaning can also be a source of contamination. Ground water is usually more contaminated as it has not been treated. Besides being a source of pathogenic microbes, the water may also be contaminated with heavy metals like arsenic and lead or even pesticide residues.

All **contact surfaces** related to food—such as counters of food preparation areas, sinks in which it is washed, chopping boards, knives, peelers, graters, grinders and utensils—could add to the microbial load. If the residues of cleaning agents are left on these surfaces or residues of pesticides which were sprayed in areas where food is prepared, the same could be transferred to the food. Utensils, if made of cheap recycled metal, could leach heavy metals like lead, chromium or aluminium into the food.

The people who handle food become the biggest source of contamination if they do not follow good hygiene practices. Hands, skin, hair, clothes and nails can potentially harbour various disease-causing microbes. If the **food handler** is suffering from or is a carrier of a disease which can be transmitted through food, he is likely to contaminate the food.

Poor handling practices like not washing and cleaning raw food properly, cooking inadequately, keeping food at inappropriate temperatures, not adequately reheating the food, not maintaining strict hygiene and sanitation, can all contribute to serious food-borne disease outbreaks. During storage or even during preparation, if raw food with a high microbial load comes in contact with cooked food, the latter is likely to get contaminated as well.

Pests (flies, cockroaches, rats, mice, etc.) are another serious source of contamination. They can physically damage the food. The more serious damage is the transfer of microbes from the pest to the food. Serious diseases like typhoid, diarrhoea and dysentery have resulted from the contamination of food by pests.

If an establishment gets linked to a major food-borne disease outbreak, it is the end of business for that operation. That is why large-scale operators like hotels and restaurant chains have elaborate food safety management systems in place. The same logic applies to the street food vendor and small-scale food establishments as well. If the food served by a vendor is safe and wholesome, his business is more likely to grow. Besides the unpleasant experience of illness for the consumer, food safety lapses can have disastrous economic consequences for the food business operator.

Practices which are likely to reduce the risk of contamination include:

- Using only clean potable water for cooking and cleaning of raw ingredients, and using clean pots and pans for cooking, storing and eating food.
- Thoroughly washing raw vegetables, fruits and grains to get rid of germs and parasites like worms. This also helps in removing pesticides, at least partially.
- Purchasing ingredients used in food preparation from reliable sources to make sure that they are free of adulterants and contaminants.
- Thoroughly cooking the foods to ensure that all germs have been killed.
- Keeping the premises thoroughly clean, sanitised and free from pests.
- Having an efficient waste disposal system.
- Storing foods in a cool, dry atmosphere or refrigerating them to discourage microbial growth.
- Good personal hygiene of all food handlers.
- Not allowing people suffering from any contagious disease to handle food.

The standard test organisms used for evaluating the safety of foods are many (see Table 14.1). In the case of drinking water, *E. coli* is an indicator of faecal contamination and must not be detectable in a 100 ml water sample (BIS 2012). Enteric viruses and protozoa are more resistant to disinfection than *E. coli*. Thus, it has been recommended that more resistant indicators, such as bacteriophages and/or bacterial spores, should be considered. Other contaminants in water include protozoan oocysts such as *Cryptosporidium* spp., *Giardia lamblia*, *Legionella*, and enteric viruses.

FSSAI (2011b) provides microbiological standards for a number of foods. Total plate count, and yeast and mould count are indicative of the microbial load of the food product (number of microbes present per unit weight in the food). Coliforms are considered to be **indicator organisms**. These bacteria are always present in the digestive tracts of animals, including humans, and are found in their wastes. Since there is a large number of pathogens which can be present in our food or water, and it is not practical to test for all of them, the presence of pathogens is determined with indirect evidence by testing for an 'indicator' organism such as coliform bacteria. Coliforms come from the same sources as pathogenic organisms and are relatively easy to identify. This is because they are usually present in larger numbers than the pathogens and respond in a similar manner to many pathogens. So, testing for coliform bacteria can be a reasonable indication of whether other pathogenic bacteria are present in a food or beverage. *E. coli* is the best indicator of faecal pollution.

Table 14.1: Microbiological Standards for Some Commonly Used Food Products

Food	*Total plate count*	*E. coli*	*Staphylococcus aureus*	*Salmonella, Shigella*	*Vibrio cholerae*	*Vibrio parahaemolyticus*	*Clostridium perfringens*
Raw seafood: fish, prawn, shrimp, lobster, squid	Not more than 5 lakh/g	Not more than 20/g	Not more than 100/g	Absent in 25g	Absent in 25g	Absent in 25g	–

Food	*Total plate count*	*Coliform count*	*E. coli*	*Staphylococcus aureus*	*Salmonella*	*Yeast and Mould count*	*Listeria monocytogenes*
Pasteurised milk/ cream/flavoured milk	50,000/g	Less than 10/g	Absent/g	Less than 10/g	Absent/25g	–	Absent/g
Pasteurised butter	50,000/g	50/g	Absent/g	50/g	Absent/25g	50/g	Absent/g
Ice cream	2,50,000/g	100/g	Absent/g	Less than 10/g	Absent/25g	Less than 10/g	Absent/g
Processed cheese	75,000/g	Less than 10/g	Absent/g	Less than10/g	Absent/25g	Less than10/g	Absent/g
Paneer	5,00,000/g	90/g	Less than 10/g	100/g	Absent/g	250/g	Absent/g
Ready-to-serve beverages	Not more than 50/ml	Absent in 100ml	–	–	–	Not more than 2/ml	–

Source: Adapted by Author from FSSAI 2011b.

Staphylococcus aureus (coagulase positive), *Salmonella, Shigella, Clostridium perfringens, Vibrio cholera, Vibrio parahaemolyticus* and *Listeria monocytogeness* are the other pathogens usually tested for in most foods.

WATER QUALITY

Water is an important component of not just the food preparation process, but also the cleaning and sanitising processes. Hence, the quality of water used is very important as it can become a significant source of contamination. The following steps can be taken to ensure good quality of water:

- Water supply should be from a trusted source like the municipal supply.
- If using ground water, it should be properly tested for the presence of contaminants and adequately treated before use.
- All plumbing and water pipes should be checked to ensure there is no leakage or cross-contamination with other pipes, such as those carrying waste water.
- The underground and overhead tanks should be periodically cleaned and records kept indicating the date of each cleaning.

The important aspects of water quality which need to be considered are shown in Figure 14.2. The water used for cooking and cleaning should have no pathogens and should not have chemical contaminants like heavy metals and pesticide residues beyond permissible limits. 'Potable' water is water fit for drinking. The Bureau of Indian Standards lays down the standard for water that is suitable for drinking. The latest revision took place in 2012, with an amendment in 2015.

Figure 14.2: Quality Parameters of Water that Need to be Checked

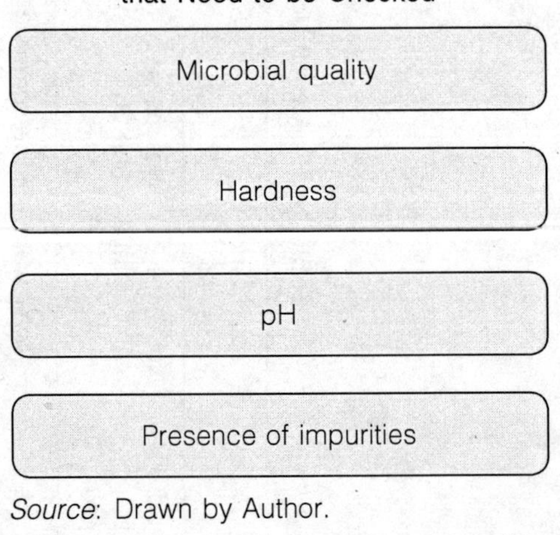

Source: Drawn by Author.

According to the BIS (2012), drinking water should not have any *E. coli* or thermotolerant coliform bacteria or coliform bacteria detectable in any 100 ml sample of water. Immediate investigative action needs to be taken if these are detected. Treatment or sanitisation of water prior to use in any cleaning regime may be required in case the water is not of satisfactory quality. Water hardness has a direct effect on the chemical action of sanitisers. Often, food service establishments put up a water softening plant to deal with the situation. Other impurities present in water can also adversely affect the effectiveness of detergents and sanitising agents. The pH of water generally ranges from 5 to 8.5 and this does not affect cleaning or sanitising. However, if the water is highly acidic or alkaline, buffering agents may need to be added in order to make the water usable.

HYGIENE AND SANITATION OF PREMISES

Not just the food preparation and storage areas, but all areas surrounding the establishment need to be kept clean and hygienic. This is because it does not take long for pests and pathogens in waste materials dumped in the surroundings to gain entry into food preparation and storage areas. Equipment which is not in operation, such as containers and other articles which are not in use, should not be unnecessarily stacked on the premises, as they become a breeding ground for pests. The building has to be constructed and maintained in such a manner that there is no corner or crevice which can harbour rodents, cockroaches, etc. The aspects which specially need our attention have been listed in Figure 14.3.

Figure 14.3: Features that Help Keep the Premises Clean and Hygienic

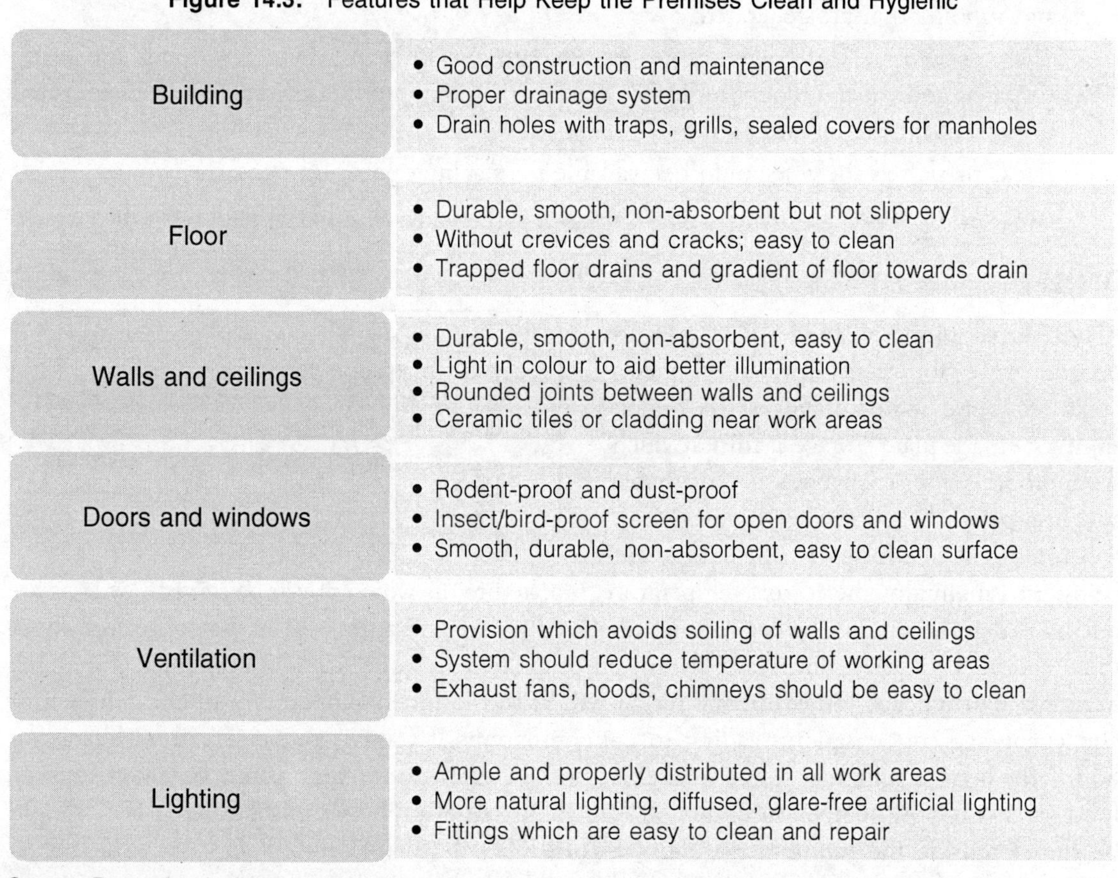

Building	• Good construction and maintenance • Proper drainage system • Drain holes with traps, grills, sealed covers for manholes
Floor	• Durable, smooth, non-absorbent but not slippery • Without crevices and cracks; easy to clean • Trapped floor drains and gradient of floor towards drain
Walls and ceilings	• Durable, smooth, non-absorbent, easy to clean • Light in colour to aid better illumination • Rounded joints between walls and ceilings • Ceramic tiles or cladding near work areas
Doors and windows	• Rodent-proof and dust-proof • Insect/bird-proof screen for open doors and windows • Smooth, durable, non-absorbent, easy to clean surface
Ventilation	• Provision which avoids soiling of walls and ceilings • System should reduce temperature of working areas • Exhaust fans, hoods, chimneys should be easy to clean
Lighting	• Ample and properly distributed in all work areas • More natural lighting, diffused, glare-free artificial lighting • Fittings which are easy to clean and repair

Source: Drawn by Author.

Kitchen

Only authorised personnel directly involved with the food preparation process should be allowed to enter the kitchen area. It should not be a thoroughfare to get to other parts of the establishment. The likelihood of contamination increases when more people enter the kitchen. The layout of the kitchen should be such that it ensures a smooth workflow. The points to be kept in mind include:

- Best use should be made of natural lighting and ventilation by appropriate positioning of doors and windows.
- Drainage systems should be well designed to carry waste water away. There should not be long channels running through the kitchen.
- Free-standing kitchen units are generally more hygienic than those fixed close to walls.
- An 'island' layout with a work table or equipment like ovens and mixing machines in the centre is easier to keep clean. Aisles should be wide to make movement free.
- All cooking ranges and stoves need hoods with ventilation systems to suck out the fumes and vapours that are generated.
- There should be clear demarcation of areas in the kitchen where raw foods are being prepared and cooked foods are stored. Plant and animal products should also be segregated to prevent cross-contamination.
- Racks or slatted shelves should be available for stacking pots and pans.
- Appropriate storage facility for fresh and dry ingredients should be made available.

Storage

> Thawed food should not be refrozen. It should be cooked immediately. Upon thawing, the microbes, especially spores, become active again and multiply rapidly. If frozen again, the food would have a much higher microbial load than earlier. Foods are best thawed in a refrigerator or in a microwave.

If not stored properly, food will spoil and become unfit for consumption. It makes great economic sense for an establishment to invest in adequate storage facilities which are appropriate for perishable, semi-perishable and non-perishable foods (see Figure 14.4). It is important to ensure that the equipment being used maintains the correct temperature. Cooked foods which are to be served hot later are refrigerated and then, just before serving, re-heated to a temperature >70°C. Before refrigeration, these should be cooled down rapidly by putting them in wide shallow containers for quick heat loss. Putting hot foods directly inside will raise the inner temperature of the refrigerator and encourage condensation, leading to contamination. If food is to be served within a few hours, the service unit may want to keep it hot. In such cases, care should be taken to keep food (even the core temperature) at >60°C. All **Potentially Hazardous Foods** (**PHF**) should be stored outside the **temperature danger zone** (**TDZ**) (5°C/41°F–60°C/140°F). The FSSAI recommends storing hot foods at >63°C and reheating/cooking till the core temperature of foods is a minimum of 75°C.

The stacking of different foods in a refrigerator should be such that there is no chance of cross-contamination. For instance, the raw meats should be kept away from vegetables and cooked preparations. Separate refrigerators should preferably be used for cooked and raw product storage. Drippings from meat should not fall on any other food; hence, it should be stored on another

Figure 14.4: Conditions for Storage of Different Types of Foods

Type of food	Storage conditions
Perishable food (vegetables, fruits, seafood, milk, meat, poultry, cooked food, etc.)	• Refrigerated storage (<5°C): Walk in chillers, cold room, refrigerators and display cabinets • Freezer storage (< –18°C): deep freezing cabinets, walk in freezers, display freezers • Hot storage: where temperature is kept >60°C like bain marie, heated service cabinets
Semi-perishable (Some vegetables (onion, potato, beetroot, etc.) flour, etc.)	• Dry storage: in containers kept in well ventilated rooms or cabinets • Refrigerated storage: for packaged products which, when opened, need to be refrigerated
Non-perishable (grains, dals, spices, tea, coffee, oil, etc.)	• Dry storage: in containers kept in well-ventilated rooms or cabinets

Source: Drawn by Author.

shelf and below other foods. Ideally, the refrigerator or freezer for non-vegetarian foods should be separate from that for vegetarian foods. All food should be covered and stored to prevent contamination and drying of surfaces. Also, refrigerators and freezers should not be overloaded as doing this reduces the effectiveness of cooling. The dry storage area should be well lit and ventilated. No container or package of food should be stored on the floor of the refrigerator. Racks or shelves should be available for stacking packages and containers. The lowermost shelf should be at least six inches above the ground to ensure thorough cleaning under the rack of shelves and to protect containers from splash and flooding.

When food is received, it should be inspected for its freshness and quality. As far as possible, packaged, well-labelled products should be purchased as these are likely to be of better quality (as has been discussed in the chapter on adulteration). When a manufacturer puts his name on a package, he becomes liable for the safety of the product. Things to look out for include:

- The packaging or container of the food product should not be damaged.
- The food product should not visibly show signs of insect infestation, mould growth or other physical damage.
- Frozen foods should not show signs of thawing (package is soft when pressed) and refreezing (presence of ice crystals; food is misshapen).
- Visibly dirty foods should first be cleaned and then sent to the storage area.

When taking food out of the storage areas, one should follow the principle of '**First in, first out**' or **FIFO**. This means that food which was brought into the kitchen store earlier should be used first, and then the newly bought stock. This is done to reduce spoilage and wastage. If fresh purchases are kept in the front or top of chillers and freezers every time, the tendency is to reach out for these first. The old stock may keep lying at the back/bottom and not get used for several days together. It may even spoil in the process. So, it is very important to put the date of receiving/preparation on the packages of food received/prepared. The expiration date should also be clearly marked and the principle of FEFO or 'First Expired First Out' followed. If there is any doubt about whether the product has expired or is still suitable for consumption, it should simply be discarded.

Equipment and Utensils

Special attention also needs to be paid to the various equipment and utensils used for the purpose of food preparation. These can serve as major sources of contamination and hence, there needs to be a specific cleaning protocol for each one of them depending upon their construction and use. For instance, equipment with several pipes or tubes would regularly need to be flushed clean so that **biofilms** do not form in the tubing. Other things to be kept in mind while selecting equipment/utensils, or installing and maintaining them are listed here:

- Utensils should be made of durable material which resists denting, pitting, chipping, scratching, etc. They should be able to handle rough handling, and repeated scouring and scrubbing. If the surface of utensils and containers is not smooth, pits and dents tend to harbour microbes.
- Utensils should be made of material which does not leach chemicals, metals, etc. into the food during the cooking or holding process.
- All food contact surfaces of equipment should be accessible for easy cleaning without having to take apart the parts of the machine each time. This encourages better cleaning by personnel.
- Equipment should be placed on tables, counters or mounted on platforms or stands which are at least six inches above the ground. If they need to be placed on the floor, they should be sealed on the floor. All this is to ensure that cleanliness is maintained in the surrounding and adjacent areas.

PERSONNEL HYGIENE

Food handlers are a major source of contamination and hence, good personal hygiene of handlers goes a long way in ensuring safety of food. People who handle food should be healthy (that is, not suffering from contagious diseases). When suffering from any ailment, they should either not come to work or be assigned some other duty where they are not directly involved in handling food. They should be prevented from directly handling food even after they recover, because in the case of some diseases like hepatitis or typhoid, the patient remains a carrier of the disease for some time. In addition, boils, carbuncles, cuts and septic spots on hands can become sources of bacteria like pathogenic staphylococci. Fingernails are another place where microbes accumulate and that is why food handlers are asked to keep them short and clean. Hair also needs to be kept covered as it can fall into the food and contaminate it. To avoid this, handlers are required to wear hair nets, caps or other types of head gear. Handlers who dig their hands into the food while processing should also remove their watches and jewellery like rings and bangles. Not only does the jewellery harbour microbes, stones or clasps could also fall into the food and become a physical hazard. The personnel involved in cooking should also wear uniforms or aprons so that their street clothes, which may be contaminated, are not in direct contact with the food.

Several food processing methods require that the cooks or handlers make use of their hands in the operation. Hand hygiene is, therefore, of prime importance. Hand washing has been recognised as one of the most effective measures in keeping food safe. Hands need to be washed regularly during the whole food processing operation, in fact, every time the personnel touch the food. Figure 14.5 lists the occasions after which hand washing is crucial to prevent contamination.

Figure 14.5: Hand Washing is Important to Prevent Contamination of Food

Food handlers should wash their hands and wrists

- Before engaging in food preparation activity
- When changing tasks like handling vegetables after meat, or handling raw and then cooked food
- After using the toilet
- After sneezing, coughing or blowing one's nose
- After handling money, garbage, waste material, cleaning chemicals or even a piece of cloth used to wipe counters

Source: Drawn by Author.
Image Source: 'Hand Wash Sign' by ozhank (CC0 1.0; Openclipart).

For effective hand washing and, indeed, maintaining good personal hygiene among food handlers, the establishment should provide basic amenities such as:

- adequate number of clean and well-maintained washrooms/toilets which the personnel are encouraged to use;
- a separate sink for hand washing outside the toilet for employees so that they do not have to visit the toilet each time they want to wash hands.
- The sink for hand washing should preferably have hands-free taps which either operate based

> An average hand harbours more than 1,000 bacteria per sq cm. Washing hands effectively can reduce this microbial load significantly.

on a sensor or can be turned on and off with the help of foot pedals or using the elbow. This prevents recontamination of hands from the tap itself.

- There should be liquid soap available in a dispenser to encourage proper hand washing.
- The personnel should be made aware of not only the importance of washing hands, but also the correct way of washing hands, to get rid of microbes lodged on their skin, between their fingers and beneath their nails. The cleaning action should last a minimum of 20 seconds.
- A hot air blower or paper towel should be available to dry their hands. Cloth towels can get contaminated if multiple users dry their hands with the same towel. If nothing is available, the personnel will wipe their hands dry on their clothes or apron, which is again not recommended due to the fear of re-contaminating the hands.
- Any refuse bin should also be foot operable so that hands do not touch such highly contaminated surfaces.

In addition, some other facilities, which also contribute to improving the safety of food served in the establishment, should be provided. These are:

- Protective clothing/uniform or aprons and head gear. The management should ensure that these are freshly laundered for every use. There should be a changing room available for them to change out of their street clothes.
- Locker facilities so that personnel can put their personal belongings and street clothes in them, rather than carrying these with them into the food preparation areas.
- A first-aid room to handle minor problems such as cuts and bruises. In addition, there should be a facility for a regular screening for contagious diseases and their treatment by a medical professional.

Food handlers are also required to follow good hygienic practices, such as having a bath daily, not indulging in smoking, picking their nose, scratching their head and other such practices which can promote the transfer of harmful microbes from their person to food. They should also avoid touching the food directly as much as possible—not to dip their finger into food to test temperature, not to hold utensils by placing their hands on inner surfaces where the food may touch the utensil (holding glasses with fingers inside or holding spoons from the end which goes into the mouth) and not tasting food by licking their fingers. Eating, chewing, smoking, spitting and nose blowing should be prohibited within the premises, especially while handling food according to FSSAI (2011b) regulations.

Training personnel about good hygienic practices is important to ensure safety of food. They need to understand the need for all the dos and don'ts. Sensitisation to food safety issues can ensure better compliance. Routine supervision is vital to ensure that food safety practices are being duly followed. The FSSAI has made it mandatory for food business operators to have a Food Safety Supervisor for every 25 food handlers on their premises.

CLEANING AND SANITISING AGENTS

The objective of **cleaning** is to remove food, dirt, grime and filth from all surfaces in and around the food production area. This can be achieved by physical, chemical or mechanical methods. The term '**soil**' is used to describe all the undesirable materials like food residue, dirt, deposits, etc. which cling to surfaces. Special care is taken to sanitise the surfaces which directly come into contact with food. The aim is not just to remove visible dirt/food but also to destroy microbes present on these surfaces. Different terms are used to describe the different levels of cleaning (see Figure 14.6).

Figure 14.6: Different Terms Used for Cleaning and Sanitising

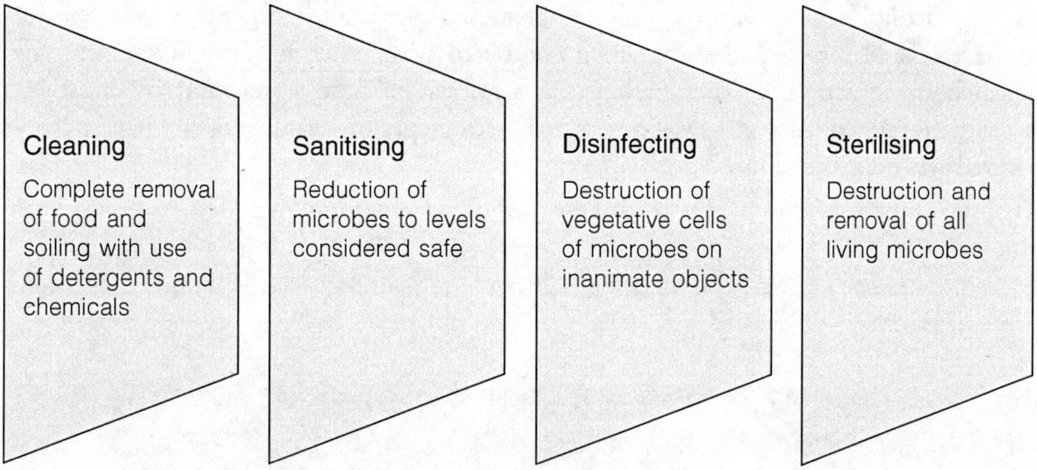

Source: Drawn by Author.

The definition given by the Association of Official Analytical Chemists of sanitising for food product contact surfaces is '*a process which reduces the contamination level by 99.999% (5 logs) in 30 seconds, and for non-product contact surfaces the process requires a contamination reduction of 99.9% (3 logs)*' (EPA 2012). Disinfectants are considered stronger than sanitisers. While sanitisers mostly kill bacteria, disinfectants can kill both bacteria and viruses. The key difference lies in the kind of chemicals used. The process of sterilisation kills all microbes and their spores. Steam, heat, radiation or chemicals are used for this.

Cleaning agents need to have different properties to be effective. The cleaning agent needs to *emulsify* the fat drops into smaller droplets which are then dispersed in the cleaning solution along with adhering dirt or soil. The cleaning compound should also have the property of **rinsibility**, that is, it should be easily removed from the surface without leaving a residue. It helps if the agent also has a **sequestrant**, which prevents calcium and magnesium salts in hard water from forming deposits on surfaces of equipment and utensils. A **surfactant** breaks the surface tension and allows greater contact between the cleaning compound and soil. It increases the ability for wetting, dispersing and rinsing.

Different types of cleaning agents are used in food service establishments and processing plants (Marriott 1997). **Alkaline cleaning solutions** are best suited for organic soil (heavy deposits of fats and proteins). These may be of different strengths. *Strongly alkaline cleaners* (such as sodium hydroxide) are very corrosive and used only for heavy soils in commercial ovens, smokehouses, etc. *Heavy duty alkaline* cleaners (such as sodium carbonate) are not that corrosive and are used in mechanised and/or high pressure cleaning systems, and these are very good at removing fats. *Mild alkaline cleaners* (such as sodium bicarbonate) are used to clean lightly soiled areas by hand. **Acid cleaning agents** are effective in cleaning mineral deposits (scaling) or inorganic soil. Inorganic acids (such as phosphoric acid and hydrofluoric acid) can be very corrosive to surfaces and irritating to the skin. Mild acid cleaners (such as hydroacetic acid, acetic acid, gluconic acid and organic acids) are slightly corrosive and may cause mild irritation to the skin. **Solvents** based on ether or alcohol help in removing oils and greases. **Soaps and detergents** help in emulsifying oil and grease and improve cleaning when combined with other additives. Detergents have a stronger cleansing action, are better than soaps for use in hard water, and are mostly made from synthetic ingredients, as opposed to soaps. Most types of cleaning agents have phosphates complexed with organic chlorine.

The cleaning procedures can be dry or wet. **Dry cleaning** includes sweeping, wiping, brushing or vacuum cleaning of surfaces or equipment. **Wet cleaning** involves cleaning with water and chemical agents. This may be achieved in two ways for equipment as shown in Figure 14.7.

Figure 14.7: Cleaning of Equipment—Comparison of CIP and COP

Clean in place (CIP)	Clean out of place (COP)
• Does not require disassembly for cleaning inside the equipment • Cleaning is faster, less labour-intensive and more repeatable • Beneficial for equipment with pipes, tubes and interior parts that are difficult to reach • Can be fully automated • Used mostly in industries like dairy, beverage, brewing and other processed foods	• Needs to be partially disassembled to clean inside the equipment • Cleaning more labour-intensive as parts have to be disassembled • Used for pieces of equipment that are hard to clean • More of manual cleaning • Used in food service establishments for most equipment

Source: Drawn by Author.

Sanitising refers to reducing the microbial load of surfaces by use of physical and chemical agents. This tends to kill vegetative cells though some spores may still survive. Sanitising is essential after the cleaning process as simply cleaning may not substantially reduce the microbial load. Sanitising helps prevent food-borne disease outbreaks and improves the shelf life and quality of products. Different types of sanitisers are used in the food industry (see Figure 14.8).

Figure 14.8: Types of Sanitisers

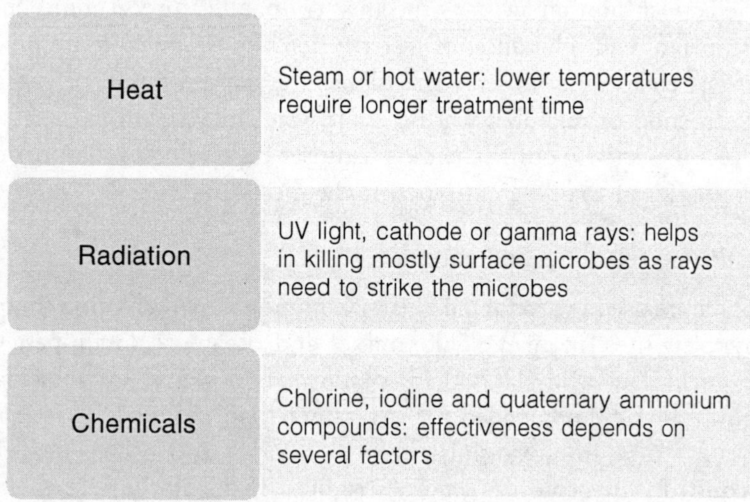

Source: Drawn by Author.

The effectiveness of all sanitisers depends on the time for which the microbes are exposed to the sanitiser, whether it is heat, radiation or a chemical. Efficiency of heat as a sanitiser also depends on the humidity and temperature. Most commonly, steam or hot water is used to sanitise as the presence of moisture makes heat more effective. Radiation is perhaps the least used method as many bacteria are resistant to radiation and need longer direct exposure to actually be killed. The effectiveness depends on cleanliness of the surface to be sanitised. If the surface has not been previously cleaned, it will be much more difficult to sanitise it. Dust, grease and grime tend to absorb radiation and also make certain chemical sanitising agents less effective. Therefore, the cleaning and sanitising process follows the steps as shown in Figure 14.9. After any wet treatment, it is preferable that the equipment and surfaces are allowed to air dry. Wiping them may re-introduce germs if the cloth used is not clean. After drying, they still need to be protected from recontamination.

Figure 14.9: The Cleaning–Sanitising Sequence for Equipment

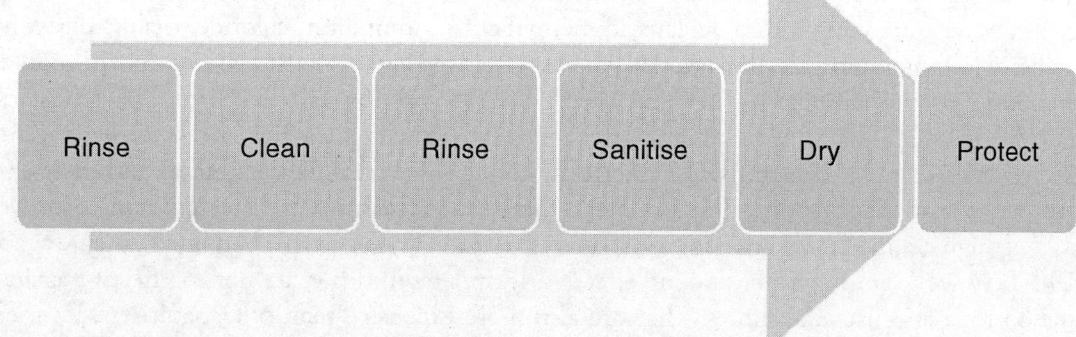

Source: Adapted by Author from Schmidt 2015.

The effectiveness of different chemical agents also depends on their concentration (and hence, the correct dilution factor as specified by manufacturers should be used), the pH of the medium, temperature and hardness of water. Microbes are killed more quickly at higher temperatures by use of chemical sanitisers. The higher the concentration of the sanitiser, the faster the rate of destruction of microbes will be. Hard water makes sanitisers less effective. Changes in pH also affect the activity of the chemical sanitiser depending on nature of the compound. Let us see the properties of the different types of chemical sanitisers.

Chlorine-releasing Compounds

These are used in several industries. Commonly used chlorine compounds include liquid chlorine, hypochlorites, inorganic chloramines and organic chloramines. Chlorine-based sanitisers form hypochlorous acid (HOCl) in solution has powerful microbicidal activity. Chlorine dioxide is now being recommended for use rather than chlorine, as it is more environment friendly. It has 2.5 times the oxidising power of chlorine and hence, smaller amounts of the chemical are required. Hypochlorites (such as sodium hypochlorite) are the most powerful and commonly used sanitising agents in the food industry, with a wide range of anti-bacterial activity. They are effective in hard water too, are relatively cheap and easily available. They are, however, unstable and become less effective when exposed to heat and light. They can also corrode steel and other metals and hence must be in contact with metallic surfaces only for a short time.

Iodophors

These are used as sanitising agents, chiefly in the dairy industry and as hand sanitisers in the form of hand-dipping solutions (examples include alcohol-iodine solutions and aqueous iodine solutions). These solutions can be used on hands as they do not irritate the skin. However, these are not as effective as hypochlorites against bacterial spores. They are also more expensive. They have some other disadvantages as well: they may cause off-flavours in some food products, they are sensitive to pH changes, and iodine tends to vapourise at about 50°C, making the sanitising agent less effective. Iodine can also cause staining of some surfaces like plastics.

Quaternary Ammonium Compounds (QACs)

These are used primarily for cleaning and sanitising floors, walls and equipment; for instance, cetyltrimethyl ammonium bromide, lauryldimethylbenzyl ammonium chloride, n-alkyl dimethyl ethylbenzyl ammonium chloride, etc. They are natural wetting agents and are especially good at penetrating porous substances. They also have a detergent action and can form a bacteriostatic film over surfaces. This helps in killing bacteria even after the application process as these agents have residual action. These sanitisers are better at killing some bacteria than others and these also work better than chlorine or iodine-based sanitisers for soiled surfaces. They are non-corrosive, stable at high temperatures and do not irritate the skin. When properly diluted, they do not smell. They work at a high pH and are effective against moulds but are not so effective against some bacteria and bacterial spores. They are also more expensive than other sanitisers. Further, many QAC formulations can cause foaming problems in CIP applications.

In addition to the above, acid-anionic sanitisers, fatty acid sanitisers, hydrogen peroxide, ozone and peroxyacetic acid are finding use in the food industry. Careful study of the properties of the chemical should be done before using it as a sanitising or cleaning agent.

It is important to note here that all cleaning and sanitising agents and pesticides should be stored in a separate area away from food ingredients and the main food preparation area. Several food poisoning outbreaks have been reported where sanitisers/pesticides have been mixed with food accidentally since they were mistaken for food ingredients. This may also occur if old food containers like oil drums and cans are used for storing these chemicals.

It is important for any food service establishment to establish proper cleaning and sanitising protocols. This means that the method, procedure and schedule for cleaning and sanitation need to be spelt out to ensure safety. These also need to be monitored to make sure that they are effective.

The Agri-Food and Veterinary Authority and National Environment Agency, Singapore has recommended the following frequency for cleaning different equipment and premises, as given in Figure 14.10. Colour-coded cleaning tools are recommended to help the personnel in charge of cleaning (who are often not very educated) to prevent cross-contamination. Colour-coding helps in keeping tools separate for general cleaning, for food processing areas, meat processing and seafood processing areas. Suitable tools should be kept for different types of surfaces and cleaning actions. For instance, a brush with stiff bristles may be required for removing tough grime which really need to be scrubbed clean. Softer bristles or pads may be required for surfaces which can easily be scratched. This is important to observe not just from the aesthetic point of view, but also because scratches tend to attract more soiling and hence, microbial contamination. The cleaning tools—brushes, brooms and cloth or pads—themselves need to be kept clean and sanitised. Otherwise, they may become a source of contamination. Also, they should be durable and not introduce physical hazards like bristles or metal/fibre pieces into the food or equipment.

Figure 14.10: Recommended Frequency of Cleaning of Premises and Equipment

Daily or after operation	Weekly	Monthly
• Floor and wall next to food preparation area • Food processing equipment • Utensils and containers • Sinks, taps, gullies and drains • Tables and work counters • Sinks, toilets • Interior cabin of delivery truck	• Doors	• Windows • Ceilings • Overhead fixtures (lighting covers and fans) • Exhaust hood and ventilation system • Refrigerator, freezer, dry storage areas

Source: Adapted by Author from AVA/NEA.

WASTE DISPOSAL

All food service establishments need an efficient system for the disposal of waste generated during operations. The waste material includes food scraps, peels, inedible portions of fruits and vegetables, egg shells, bones, empty packaging material (paper, cardboard, plastic, tin, etc.) and waste water from washing and cleaning. Proper waste disposal is important to ensure that the establishment does not pollute the ground surface and water supply or create unsanitary conditions. Waste water usually drains into the sewage lines. Waste released into the sewage system should conform to the local sanitary laws. Solid waste should be collected in foot-operable waste bins made of durable, easy-to-clean material which is leak-proof. Bins should have tight-fitting lids. These bins should be lined with plastic bags. There should be separate waste bins for biodegradable waste (vegetable matter, paper, etc. so that it may be composted later) and recyclable waste (polythene, cardboard, glass, etc.). These bins should be frequently emptied into bigger waste bins kept outside the food preparation area. All bins are to be kept thoroughly clean and covered so that they do not attract pests. These would also need to be disinfected regularly and the area should be kept odour-free by not letting garbage accumulate for long. The collection containers should be large enough to accommodate waste generated during the day, and there should not be any spill-overs. They should be placed on platforms made of concrete or non-absorbent material. The ground should be such that there is no low-lying area where liquid waste may accumulate.

PEST MANAGEMENT

One can expect the presence of pests wherever food is being stored or prepared. Control measures to reduce or eradicate these pests need to be in place to reduce the risk of a food-borne illness. Pests, as we have already seen, can be vectors for dangerous pathogens. They can also cause substantial damage to equipment by damaging wires and tubes. Pests may also leave behind droppings, hair, eggs, etc. in the food. In addition, by feeding on the food stored in the premises, they can render it unfit for consumption, resulting in financial losses. Common pests found in food service/processing establishments include rodents (rats and mice), birds and insects (flies, weevils, cockroaches, ants, etc.). The bigger pests feed on the food, while the smaller ones basically live and reproduce in the food (like weevils in grain and flour).

For managing the problem of pests, certain control measures need to be adopted. The methods can be classified as environmental, physical and chemical as shown in Figure 14.11. The **environment** or surrounding areas of the premises and food preparation and storage areas should be kept clean by removing potential breeding grounds for pests, such as heaps of refuse, empty containers and old equipment. Waste should not be allowed to accumulate anywhere on the premises and all spillages should be promptly cleaned. Too much wild vegetation around the building or open ground can increase the number of pests which dwell in the ground. Temperature and humidity control in storage areas can also discourage the multiplication of pests. Warm temperatures and higher humidity favour the multiplication of pests like insects, besides encouraging the growth of microbes.

Physical control methods start in fact with the construction of the premises. The construction should be strong and durable in such a way that pests cannot gain entry (for example, rats borrowing in through the walls or flooring). The doors and windows should not have gaps through/under which they can slip in. These, if present, need to be sealed or covered suitably with rubber padding. Meshes and screens also keep out pests if doors and windows need to be kept open for ventilation. Doorways can also be protected by hanging plastic strips or air curtains. The drains should be fitted with traps which do not allow the entry of pests.

Figure 14.11: Methods of Pest Control

Environmental	Physical	Chemical
• Sanitation in surrounding areas • Destruction of their habitat • Storage temperature, humidity, humidity control	• Killing them with mechanical devices like fly swatters • Laying traps • Preventing their physical access into premises and containers	• Use of insecticides, rodenticides as aerosol sprays • Fumigation with pesticides • Use of baits and repellents

Source: Drawn by Author.

Fly swatters of different kinds are now available in the market, including ones which are electrified to kill flying pests. Electric fly-killers can also be installed on walls, especially near the doors. Ultraviolet light is also used to kill insects present inside foods. Sticky traps for insects and mechanical traps for rodents are commonly used. Storing food in pest-proof packaging and containers is also a way to keep them safe. Storing food at a height from the ground facilitates easy cleaning and detection of tell-tale pellets of excreta, or gnawing marks or debris, which are the first indications of a pest problem.

Pest control using chemicals becomes essential when pests have already gained entry into the premises. Physically trying to catch them is difficult, especially if they are in large numbers. Rodenticides are used to kill rodents, while insecticides are chemicals used to kill insects. Some of these chemicals can also be used to simply repel the pests. Fogging, fumigation and aerosol sprays are also used, depending on the extent of infestation. Care should be taken to remove all food, beverages and even small utensils from the area before fumigation or spraying. As already discussed in the chapter on pesticides, humans can be harmed as well if the pesticides or their residues get mixed with the food. The premises should be thoroughly cleaned after application of pesticides. Baits and poisons for rodents should not repel the animal and should make the animal go out of the premises into the open to die. The staff should be sensitised to and trained in the usage of pest-control measures and the possible hazards due to pesticide residues in food. A record should be kept of all pest-control treatments done. Only safe and approved pesticides should be used.

SUMMARY

- With an increase in the number of people choosing to eat meals prepared outside their homes, the need to look at the safety of food served by these establishments is increasing.
- Food is being served on 'wheels, wings and waves' (trains/buses, aeroplanes and ships) in addition to food service establishments like hotels, restaurants, canteens of offices, schools, colleges, hostels, hospitals, and small kiosks and street food vendors.
- Food hygiene is defined by Codex as the conditions and measures necessary for the production, processing, storage and distribution of food designed to ensure a safe, sound, wholesome product fit for human consumption.
- Food service establishments can be temporary/mobile units or those which are fixed and so, more or less permanent.
- Food can become contaminated during preparation, storage and service from various sources.
- If raw ingredients are heavily contaminated, cooking may not destroy all microbes.
- If any of the surfaces which come in contact with food—chopping boards, knives, peelers, graters, blenders, utensils—are unclean, the food becomes contaminated.
- Adequate cleaning and sanitisation procedures need to be followed to reduce microbial load of ingredients and equipment.
- Cleaning is the removal of food and soiling. Sanitising ensures decrease in microbial load to acceptable levels. Disinfection is the destruction of harmful microbes on inanimate surfaces. Sterilisation is the complete destruction of all microbes in food or on surfaces.
- The effectiveness of all sanitisers depends on the time for which the microbes are exposed to the sanitiser, whether it is heat, radiation or a chemical.
- Effectiveness of different chemical agents also depends on their concentration, pH of the medium, temperature and water hardness.
- Food handlers can be a major source of contamination and hence, need to maintain strict personal hygiene. Hands, skin, hair, clothes and nails can potentially harbour various disease-causing microbes.
- Hand washing is one of the best measures of ensuring food safety. For effective hand washing and, indeed, maintaining good personal hygiene among food handlers, the establishment should provide basic amenities.
- Proper waste disposal is important to ensure that establishments do not pollute the ground surfaces and water supply or create unsanitary conditions. Poor waste disposal practices can attract pests.
- For managing the problem of pests, certain control measures need to be adopted. These may be classified into environmental, physical and chemical measures. Environmental measures include maintaining sanitation in and around the food establishment and controlling the ambient temperature and humidity. Physical measures include devices which trap or kill the pests, and prevent physical access to the premises by covering drains,

securing doors and windows. Chemical measures include use of pesticides in the form of baits, repellents or sprays.

- Care should be taken to remove all food, beverages and even small utensils from the area before fumigation or spraying pesticides.
- Water quality needs to be maintained for its use in different operations. The microbial quality, hardness, pH and presence of impurities can affect its quality and usage.
- The presence of pathogens is determined with indirect evidence by testing for an 'indicator' organism, such as coliform bacteria.
- *E. coli* is the best indicator of faecal pollution.
- The building, floor, walls, ceilings, doors, windows, ventilation system and lighting are important areas of the premises to be kept clean.
- There should be clear demarcation of areas in the kitchen where raw foods and cooked foods are being processed or stored. Plant and animal products should also be segregated to prevent cross-contamination.
- When taking food out of the storage areas, one should follow the principle of 'First in, first out' or FIFO, or 'First expire, first out' (FEFO).
- If there is any doubt about whether the product has expired or is still suitable for consumption, it should simply be discarded.

KEY WORDS

Bain marie: A pan of hot water in which a cooking container is placed for heating it or for the purpose of slow cooking.

Biofilms: A thin film of microbes which forms sticking to a surface, such as inside tubes, pipes of equipment for storing, processing or dispensing food.

Carbuncle: A cluster of boils.

Core temperature: The temperature at the centre of the food product; so for a samosa, it would mean the temperature of the filling at the centre of the samosa.

Cross-contamination: When a food gets contaminated in contact with another food or surface.

Food handler: Anyone who handles the food, like the cook, helper or server.

Food hygiene: All conditions and measures necessary to ensure the safety and suitability of food at all stages of the food chain.

Insecticide: Substance used for killing insects.

Pathogenic: Disease causing.

Rodenticide: Substance used for killing rodents.

Soil: A term used to describe all the undesirable materials, such as food residue, dirt, deposits, etc., which cling to surfaces of utensils, equipment, etc.

Waste: Unwanted, unusable material.

Wholesome food: Food good for your health; it refers here to food that is intended for human consumption and that meets all quality standards.

EXERCISES

1. Comment on the different sources of contamination likely to be seen in a food service establishment.
2. What is the difference between cleaning, sanitisation and disinfection?
3. What are the different types of cleaning and sanitising agents used in the food industry?

4. What points would you keep in mind while organising a safe waste disposal system for a food service establishment?
5. What are the different methods used for controlling pests in establishments?
6. How can hazards associated with food handlers be minimised?

REFERENCES

AVA/NEA, *Good Cleaning and Sanitation Practices*, Singapore: Agri-Food and Veterinary Authority and National Environment Agency, Available at http://www.ava.gov.sg/docs/default-source/tools-and-resources/resources-for-businesses/(english)-good-cleaning-and-sanitation-practices (accessed 20 January 2017).

BIS, *Drinking Water—Specification*, Second Revision, New Delhi: Bureau of Indian Standards, 2012.

EPA, 'Product Performance Test Guidelines Ocspp 810.2300: Sanitizers for Use on Hard Surfaces Efficacy Data Recommendations', USA: Environment Protection Agency, 2012.

FAO/WHO, 'Codex Alimentarius', *Food Hygiene—Basic Texts*, 4e, Rome: World Health Organization Food and Agriculture Organization of The United Nations, 2009.

———, 'Definitions for the Purposes of the Codex Alimentarius', *Codex Alimentarius Commission. Procedural Manual*, 24e, Rome: Joint FAO/WHO Food Standards Programme, 2015.

FSSAI, 'Food Safety and Standards (Licensing and Registration of Food Businesses), Regulations 2011', *The Gazette of India: Extraordinary Part III—Sec. 4*, New Delhi: Ministry of Health and Family Welfare (Food Safety and Standards Authority of India), 1 August 2011a, Available at http://www.old.fssai.gov.in/Portals/0/Pdf/Food%20safety%20and%20Standards%20(Licensing%20and%20Registration%20of%20Food%20businesses)%20regulation,%202011.pdf (accessed 11 April 2018).

———, 'Food Safety and Standards (Food Products Standards and Food Additives) Regulations, 2011', Gazette Notification of Ministry of Health and Family Welfare (Food Safety and Standards Authority of India), New Delhi, 1 August 2011b. Available at http://www.old.fssai.gov.in/Portals/0/Pdf/Food%20safety%20and%20standards(%20Food%20product%20standards%20and%20food%20additives)%20regulation,%202011%20(part%20II).pdf (accessed 11 April 2018).

———, 'Training Manual Food Safety Supervisor Course Advance (Level 2) Catering'. Available at http://www.fssai.gov.in/home/capacity-building/e-library/training-manual.html (accessed 27 May 2018).

Marriott, N. G., *Essentials of Food Sanitation*, New York: Chapman & Hall, 1997.

Schmidt, R. H., *Basic Elements of Equipment Cleaning and Sanitizing in Food Processing and Handling Operations*, 2015, FS14 series of the Food Science and Human Nutrition Department, UF/IFAS Extension, Original publication date July 1997, Revised March 2009, Reviewed June 2015, Available at http://edis.ifas.ufl.edu/pdffiles/FS/FS07700.pdf (accessed 11 April 2018).

ONLINE SOURCES

Animation of the National Health Service Routine of Washing Hands, Available at https://www.youtube.com/watch?v=oGQpJafaWj0 (accessed 15 April 2018).

Application for Registration of a Food Business to FSSAI—Forms and Rules, Available at http://www.old.fssai.gov.in/Portals/0/Pdf/Food%20safety%20and%20Standards%20(Licensing%20and%20Registration%20of%20Food%20businesses)%20regulation,%202011.pdf (accessed 11 April 2018).

FSSAI Checklist for Routine Inspection of Catering/Food Service Establishment, Available at http://old.fssai.gov.in/Portals/0/Pdf/Catering_Establishments(23.10.13).pdf (accessed 26 October 2017).

FSSAI Guidance Document Food Safety Management System. Food Industry Guide to Implement GMP/GHP Requirements, Catering Sector. October 2017. Available at http://www.fssai.gov.in/home/safe-food-practices/FSMS-GUIDANCE-DOCUMENTS-FOR-THE-FOOD-BUSINESSES.html (accessed 27 May 2018).

Training Initiatives Launched by FSSAI, Registering for Training for Food Safety Supervisor, Available at https://fostac.fssai.gov.in/ (accessed 15 April 2018).

15

STREET FOOD SAFETY

HIGHLIGHTS

- The special case of street foods
- Microbiological quality of street foods
- Challenges in improving quality and safety
- Communicating food safety measures

Street foods are foods and beverages sold by vendors and hawkers on the streets or other similar public places. These may be prepared on the street or some other location and then sold in public places. Street-vended foods are a reality in every country of the world. They are now recognised as a convenient and economical source of food for the urban population of most developing nations. Street vending was mostly an urban phenomenon, especially in India, but it is now being seen in rural communities as well. The Ministry of Urban Poverty Alleviation, Government of India has estimated that there are about 20 lakh street food vendors in the country.

This informal food service sector has raised several concerns regarding both the quality as well as safety of the foods vended. Street foods can be a boon or bane depending on whether they feed the food insecure, providing them with affordable meals, or increasing the food-borne disease burden among the already malnourished urban poor. This chapter will introduce you to the world of street food vending, the benefits and limitations of this type of food supply, challenges faced in improving safety and quality, and what can be done to improve the state of affairs. The task of improving food quality will have to be accomplished using the minimum resources available to the street vendors in this unorganised sector.

THE SPECIAL CASE OF STREET FOODS

There is no doubt that street foods are culturally and nutritionally very important in most developing countries like India, as well as developed nations of the world. They provide meals to several people in a community—the office goer who did not have time in the morning to eat breakfast or pack lunch, the labourer who does not have the means to cook a full meal, the beggar, and so many others whose job keeps them on the move the whole day. Street food vending provides food at the workplace and at other important locations in the city, like tourist spots, educational institutes, hospitals, railway stations, bus terminals and market areas. The vendors may put up stalls or use pushcarts, stands or simply vend out of baskets they carry. Some others may sell out of vans or car trunks as well. For families on an outing, street food is an added attraction. The food is cheaper than the food sold in the formal sector (restaurants, cafes and hotels). It is sometimes even cheaper than trying to cook the same at home.

Street food vending is an important source of livelihood for millions of people around the globe. In many cases, women are involved in the business of vending food. This provides economic independence to the women and has positive social implications for the community. It needs low capital investment and hence, provides a chance for self-employment for many people. Overall, economic implications are immense, with a big impact on local agricultural production as well. Middle- and low-income sections of the population tend to depend heavily on street foods for at least one meal in the day. A significant proportion of the daily nutritional requirement of adults is sometimes met by street foods.

The variety of foods and beverages which are street vended in each country is also mindboggling. Each country has its own specialities, the kind and variety of the items depending on local eating habits and trends in lifestyle. For a review on types of street foods sold in different countries, refer to the relevant article in the *World Review of Nutrition and Dietetics* (Simopoulos and Bhat 2000). In India, the items range from cut fruits and vegetables, *chat* items, fried snacks (*pakora*s, bread pakoras, *wada*s, *samosa*s, *kachori*s, *tikki*s, etc.) and egg preparations, to full meals. Meat and meat products are also quite popular. In addition, one sees a lot of *namkeen*s (savouries) as well as sweet preparations like *jalebi*s, *kulfi*, *rasgullas* and *burfi* being sold on the streets. A variety of cuisines can be seen on the streets, depending on the local eating habits. International cuisine adapted to Indian flavours—such as Chinese, Tibetan, Afghani, Continental preparations—are also seen.

The kinds of foods and beverages sold vary with season. So, for instance, in summers, you may find a lot of vendors selling sherbets, *jaljeera*, lemon juice, mango shake, *sattu*, etc., while in winters, you may notice big woks (*kadai*s) with hot almond-flavoured milk being sold, especially in north India. The kinds of dishes and preparations vary with the region in a culturally diverse country like India. It also tends to change with festivals. It is like a gastronomical treat on the streets during festivals in India. Special preparations of kebabs and *haleem* flood the streets in the evenings during Ramadan, when Muslims break their fast. Food walks/trips are specially organised to help people savour some of the best street foods a city/region has to offer. The National Association of Street Food Vendors of India (NASVI) organises a National Street Food Festival every year in New Delhi to promote street food vendors from across the country.

Although they play such an important socio-economic role in the community, street food vendors can create a nuisance. Their tremendous unlimited and unregulated growth is a major strain on the city's resources. They increase the congestion in already crowded spaces, often creating a sanitation problem due to littering. Customers throw the disposables plates, spoons and glasses on the street, or the vendors themselves dump leftovers on the street or create a mess trying to cook and wash on the street itself. They may illegally use water and electricity without paying for it and encroach upon pavements. To make matters worse, due to shortage of potable water and lack of cleanliness, the food prepared by the vendor may be contaminated and lead to the spread of food-borne infections. Improper use of food additives like food colour and the presence of other physical and chemical contaminants like insects, dust, filth, chemicals from plastics or metals leaching from utensils into the food and adulterants added to substandard ingredients used in food preparation can all make the food unfit for human consumption.

Food preparation operations often involve the vendor's entire family. Due to a lack of space in the street or place where the food is vended, the preparation of the dishes to be sold is sometimes done in the homes of the vendors. Most of these vendors are poor, living in single room tenements in the slums of cities. The vendor and his family, in most cases, have not received any formal training in food preparation, food catering or food safety. So, from the viewpoint of food safety, street food regulation becomes very important.

MICROBIOLOGICAL QUALITY OF STREET FOODS

Review of literature reveals several food poisoning episodes due to consumption of contaminated street foods. Different studies on street foods have revealed the presence of pathogens responsible for diseases, such as *Bacillus cereus*, *Clostridium perfringens*, *Staphylococcus aureus*, *Campylobacter* and *Salmonella spp.* in a variety of foods. Street foods were responsible for 691 food poisoning outbreaks and 49 deaths from 1983 to 1992 in Shandong Province, China (Lianghui et al. 1993). In another study, a cholera epidemic in Pune, India was traced to contaminated sugarcane juice served with ice (FAO 1986). Food-borne diseases like diarrhoea, cholera, typhoid fever and food poisoning are common in people, but linking them to specific street foods is difficult due to poor reporting of such episodes and long incubation periods for some of these illnesses. It becomes difficult to pinpoint a particular food or vendor unless several people take ill simultaneously and that too, soon after consumption of the contaminated food.

Several studies done on the quality of street foods in cities like Kolkata, Agra, Allahabad, Bangalore, Mumbai, Lucknow, Tirupati, Udaipur, Pune, New Delhi, Hyderabad, Amravati, Chandigarh, Chennai and Coimbatore have shown the presence of hazards like adulterants, unpermitted additives and a variety of pathogenic bacteria in a number of street foods sold in these cities (Chakravarty and Canet 1996; Bhat and Waghray 2000; Tambekar et al. 2008). Kaul and Aggarwal (1988) have reported the poor microbiological quality of *chat* items in Chandigarh. In addition to bacteria, yeast and mould counts have also been found to be high, especially in sweet preparations and beverages like fruit juices. Milk and milk products like curd-based preparations, ice creams and other dessert preparations have also been shown to have high counts of bacteria, as milk is a very good medium for the growth of microbes.

Personal Hygiene and Health Status of Street Food Vendors

Personal hygiene and health status of the food handler has a very important role to play in the safety of street foods. Food handlers need to take care of the following in order to ensure that they are not the source of contamination or the mode of transmission of infections:

- *Wear clean clothes*: It is better that the handlers wear clothes other than their home attire during food processing and service operations. This way, they would not carry germs with their clothes into food preparation and storage areas. They could also use aprons.
- Keep their *hair trimmed* and wear *protective caps/nets* or *head gear* which prevents hair from falling into food. Hair is not just a physical contaminant, but also a source of microbial contamination.
- Keep *nails short*, as long nails can harbour several bacteria.
- Preferably wear *clean gloves* when touching food. The skin also harbours a variety of microbes. Touching door knobs, mobile phones or any surface can transfer millions of bacteria onto the hand.
- *Bathing* daily and washing hands frequently will keep the skin microflora of the handler in check.
- Handlers need to *wash hands* every time before touching food with bare hands. Hands should also be washed after visiting the toilet, touching dirty surfaces, raw meat and vegetables.
- Hands need to be thoroughly washed if handlers have been scratching themselves or picking their nose, etc.
- In case of *skin infection*, boils, cuts and wounds, the handlers should avoid touching food with bare hands. These boils and cuts can harbour a variety of bacteria, some of which are pathogenic.
- *Sick handlers*, such as those suffering from colds, coughs, gastroenteritis and diarrhoea should not be permitted to come in contact with the food at all as they are carriers of disease-causing microbes.
- They should not blow air into the food or packaging while trying to cool the food or trying to open a plastic packaging bag, as this, too, transmits germs.

Risk Assessment of Street-vended Foods

The science of risk assessment needs to be used in order to identify foods which can be classified as 'high risk foods'. Most of the food-borne illnesses are due to microbial contamination of foods. Foods with high water activity kept at ambient storage temperatures are likely to have high microbial loads. Improper handling further increases contamination levels. Conditions which increase the risk include:

- holding cooked food at room temperature for several hours
- inadequate reheating of foods before serving

- storing foods in bulk in large pots in refrigerators or ineffective cooling
- foods to be kept hot not being kept at sufficiently high temperatures
- cross-contamination between raw and cooked foods

Several vendors fully process and cook foods in advance, while others partially cook and then cook/reheat foods just before serving. Often, the temperatures achieved during this heat treatment are not high enough to destroy spores which have germinated, or the microbes which have multiplied while the product was being held at room temperature.

In addition, the hygiene and sanitation of the environment and that of the food handler are of utmost importance in determining the risk posed by these foods. Foods vended in filthy surroundings like garbage dumps, open drains or in proximity to public toilets or busy roads are at a higher risk of getting contaminated. Waste generated by the vendors is usually dumped in the vicinity (see Figure 15.1). Waste water thrown in streets or open gutters nearby becomes a breeding ground for pests like rodents, cockroaches and flies. Thus, sources of microbial hazards are the **vendor site or location**, the raw materials used for preparation, including water, utensils and equipment used for food preparation, and the food vendor himself.

The **quality of the raw material** is very important to monitor, since microbes are sometimes known to survive cooking and processing, especially if cooking involves only mild heat treatment. Unavailability of potable water for the use of vendors is another major concern. Using **unsafe water** for food preparation, hand washing or cleaning of food ingredients, dishes and utensils significantly increases the microbial load of the food. Several studies have shown the presence of coliform bacteria, including faecal coliforms (indicative of faecal contamination), enteropathogenic *E. coli*, *Salmonella* and *Shigella* in the water being used by street food vendors. Such heavily contaminated water is responsible for diarrhoeal diseases in the consumers of street foods. The raw vegetables, meat and poultry are all likely to be heavily contaminated with microbes. If not washed properly, the pathogens can contaminate the final product or any other food kept in close vicinity, especially if the same chopping boards, knives and utensils are used for cooked and raw foods, or for meats and vegetables. Dry ingredients like spices are also known to be heavily contaminated due to **poor handling practices**. These can further add to the microbial load of the final food product. Some organisms which contaminate the spices may survive cooking temperatures, as they are spore-formers.

Street foods also have a higher risk of being contaminated with **physical and chemical contaminants.** To keep costs low, the vendors may choose low-cost, poor-quality ingredients which have a greater chance of being adulterated, sometimes with harmful chemicals like unpermitted colours or preservatives. As there is no quality control check of the ingredients sold loose (unpackaged), there is a greater likelihood of these being of poor quality.

Most countries have limited personnel available with the regulatory authorities who can inspect and monitor the quality of the street foods. Hence, the proactive approach which anticipates problems before they occur is much better than punitive action later by a regulatory authority, in case food is not found to be safe. **Hazard Analysis Critical Control Point (HACCP)** studies

Figure 15.1: Most Street Food Vendors in Indian Cities are Found in Congested, Busy Areas with Filthy Surroundings

Source: Author.

have highlighted the critical points at which a vendor needs to have control measures in place to reduce the risk of contamination of his foods and decrease the likelihood of a food poisoning episode. In several studies which looked at the critical point at which the contamination took place in a number of food products, post-cooking contamination due to poor handling practices was identified as the major source of contamination.

In addition to improving the personal hygiene of handlers and the cleanliness of utensils and equipment, reheating foods to temperatures above 70°C also helps in reducing contamination levels. Dishes or preparations which involve sieving or straining the food through a strainer or cloth like *paneer* or *channa* (cottage cheese) based sweetmeats are likely to get contaminated if the cloth or strainer is not kept clean. Similarly, juicers and other such equipment, if not kept clean or not frequently

Figure 15.2: Street Food Vending is Very Organised and Clean in Some Countries

Source: www.flickr.com (accessed 15 April 2018).

washed with potable water, may contaminate the juice or puree being prepared using the equipment.

Foods which have a high moisture/water content (like *golgappas*), foods which are served at ambient temperatures without reheating (like most *chat* items), foods which are handled with bare hands while serving, foods served raw like cut fruits, vegetables, fruit *chats*, etc. are likely to be more heavily contaminated and hence considered to be high-risk foods. Foods to which ice has been added also tend to be at a high risk of being contaminated with pathogens. Ice may be made from contaminated water or may have been kept or handled under insanitary conditions. Of course, foods which are displayed in the open, exposed to flies and insects are at a greater risk. These pests sit on garbage and filth lying in the vicinity and carry microbes to the food.

CHALLENGES IN IMPROVING QUALITY AND SAFETY

Street foods are a cheap and good source of nutrition for the poor. Several people are dependent on these readily available street foods for their daily meals. However, if these foods endanger the health of people, all these benefits are of no use. Sometimes, the knee-jerk reaction of some authorities is to simply ban the vendors from an area, rather than invest time, effort and resources to improve the vending. So, for instance, vendors outside schools are generally driven away so that children may not be tempted by the unsafe food. The vendors simply move to the next lane where children find them in no time and the practice continues. Instead, school authorities can choose the vendors who may be allowed near their schools by asking them to follow certain terms and conditions which will ensure that the food served by them is nourishing and safe.

The consumer identifies street food with good taste, variety, low cost and easy availability. He is rarely concerned about its safety or nutritional value. So, he does not demand a certain level of hygiene from the vendor. How many consumers, for instance, insist that the vendor puts on gloves before dipping his hands in the spicy water served with *golgappas*? How many point out to the vendor of *petha*, a popular sweetmeat in the northern part of the country, that he should cover the sweets with a net so that flies and bees do not sit on it? The consumer needs as much sensitisation to the issues of food safety as does the vendor. As street food vending is a business, the biggest incentive the vendor can have to improve his food handling practices is to have his customers insist upon it! Thus, to make the customers more discerning, the national food regulatory authority (FSSAI) has intensified its efforts to raise awareness levels of the public about food safety issues.

There are several things which a street food vendor has to consider to improve the safety of the food he vends. The regulatory authorities need to facilitate these as well so that the vendor is encouraged to comply with food safety norms. The different aspects to be considered include:

- *Availability and storage at site of potable water*: The authorities have to make sure that there is a source of water supply near the designated vending location from where the vendor can draw and use water for washing and for preparing food. If the source is at some distance from his cart, his cart should have a mechanism to store the water and draw it preferably from a tap so that dipping into the water can be avoided.

> **International organisations involved in improving safety of street-vended foods:**
> - World Health Organization (WHO)
> - Food and Agriculture Organization (FAO)
> - FAO/WHO Coordinating Committee for Near East (CCNEA)
> - FAO/WHO Coordinating Committee for Africa (CCAFRICA)
> - FAO/WHO Coordinating Committee for Latin America and the Caribbean (CCLAC)

- *Appropriate utensils for cooking and storing*: The vendor should have appropriate utensils for storing and cooking food, which are not dented and damaged, and are easy to clean and maintain. Residue build-up due to the presence of crevices in the design of the utensils is undesirable as this encourages the growth of microbes. The material of these utensils should be such that it does not leach dangerous chemicals or metals (like copper, cadmium and lead) into the food. The utensils should have a provision to be covered tightly with a lid to avoid physical contaminants from falling into the food or beverage.
- *Means of keeping food either hot or cool*: One of the prime principles of keeping food safe is to keep it at an appropriate storage temperature. Ingredients and prepared food need to be kept either cold or hot, depending on their nature, to prevent them from microbial spoilage. The vending carts may hence need either an energy source for keeping food warm or a cooling technology to keep things at a low temperature. The design of the vending cart or the stall has to be appropriate, keeping these requirements in mind.
- *Means of food service*: The kind of utensils and cutlery the food service vendor uses has a significant impact on the safety of the food. Most vendors may use disposable service utensils. The disposable items can create a garbage disposal problem, while reusable washable dishes may be difficult to keep clean for every service due to lack of running water in the vicinity. In many instances, the vendors simply dip the plates, spoons and glasses in a bucket of already dirty water and then wipe them clean with a not-so-clean piece of cloth. Cleaning detergents are rarely used because the vendor does not want to spend a lot of money. Whether he reheats his food adequately is also a matter of concern due to lack of fuel/source of heating available. So, for instance, *samosa*s fried at a different location may be vended for many hours after preparation without any reheating, and can serve as a potential source of food-borne infection.
- *Wrapping and packaging applied to food*: Sometimes, the customer may not want to eat the food immediately and may want it packed to take away with him. Street food vendors may not want to invest in elaborate packing jars, cups, etc. You may have noticed how tea, dal, curry and fluid preparations are packed in polythene bags. Some vendors use pieces of newspapers which tend to leach ink into the food. Some others may use cheap plastic plates and spoons. Chemicals are known to leach out from the plastics into even water stored in plastic bottles, and these are food materials, some acidic in nature which can easily cause a

number of chemicals to react with it. Safer, low-cost packaging alternatives made of dried leaves, impervious paper and cardboard need to be made available to the vendors.

- *Cleaning facilities and waste disposal*: In many instances, the vendors do not have running water to perform their cleaning operations. Cleaning detergents are rarely used because the vendor does not want to spend a lot of money and also does not have a lot of time to clean his utensils very thoroughly. Dustbins are rarely carried by vendors as they increase their work of disposing off the garbage collected during the day. Bins placed by the local authorities may not be at a suitable location for the customers to locate and dispose their plates. A general lack of civic sense also prevents them from using dedicated bins for garbage disposal. As a result, most food vending sites are littered and unclean. This is what distinguishes most Indian street-vending sites from vending sites in Singapore, Malaysia, Thailand, Vietnam and countries of the European Union or North America (see Figure 15.2). Food poisoning episodes are also fewer in these countries as opposed to where there is no regard for hygiene and sanitation.
- *Toilet facilities*: These are extremely important and should be available in the near vicinity of the vending location. This encourages the vendor to use the facility for visiting the toilet (as opposed to relieving oneself on the street).

New, practical, cost-effective technologies need to be developed to enable the street food vendor to keep high-risk foods hot or cold, store sufficient water for use, as well as food display cases which can attract customers, but at the same time keep food safe from flies and other pests (see Figure 15.3). Vendors are known to use drums and tin containers which had been used for

Figure 15.3: Elements of a Smart Cart which can be Used for Street Food Vending

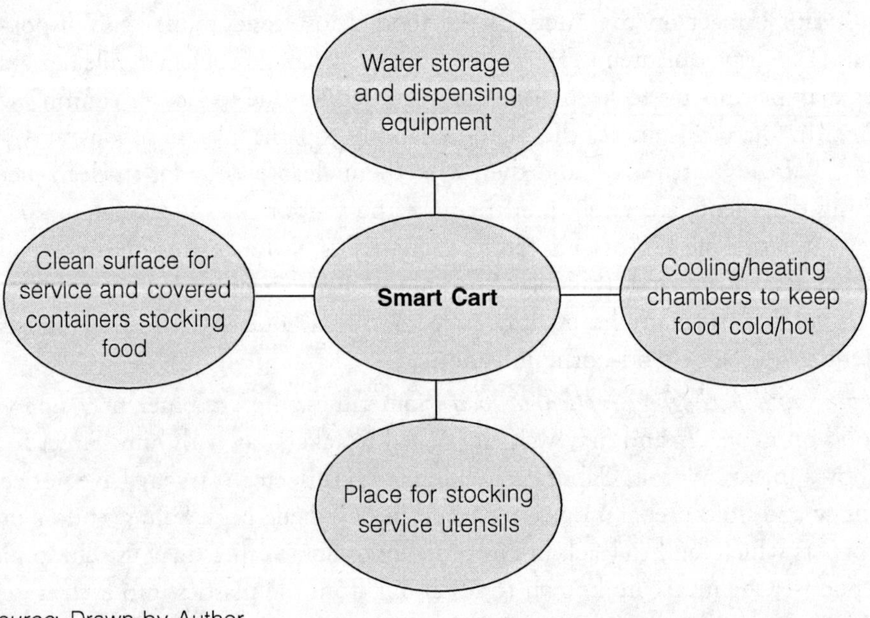

Source: Drawn by Author.

other purposes to cook or store food, use sticks of wood or rods for stirring and sheets of tin/plastic as lids. Appropriate utensils and simple food-processing machines will also assist the vendor in handling preparation of food in large quantities.

Regulations for street food vending

Food Safety and Standards (Licensing and Registration of Food Businesses) Regulations 2011: requires all street food vendors and small food businesses to be registered with the FSSAI.

Street Food Vendors—Food Safety Requirements: standards developed by BIS, 2012.

Street Vendors (Protection of Livelihood and Regulation of Street Vending) Act 2014: provides for demarcation of vending zones to protect the vendors from undue harassment.

Street foods play a very significant part in the socio-economic scenario and trying to do away with them is not a desirable solution. Instead, all energy and resources available need to be focussed on what can be done to improve their quality and safety. The vendors need to be provided with demarcated areas where food can be vended. Such food parks need to be in areas where the vendor will get enough customers. These areas should provide adequate space, infrastructure and basic amenities like toilets, potable water, garbage disposal facilities, etc. within the city or town's masterplan. The local authorities then need to facilitate the smooth functioning at these vending sites, preventing any harassment of the vendors or the public.

Public health authorities should provide technical guidance to the vendors to improve the quality of foods and the kind of carts and utensils to be used to keep food fresh longer and contamination free. Regular awareness drives to educate the vendors about food safety and, perhaps, even new culinary skills could greatly contribute to improving food quality and safety. Active cooperation by vendors is very important for this. Cooperatives and associations of vendors could greatly facilitate the process, look after their interests and protect them from exploitation. In India, NASVI is one such body, which was registered as a society in 2003 but took root as a network in 1998. NASVI is a national federation of street vendor organisations. It is a coalition of trade unions, community-based organisations (CBOs), non-government organisations (NGOs) and professionals. NASVI aims to protect the right to livelihood of the millions of street food vendors in the country and bring about macro-level changes in laws and policies which will benefit the food-vending sector.

The Street Vendors (Protection of Livelihood and Regulation of Street Vending) Act of 2014 protects the right of urban street vendors and regulates street vending activity. Street vendors are issued vending certificates after they pay a vending fee specified in the scheme. There are terms and conditions specified in the scheme which the vendor needs to follow. The certificate entitles the vendor to sell products at earmarked locations without any harassment by police or other authorities. It would also protect the vendors from anti-social elements who levy 'protection money' to keep the police and health authorities from harassing the vendors.

Regulations which come into place must involve all stakeholders, whether it is the vendors themselves or the consumer fora. Licensing gives legitimacy to the business and brings a certain amount of security and confidence for the vendor. The vendor may then feel more motivated to improve his business style, invest in improving the kind of foods he vends, and go in for simple technologies which suit his vending operation.

Regular training in food handling practices to the food vendors would go a long way in improving the safety of street-vended foods. Inspectors involved in the actual implementation of the Act would also need to be trained so that they are looked at as facilitators who improve compliance by the food vendors, rather than people to be bribed. Along with training, monitoring is as important to see that the vendors are following the rules and regulations.

COMMUNICATING FOOD SAFETY MEASURES

Training has to have a strong practical and skill-building component. Both the vendor and the food safety officer who monitors the vendor should be trained to identify potential sources of hazards in the vending operations and what control measures need to be implemented in order to reduce the risk of food-borne illnesses. Training also demands a major change in attitude and practices of vendors, and staff of the regulatory authorities. Research and educational institutes working in the field of food safety, and that of the private sector, should collaborate, especially for funding initiatives. A participatory approach to communicating food safety, involving all stakeholders, will improve compliance to norms and regulations.

Figure 15.4: Elements of Training to be Imparted to Street Food Vendors

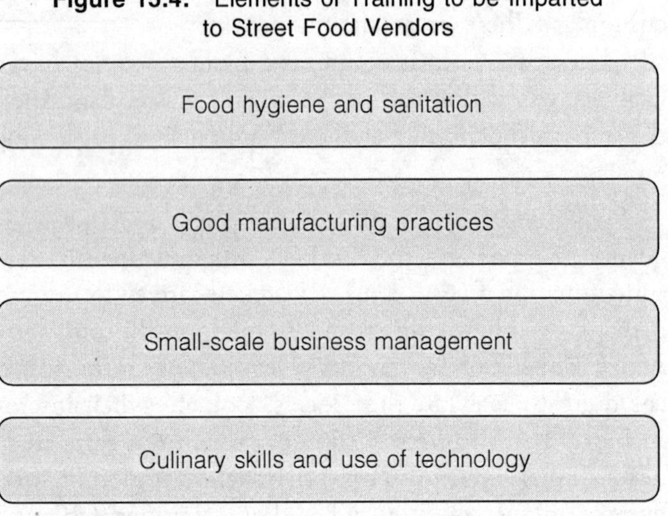

Source: Drawn by Author.

Model vending areas like food parks can be used to communicate the model to the public as well as to other street food vendors. Both stakeholders need to see visible benefits to make such initiatives a success.

In 2006, the WHO came out with a manual for keeping foods safer, which is applicable to street foods as well. There are 'Five Keys' which can help in keeping food safe. The first key is to '**keep clean**' the vending unit and location and all work surfaces:

Five keys to safer food, WHO (2006)

- Keep food clean
- Separate raw and cooked foods
- Cook thoroughly
- Keep food at safe temperatures
- Use safe water and raw materials

- The vendor should not stand near rubbish dumps, open drains and toilets, which are all reservoirs of germs.

- He should keep the food at a height above the ground, which tends to be heavily contaminated.
- Food should also be protected from dust, insects, dirt and direct sunlight.

The second key is to '**keep raw and cooked foods separated**' by using separate knives, chopping boards and utensils for handling them. Raw foods tend to be heavily contaminated with microbes and they can transfer the microbial load to cooked foods.

Good personal hygienic practices, such as short fingernails and hair, daily bathing, washing hands thoroughly before handling food, are all important. Convincing vendors to avoid smoking or chewing tobacco, nose picking, coughing and sneezing, spitting over food and tasting food with fingers is difficult, but vital to ensure safe food.

'**Cooking food thoroughly**', especially meat, poultry, eggs and seafood, to at least 70°C, is essential to destroy microbes. Boiling liquid preparations like soups and gravies for at least two minutes is recommended. Foods with stuffing, such as *samosa*s, need to be heated in such a way that even the core of the stuffing gets heated to a high temperature. Foods should be kept at safe temperatures. Cooked foods should be kept piping hot (above 60°C) until served to prevent growth of microbes or their spores. They should not be left at room temperature for more than two hours. Perishable foods are best stored in a refrigerator (best below 5°C) until consumption, and they can be reheated before serving. By **holding at temperatures below 5°C or above 60°C**, the growth of microorganisms is slowed down or stopped.

'**Using safe water and raw material**' to start with goes a long way in ensuring safe food. If unsure about the quality of water, boiling and filtering it before use in foods is better. Raw ingredients should be purchased from reliable sources. They should be fresh and of good quality to obtain a good quality final product.

Malaysia, Philippines and India are the three countries which have regulations for protecting street vendors. In India, the **CII Institute of Food Safety and Quality** (**FSQ**) has taken an initiative to create awareness among consumers and street food vendors, and it has issued a simple informative checklist of hygienic practices called the 'CII-14 point checklist on food safety for street vended food'. This lays down the hygiene standards that should be followed by street food vendors.

The All India Institute of Hygiene and Public Health, Kolkata was given the FAO/Edouard Saouma Award in 1995 for improving the safety and quality of street foods in the city of Kolkata. The initiative began in 1992 as a FAO-funded project. The Institute involved all the important stakeholders—the vendors, the Kolkata police, the Mayor and the municipal authorities—in the implementation of its strategy, which was one of the major reasons for the success of the project. Several other initiatives were also taken in cities like New Delhi, Mumbai, Pune and Hyderabad to study the socio-economic aspects of street foods and try out strategies to improve the safety and quality. Numerous studies have been conducted by Lady Irwin College, University of Delhi to apply HACCP principles to the food vending operations and identify critical control points which need to be monitored, and control measures which are low cost and easily implemented in the small-scale and unorganised sector. Training modules for street food vendors have also been developed and implemented by the college.

Several initiatives have been taken up by the Indian government, such as the ***Swachh Bharat Swachh Pakwan*** (***Hunar Zaika***) Project of the Ministry of Tourism to upgrade the skills and improve the hygiene standards of street food vendors. Also, the Ministry of Consumer Affairs, Food and Public Distribution in collaboration with Confederation of Indian Industries (CII), NASVI and Voluntary Organization in Interest of Consumer Education (VOICE) have launched a ***Surakshit Khadya Abhiyan*** to promote awareness about food safety with a special focus on street foods. The FSSAI also launched an initiative called '***Project Clean Street Food***' in 2016 to improve the safety of foods vended on streets. The project envisages training street food vendors in aspects of food safety and improving the quality of their food so that they attract more customers and their business improves. Under the country's *Pradhan Mantri Kaushal Vikas Yojana*, they will be imparted the necessary entrepreneurial skills which will boost the social and economic status of the vendors. The goal is also to make a global brand of Indian street foods. In the first phase of the project, the vendors will be mobilised and enrolled, followed by the second phase of capacity building and skill enhancement by training. The third and fourth phases will focus on quality assurance and sustainability, respectively.

SUMMARY

- Street foods are foods and beverages sold by vendors and hawkers, especially on the streets or other similar public places.
- The variety and form of street food depends on local eating habits.
- Street foods can significantly contribute to the daily nutritional intake of several people whose income or job profile necessitates that they consume street foods as a major part of their daily diet.
- Street food businesses provide livelihood opportunities for lakhs of people in the country and they are a boost for the local economy.
- However, their unregulated growth can be a major strain on the resources of the city. Hygiene and sanitation of the streets and safety of the foods served are the primary concerns.
- Contaminated street foods have been the cause of several food poisoning outbreaks and have resulted in a lot of misery to those affected.
- Sometimes, the use of sub-standard quality of food ingredients and/or the serving or packaging material results in the introduction of physical and chemical hazards in food.
- There are several regulations in place to ensure safety of street-vended foods and the government has launched new initiatives to improve the quality of these foods.
- Simple precautions followed by street food vendors can help in improving their business and the safety of their customers.

KEY WORDS

Capacity building: Developing the knowledge, skills and other capabilities of people and institutions.

HACCP: Hazard Analysis Critical Control Point; helps to identify hazards in a food supply chain and the critical points at which these can be controlled.

Quality assurance: The maintenance of a desired level of quality in a product or service.

Stakeholder: A person or group that has an investment, share or interest in a business or industry; for instance, the business operator, the consumer and the regulating authority.

EXERCISES

1. List the foods that you have seen being sold on the streets of your city. Is there a difference between foods and beverages sold in summers and winters?
2. What challenges does street food vending pose in terms of food safety?
3. How can street food vendors be facilitated in improving the safety and quality of their food?
4. Outline certain points to remember for safe food handling by street food vendors.
5. What training can be imparted to street food vendors which will help improve their business?
6. What changes in design would you like to suggest in the typical pushcarts that vendors use in your city, to improve the safety of foods being sold?
7. List the initiatives taken by the Indian government to improve the safety of street-vended foods.

REFERENCES

Bhat, R. V., and K. Waghray, 'Profile of Street Foods Sold in Asian Countries', *World Rev Nutr Diet* 86, 2000, pp. 53–99.

Chakravarty, I., and C. Canet, 'Food, Agriculture and Nutrition', FAO Corporate Document Repository, 1996.

CII, 'CII-14 Point Checklist on Food Safety for Street Vended Food', 2008, Version 1.0, Available at www.cii-iq.in (accessed 11 April 2016).

FAO, 'Study on Street Foods in Pune India', Food and Agriculture Organization of the United Nations and State Public Health Laboratory Pune, Government of Maharashtra, India, 1986, pp. 1–133.

———, 'Street Foods', Report of an FAO Technical Meeting on Street Foods, Calcutta, India, November 1995, FAO Food and Nutrition Paper 63, Rome: Food and Agriculture Organization, 1997.

FAO/WHO, 'General Requirements (Food Hygiene)', Codex Alimentarius (Supplement to Volume 1B), Rome: FAO/WHO, 1997, Available at http://www.fao.org/docrep/w6419e/w6419e00.htm (accessed 3 February 2017).

INFOSAN, 'Basic Steps to Improve Safety of Street-vended Food', International Food Safety Authorities Network, INFOSAN Information Note No. 3/2010—Safety of street-vended food, Geneva: FAO/WHO, 2010.

Kaul, M., and G. Aggarwal, 'Microbial Load of Common Chat Products', *Ind J Nutr Diet* 25 (6), 1988, p. 197.

Lianghui, X., S. M. Xingling, C. Yuju, L. Zhang, and W. Haiyan, 'Analysis of Street Food Safety in Shandong Province, Abstracts', In *Final Programme Street Foods Epidemiology, Management and Practical Approaches*, Beijing, 19–21 October 1993, p. 15.

MFPOI, 2009, 'Upgradation of the Quality of Street Food', Available at http//mofpi.nic.in (accessed 1 February 2017).

Rane, S., 'Street Vended Food in Developing World: Hazard Analyses', *Indian J Microbiol* 51 (1), 2011, pp. 100–06.

Simopoulos, A. P., and R. V. Bhat, 'Street Foods', *World Review of Nutrition and Dietetics* 86, 2000.

Tambekar, D. H., V. J. Jaiswal, D. V. Dhanorkar, P. B. Gulhane, M. N. Dudhane, 'Identification of Microbiological Hazards and Safety of Ready-to-eat Food Vendee in Streets of Amravati City, India', *J ApplBiosci* 7, 2008, pp. 195–201.

WHO, 'Essential Safety Requirements for Street-Vended Foods', revised edition, Geneva: WHO, 1996.

———, 'Five Keys To Safer Food Manual', 2006, Available at http://www.who.int/foodsafety/publications/5keysmanual/en/ (accessed 26 July 2016).

ONLINE SOURCES

FSSAI IEC Material on Safe Food for Capacity Building of Food Handlers, Available at http://www.fssai.gov.in/home/capacity-building/iec/awareness-materials.html (accessed 15 April 2016).

FSSAI Project Clean Street Food Brochure, Available at http://www.old.fssai.gov.in/Portals/0/Pdf/IEC_Awareness_Materials/Leaflets/Clean_Street_Food_Brochure.pdf (accessed 20 December 2016).

National Association of Street Vendors of India—NASVI, Available at http://nasvinet.org/newsite/ (accessed 15 April 2016).

16

QUALITY MANAGEMENT

HIGHLIGHTS

- Quality Control and Assurance
- Total Quality Management—concept, need and components
- ISO 22000 Food Safety Management System
- Good Manufacturing Practices
- Hazard Analysis Critical Control Point System
- Accreditation and Auditing

Safe and wholesome food is a basic need of consumers and should be a major concern of all food processors. Whether it is the farmer or the local milk vendor, the office canteen caterer or the restaurant owner, the women's self-help group making pickles to sell or the multinational company selling biscuits and bread—all need to assure the consumer that their food products are of good quality. Food reaches the consumer via supply chains that link different types of people and organisations. These include the primary producer of the food, the processing plant where the primary food (for example, wheat) is transformed into a food product (such as bread), the distributor who transports the product and takes it to storage setups or to the retailers, caterers, etc. Controls need to be exercised throughout the supply chain and these are mainly based on laboratory testing. In the preceding chapters, we have already looked at the various hazards which can be present in our food and how food service establishments need to maintain hygiene and sanitation in order to serve safe food. You have also been introduced to various laws, regulations as well as international bodies responsible for laying down food standards as well as trade agreements between nations. In this chapter, we will learn more about the concepts of food safety management systems, about methods of assuring quality and safety of products and services by the food industry, as well as about auditing and accreditation.

QUALITY CONTROL AND ASSURANCE

Small- and medium-sized food producers and manufacturers are increasingly considering ways and means of improving the quality of their foods in order to compete with larger companies that have global presence. In fact, supplying good quality safe food has become essential to their survival. Earlier, the local grocer would not be too bothered about the quality of his food products as, perhaps, his was the only shop in the neighbourhood, and he was not too worried about his clientele going elsewhere. The pulses (*dals*) and rice he sold would have physical hazards like small stones, pieces of straw, husk and even weevils. The consumer was expected to go home and clean the same before consumption. When supermarkets and big grocery stores made an advent in India, the customer was offered clean, packaged grains which he did not have to clean further before use. The customer obviously chose to buy provisions from the big grocery stores/supermarkets as he was being assured better quality and safer food products. The small retailer had to adapt and improve the quality of grains he sold—he started cleaning and packaging his grains as well!

Quality is a subjective as well as objective measurement of a food—its flavour, colour, maturity, purity, safety, wholesomeness, nutrition and other attributes or characteristics. It is the degree or extent to which the characteristics of the product fulfil the customer's requirements.

Initially, to check the quality of goods and services, there would be an **inspection**. If the end products or services did not comply to set standards, then corrective actions could be limited. For products, it would imply whatever can be salvaged by sorting, grading and re-blending. The concept of **quality control** includes development of a quality manual, use of process performance data and product testing along with self-inspection. The approach is to first detect the problem/defect and then look for solutions to the problem. The effort is to make the product or process conform to specified standards and prevent sub-standard service or product from reaching the customer. Not using either inspection or quality control may result in heavy losses to the manufacturer or food service operator as products found to be unsafe or of poor quality would be rejected by the consumer. **Quality assurance**, on other hand, involves advanced quality planning and quality systems development with comprehensive quality manuals. It is a process-oriented approach and creates conditions which ensure that the preparation of the food product conforms to the desired specifications.

Taking an example of the meat processing industry, we can see the difference between these terms:

Quality control: Testing the carcass of the animals for veterinary drug residues or testing meat products for salmonella prior to marketing.

Quality assurance: Implementation of production procedures at farm level which minimise/avoid drug residues/pathogens in meat, as well as SOPs for good hygienic practices.

Food businesses meet their food safety and quality responsibilities by implementing quality assurance systems along the food production chain. Quality assurance systems enable application and verification of control measures intended to assure the quality and safety of food. These sets of controls may include prerequisites like Good Agricultural Practices (GAP), Good Manufacturing Practices (GMPs), Good Hygienic Practices (GHPs), and Hazard Analysis and Critical Control Point (HACCP) systems. Many businesses can face challenges but, in particular, small-scale producers and traders in developing countries need support in planning and implementing food safety management systems in line with national and international regulatory requirements and customer expectations.

International organisations working towards quality and safety assurances include the Codex Alimentarius Commission and under it the Joint FAO/WHO Food Standards Program, organisations like the International Organization for Standardization (ISO), the World Trade Organization (WTO) and the SPS and TBT Agreements (discussed in a previous chapter). Food safety standards have become the key operating principle of these agreements which affect world trade. Global assurance systems are based on science-based standards. Codex standards have been considered as a benchmark. They adopt the 'farm to fork' or the food chain approach (see Figure 16.1). The concept of sampling only the end-product and testing its safety and quality is no longer considered adequate. The quality and safety systems work on different aspects:

- preventing or minimising contamination
- setting limits for use of food additives
- following labelling requirements
- looking into minimum legal requirements of the product quality attributes

Quality assurance is an ongoing process and focuses on preventing problems. It requires a deep understanding of and involvement in the product compositional requirements and compliance to regulatory standards of the country, and monitoring the inputs and every unit operation during production. Governments have an important role to play in providing policy guidance on the most appropriate quality assurance systems and monitoring their implementation.

Figure 16.1: Quality Assurance along the Entire Food Chain

Source: Drawn by Author.

To ensure food safety, we need to look at the entire food chain, from the place of production of the food at the farm level to the consumer's plate just before consumption. To achieve this, there needs to be an integration of various quality and food safety management tools, practices and systems such as:

- Good Hygienic Practices (GHP)
- Good Manufacturing Practices (GMP)
- Good Agricultural Practices (GAP)
- Good Animal Husbandry (GAH) or Good Veterinary Practices (GVP)
- Hazard Analysis Critical Control Point (HACCP)

- Risk Analysis
- ISO 22000 Food Safety Management System
- ISO 9000 Quality Management System
- Total Quality Management

TOTAL QUALITY MANAGEMENT: CONCEPT, NEED AND COMPONENTS

Total Quality Management (TQM) is a continual activity which seeks the involvement of suppliers, customers and all employees to improve the quality of the products and/or services. In all operations, there is emphasis on teamwork and employee involvement. In a TQM effort, all members of an organisation participate in improving the processes, products, services and work culture. Each employee recognises their personal responsibility towards ensuring quality and safety. This helps the company as a whole in achieving uniformity, quality and hence safety of the product.

TQM is a management approach of ensuring long-term success through customer satisfaction. There are eight primary elements of TQM, according to ASQ (2016):

- CUSTOMER-FOCUSSED
  - ➢ Customer determines the level of quality and needs to be satisfied
- TOTAL EMPLOYEE INVOLVEMENT
  - ➢ Empowerment of and conducive environment for all employees to work towards a common goal
  - ➢ A spirit of teamwork based on ethics, trust and integrity
  - ➢ Team leaders act as a source of inspiration and provide direction
- PROCESS-CENTRED
  - ➢ Steps of the process are defined and performance measures are monitored
  - ➢ Use of high quality ingredients, equipment, utensils, etc. to produce a good quality product
- INTEGRATED SYSTEM
  - ➢ Different functional units which are all interconnected
  - ➢ All departments of the food industry work in unison
- STRATEGIC AND SYSTEMATIC APPROACH
  - ➢ Formulation of a strategic plan to achieve vision, mission and goal of establishment is important
- CONTINUAL IMPROVEMENT
  - ➢ A drive to be more competitive and effective in the market
  - ➢ Training of employees to improve their performance

- FACT-BASED DECISION-MAKING
  - Continual collection and analysis of data in order to improve decision making accuracy
  - Use of science-based standards
- COMMUNICATIONS
  - Communicating strategies and procedures to maintain the morale and motivate employees at all levels

TQM is totally dependent on a quality assurance system. The ISO 9000 and ISO 22000 series of standards can be used for designing the TQM programmes. TQM has a major role to play in the food industry. Products need to be manufactured keeping in mind preferences of the consumer regarding quality attributes and the fact that along with quality, the consumer also desires a safe food product. This concept also helps the industry in making superior products, as one of the features of TQM is 'continuous improvement'. This is possible only through research and taking feedback from customers. With customer satisfaction comes long-term customer loyalty. TQM builds trust in the mind of the customer, making him select products of the same brand because the customer is sure of the quality. This is how some food companies have built a brand following for some of their products.

Kaizen (*Kai*-change, *zen*-good) is a Japanese term which means 'improvement' or a 'change for the better.' It is similar to TQM, where all employees of an industry put in a continuous effort to improve all processes and systems of the organisation. Kaizen works on the basic principle that change is for the good of the business and hence, should be readily adopted. It is only through change that the processes and functions of an organisation can be improved. The process of Kaizen plays an important role in improving employee and customer satisfaction. It gives rise to a well-organised workplace, resulting in better productivity and better results. The employees also feel strongly attached and loyal to the organisation.

ISO 22000 FOOD SAFETY MANAGEMENT SYSTEM

In today's globalised world, with food products readily crossing international borders, the risk of unsafe food can get multiplied several times in a short span of time. The consequences of unsafe food and hygiene can be very serious. Adopting and adhering to a standard for food safety management can help organisations identify and control hazards pertaining to food.

ISO (International Organization for Standardization) is a global federation of national standards bodies. The ISO technical committees are responsible for preparing and issuing international standards which they do in collaboration with numerous international organisations, both governmental and non-governmental.

The **ISO 22000 FSMS** (**Food Safety Management System**) specifies the requirements for a food safety management system. This standard is meant for any organisation in the food chain which desires to prove its ability to control food safety hazards to ensure that food is safe at the time of human consumption. Specifically, such an organisation can derive the following benefits from adopting this standard:

- systematic identification and management of food safety hazards
- greater confidence for safety of food and related products served and delivered through the food chain
- better technological discipline across the organisation
- compatibility with the system of quality management as per the ISO 9001 standard and therefore, the possibility of a fully integrated management system

ISO 22000 contains several standards, each with a different focus on food safety management (see Table 16.1).

Table 16.1: The ISO 22000 Family of Standards

Standard	*Focus*
ISO 22000:2005	Overall guidelines for food safety management
ISO 22004:2014	Generic advice on the application of ISO 22000
ISO 22005:2007	Traceability in the feed and food chain
ISO/TS 22002-1:2009	Specific prerequisites for food manufacturing
ISO/TS 22002-2:2013	Specific prerequisites for catering
ISO/TS 22002-3:2011	Specific prerequisites for farming
ISO/TS 22002-4:2013	Specific prerequisites for food packaging manufacturing
ISO/TS 22003:2013	Guidelines for audit and certification bodies

Source: Compiled by Author.

ISO 22000:2005 incorporates the seven principles of the HACCP system and the application steps of the Codex Alimentarius Commission and combines the same with Pre-Requisite Programmes (PRPs). PRPs must be functioning effectively within the system before ISO or HACCP can be introduced. PRPs in ISO 22002-1, for instance, include requirements for construction and layout of building, layout of premises and workspace, waste disposal, equipment suitability, cleaning and maintenance, measures for prevention of cross-contamination, cleaning and sanitising, pest control, personnel hygiene and employee facilities, among others.

> There is a need to continuously evaluate and update food GMP regulations to ensure that they take today's technologies and food safety hazards into account.

Conducting a hazard analysis helps in organising the knowledge required for a good combination of control measures. The standard requires all hazards that are expected to occur in the food chain, including those that are linked to the type of process used, to be systematically identified and assessed. In this way, it provides the means to determine why certain hazards should be controlled and why others need not. During the process of hazard analysis, the organisation determines the strategy to enforce hazard control by combining the PRPs and the

HACCP plan. HACCP systems or HACCP-based systems are considered an important tool for food safety management. GAP, GMP and GHP are PRPs for HACCP.

ISO 9000 is a set of quality management standards. They are a process standard (and not a product standard). These are applicable to all kinds of organisations. The standards require you to establish a Quality Management System and documentation process. The system should support quality, satisfy the customers by meeting their requirements, establish a quality policy, formulate quality objectives, plan the development of the system, communicate responsibilities to those involved and perform reviews intended to improve upon the system. The ISO 9000 family includes the following standards—ISO 9001:2015 (which gives requirements of a quality management system), ISO 9000:2015 (which covers the basic concepts and language), ISO 9004:2009 (which focuses on how to make a quality management system more efficient and effective), and ISO 19011:2011 (which sets out guidance on internal and external audits of quality management systems). Similarly, the ISO 14000 family of standards provides practical tools for companies and organisations of all kinds looking to manage their environmental responsibilities.

GOOD MANUFACTURING PRACTICES

Good Manufacturing Practices (GMP) is a system for ensuring that products are consistently produced and controlled according to quality standards. Several industries adopt GMP to maintain product quality. Applicable for food processing industries, GMP must be used by all establishments involved in pre-preparation, preparation, packaging, handling and storage of food. The concept of GMP is being replaced by cGMP, meaning current Good Manufacturing Practices. It covers all aspects of production starting from the raw materials, premises (building and facility design), equipment, utensils, sanitary and cleaning operations, production and process control to the training and personal hygiene of staff.

Manufacturing processes need to be defined well. All processes which are critical in food production need to be under control. The environmental conditions should be adequately controlled to prevent contamination of food. This is ensured by maintaining a clean and hygienic manufacturing area. It also involves testing of food to ensure that it is according to product specifications. There should be clarity in the documentation process and maintenance of records. The components of GMP are given in Figure 16.2. In India, GMP inspections are carried out by state Food and Drugs Administrations (FDA) and these FDAs report to the Central Drugs Standard Control Organization for pharmaceutical industries.

Good Agricultural Practices (**GAP**) improve the production of safe and good quality produce. These practices are usually environment friendly. They also address issues of economic and social sustainability. They encourage controlled use of agricultural chemicals in approved dosages which are unlikely to result in residues in food, or be harmful for the soil, surrounding water bodies, plants and animal life. Consumers' growing concern regarding food safety had led European nations to form EUREPGAP in 1997. The EUREPGAP standards helped producers comply with criteria accepted across Europe for food safety, sustainable production methods, worker and

Figure 16.2: Components of Good Manufacturing Practices to Ensure Food Safety

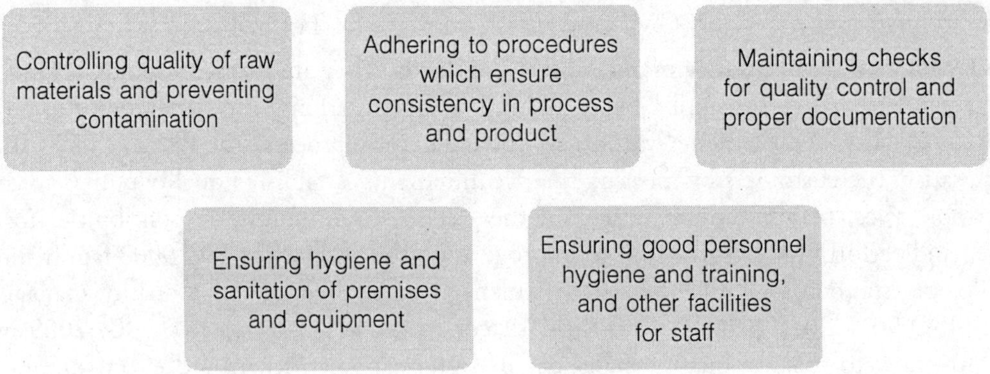

Source: Drawn by Author.

animal welfare, and responsible use of water, compound feed and plant propagation materials. In 2007, its name changed to GLOBALG.A.P, reflecting its global outreach with more than 100 countries adopting these standards. As more and more food service buyers and retailers are demanding a certain level of quality and safety from agricultural food products, and are hence looking for GAP-certified products, the Quality Council of India launched a standard, INDGAP, in September 2014. This hopes to empower small farm holdings and enable them to ensure safety and hygiene in their farming systems.

Similarly, **Good Animal Husbandry** (**GAH**) or **Good Veterinary Practices** (**GVP**) have been established to assure consumers that foods derived from animals meet acceptable levels of quality and safety. The focus is on safe animal feed, healthy living conditions and treatment/ monitoring of diseases which afflict them. The aim is to reduce veterinary residues, pesticide residues, pathogens, mycotoxins and other contaminants in animal products.

HAZARD ANALYSIS CRITICAL CONTROL POINT (HACCP) SYSTEM

The HACCP system is actually a risk management tool which is tailored to individual food operations. It is used to identify specific hazards such as microbiological, chemical and physical hazards, and put in place measures for their prevention and control to ensure safety and quality of food. The HACCP system can be regarded as a general approach to problem solving and also an effective means of ensuring product safety.

It has its origins in the space exploration programmes of the National Aeronautics and Space Administration (NASA) of the United

> Traditionally, quality checks would involve an inspection team performing spot checks of conditions during different stages of manufacturing and of a random sample of the finished product. This is a reactive approach in which the company tries to handle a situation of food contamination after it has happened. HACCP, on the other hand, is a preventive approach which aims to control the production process and prevent contamination from occurring. It anticipates that a problem will occur and then takes corrective measures to prevent it from happening.

States of America. Sending a manned mission was fraught with dangers if the safety of the food meant for astronauts could not be ensured. Remember that such missions last for months and cooked food would have to be kept in a form which was fit for human consumption. Together with the Pillsbury company and the US Army Laboratories in Massachusetts in 1959, a new method of food safety was developed. It was based on the identification of critical control points (CCPs) for system failures. Pillsbury later adopted the CCPs and the 'System Safety Approach' in its own food manufacturing operations. Slowly, people starting understanding the importance of this approach and the first publication which used the term 'HACCP' was printed in 1973 by the Food and Drug Administration (FDA). It was on a training programme which Pillsbury conducted to train inspectors following an investigation into a contamination of canned goods with *Clostridium botulinum* (Knechtges 2012).

> To produce the safest food possible, one needs to have control over the production process, the raw materials, the environment and the food handlers.

The failure of inspection methods in the United States in 1993 led to an outbreak of *E. coli* O157:H7 in hamburgers in the north-western part of the country, affecting more than 500 people and killing four. This provided the final push needed for the US Department of Agriculture (USDA) to issue the Pathogen Reduction: Hazard Analysis and Critical Control Points (HACCP) System rule in 1996. Under HACCP regulations, the food processing industry assumes primary responsibility for the safety of the food it produces. The government's role is to verify that the industry is carrying out its responsibility and to initiate appropriate regulatory action if necessary. Eventually, most regulatory authorities of the world, and the Codex Alimentarius Commission, have mandated or recommended the use of HACCP for food operations. In India, HACCP was introduced in some industries in the 1990s. We now see several food products which are HACCP certified. Most of these are restricted, however, to large-scale manufacturers and some multinational food companies. HACCP needs to be adopted by the small-scale food producer and other food service establishments.

The rationale of HACCP involves conducting a study to identify all existing or potential hazards within the process, identifying effective control measures and designating critical control points where these measures may be implemented. The guiding document for implementing a HACCP system is called a HACCP plan. To develop and implement a HACCP plan, standard operating procedures (SOPs) for sanitary practices and compliance with GMPs is a prerequisite. For the development of the HACCP plan, several **preliminary steps** are needed.

A **HACCP team needs to be assembled** first, comprising members representing key operations and departments of the food processing plant or food service establishment. It pays to have food safety experts like microbiologists and quality assurance representatives on your team. Nevertheless, at least one member on the team should have had a proper training in HACCP principles. The next step involves **describing the food products** and the details about how they are produced/prepared and distributed/served. The description includes sources of procurement of raw materials, storage temperatures and time, steps of processing, packaging/service, dispatch, and other important information. **Intended uses for the product** by the consumers should also be identified.

Finally, the HACCP team would need to prepare a 'process flow diagram' of the food product, which lists all the stages in the process of preparation of the product. This is verified by a 'walk-through' of the entire process to make sure all steps have been incorporated. The seven principles of HACCP, as listed in Figure 16.3, are then used to develop the HACCP plan.

Figure 16.3: The Seven Principles of HACCP

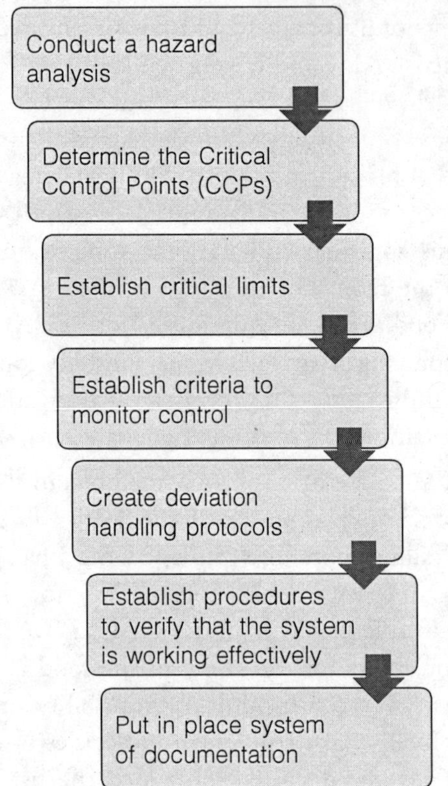

Source: Adapted by Author from FAO/WHO 2006.

Conducting a hazard analysis involves two steps—the **identification** of the hazards and **evaluation** of the hazards. The types of hazards—physical, chemical or biological—which are present or are likely to be introduced during the processing of the food are determined (see Figure 16.4). These could be coming in through the raw materials used to prepare the product or from equipment, processing environment or handlers at different stages of the process. For instance, the chicken used to prepare *momo*s (dumplings) may have a heavy microbial load at the beginning of the process, which may not all get destroyed during the preparation of the filling for the dumpling. Contaminants like aluminium could be introduced into the dumpling while cooking in utensils made of this metal. In addition, food handlers, while folding the casing of the dumpling and putting the stuffing, could introduce fresh pathogens from their hands. Inadequate heating during the steaming process, especially of the core of the filling, could produce contaminated dumplings.

Hazard evaluation involves determining the magnitude of the risk posed by the identified hazards, that is, the likelihood of occurrence of the hazard as well as the possible adverse consequences.

The second principle is to **identify CCPs** in the process flow diagram where hazard analysis has indicated the possible introduction/exacerbation (increase in concentration/toxic potential) of a hazard. For most of these points, observance of basic principles of hygiene and sanitation will minimise risks. For some points, however, dedicated monitoring is required. These points are critical in preventing food-borne disease outbreaks. Examples of CCPs include thermal processes (like pasteurisation, freezing, sterilisation, cooking and reheating), time and temperature conditions for storage, pH adjustment, water activity, salt concentration and detection of contaminants. To determine whether a processing step can be considered critical or not, asking

Figure 16.4: Identifying Potential Hazards

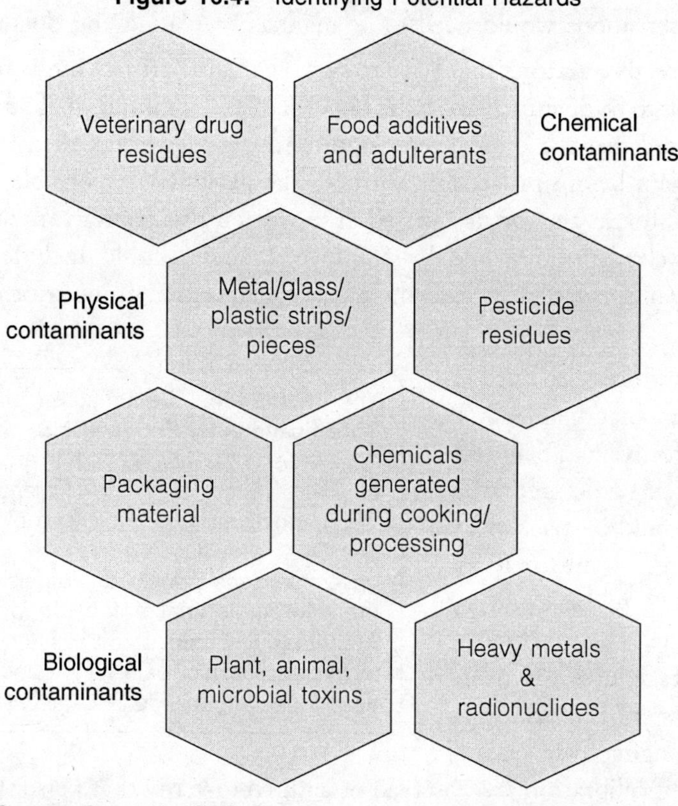

Source: Drawn by Author.

some basic questions helps. For instance, we must find out if the step is significantly designed to eliminate or reduce the likely occurrence of a hazard to an acceptable level. If yes, this can be considered a CCP. We also need to check if a subsequent step in the processing could eliminate the identified hazard. If the answer to this question is no, then again, the step would be considered a CCP (see Appendix for the HACCP decision tree).

Appropriate **critical limits** need to be established for each CCP. These are minimum or maximum values for parameters at each CCP that must be controlled to prevent, eliminate or reduce a food safety hazard to an acceptable level. For a cooked food, this might include setting the minimum cooking temperature and time required to ensure elimination of harmful microbes. Critical limits could be derived from regulations or safety-related product specifications available in credible scientific literature. They should be precise and not a range of possible values.

Establishing monitoring procedures is important to see if deviations from critical limits are occurring; for instance, measuring of temperature using computer-controlled sensors to detect deviations in real time. Advanced technology has made it possible for suitable alarm systems to be triggered whenever a critical limit is crossed. This alerts the team to take corrective action. In smaller establishments, it may be important to designate a person for each CCP, who would monitor time and temperature on a regular basis and alert the team if there was loss of control at that point. All observations would need to be manually recorded and documented.

Establishing corrective actions that have to be taken when critical limits have not been met is important and needs to be documented in the HACCP plan. For instance, if during pasteurisation of milk, it was detected that the critical temperature was not achieved, then the milk may need to be heat treated again before proceeding further. The person(s) responsible for implementing the corrective action should also be designated. The written procedures for corrective actions to be taken should be clearly understood by employees. These should include details of whose technical expertise can be availed in case the cause for deviation from critical limit cannot be determined.

Verification procedures also need to be established to ensure that the HACCP system is working effectively as planned. The decisions for choosing process controls and critical limits should be backed by valid scientific sources of information. Also, validation needs to be done by in-plant observations, measurements, testing and other procedures to ensure that the HACCP system is working as planned. Activities ranging from record-keeping to instrument calibration are observed or audited to verify that personnel are performing them as prescribed by the HACCP plan. Verification also involves microbiological testing of foods. Microbiological criteria (levels of microbes acceptable in a particular food) are required to see if the system is working effectively in preventing/reducing microbial hazards.

The International Commission on Microbiological Specifications for Foods (**ICMSF**) was established in 1962 through the action of the International Committee on Food Microbiology and Hygiene, a committee of the International Union of Microbiological Societies (IUMS). It provides science-based guidance to the government and industry on appraising and controlling the microbiological safety of foods. **The Codex Alimentarius Commission** has become the reference for international food safety and its principles have been used for setting microbiological criteria.

The importance of **keeping records** diligently cannot be overemphasised. There should be a method and procedure for record keeping that needs to be followed by the employees concerned. It is recommended that records be maintained in a tabular format for clarity and easy retrieval of information. Bigger establishments prefer to computerise the records and have automatic recording.

Case Studies on HACCP

In a case study of the traditional *khoa* industry in two districts of Andhra Pradesh, HACCP was used to understand risks and provide solutions (Sudershan et al. 1997). The process of *khoa* preparation in the area was studied. The CCPs were identified as storage of *khoa* at room temperature for up to three days, contamination due to handling by multiple food handlers and unclean vessels being used for storage. During transportation, the vendors mixed *khoa* from different sources, thus increasing the chance of cross-contamination. They were found to be selling the *khoa* by laying it out in the open, exposed to dust and flies. Installation of cold storage at the village level and improving the packaging system, besides imparting education to food handlers on the microbiological and hygiene aspects, were suggested as measures to improve food safety.

Similarly, HACCP has been used to identify solutions to food poisoning outbreaks due to contamination of a variety of foods. It has also been applied to ensure the safety and other quality aspects of different kinds of food packaging materials. Let us consider the example of preparation of an Indian sweet preparation, *besan ladoo* or sweet balls made of bengalgram flour, to understand a HACCP plan (see Table 16.2). The first step is to make a process flow diagram (see Figure 16.5).

Figure 16.5: Process Flow Diagram for Making *Besan Ladoo*

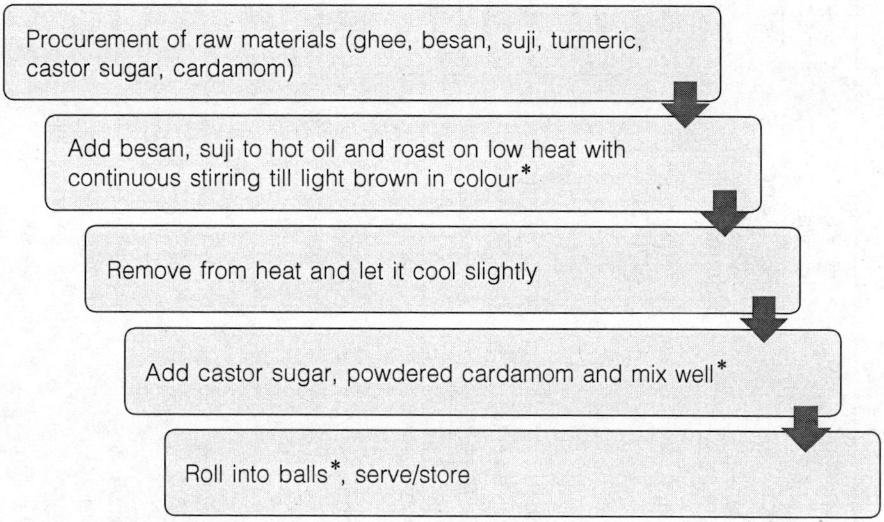

Procurement of raw materials (ghee, besan, suji, turmeric, castor sugar, cardamom)

↓

Add besan, suji to hot oil and roast on low heat with continuous stirring till light brown in colour*

↓

Remove from heat and let it cool slightly

↓

Add castor sugar, powdered cardamom and mix well*

↓

Roll into balls*, serve/store

Note: *Critical Control Points.

Source: Adapted by Author from Jyoti and Mathur 2010.

Thus, during preparation of the *ladoo*s, as can be seen from the process flow diagram and the HACCP plan, microbes may enter at multiple points, especially when bare hands touch the ingredients/finished product. Cross-contamination from unclean utensils or unhygienic environment may also add to the microbial load. Washing hands each time there is physical contact with ingredients/product may reduce the risk of transfer of harmful microbes. Keeping the surroundings and all food contact surfaces clean is, of course, vital to a safe product.

Benefits and Limitations of the HACCP Approach

The application of HACCP for foods served in food service establishments can address many of the difficulties faced in ensuring safety. Figure 16.6 enumerates the various benefits of using this approach to tackle food safety issues.

Table 16.2: HACCP Plan for *Besan Ladoo*

Process step	*Hazards*	*Preventive measures*	*CCP*	*Critical limits*	*Monitoring*	*Corrective action*
Receiving raw materials	• Physical hazards (foreign particles, insects) • Microbial hazards	• Visual inspection • Specification compliance • Product labeling and expiry check	No	• No visible insect infestation • No foreign objects in material	• Visual daily inspection/ sampling	• Reject, if insect infestation, dirt/ foreign objects found • Vendor quality assurance
Heat fat and roast ingredients	• Microbial hazards—cross-contamination from dirty equipment	• Temperature control • Use of clean equipment	Yes	• Temperature (>70ºC)	• Temperature checks • Visual inspection of equipment	• Reheat to temperature >70ºC
Cool and mix remaining ingredients	• Microbial hazards—airborne, cross-contamination from ingredients, and dirty equipment	• Use of good quality ingredients, clean equipment • Proper covering during cooling	Yes	• No insects or pests • Microbial standards	• Visual inspection • Random microbiological tests	• Reheat mixture • Discard if in doubt
Make balls	• Microbial contamination from dirty hands	• Wash hands properly	Yes	• Microbial standards	• Inspection of hands before preparation • Check provision of soap, clean towels	• Reheat if in doubt
Cool and store in display utensil	• Microbial contamination from utensil and handling • Air-borne contaminants while cooling • Flies	• Use of clean equipment • Proper covering during storage • Use of disposable gloves if using hands to serve	Yes	• No pests in display/storage area • Display cases clean and fully closed	• Visual inspection • Random microbiological tests	• Reheat

Source: Adapted by Author frcm Jyoti and Mathur 2010.

Figure 16.6: Benefits of Using the HACCP Approach

- Implementation and monitoring by persons handling food operations
- Proactive approach which anticipates problems before they occur
- Less expensive than traditional inspection, chemical and microbiological analysis
- Control mechanisms are documented and hence easy to monitor for compliance over extended periods of time
- Useful in predicting potential hazards
- Identifies critical food safety risk factors useful for training and education

Sources: Adapted by Author from Knechtges 2012 and Roberts 2003.

The major benefit of HACCP is that it is a **systematic approach** for identifying, analysing and controlling hazards within a food processing/service establishment. It is useful for new operations and also allows for identification of all expected hazards which have never been previously experienced or documented. It is sufficiently **flexible** to allow changes in processing technology. The HACCP plan provides **direction and guidance** for food safety activities, through the entire food chain, to minimise the risk of distributing/serving unsafe food. Record keeping helps ensure continuity in the process control of hazards and provides an **auditable record**. It is a **preventive approach** and hence, works out to be more beneficial for business than the traditional inspection approach. It helps save money and resources for the establishment and has considerably **decreased financial loss** (monetary loss in rejection, recall of products and legal expenses in case of prosecution) in several food industries. HACCP-certified products and companies **inspire confidence among consumers** regarding quality and safety of the product. For the consumer, the benefits include a reduced risk of food-borne diseases and an increased quality of life. The government also stands to gain by **improved public health** with reduced costs of dealing with food-borne diseases and **facilitation of international trade.**

The primary **limitation of HACCP** is that it is not a standalone programme. Other efforts such as GMPs, cleaning and sanitisation of premises and equipment, personnel hygiene, waste management, pest control and maintenance of water quality are vital for any HACCP plan to work. Failure to keep abreast of developments in the field of food safety, such as the emergence of new hazards, better measures for controlling a hazard, deeper understanding of how hazards can increase in severity under certain conditions can make the control measures in a HACCP plan outdated. Another limitation of HACCP is that not everyone agrees on which control points in a process flow are 'critical enough' to be designated as CCPs. Some may insist on most steps in the production process being considered CCPs. This would, however, increase the burden of monitoring and record keeping. As it is, record keeping can be very cumbersome and is considered a major limitation from the point of view of the burden on personnel. If some control points are not designated as critical, it still means that other food safety controls must be maintained at these points. For instance, the first step of any preparation process is checking the quality of raw ingredients. It may not be designated as a CCP. However, one still needs to check the microbiological quality of all ingredients likely to be contaminated and ensure adequate cleaning of ingredients like vegetables. Trained personnel need to be involved in the development, implementation and maintenance of HACCP systems. In small establishments, the lack of scientific expertise could become an obstacle to developing an effective HACCP plan.

ACCREDITATION AND AUDITING

A system should always be subject to independent audit for evaluation at different levels of inspection and certification system. Internationally recognised assessment and verification procedures need to be used for the same.

Certification is the process of providing a written testimony or assurance that an organisation's product, service or system meets the requirements of an independent, widely accepted standard. It demonstrates that the product, service or system meets the expectations of the organisation's customers. In fact, in many cases, certification may even be a legal or contractual requirement. Typically, this testimony is provided by way of a written certificate. The certification is performed by an independent body, distinct from the body responsible for issuing the standard.

The ISO 22000:2013 standard outlines the requirements for certification agencies responsible for the audit and certification of the food safety management system (FSMS). It assists in the certification process. Certification of the FSMS of an organisation is one means of providing assurance that the organisation has implemented a system for the management of food safety in line with its policy.

Auditing is the process by which a certification body assesses whether the product, service or process of an organisation meets the requirements of a standard. It involves studying the systems and processes of the organisation, interviewing of key personnel and documentation to evaluate whether the standard has been implemented well or not. In order to prepare for the audit by an independent certification body, most organisations set up their internal teams which are tasked with implementing the standard and with carrying out **internal audits** to help prepare for the audit by the certification body.

Certification requires the certifying agency to audit the organisation's FSMS. The result of a successful certification process is usually a certification document which attests to the conformance of the organisation's FSMS with a specific FSMS standard like ISO 22000. In India, ISO certification is offered by a host of certification bodies such as Bureau Veritas Certification, Det Norske Veritas, Indian Register Quality Systems, Intertek India, SGS India, TUV, to name a few.

Figure 16.7: Some Certification Systems around the World

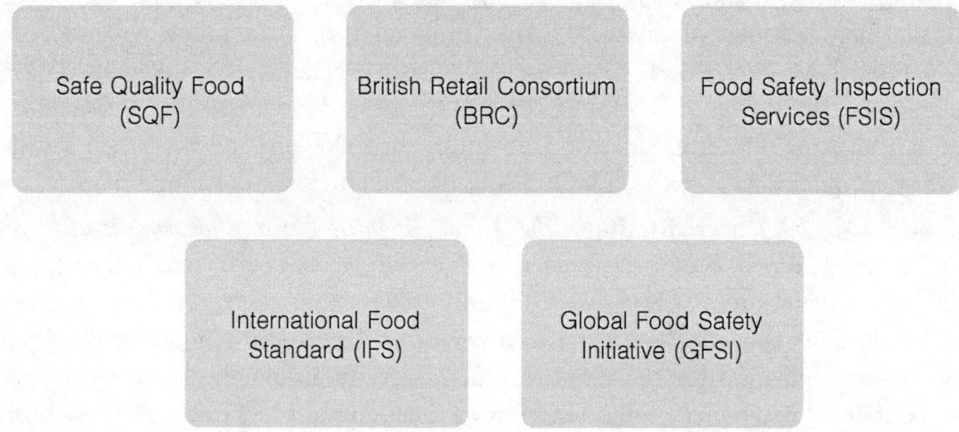

Source: Adapted by Author from Jaiswal 2009.

Some of the other certification systems being used across the globe have been shown in Figure 16.7. A few of them are discussed here.

The Safe Quality Foods Programme (SQF)

The SQF Code is administered by the SQF Institute and is relevant for retailers and food service providers around the world. There are two codes under this:

SQF 1000 Code

This code is designed for primary producers and requires them to develop GAPs and maintain plans to control their critical operations.

SQF 2000 Code

This code is applicable to food manufacturing and distribution organisations and requires them to develop GMPs and to maintain plans to control their critical operations.

The code is divided into three levels of certification, indicating the extent of development of the safety and quality systems of an organisation. The SQF certification bodies need to attain international accreditation. Every assessment is reviewed by a review panel of the certification body, which issues SQF certificates to successful suppliers and manufacturers. Some of the SQF certification bodies in India are BSI Group, Mérieux NutriSciences Certification, NSF Food Safety Certification, Perry Johnson Registrars Food Safety, SAI Global, SGS Systems and TUV NORD.

International Food Standard (IFS)

The members of the German retail federation HDE, the French FCD and the Italian COOP, CONAD and Federdistribuzione have collaborated on a food safety and quality standard called the International Food Standard (IFS). It is most suitable for suppliers of German, French or Italian retailer-branded food products. The IFS family comprises the following standards—IFS Food, IFS Global Markets Food, IFS Wholesale/Cash & Carry, IFS Logistics, IFS Global Markets Logistics, IFS Broker 2, IFS HPC, IFS PACsecure and IFS Food Store. There are several certification bodies for IFS across the world. In India, the following bodies provide certification: Bureau Veritas Polska, DNV, DQS, ECOCERT, Food Cert, SAI Global and SGS.

According to the ISO, **accreditation** *is the formal recognition by an independent body, generally known as an accreditation body, that a certification body operates per international standards.* ISO 17000:2004 defines terms related to conformity assessment. Accreditation must be a very objective, transparent and effective exercise. It serves as the basis for policy making and as a means of market regulation for the regulatory authority. It ultimately facilitates trade, builds consumer confidence and increases the credibility of the food industry/food service establishment. The organisation responsible for the accreditation of certification bodies is called the National Accreditation Board for Certification Bodies (NABCB). The organisation responsible for the accreditation of laboratories is called the National Accreditation Board for Testing and Calibration Laboratories (NABL).

The Quality Council of India (QCI) was set up in 1997 by the Government of India, jointly with the Indian industry to establish and operate the National Accreditation Structure for conformity assessment bodies. QCI has a pivotal role to play in propagating, adoption and adherence to quality standards in all important spheres of activities.

The Food Safety and Standards Authority of India is established under the Food Safety and Standards Act, 2006 and has the mandate for laying down scientific standards for food articles and to regulate their manufacture, storage, distribution, sale and import to ensure availability of safe and wholesome food. Section 3(1)(s) of the Act defines 'Food Safety Management System' as the adoption of GMPs, GHPs, HACCP and other specified practices for the food business. Regulation 2.1.2 of the Food Safety and Standards (Licensing & Registration of Food Businesses) Regulations, 2011 mandates the licensing of food businesses, provided their FSMS is compliant with the GMPs and GHPs detailed in Schedule 4 of the same regulations. Section 16(2)(c) of the FSS Act, 2006 provides for the mechanism for accreditation of certification bodies for FSMSs and Section 44 of the Act provides for recognition of an organisation or agency for food safety audit and checking compliance with the FSMS required under the Act or the rules and regulations made thereunder.

SUMMARY

- Safe and wholesome food is a basic need of consumers.
- Quality is a subjective as well as objective measurement of a food. It is the degree or extent to which characteristics of the product fulfil the customer's requirements.
- Quality control is different from quality assurance as it relies more on end-product testing and then fire-fighting in case of a problem.
- Quality assurance systems enable application and verification of control measures intended to assure the quality and safety of food.
- Global assurance systems are based on science-based standards. Codex standards have been considered as a benchmark. They adopt the 'farm-to-fork' or the food chain approach.
- Some of the various food safety management tools/practices are Good Hygienic Practices (GHPs), Good Manufacturing Practices (GMPs), Good Agricultural Practices (GAPs), Good Animal Husbandry (GAH) or Good Veterinary Practices (GVPs), Hazard Analysis Critical Control Point (HACCP), Risk Analysis, ISO 22000 Food Safety Management System, ISO 9000 Quality Management System and Total Quality Management (TQM).
- TQM is a continual activity which seeks the involvement of suppliers, customers and all employees to improve the quality of the products and/or services.
- Kaizen works on the basic principle that change is for the good of the business and hence, should be readily adopted.
- The ISO 22000 FSMS (Food Safety Management System) specifies the requirements for any organisation in the food chain which desires to prove its ability to control food safety hazards to ensure that food is safe at the time of human consumption.
- ISO 9000 are a set of process standards. The standards require you to establish a Quality Management System and documentation process.
- GMP is a system for ensuring that products are consistently produced and controlled according to quality standards.
- The HACCP system is actually a risk management tool which is tailored to individual food operations. It is used to identify specific hazards—microbiological, chemical and physical—and put in place measures for their prevention and control to ensure safety and quality of food.
- There are certain prerequisites to the seven principles of HACCP.
- Certification is the process of providing a written testimony or assurance that an organisation's product, service or system meets the requirements of an independent, widely accepted standard.
- Auditing is the process by which a certification body assesses whether an organisation's product, service or process meets the requirements of a standard.
- Some certification systems include SQF, BRC, FSIS, IFS and GFSI.
- Accreditation is the formal recognition by an independent body—generally known as an accreditation body—that a certification body operates as per international standards.

KEY WORDS

Control measure: Any action and activity that can be used to prevent or eliminate a food safety hazard or reduce it to an acceptable level.

Corrective action: Any action to be taken when the results of monitoring the CCP indicate a loss of control.

Critical Control Point (CCP): A step at which control can be applied and is essential to prevent or eliminate a food safety hazard, or to reduce it to an acceptable level.

Critical limit: A criterion which separates acceptability from unacceptability.

Deviation: Failure to meet critical limit.

HACCP: A system which identifies, evaluates and controls hazards which are significant for food safety.

HACCP plan: A document prepared in accordance with the principles of HACCP to ensure control of hazards which are significant for food safety in the segment of the food chain under consideration.

Hazard: A biological, chemical or physical agent in, or condition of, food with the potential to cause an adverse health effect.

Hazard analysis: The process of collecting and evaluating information on hazards and conditions leading to their presence to decide which are significant for food safety and therefore should be addressed in the HACCP plan.

Radionuclides: Unstable form of a chemical element that radioactively decays, emitting radiation; may be present in food, water and milk as a result of accidently or irresponsibly dumped radioactive waste in soil, air or water.

Validation: Obtaining evidence that the elements of the HACCP plan are effective.

Verification: The application of methods, procedures, tests and other evaluations, in addition to monitoring to determine compliance with the HACCP plan.

EXERCISES

1. What do you understand by Total Quality Management?
2. List the seven principles of HACCP.
3. Why is documentation an important component of the HACCP plan?
4. What are Good Manufacturing Practices? How do they contribute to making food safe?
5. Describe the SQF and IFS standards. How does a food processing unit get certified under these?
6. 'ISO 22000 is a family of standards'. Justify the statement giving suitable examples.
7. What does auditing mean and who does it?

REFERENCES

ASQ, *Total Quality Management*, 2016, American Society for Quality, Available at http://asq.org/learn-about-quality/total-quality-management/overview/overview.html (accessed 25 January 2017).

CAC, *General Principles of Food Hygiene*, 2003, revised version, Codex Alimentarius Commission, Available at http://www.fao.org/input/download/standards/23/CXP_001e.pdf (accessed 1 February 2017).

FAO/WHO, 'Guidance to Governments on the Application of HACCP in Small and/or Less-developed Food Businesses', FAO Food and Nutrition Paper 86, Rome: FAO/WHO, 2006.

Forsythe, S. J., *The Microbiology of Safe Food*, 2e, UK: Wiley-Blackwell, 2010.

IFS International Food Standard, Available at https://www.ifs-certification.com/index.php/en/partners/certification (accessed 28 January 2017).

ISO 22000—Food Safety Management System, Available at http://www.isocertificationindia.in/ISO_220002005%20.html (accessed 15 April 2018).

ISO 9000-Quality Management, Available at http://www.iso.org/iso/iso_9000 (accessed 30 January 2017).

Jaiswal, P. K., 'Total Quality and Safety Management System', in *Food Quality and Safety*, Noida: CBS Publishers, 2009, pp. 93–100.

Jyoti and Mathur, P., *Microbiological Quality of Selected Sweetmeats Sold in Delhi*, M.Sc. Dissertation in Partial Fulfilment of M.Sc. Food and Nutrition, submitted to Department of Home Science, Lady Irwin College, University of Delhi, New Delhi, 2010.

Knechtges, P. L., 'Risk and Hazard Analysis of Food', in *Food Safety—Theory and Practice*, USA: Jones & Bartlett Learning, 2012, pp. 278–300.

Roberts, C. A., 'Food Safety', *Encyclopedia of Food and Culture*, 2003, Available at http://www.encyclopedia.com (accessed 8 February 2016).

SQF, *The Safe Quality Foods Program*, Available at http://www.22000-tools.com/sqf-levels.html (accessed 28 January 2017).

Sudershan, R.V., R. N. Rao, and R. V. Bhat, 'Concepts of HACCP and Traditional Food Industry—A Case Study of Khoa', *Indian Food Industry* 16 (4), 1997, pp. 40–45.

ONLINE SOURCES

Codex Alimentarius Commission—General Principles of Food Hygiene CAC/RCP 1-1969 rev. 4 (2003), Available at http://www.mhlw.go.jp/english/topics/importedfoods/guideline/dl/04.pdf (accessed 1 February 2017).

Food Safety Management System Manual FSS Act 2006, Available at http://old.fssai.gov.in/Portals/0/Pdf/manual%20of%20food%20safety%20management%20system,%20fss%20act%202006.pdf (accessed 26 October 2017).

Food Safety Related Websites:

http://www.foodsafety.gov (accessed 15 April 2018).

http://foodsafety.nal.usda.gov (accessed 15 April 2018).

FSSAI, Available at http://www.fssai.gov.in/home/about-us/introduction.html (accessed 14 April 2018).

Good Manufacturing Practice (GMP) Resources, Available at http://www.ispe.org/gmp-resources (accessed 15 April 2018).

Microbiological Risk Assessment by Joint FAO/WHO Expert Meetings on Microbiological Risk Assessment (JEMRA), Available at http://www.fao.org/food/food-safety-quality/scientific-advice/jemra/en/ (accessed 15 April 2018).

Requirements For A HACCP Based Food Safety System. Compiled by the National Board of Experts—HACCP, The Netherlands. 3rd Version2, September 2002, Available at http://www.foodsafetymanagement.info/bron/cms_file/Requirements%20HACCP%20versie%203.pdf (accessed 15 April 2018).

Understanding Total Quality Management, Available at http://www.managementstudyguide.com/total-quality-management.htm (accessed 15 April 2018).

Video on Food Service Establishment Inspection, Available at https://www.youtube.com/watch?v=R64cp6_NyQk (accessed 15 April 2018).

Video on HACCP - Making Food Products Safe

Module 1, Available at https://www.youtube.com/watch?v=7nbjd_TnU8o (accessed 15 April 2018).

Video on HACCP Training for Food Handlers Module 2, Available at https://www.youtube.com/watch?v=gRJ7q_2Vkrc (accessed 15 April 2018).

https://www.youtube.com/watch?v=mE-q9W4jqQg (accessed 15 April 2018).

Appendix: CCP Decision Tree

A decision tree helps in the identification of critical control points (CCPs) in a process-flow diagram. A set of questions needs to be answered to arrive at the decision. The figure below illustrates this decision-making process.

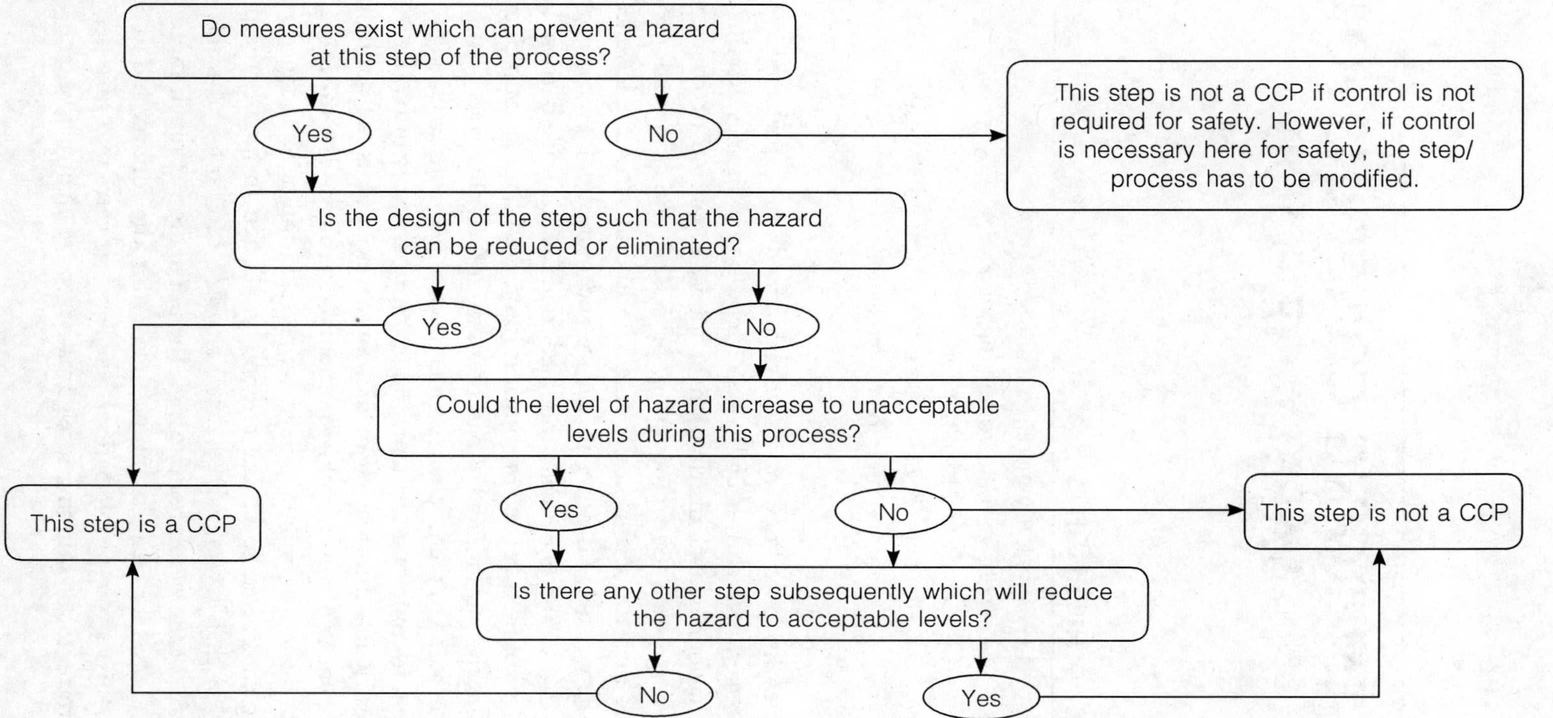

Source: Adapted by Author from from 'Hazard Analysis and Critical Control Point Principles and Application Guidelines', Adopted 14 August 1997, National Advisory Committee on Microbiological Criteria for Foods, *Journal of Food Protection* 61 (9), 1998, pp. 1246–59, Available at http://jfoodprotection.org/doi/pdf/10.4315/0362-028X-61.9.1246 (accessed 16 April 2018).

17

EMERGING CONCERNS FOR SAFETY OF FOOD

HIGHLIGHTS

- Genetically modified foods
- Prions and emerging pathogens
- Contaminants of concern
- Reasons for emergence of food-borne illnesses
- Prevention and control measures

In the 1950s, scientists only knew of a few major food-borne pathogens. We now have a list which is much longer, with almost 250 types of food-borne diseases described. Changes in food consumption behaviour, global distribution of foods, expansion of commercial food services, new methods of large-scale food production, processing and preservation, increasing mobility of population and a greater strain on the public health infrastructure have led to the emergence of newer food safety issues. Advances in science and biotechnology have introduced new food products, crop varieties and genetically modified foods. With trade barriers being lifted, there is a greater movement of food between nations. It is, no doubt, an encouraging trend. However, it has brought with it the transmission of pathogens from their countries of origin to nations which were hitherto unexposed to them. There is emergence of new infectious agents or re-emergence of strains which are now antibiotic-resistant. Indiscriminate use of antibiotics in animal husbandry, the poultry industry and through self-medication or other abuse of antibiotics by humans has led to the development of antimicrobial-resistant 'superbugs'. The microbes have also learnt to adapt in unfavourable environments. They have mutated and new, stronger strains have emerged. Some foods long considered to be safe are now implicated in food-borne disease outbreaks. It was not until 1989 that it was realised that *Salmonella* can be found inside raw eggs, and that raw or undercooked eggs were unsafe to eat. The population is much more mobile now than a few decades ago. Travel for business and pleasure within the country and to other nations is now quite common. This can be problematic if people act as carriers of diseases, spreading them in the places they travel to, or bringing foreign pathogens to their native land.

This chapter looks at some of these food safety issues which have shaken old concepts and sometimes, the whole foundation of our knowledge base. New bugs, and in food vehicles which were hitherto considered to be safe, have changed the way we formulate policies and standards. Let us look at some of these issues in detail.

GENETICALLY MODIFIED (GM) FOODS

According to the WHO, '*Genetically modified organisms (GMOs) can be defined as organisms (i.e. plants, animals or microorganisms) in which the genetic material (DNA) has been altered in a way that does not occur naturally by mating and/or natural recombination.*' Foods produced from or using GM organisms are often referred to as GM foods. Advances in food biotechnology have led to the application of techniques of genetic engineering in developing new plant varieties. The technology basically allows for selected genes to be transferred from one organism to the other even if the two species are unrelated. These genetically modified foods of plant origin have improved qualities like greater nutritional value, shorter growing and maturation period, greater resistance to pest and disease, and lower levels of anti-nutritional compounds.

> In 2016, GM crops were being grown in 26 countries and the total global area under GM crops was 185.1 million hectares. USA led the list of countries and produced GM maize, soybean, canola, sugarbeet, alfalfa, papaya and squash, followed by Brazil, Argentina and Canada. India had the fifth largest area planted with GM crops until the end of 2017, but grew only cotton. Cultivation of no other GM crop was permitted.

Opponents of this field of biotechnology feel that altering or disrupting an organism's genetic blueprint by genetic engineering is an inherently unpredictable and dangerous procedure. It may lead to production of unknown compounds which might harm us in the long run. GM foods may not have been adequately tested for their safety and as most of the research on this is industry sponsored, little trust can be placed in the reported research outcomes.

> India's **Genetic Engineering Approval Committee** (**GEAC**), in 2017, recommended the cultivation of GM mustard, which may become India's first GM crop. Earlier, in 2009, the body had approved Bt Brinjal. However, the government put an indefinite ban on its cultivation in February 2010 following strong protests.

The hazards of GM foods have been categorised into three types, according to people against this technology. These are human health, environmental and socioeconomic hazards. The debate is endless about how safe genetically modified foods are for **human health**. The major problem which can arise with GM foods is the use of genes from known food allergens such as milk, eggs, wheat, fish, shellfish, tree nuts, peanuts and soy. Generally, it is the protein present in these foods which acts as an allergen. If the *allergenic protein is transferred to another food*, that too can lead to allergenic responses which can be severe enough to cause death. For instance, to produce GM soybean with an improved protein content, a gene from Brazil nut was added. This put the people allergic to Brazil nuts at a great risk as they had no way of knowing that the soybean they were consuming had an allergen from Brazil nut. The gene transfers in genetic engineering can also lead to the *production of novel (new) proteins*, which may be harmful. GM potatoes made by introducing DNA from the snowdrop plant resulted in a chemically different potato. This, when fed to rats, caused damage to vital organs. Similarly, in Japan, a company used GM bacteria to produce a nutrient supplement—L-tryptophan. More than 1,500 people fell ill and 37 died after using the product. Although the exact cause remains controversial, it is believed by some scientists that the GM bacteria probably *produced a toxin* which the normal bacteria used in the production of this supplement did not.

Since most of the genes introduced into food products come from sources which have never been a part of human diet, it becomes even more difficult to predict allergenicity or, for that matter, toxicity. Also, some varieties of GM crops like soybean have shown *decreased amounts of beneficial phytoestrogen compounds* as compared to traditional soybeans. This decreases the health benefits of the crop. According to some reports, *GM crops may actually require more pesticides* as compared to the traditional crops, thus building up pesticide residues in our food supply.

Genetically engineered (GE) foods may also be potentially hazardous to the **environment**. It is possible that wind, rain, insects and birds can carry pollen from GE crops to fields planted with traditional or organic crops. This may lead to '*genetic pollution*' as there is no way of controlling this type of cross-pollination. There is also a fear that the *herbicide-resistant property* of the GE crop may get transmitted to the weed, creating weeds which will require higher doses of herbicide to be used in fields. Viruses and plant *pathogens infecting these plants may mutate* into new or stronger forms. GE plants introduced into an environment may also lead to the *decline of the native species*. For instance, GE organisms, which are hardier than the wild varieties, may lead to the latter's extinction if released into the same habitat.

It is important to determine whether the GE plant is safe for the environment. For instance, in 1996, the Environment Protection Agency (EPA) approved the use of *Bacillus thuringiensis* (Bt) in GM crops as a pesticide, since it controls pests which attack plants. This bacterium is naturally found in soil and produces a natural toxin which organic farmers use as a method of biological pest control. However, there are fears that the insects may become resistant to this toxin because of the artificial application of the bacteria.

Socioeconomic hazards are also to be reckoned with. Opponents of GM foods highlight the *crop failures* as evidence that such GE plants may not be as useful as they are touted to be. Large numbers of farmer suicides in India were linked to the failure of Bt cotton, which crumbled under a whitefly (pest) attack. It was supposed to have been immune to pests! In addition, some seed companies have been making *infertile GE crops*. This means that the farmer cannot use seeds from his harvested crop to sow for the next season. He would have to purchase a fresh batch of seeds from the company.

However, there are many benefits of using this technology, as genetic engineering may actually be a solution for improving food security, provided all the food safety issues are carefully addressed. Several studies have also shown that some fears expressed by the opponents of GM foods are unfounded and that GM foods are actually safe to consume.

PRIONS AND EMERGING PATHOGENS

Transmissible Spongiform Encephalopathies (TSEs) are a group of progressive degenerative conditions that affect the brain and nervous system of some animals and humans. The infective agent was identified as a **prion**, a type of pathogenic protein. The infectious agent induces abnormal folding of specific normal cellular proteins. These then accumulate in the brain, causing damage like holes or plaques leading to dementia and ultimately, death. These are thought to be found only in the brain tissue, spinal cord and retina of infected animals and not in meat and milk. TSEs are also referred to as prion diseases. **Scrapie** is a long-recognised disease that afflicts sheep and goats. It affects the nervous system, is degenerative and ultimately results in the death of an animal. In 1986, scientists first learnt that the disease was transmissible to other species (usually, diseases are not transmitted from one species to another). Cattle were being fed offal (intestine and internal organs), meat and bone meal from sheep and goats to increase the amount of protein in their diet. This probably resulted in the transfer of the infective agent. Cattle that ate the feed made from infected animals developed **Bovine Spongiform Encephalopathy** (BSE) or 'mad cow disease'. This is a fatal brain disease of cattle in which the brain appears sponge-like if seen under the microscope. The disease was first reported in the United Kingdom, and by 1992, more than 30,000 cattle were afflicted per year. Despite intensive control efforts, the disease spread across international boundaries to more than 24 countries by 2006. The export of animal feed products made in the UK to other countries had apparently resulted in export of the disease as well!

In Papua New Guinea, CJD is known as *kuru.* It was believed to be transmitted through cannibalism, with women somehow being more affected by this disease. Scientific investigations revealed that during funeral ceremonies, women traditionally ate the brain of the dead person, while the men ate the muscle. This tradition has now been curtailed.

In humans, a similar disease is called the Creutzfeldt Jakob disease (CJD). A new variant of this disease (vCJD) which affected younger people was identified and was linked to BSE. This meant that the infective agent had jumped species again and was now infecting humans. Symptoms included memory loss, dementia, anxiety, depression and personality changes. These were accompanied with physical problems like change in gait, coordination dysfunction, problems in speech and seizures. These outbreaks happened in the UK and some other countries of Europe in the early 1990s. They were attributed to the consumption of beef from infected cattle. This discovery nearly destroyed the meat industry of the UK, with all countries banning imports and the locals shunning beef. Besides European countries, the disease has also been reported in the USA and Canada. The use of rendered feeds prepared from certain mammalian tissues is now banned in most countries. The food safety strategy also focuses on banning certain bovine tissues from entering the human food chain. Regular checking of cattle for infection and occasional analysis of the meat products for detection of BSE is also encouraged.

Emerging pathogens of concern refer to those pathogens which are either causing a new illness or the number of cases is now increasing sharply. The increase in number could also be because the pathogens are spreading the disease over a wider geographical area. For instance, the number of people falling ill due to *Listeria* is nearly doubling every year. *E. coli* O157:H7 has caused multiple outbreaks. Multidrug resistant microbes like *Salmonella* and *Brucella* are causing major problems. Bird flu and swine flu have been making appearances, throwing the poultry and pork industries out of gear, with consumers shunning these meats during outbreaks. Let us learn a little more about some of these pathogens.

***Escherichia coli* O157:H7**, originally called the 'hamburger disease' due to its presence in undercooked ground beef used to make burgers, has shown up in a variety of foods. Salami, raw milk, apple cider, lettuce, brussel sprouts, uncooked sprouts and soft cheeses made from raw milk have shown contamination with this bacterium although some of these foods have an acidic pH. *E. coli* are present in the normal gut flora of all mammals. Entero-pathogenic *Escherichia coli* (EPEC) is the strain which has been linked to a number of the gastroenteritis cases. One of the types of EPEC, *E. coli* O157:H7, has emerged as a pathogen causing great concern. Identified in 1982, this organism is considered to be a leading cause of diarrhoea and hemolytic uremic syndrome, the primary cause of renal failure in children.

Listeriosis is a serious infection caused by eating food contaminated with the bacterium ***Listeria monocytogenes.*** The disease primarily affects pregnant women, newborns and adults with weakened immune systems. Healthy adults and children occasionally get infected with *Listeria*, but they rarely become seriously ill. The symptoms include fever, muscle aches, and sometimes gastrointestinal symptoms such as nausea or diarrhoea. It has been detected in foods like milk, soft cheeses, salads, processed meats and ready-to-eat chicken and meat preparations (which are contaminated after cooking).

New parasites are now turning up in new environments and with new resistance capabilities. ***Cryptosporidium parvum***, a one-celled parasite, first documented to have infected humans in 1976, led to a large-scale outbreak of watery diarrhoea in 1993 in Wisconsin, USA, affecting nearly 4 lakh people. What was scary was that the pathogen was found in the treated water which the municipal corporation supplied, that is, water which was found to have met the state standards. It highlighted the need to start testing for this parasite which was resistant to chlorine and other disinfectants. Since then, there have been many outbreaks, several of them linked to accidental intake of contaminated recreational waters (like in water parks and swimming pools) which have increased in number in India recently.

North American outbreaks of **cyclosporiasis** provide another example of a new and novel agent. The infection is caused by a protozoan parasite, *Cyclospora cayetanensis,* that produces prolonged watery diarrhoea after incubating in the host for more than a week. Other accompanying symptoms include low-grade fever, fatigue, weight loss and loss of appetite. The organism was first detected in Papua New Guinea in 1979; the disease is now endemic in more than 27 countries.

Even previously recognised pathogens are posing new problems. For example, we know that the increasing consumption of chicken has been accompanied by an increased incidence of ***Campylobacter jejuni*** infection. The bacterium has also been detected in red meat and raw milk. *Campylobacter* now exceeds *Salmonella* as the most common bacterial food-borne pathogen in most countries. Emergence of antibiotic-resistant *Campylobacter* spp. has further created problems for health professionals.

***Salmonella typhimurium* DT104**, widely distributed in wild and farm animals, is now increasingly making people sick as well. To make matters worse, it is resistant to several common antibiotics. Non-typhoidal strains of *Salmonella* are also increasingly leading to illness. This is being attributed to the consumption of undercooked meat, poultry products and use of raw eggs in food preparation. Eating half-boiled or 'sunny-side-up' eggs with a runny yolk is not recommended because of the risk of *Salmonella* infection.

The threat of animal diseases being transmitted to humans has also been in the limelight in recent years. Reports of '**Bird Flu**' infecting humans have been highlighted by the media. Confirmed instances of the avian influenza viruses infecting humans have been documented since 1997. The type of virus with the greatest risk is the highly pathogenic avian influenza HPAI strain, H5N1 (see Figure 17.1A). This strain appeared in China in 1996. Between 1996 and 2008, HPAI outbreaks in poultry have occurred at least 11 times and four of these outbreaks have involved millions of birds. Outbreaks have become more common due to the high density and frequent movement of flocks from intensive poultry production.

The virus mostly infects domesticated birds like chicken and turkey. It spreads among susceptible birds when they come in contact with contaminated saliva, nasal secretions and faeces. It is not absolutely clear how humans get infected, but it is proposed that any contact with infected birds can transmit the infection, especially during operations like slaughter and plucking. The influenza

Figure 17.1: Bird Flu and Swine Flu Viruses

A: Avian influenza A H5N1 viruses

Source: 'Avian influenza A H5N1 viruses' by US Centers for Disease Control and Prevention (CC0 1.0; Wikimedia Commons).

B: H1N1 influenza viruses

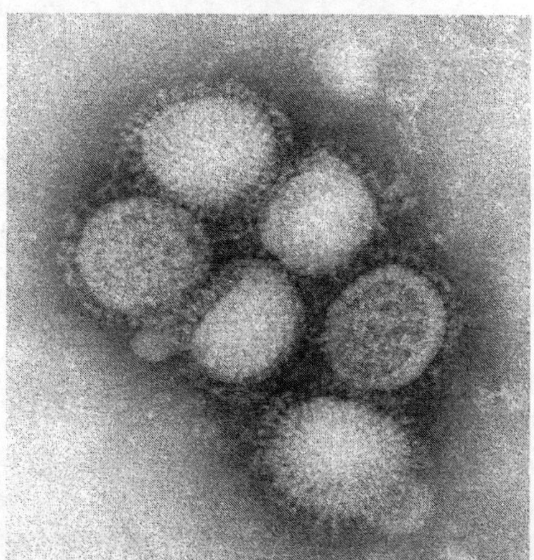

Source: 'Image of the newly identified H1N1 influenza virus' by US Centers for Disease Control and Prevention (CC0 1.0; Wikimedia Commons).

virus has shown presence of genes that have been adapted from both human and avian strains. The reported symptoms in infected individuals range from fever, cough, sore throat and muscle aches to eye infections, pneumonia and other life-threatening complications. Human infections were first reported in 1997 in Hong Kong. Since 2003, more than 700 human cases of Asian HPAI H5N1 have been reported to the WHO, primarily from 15 countries in Asia, Africa, the Pacific, Europe and West Asia, though over 60 countries have been affected. The mortality rate for humans with H5N1 is 60 per cent.

Pigs can also be infected with human, avian and swine influenza viruses, allowing for mixtures of genes (reassortment) to create a new virus. **Swine influenza**, also called pig influenza, swine flu, hog flu and pig flu, is an infection caused by any one of several types of swine influenza viruses. As of 2009, the known causative strains included influenza C and the subtypes of influenza A known as H1N1, H1N2, H2N1, H3N1, H3N2, and H2N3.

The swine flu was initially seen in humans in Mexico in 2009 and the strain was identified as H1N1 (see Figure 17.1B). People with regular exposure to pigs are at increased risk of swine flu infection. Symptoms resemble that of any flu—chills, fever, sore throat, muscle pains, severe headache, coughing, weakness and general discomfort. Cases of swine flu have been reported in India, with a massive outbreak in almost all states of India in 2015. Thousands of people tested positive and more than 2,000 people died as a result of the infection. Scientists reported that the virus had probably acquired a mutation which made it easier to infect humans. The need for strict monitoring and surveillance was felt to prevent outbreaks in the future.

A number of other microbes can be added to the list of emerging pathogens—*Toxoplasma gondii*, *Shigella*, *Vibrio parahaemolyticus*, *Yersinia enterocolitica*, etc. These have been discussed in earlier chapters as well. The concern for microbes which have developed antibiotic resistance is also growing. These bacteria, fungi, viruses and parasites which have acquired resistance to antimicrobial substances are referred to as '**Antimicrobial Resistant (AMR)' microbes.** This can happen naturally with microbes adapting to changes in their environment as a basic survival strategy. However, humans are also responsible for the creation of these 'superbugs' or pathogens which cannot be killed using normal drugs and disinfectants. Over-the-counter sale and now, sale through the internet, of antimicrobial drugs, self-medication, poor adherence to therapy (the doctor tells you to have the antibiotic for five days and you stop it after 2–3 days when you feel better!), poor quality antimicrobials and use for non-therapeutic purposes in both humans and animals has led to AMR.

The consequences of AMR include failure to treat infections, often leading to the death of the patient. Others may have a prolonged illness leading to production losses and increased medical costs borne by individuals and the government. In May 2015, the World Health Assembly adopted a global action plan on antimicrobial resistance, with the objective to improve awareness, strengthen surveillance and make sanitation and hygiene more effective.

One of the valid fears of the government is bioterrorism. Use of highly pathogenic microbes for contaminating the water or food supply of cities is a plausible threat. Food safety practices and management of the food supply must include reducing the vulnerability to deliberate introduction of hazards.

CONTAMINANTS OF CONCERN

Use of newer chemicals in food production, processing and packaging is introducing newer contaminants into our food supply. Earlier chapters have highlighted these concerns regarding pesticide residues, drugs used in animal husbandry and other chemical contaminants. Some of these contaminants have probably always been there in our food; only, we did not have the advanced instruments and technology to detect them. Others have been introduced into food in recent times due to their increased production and use.

Growth **hormones** used to increase size of meat-producing animals and oxytocin used to increase milk yield find their way into the foods of animal origin like meat, milk and eggs. How much of a human health risk these pose is debatable. According to some research evidence, these hormones present in food are digested like any other protein in the human digestive tract. **Antibiotic residues** are also increasingly being detected in newer foods. Milk, meat and eggs had been detected with residues of veterinary drugs; however, in 2010, there was a report of antibiotic residues in honey in India. In commercial beekeeping, the bees are susceptible to infections which can wipe out entire hives. Antibiotics are regularly used to tackle infections and these are finding their way into the honey produced by the bees. Similarly, pesticide residues are also finding their way into a greater number of foods (soft drinks and processed foods, besides being present in fruits, vegetables and grains) and are being detected at much higher concentration levels.

Harmful chemicals leaching from plastics into the food and into water stored in plastic bottles is becoming a serious concern. In a study by Zota et al. (2016), it was observed that people who ate high amounts of fast food had higher levels of phthalates (industrial chemicals) in their urine.

Plastic debris in the marine environment including resin pellets, fragments and microscopic plastic fragments containing a cocktail of chemicals and organic compounds is contaminating the fish and other seafood we eat. The United Nations Environment Program called marine plastics the 'new toxic timebomb'. In addition to the chemicals which are used to make plastics, **Persistent bioaccumulative toxins (PBTs)** tend to contaminate all forms of marine plastics. These contaminants present in sea water concentrate in the microfragments of plastic due to their high surface area. Similarly, pesticides and heavy metals also adhere to the surface of these plastics. Marine organisms which feed on these plastics then concentrate the plastic additives, pesticides, metals and other toxins. These ultimately land up on our dinner plate. These chemical hazards have been linked to hormonal disturbances, damage to vital organs and cancer in humans.

Packaging, serving and storage **utensils/materials** have also been under the scanner of regulatory authorities working to ensure the safety of consumers. Use of newspaper for wrapping or serving food has now been banned in India (as late as 2016!) after the realisation that this practice had become increasingly prevalent, especially among street food vendors. **Newspapers** leach out harmful chemicals contained in their ink and the paper into food, which comes in contact with it. A similar ban needs to be imposed on inferior quality plastics used by small-scale food service establishments for packing food and as disposable utensils for serving food.

Opponents of **food irradiation** fear that the process may lead to the production of new chemicals in food due to exposure to radiation. Furthermore, viruses and bacterial spores not killed by the process may actually mutate into 'superbugs'. Long-term studies that demonstrate the safety of irradiated foods need to be carried out.

REASONS FOR EMERGENCE OF FOOD-BORNE ILLNESSES

According to the Institute of Medicine (IOM), USA, certain food-borne diseases have emerged as major threats to public health in the recent past. As some diseases are controlled, others may emerge and increase in incidence. The incidence of diseases is thus not static and the disease profile changes over time due to several factors in the environment. Figure 17.2 highlights some of these factors which have led to the emergence of microbial threats.

The **demographics** in most countries is changing. With increase in the number of elderly persons, a larger proportion of the population is now at a greater risk of food-borne infections due to their lower immunity and hence, higher susceptibility to illness. **Behavioural changes** in food habits—such as health-conscious people eating more of raw fruits and vegetables, minimally

Figure 17.2: Factors Facilitating the Emergence of Microbial Threats and Diseases

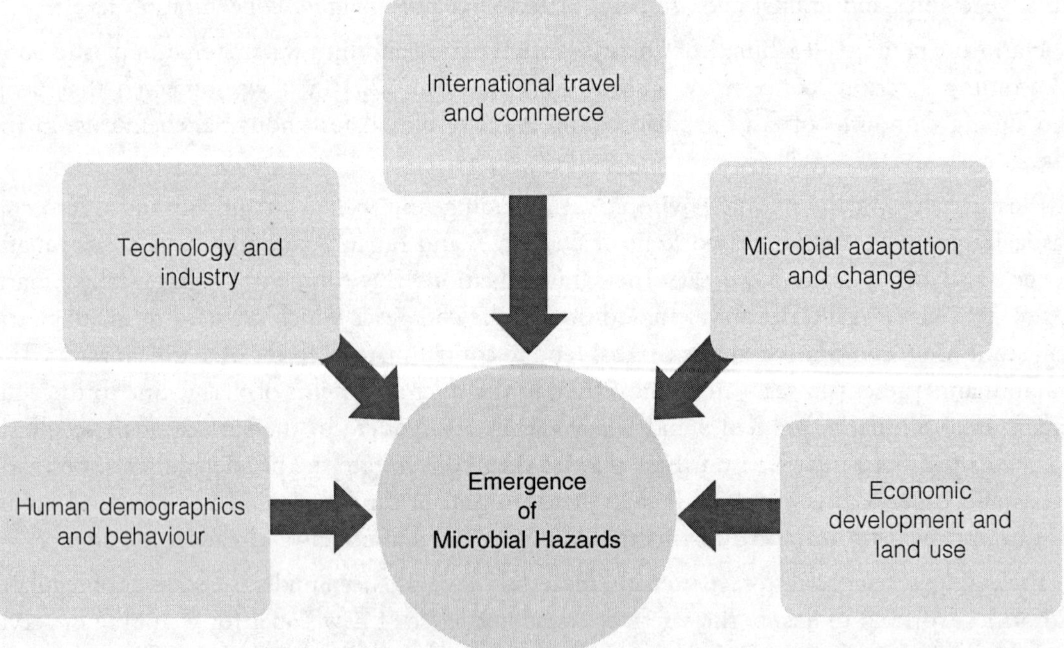

Source: Adapted by Author from Knechtges 2012.

processed juices and other foods—has put them at a higher risk of eating pathogen-contaminated foods. Likewise, the trend to eat meals away from home puts people at a greater risk of eating contaminated food.

Advances in the **technology of food production and processing** have helped increase food production. A lot of automation has been introduced in food-producing factories. However, food safety practices have not been adequately adopted by most industries. Strict cleaning protocols for maintenance of machines, if not followed, would lead to an increase in contamination of food. Pathogenic bacteria which form surface films in pipes and crevices of equipment can then contaminate food and beverages being processed in them. Also, increase in production has been accompanied by increase in distribution across a greater geographical area. The pathogens have consequently caused outbreaks in a higher number of cities.

International trade and commerce has also resulted in the world becoming a smaller place. Tourists have also started venturing across international boundaries, exploring the cuisines of other countries. These travellers can unknowingly become carriers of pathogens, carrying them back to their own countries. In addition, import of food from other nations and trade in animals for breeding is also helping in the spread of diseases. The pandemic of salmonellosis is blamed on the sale of egg-laying hens for breeding purposes.

Microorganisms are also rapidly **adapting to changing environmental conditions**. Some are increasing in virulence, while others are now showing the ability to survive and thrive in acidic conditions, temperature extremes and dry conditions. Foods previously believed to be inhospitable for microbes or not supporting the growth of certain kinds of microbes are testing positive for microbial contamination. The microbes are also becoming resistant to disinfectants used in the food industry and to antibiotics used to treat infections.

Manure generated on animal farms is a reservoir of pathogens like pathogenic species of *E. coli*, *Salmonella*, *Camplylobacter* and others. If the **waste management** is improper, it results in a spread of infection among the farm animals. Similarly, if human waste or sewage is not treated properly and waste water from animal farms or from sewage treatment plants is allowed to reach farms where food crops are growing or water bodies where shellfish and fish are being reared, it can lead to contamination of food.

The war on infectious diseases can be won only by taking effective public health measures to ensure food safety at all levels of food production (literally from 'farm' to 'fork'). This puts a lot of emphasis on regulatory measures enforced by governments of countries and on food business operators, who need to be sensitised to food safety issues.

PREVENTION AND CONTROL MEASURES

Food-borne disease prevention involves a thorough understanding of the production chain, the implementation of Hazard Analysis Critical Control Point (HACCP) strategies and use of appropriate food preservation methods without undue increase in the number of chemicals added. We need to look at each food product from its first possible ingredient to its eventual consumption. The science-based approach of HACCP for reducing the risk of food-borne disease identifies critical control points (CCPs) where problems can arise. Appropriate food safety measures are then designed for these CCPs.

Predictive microbiology utilises mathematical models and computer software to describe responses of microbes to environmental conditions such as temperature, pH and water activity. A prediction is used as a guide to the response of microorganisms to a particular set of environmental conditions. This information is used to judge whether food exposed to certain conditions would have resulted in the food becoming unsafe due to high microbial load or toxin production. ComBase is a database of microbial behaviour in different environments. Its software models help to predict the growth or inactivation of microorganisms. Predictive microbiology has numerous practical applications and is an active area of research. For instance, the data on time taken and temperature at which a batch of cheese got transported from factory to the retail outlets could be used in a predictive model. The modelling would then let the risk manager know whether the cheese was at any point in time exposed to temperatures which would have encouraged microbial growth.

Education of industrialists, the healthcare community, public health agencies, and consumers is paramount. The food growing, production, processing, transportation and preparation industries need to understand food-borne disease and how to prevent it. Public health officials need to coordinate efforts among private and government agencies involved in food-borne disease investigations. There is a need to convey, in a meaningful way, the importance of hand washing and the risks for cross-contamination among various food items in the kitchen.

With a multitude of food products swarming the market and a significant portion of these being imported from other countries, the consumer needs to be vigilant about food hazards he is likely to be exposed to. Labels on these foods are the only means of knowing the composition of the food product you are about to consume. You may have noticed that some labels of these products are in foreign languages, without any English translation. The labelling regulations need to be implemented very strictly so that the consumer is provided with adequate information about the ingredients and additives used to prepare the product, besides highlighting the best before date and instructions for storage and use. Information about presence of possible allergens in the food is vital for people who are hypersensitive.

Cold plasma is a novel non-thermal food processing technology that uses energetic, reactive gases to inactivate contaminating microbes on meats, poultry, fruits and vegetables and even packaging material. This flexible sanitising method uses electricity and a carrier gas, such as air, oxygen, nitrogen or helium. The primary modes of action are due to ultraviolet light and reactive chemical products of the cold plasma ionisation process. Reductions of greater than five logs can be obtained for pathogens such as *Salmonella, Escherichia coli* O157:H7, *Listeria monocytogenes and Staphylococcus aureus.* This new technology may prove to be one of the most effective measures of microbial control in the food industry.

The complex and changing biological web of the human food supply means that we can expect new pathogens to emerge and novel food vehicles to be identified. However, we need to be vigilant and take preventive measures to minimise damage to human and animal health (see Box 17.1). Hospitals and physicians play an important role in notifying the government about any new disease or pathogen they suspect. The consumer also needs to be aware of hazards in foods and practices which would increase contamination of his food supply. Any information which the government has with regard to the presence of a contaminant in the food supply needs to be communicated to the public with guidelines on how to manage the risk. This needs to be done carefully without creating a situation of panic in the country. Sometimes, it is seen that the silence of the government regarding a food safety hazard leads to greater chaos. Effective communication is the key to effectively controlling and limiting disease outbreaks, and minimising consequent economic losses. Better methods of traceability of food products can also limit economic damage. If food coming from a particular source is found to be contaminated, then similar foods from other sources need not be shunned or recalled from the market.

Box 17.1: Preventive Measures to Improve Food Safety

Progress in the field of food safety will depend on:

- focused efforts to reduce contamination after harvest
- better sanitation and process control for meat and poultry
- understanding the biology of pathogens for effective control measures
- a robust public health surveillance
- vigilance of global food trade
- identification of newer challenges
- protocols to deal with food safety emergencies like food-borne disease outbreaks
- effective communication with consumers about risks and ways of managing risks
- efficient system for traceability of foods and ingredients

Radiofrequency Identification (**RIFD**) **Technology** is increasingly being used to trace products in the supply chain. RFID is a form of auto-identification, like a bar code or a license tag containing a unique serial number. Efforts are on to develop mobile apps which can be used to check whether, for instance, the packet of cheese you are buying was kept chilled throughout its journey from the factory to the supermarket shelf! You would probably not buy the cheese if you discovered that it was kept without refrigeration in a warehouse for more than 24 hours during its journey to the supermarket. Another new technology is that of **thermochromic labelling**, which uses a special ink on the package of food products. These are used for products which need to be kept at certain temperatures during storage or need to be served at a particular temperature. The ink changes colour when the threshold temperature is reached, informing the consumer whether the food is now safe to eat, or if the food is at the right temperature to be served. It is being used in some countries to let the consumers know, for instance, whether their pizza is hot enough to eat or their beer is chilled enough to drink.

SUMMARY

- Several factors may contribute to an increasing incidence of food-borne diseases due to new pathogens or pathogens in foods hitherto believed to be safe.

- These factors include changes in the food consumption behaviour, global distribution of foods, expansion of commercial food services, new methods of large-scale food production, changing demographic profile of the population, increasing mobility of population and a greater strain on the public health infrastructure.
- Genetically modified foods are still not permitted for sale and local consumption in a number of countries, including India, because of fears of allergenicity and long-term toxicity besides other environmental and socioeconomic concerns.
- *Listeria monocytogenes, Campylobacter jejuni, E. coli O157:H7, Cryptosporidium parvum, Toxoplasma gondii, Salmonella, Shigella, Vibrio parahaemolyticus* and *Yersinia enterocolitica* are some of the emerging pathogens of concern. In addition to the usual gastrointestinal symptoms of diarrhoea and vomiting, these pathogens can lead to life-threatening complications.
- Antimicrobial Resistant (AMR) microbes are also creating havoc across the world. Over-the-counter sale of drugs, self-medication, poor adherence to therapy, poor quality antimicrobials and use for non-therapeutic purposes in both humans and animals has led to AMR.
- Transmissible spongiform encephalopathies (TSEs), bird flu and swine flu are other concerns which have had widespread economic and health implications.
- Chemical contaminants are increasing in concentration and in the number of foods in which they have been detected. Some of these contaminants are pesticide residues, veterinary drug residues and plastics.
- Pathogens can be kept in check only by improved surveillance, education of the food producers, handlers and the common man, thorough understanding of the food production and distribution chain, and better methods for reducing the microbial contamination.
- Hospitals, physicians and the consumers play a crucial role in surveillance and early reporting.
- Educating the public about the basics of food safety is very important.

KEY WORDS

Bioterrorism: The intentional release of viruses, bacteria or other germs into the food, water or air with the intent to sicken or kill people, livestock or crops.

Demographics: Statistical data relating to the population.

Entero-pathogen: Any microorganism that causes intestinal disease.

Hemolytic uremic syndrome: A condition characterised by abnormal destruction of red blood cells, low platelet count and kidney failure.

Irradiation: (here) Exposure of food to ionising radiation to kill all pathogens and extend shelf life.

Rendering: A process that converts waste animal tissue into stable, value-added materials.

Super-bug: Strain of bacteria that has become resistant to most antibiotic drugs.

Surveillance: Close observation and inspection.

EXERCISES

1. How does one decide whether a pathogen is an emerging concern or not?
2. List the factors facilitating the emergence of microbial hazards in the world.
3. What do you understand by AMR microbes? Why are they such a big threat to our health?
4. What steps should be taken to reduce the creation of AMR microbes?

5. What are transmissible spongiform encephalopathies? Describe giving examples.
6. Why are GM foods considered to be harmful by some?
7. Discuss the preventive measures that can be taken to ensure protection of the consumer from emerging food safety threats.

REFERENCES

Knechtges, P. L., 'Foodborne Infectious and Microbial Agents', in *Food Safety—Theory and Practice*, USA: Jones & Bartlett Learning, 2012, pp. 109–13.

Lloyd-Smith, M., and J. Immig, 'Contaminants in Marine Plastic Pollution: "the new toxic time-bomb"', 2016, *National Toxic Network*, Australia, Available at http://www.ntn.org.au/wp/wp-content/uploads/2016/05/NTN-Contaminants-in-Marine-Plastics-Report-April-2016-.pdf (accessed 26 December 2016).

Roberts, C. A., *The Food Safety Information Handbook*, USA: Oryx Press, 2001.

Zota A. R., C. A. Phillips, and S. D. Mitro, 'Recent Fast Food Consumption and Bisphenol A and Phthalates Exposures among the U.S. Population in NHANES, 2003–2010', *Environ Health Perspect* 124 (10), 2016, pp. 1521–28.

ONLINE SOURCES

Cold Plasma Technology, Available at https://www.foodonline.com/doc/cold-plasma-technology-will-benefit-the-food-processing-industry-0001 (accessed 15 April 2018).

Predictive Microbiology, Available at http://www.fao.org/docrep/006/y4743e/y4743e0o.htm (accessed 15 April 2018).

Smart Packaging, Available at http://www.packageprinting.com/article/smart-packaging-thermochromic-inks-53226/all/ (accessed 15 April 2018).

Video on Cold Plasma Technology, Available at https://www.youtube.com/watch?v=HPcsTav95nc (accessed 15 April 2018).

Video on How Crops are Genetically Modified, Available at https://www.youtube.com/watch?v=2G-yUuiqIZ0 (accessed 15 April 2018).

Video on Prions—Incurable Brain Dissolving Proteins, Available at https://www.youtube.com/watch?v=micLucwLGgI (accessed 15 April 2018).

INDEX